The Author

Gladwyn Turbutt is well known in local history circles for his impressive four-volume *History of Derbyshire*, for which he received the Marsh/Country Life Book of the Year Award in 2000, and for his subsequent books on *The Hospitaller Order of St. John of Jerusalem in Derbyshire History* (1999) and *Superstition and Religion in Early Derbyshire History* (2006). He is an MA of Oxford University and an Hon. DLitt of the University of Derby.

Summary

This challenging book by historian Gladwyn Turbutt examines why 'conventional' Christianity has now lost its appeal for many. He begins by tracing the growth of spirituality from pagan times; depicts the struggle of the early Church against its pagan rivals, and the subsequent adoption of a number of pagan beliefs (virgin birth, star in the east, resurrection after three days, communion ritual); describes the formation of a church hierarchy and the definition of Christian 'doctrines'. It goes on to discuss the philosophical arguments about God and of the concept of Transcendental reality, and then examines the historical records of Jesus of Nazareth. He uses the findings of biblical scholars and theologians to show up subsequent interpolations into the early narratives of Jesus' life and death, and the unsustainability of a number of hallowed doctrines. He maintains that Jesus was not the immaculately conceived son of Mary but was rather the normally conceived son of her husband Joseph; nor, he maintains, did Jesus ever claim to be 'God incarnate' nor the second person of the man-made concept of the Holy Trinity. He was in fact fully mortal and a charismatic prophet, a man 'approved by God' whose moral teaching and promises of everlasting life are of universal relevance. The author concludes by advocating a major doctrinal reform and by suggesting fresh ways in which Christianity might be presented to a younger and increasingly sceptical generation. The book follows in the footsteps of earlier examinations of contemporary Christian beliefs, beginning with Gerald Priestland's *Priestland's Progress* (1981), and followed by Bel Mooney's *Devout Sceptics* (2003) and John Humphrys's *In God We Doubt* (2007)

Acknowledgements

It will be clear to readers of this book that my greatest debt must be to those biblical scholars and theologians from whose works I have freely quoted and on whose scholarship my book has been based. It is their findings, above all, to which I have given expression and which have demonstrated how many of 'conventional' Christianity's hallowed doctrines have now – after 2000 years – become untenable for many people, both lay and clerical. Any errors of fact and judgement in the text are of course my sole responsibility.

One again, I am greatly indebted to Margaret Parry for her meticulous preparation of my manuscript for publication. I should also like to thank Linda Harris, Catriona Watson and Gina Yiannis of Indepenpress Publishing and Marketing for support, encouragement and professionalism.

Gladwyn Turbutt

Contents

1. INTRODUCTION

Like many of my own generation I am puzzled by the apparent indifference of the populace at large to matters of religious belief. This disenchantment is demonstrated only too clearly by the declining membership of most Christian denominations in the United Kingdom in recent years, and the palpable disinterest of many intelligent people in the conventional Church. We may well empathise with the sentiments expressed by John Betjeman nearly fifty years ago when he wrote:

> 'Some know for all their lives that Christ is God,
> Some start upon that arduous love affair
> In clouds of doubt and argument; and some
> (My closest friends) seem not to want His love –
> And why this is I wish to God I knew.
> As at the Dragon School, so still for me
> The steps to truth were made by sculptured stones,
> Stained glass and vestments, holy-water stoups,
> Incense and crossings of myself – the things
> That hearty middle-stumpers most despise
> As 'all the inessentials of the Faith.'

Summoned by Bells (1960), 95–6

Let us now consider three examples. Firstly, for young people today (as we shall see in Chapter 6) Church services are considered irrelevant: 'you don't get anything out of it, it simply does not touch my life, it's meaningless.' Secondly, the distinguished writer and historian Karen Armstrong was a Roman Catholic nun whose 'sense of devotion was an aesthetic response to the beauty of the Gregorian chant and the liturgy'. She writes: 'I never glimpsed the God described by the prophets and mystics. Jesus Christ, about whom we talked far more than about "God", seemed a purely historical figure, inextricably embedded in late antiquity. I also began to have grave doubts about some of the doctrines of the

Church. How could anybody possibly know for certain that the man Jesus had been God incarnate and what did such a belief mean? Did the New Testament really teach the elaborate – and highly contradictory – doctrine of the Trinity or was this, like so many other articles of the faith, a fabrication by theologians centuries after the death of Christ in Jerusalem? Eventually, with regret, I left the religious life…'[1] This, it has to be said, is only one example of many academics who have felt unable to accept much of traditional Christian doctrine. Finally, for many people – not just Roman Catholics – the recent publication of Mother Teresa's 'Private Writings' will have come as a profound shock. Always assumed to have been a devout Catholic, whose exemplary faith gave her the strength and dedication to work most of her life amongst the poor and outcasts of Calcutta (for which in 1979 she was awarded the Nobel Peace Prize), we now learn that she suffered an inner torture for her love of God which she felt was not reciprocated. 'People say they are drawn close to God – seeing my strong faith – Is this not deceiving people? Every time I have wanted to tell the truth – "that I have no faith" – the words just do not come…'.[2] A comment by the late Cardinal Basil Hume comes to mind: 'There is no greater pain than the sense of having been abandoned by God: the sense that behind it all there is, after all, nothing.'[3] These three statements, displaying sincere and deeply-held beliefs of individuals, may be seen as examples of commonly-held criticisms of the Christian religion: first, incomprehension; second, intellectual doubts; and third painful disillusionment – themes which will recur throughout the chapters that follow.

However, this is not to say that there is a lack of spirituality or a sense of the numinous in today's society. It is rather that mankind's need for spirituality is now fulfilled only partially by *institutional* religion. As Michael Holloway (a former Bishop of Edinburgh) points out, spirituality and morality were always regarded as the 'traditional preserve of religion'. But not any longer. Many people (he claims) 'may or may not 'believe' in God, but they are no longer comfortable in any of the traditional religions… and they do not cease to be interested in spirituality or the inner life of the human community just because they are not members of any of the religions on offer in our society'.[4] Thus it is not necessary to be a Christian to feel as strongly as some Christians do about the need for world justice and political reconciliation. You do not need the gospel of Jesus and the power of the Holy Spirit to engage with equal ardour in such causes. As Kai Nielson has argued: 'the non-existence of God does not preclude the possibility of there being an objective standard on which to base moral judgements', and again: 'Morality has an objective rationale in complete independence of religion'.[5] This manifestly explains the current widely held sense of disillusionment with 'religion' as such; the feeling that rational agnosticism is more in keeping with the world of today, a fact illustrated with brilliance and sensitivity by the BBC Radio 4 series of interviews with a wide spectrum of distinguished guests presented by Bel Mooney and subsequently embodied in her book *Devout Sceptics* (2003).[6] Yet despite people's scepticism about belief in God and the whole edifice of the Christian Church Mooney declares: 'four elements of secular belief today (our conversations showed again and again) can lead to glimmerings of the divine: scientific knowledge, awareness of the environment, the wide availability of the arts, and the psychological study of human nature',[7] and the wisdom, imagination and tolerant attitude displayed by her invited guests were for me both remarkable and compelling. Moreover, what is so reassuring is how very few of those questioned about their faith or lack of it had dogmatic and inflexible opinions and more often appeared to have been groping for years to find meaningful answers to their doubts. This point was forcibly brought out in John Humphrys's BBC Radio 4 series *Humphrys in Search of God* in 2006, a relatively short exercise comprising only three half-hour interviews but which once again demonstrated wide interest among the public ('I have never had such a response to anything I have written or broadcast'). In his book *In God We Doubt* (2007) Humphrys elaborated in detail many of the issues which have troubled him – and clearly others as well. He is impressed by the fact that many of those who responded to his broadcast thought of themselves as neither believers nor atheists but 'doubters'.

So where did I feel I stood in this dilemma of faith when so many distinguished people were (in Bel Mooney's apt phrase) devout sceptics? If one is intellectually honest can one have unquestioning faith? This for me is the fundamental question and one that has troubled distinguished scholars, theologians and scientists over the years. It is undoubtedly a contributing factor to the public indifference to 'religion' which this book seeks to address. I don't doubt that those who have a genuine and deeply-felt vocation have little difficulty in answering 'yes'. But for the majority I suggest that, as life for many of our citizens continues on its comfortable, if not necessarily affluent, course, there is no urge to concern themselves in a rigorous (and perhaps uncomfortable) examination of where their religious beliefs may lie. There is no obvious candidate playing the role of John the Baptist or Billy Graham to spur them into such an examination. Perhaps therefore I should embark upon an exercise similar to that of *Priestland's Progress* in which the former BBC Religious Affairs correspondent Gerald Priestland (who admitted that 'I had barely paused to ask myself what I really believed, let alone why') sought to establish whether he was really a Christian at all.[8] The response to Priestland's BBC radio programmes was overwhelming: '...to my joy I seem to have brought encouragement to what I call the Great Anonymous Church of the Unchurched: those who believe, or would like to believe, but are disenchanted with the churches...'.[9] It is not without interest to note that, before his London Weekend Television broadcast in the series *Jesus, the Evidence* in 1984, Dr David Jenkins, former Bishop of Durham, said that he aimed at several types of audience: 'Mostly, religious people [who] are regarded as a closed class of enthusiasts with private interests of an esoteric but not widely significant nature... the positive unbelievers, the thoughtful atheists who settle into the habit of dismissing Christian faith and all religion as obviously unreasonable and mere superstition because of the undesirable and inhuman things perpetrated in its name.' Then there were 'the indifferent. Today these seem to be the largest category in our society...'[10] Indifferent? Disenchanted? Sceptical at the recent Lambeth Conference with bishops of the worldwide Anglican Communion bickering amongst themselves?

This book is an attempt, from an unbiased historian's point of view, to address 'the indifferent' members of our society: to make – on their behalf – a rigorous examination of some of the doctrines, beliefs and practices of Christian faith as they have been handed down to us and which I personally have hitherto passively accepted. Most will probably agree that, in all conscience, an honest doctrinal reappraisal – such as envisaged by the late Bishop John Robinson and others half a century ago – is overdue. For all thinking people it is a matter of 'facing up to the doubts'.

Wherever possible I have quoted verbatim the views of biblical scholars and theologians so as to give authority and direction to the text. Some of its findings may make uncomfortable reading for convinced Christians, but I hope it may be helpful to those who are 'devout sceptics' by illustrating how so much myth and textual interpolation into hitherto sacrosanct scriptural sources has resulted in a luxuriant historical undergrowth which now requires drastic pruning if Christianity as a religion is to remain a credible faith. Readers will have to judge for themselves as to how many of my conclusions they consider well founded. And I have been conscious throughout of John Locke's dictum:

'Bring to your enquiries a mind covetous of truth, that seeks after that impartially, and embraces it – how poor, how contemptible, how unfashionable soever it may seem.'

NOTES

[1] Armstrong, 1999, 2

[2] *Mother Teresa Come Be My Light: The revealing private writings of the Nobel Peace Prize Winner.* Ed. Brian Kolodiejchuk, 2008, 238

[3] Hume, 2002, 180

[4] Holloway, 2004, x

[5] Nielsen, K., 1973, *Ethics without God*, 48, 64

[6] Mooney, 2003

[7] Ibid., 5

[8] Priestland, 1981

---

[9]   Ibid., 9

[10]   Jenkins, 2002, 29–30

2. SETTING THE SCENE

We are all subject to a spectrum of belief in the Transcendent, in something existing apart from, and not subject to the limitations of the material universe. At one extreme there are those (e.g. Atheists) who deny the existence of any supernatural world or entity (i.e. God); at the other, those who unreservedly believe in it. Between these extremes of belief there are some who have an instinctive feeling that there *does* exist something 'other-worldly', the reality of which they are uncertain but feel bound to acknowledge in their daily lives – whether it be the 'religion' of Christianity or other faiths.

The most fortunate men and women in this world are without doubt those who have a 'calling' or 'vocation' for a spiritual life, and – for the purpose of this study – for the Christian way of life as taught and practised by Jesus Christ some two thousand years ago and subsequently codified by his later adherents into the institutional doctrines of the Christian Church. For them there is not a shadow of doubt about the 'truth' of the biblical account of Jesus and the circumstances of his life, message and death, and, more importantly, of his continuing existence in 'heaven' to which we are all bound after leaving this life. Among the most committed and devout of all professed Christians are those belonging to the contemplative cenobitic orders, both male and female. These communities, dwelling in monasteries and convents, are fortunate above all in that, unlike the majority of the secular public, they have an unshakeable faith in the efficacy of prayer and the absolute imperative of worshipping God daily and indeed hourly. For enclosed orders such as the Carthusians or Cistercians prayer is of paramount importance, lived within a largely self-sufficient community apart from the day-to-day stresses of the world. Others, like the Franciscans, Dominicans, Jesuits and some of the Benedictines (as at Ampleforth Abbey), are not confined to closed communities but go out into the world to preach, teach and heal.

The origin of the enclosed orders may be traced directly back to St Basil (*c.*329–79) of Caesarea, who was the first to abandon the eremitical life in the desert for an organised communal life governed by a set of rules. He was later followed by St Benedict (*c.*480–*c.*547) who – after living the life of a hermit in a mountain cave for three years – founded a group of like-minded communities near Subiaco in Italy. He went on to found (*c.*530) the famous monastery of Monte Casino, and drew up a set of rules (later known as the Rule of St Benedict) to which all monastic inmates should be bound, and who would take the vows of poverty, chastity and obedience on their profession, and where everything is held in common. The daily routine of prayer is focused on the Mass or Eucharist, together with the celebration of the offices of the seven canonical hours which ensures a constant cycle of prayer from the small hours of the night right through until after sunset. It is a rigorous schedule, interspersed by periods for study, meditation and physical work. If that were not enough some branches of the Benedictine community, such as the Cistercians (deriving their name from the abbey of Cîteaux), practised a life of yet greater asceticism and vicarious penance dedicated to the glory of God along with their prayers for the redemption of mankind.

What is the motivation of the devotees of enclosed orders? It could be claimed on their behalf that by disposing of all their earthly possessions and disdaining any worldly ambitions they are thereby freed to follow a life devoid of personal sin where a belief in the transcendence of God is paramount and they become aware of the reality of God's presence both in their own lives and in the persons of other members of the community; and that they seek to achieve when participating in the Mass or Eucharist a kind of orgasmic intimacy with the Divine – if that were possible – which was hinted at by mystical poets such as Francis Quarles (1592–1644) or George Herbert (1593–1633), or mystics such as Catherine of Siena (1347–1380) and Teresa of Avila (1515–1582). And if it were to be claimed that, compared with the active good works in the wider community of the unenclosed religious (the selfless, charitable work of the late Mother Teresa comes immediately to mind), such ambitions were merely a case of self-indulgent escapism, they would respond that their ceaseless offering of prayer to God on behalf of mankind is a sufficient reason. As an example of monastic dedication, the late Cardinal Archbishop Basil Hume's book *Searching for God* (2002 edn.) is instructive. Throughout his 'conferences' (OSB-speak for 'addresses'), which comprise the book, there is a constant repetition of the purpose of the monastic life – namely, a search for God:

'an exploration into the mystery which is God'
'…you have come here, as you are well aware to seek God…'
'…there is one thing only at which each of us should aim, and that is prayer. That is the *unum necessarium*: the highest form of union with God that we can attain in this world'
'the monastic life is, above all else, a search for God… the end is the search for union with God.'

After visiting the Abbey of Saint Wandrille in Normandy in 1948, the late Patrick Leigh Fermor expressed the view that 'The life of monks passes in a state of white-hot conviction and striving to which there is never a holiday; and no living man, after all, is in a position to declare their premises true or false. They have foresworn the pleasures and rewards of a world whose values they consider meaningless; and they alone have as a body confronted the terrifying problem of eternity, abandoning everything to help their fellow-men and themselves to meet it… Worship, then, and prayer are the *raison d'être* of the Benedictine order …'[1] I would conclude by asserting that only those whose Christian faith is absolute would embrace the cenobitic life and that we – the questioning outsiders – have good reason to admire their dedication.

For the unenclosed Orders (e.g. Franciscans, Dominicans and Jesuits) their preaching role is paramount. As a good example of their attitude to Christianity let us take the recent book by the Dominican Father Timothy Radcliffe, *What is the Point of Being a Christian?* (2005). Radcliffe was asked by a friend: 'Why be a Christian?' He then asked himself whether his faith was true or not. 'If it was true, that humanity was destined to share God's own unutterable happiness, then this must be the purpose of my life. If it was not true, then clearly I must leave the Church. So I replied to this friend of mine, "Because it is true".'[2] Here, then, is the subjective choice of a man who believes that we are all destined 'to share God's unutterable happiness,' and in consequence his life must be devoted to 'pointing' people to God so that they may also be partakers of the heavenly kingdom.

Which leads us on to the question of 'truth', which lay at the heart of Radcliffe's chosen calling. In matters of religion it is particularly important for the impartial observer – rather than the committed Christian – to recognise that the concept of 'truth' popularly lies in the eye of the beholder, notwithstanding the pronouncements of those in positions of religious 'authority'. There is no such thing as 'truth' in an absolute sense. It is not a verifiable concept. Even more so the term 'revealed truth' which brings into the equation the equally unverifiable concept of 'revelation'. As Richard Holloway points out: 'The root of the difficulty lies in the nature of the claims religions make about matters that are beyond verification. This uncertainty, which lies at the heart of all religious systems, famously produces compensating protestations of absolute certainty about matters that are intrinsically unknowable.'[3] However, this is clearly not a straightforward matter. Professor Keith Ward points out that: 'It is misleading to ask whether religious beliefs are true, as if that was a neutrally ascertainable matter of fact... The 'truth' of a religious belief is known in some definite psychological response to an active power, the force of whose activity itself depends upon the predispositions and receptivity of the human mind.'[4] Since psychological responses depend on the upbringing, education and preconceptions of each individual, this definition would inevitably evoke a multitude of subjective responses to the 'truth' of any religion. Which hardly gets us any further! The views of Father Timothy Radcliffe on this subject are instructive. Radcliffe states that 'Christianity stands or falls on the truth of its claims, but complex issues are raised in trying to understand the sense in which they are true... Our statements about God are only understandable in the context of lives that are pointed to God.

Outside the context of lives that reach beyond themselves, then all our statements about God will not mean much.'[5] In other words, Christian 'truth' is only comprehensible to convinced Christians. Furthermore, 'the moment that religious people start to talk about truth, then people become nervous. This is understandable. All over the world violence is associated with different faiths quarrelling about the truth... Truth claims are associated with intolerance, arrogance and indoctrination...'[6] Radcliffe continues: 'Christianity should remind our society of our buried desire for the truth, and walk with it as it searches. But we will only be able to do this convincingly if we are seen to be pilgrims ourselves who do not know all the answers in advance. Christian leaders will speak with more authority if they say more often "I do not know". We must be seen as those who not only teach but also learn',[7] and he quotes approvingly St Augustine's words 'Whoever thinks that in this mortal life he may so disperse the mists of the imagination as to possess the unclouded light of unchangeable truth... understands neither what he seeks nor who he is that seeks it.'[8] These admirable sentiments will be endorsed by many, but the problem is that not everyone shares Father Radcliffe's intuitive conviction about the reality of a future life, and we shall therefore be wise to use inverted commas in this book whenever the word *truth* occurs, unless it is a quotation, so that at least we can remain intellectually impartial. And lastly, what makes someone a Christian believer? The late Cardinal Basil Hume gives us the answer: 'and we know from experience that faith is not something we bring forth ourselves: it is something we receive, which is given to us. It is something for which we have to dispose ourselves and pray.'[9]

For those with an open and questioning mind, uncluttered by family or social influence, what intellectual choice confronts us with regard to our spiritual beliefs? Broadly, we have a choice of categorisation between Atheism, Agnosticism, Deism and Theism (in Hinduism one would add Polytheism to this list). These beliefs may be characterised as follows. Atheists take the view that, whatever definition you may care to choose, there is no God (or Gods), and that the origin of the world and the subsequent appearance of life on earth and its development into complex forms may be explained exclusively on scientific principles. There is, in their view, no reality beyond the physical. Belief in the transcendent is an illusion. Agnostics believe that nothing is known, or likely to be known, of the existence of a God or of anything beyond material phenomena. Deists believe in the existence of one God responsible for creating the universe but without accepting revelation to mankind. In effect, after the single act of creation (c.14 billion years ago) their God adopted a policy of supreme indifference towards his creation. Theists believe in the existence of one God responsible for the origin of the world and of life within it, supernaturally revealed to man and maintaining a personal relationship with his creatures. Among the Christian fraternity in the United Kingdom, apart from the mainstream Church of England with its various branches, and the Roman Catholic Church, are the Unitarians, founded in the seventeenth century by John Biddle (1615–1662) under the influence of the Dutch Catholic reformer Erasmus and the Spanish theologian Michael Servetus (who was executed in 1553 for his denial of the Trinity). Unitarians have no creed and reject the doctrine of the Holy Trinity and the divinity of Christ. They do not subscribe to the Thirty-Nine Articles of the Anglican Church and their beliefs derive ultimately from Arianism. Two of their number, Bartholomew Legate and Edward Wightman, were burnt at the stake as heretics in 1612. Their name, incidentally, was coined by the eighteenth-century chemist, Joseph Priestley. The more intolerant evangelical Christians today still regard them as heretics.[10] The Quakers are another offshoot from traditional Christianity, from whose doctrines they broke away in the seventeenth century. After the execution of King Charles I in 1649 the Puritan government found itself confronted by exceptional religious fervour amongst the army and many ordinary people who genuinely believed that the Day of the Lord was at hand and the Kingdom of Heaven was about to be established. Amongst the religious sects which sprang up at this time were the Levellers, the Ranters, the Seekers and the Quakers, the latter led by George Fox (1624–1691) and James Naylor (1616–1660) who held that every individual could achieve salvation here on earth, and preached pacifism, non-violence and egalitarianism. As Fox recalled, 'it was Justice Bennet of Derby that first called us Quakers because we bid them tremble at the word of God.'[11] Fox and his supporters, who called themselves the Society of Friends, were remarkable preachers but after the 1662 Quakers' Act was passed (which prohibited their assembly for worship) many Quakers left the country to settle in America (the Quaker William Penn, for example, founding the new state of Pennsylvania in 1682). Contemporary Quakers are few in number (about 19,000 in the UK and 340,000 worldwide in 2008); they have no hierarchy as such (although some Quaker Meetings have pastors); while rooted in Christianity they have no theological doctrine, dogma or set form of liturgy (but 'wait upon God in silence'), and do not believe in outward sacraments such as the Eucharist. Quakerism's lack of dogma is held to be essential for compatibility with a scientific world view. Quakerism is essentially a 'way', rather than a set of beliefs. Historically, Quakers campaigned against slavery, argued for religious toleration, and against discrimination by social class, gender or race. Quakers devote themselves to world-wide peace, the relief of poverty and hunger, and are active in inter-faith work.[12] Writing in 1995 Professor Monika Hellwig declared: 'My honest attempts to see what is truly happening in the Christian Churches have led to the conclusion that the Society of Friends is consistently more generous, more morally upright, more proof against worldly seductions, and more willing to take on risks and arduous work on behalf of peace and social justice.'[13] She also spoke warmly of the friendly community bond amongst members of Baptist Churches and found most Protestant sects accustomed to spending more time in Sunday worship than others. One might perhaps add Pantheism to this list, as exemplified in Spinoza's philosophy. The Greek view that creation out of nothing is impossible led to pantheism which maintains that everything – including nature itself – is an aspect of God; and all that can be hoped for is to become increasingly subsumed into the being of God.[14] This is very much in keeping with the views of most mystics who have found it hard to believe that the world is separate from God. Pantheists take the view that there can be no 'personal' immortality as is believed by Christians.

14

The development of religious thought over the past 5,000 years or so is a fascinating story, combined as it is with the history of philosophical ideas which have exercised the mind of man since he first began to live in civilised communities. The meaning and purpose of life, the possibility of a human soul and of immortality, belief in spirits and gods – all are subjects which have been addressed by those whose beliefs we have characterised above. It is therefore an essential preliminary for us to study the historical background of ideas in the West in order to appreciate the way in which Christianity as a religion has come down to us, and to enable us to make up our own minds as to its claims.

NOTES

[1] Leigh Fermor, P., 2004, *Words of Mercury*, 67
[2] Radcliffe. 2005, 1. In Chapter 6 (pp. 111–128) Radcliffe discusses the Christian attitude to 'truth'
[3] Holloway, 2004, 9
[4] Ward, 2004, 97–8
[5] Radcliffe, 2005, 209
[6] Ibid., 116
[7] Ibid., 115
[8] Ibid., 116
[9] Hume, 2007, 209
[10] Thus in 2006 the Bishop of Chester, the Rt Revd Dr Peter Forster, refused to allow a Unitarian service of the Unitarian Church's General Assembly to be held in Chester Cathedral (such a service having nevertheless been held there on three previous occasions). See Ruth Gledhill, *The Times*, 1 March, 2006
[11] For the Quakers in Derbyshire see Turbutt, G., 1999, *A History of Derbyshire*, Vol 3, 1137–1145
[12] See Dandelion, P., 2008, *The Quakers*
[13] Hellwig, M., 1995, 'Roman Catholic Christian in a World of Options', in Forward, M. (ed.), 1995, 151
[14] Russell, 1965, 553–4

3. THE HISTORICAL AND THEOLOGICAL BACKGROUND

(i)   A History of Religious Thought

All creatures in the natural world, including human beings, are born with an instinct for survival. Were they not, they would become extinct. The fundamental distinction between animals and human beings is that the latter are born with the power of consciousness. How this division occurred is at present a scientific mystery. The power of consciousness adds a further dimension to the primitive instinct for survival by instinctively persuading human beings that supernatural powers can be enlisted to protect mankind from danger and to secure for them the means by which they can survive and flourish. To ensure that this was so, primitive man devised sacrificial rituals to appease and worship these supernatural gods. This was the beginning of 'religion'. Thus it has often been said that 'man is a religious animal'. Primitive man also believed in an afterlife. As early as c.60,000 BC Neanderthal people in the Kurdish area of northern Iraq appear to have ceremonially buried their dead (remains of funeral feasts have been noted and, rather touchingly, with one burial were discovered the remains of a garland of flowers[1]). From the prehistoric period in Western Europe weapons, implements, joints of meat and pottery drinking cups (e.g. Bronze Age 'beakers') have been found frequently with burials, along with evidence of funeral feasts, and the burial of bodies in the foetal position (to facilitate a re-birth into a new life) have frequently come to light. These examples show the gradually evolving theme of death and re-birth amongst such early peoples. It is therefore abundantly clear that belief in the supernatural and in an afterlife had developed in mankind by the time of the last Ice Age, and was to be elaborated in the early civilisations of Mesopotamia and Egypt before passing into the mainstream of Western European thought. Whether – as atheists like to maintain – these 'religious' impulses may be seen as the last vestiges of primitive man's defence mechanisms, the historical evidence for man's religious belief cannot be denied.

In her impressively researched book *A History of God* Karen Armstrong believes that human beings 'are spiritual animals… Men and women started to worship gods as soon as they became recognisably human; they created religions at the same time as they created works of art. This was not simply because they wanted to propitiate powerful forces … religion … seems to have been something that we have always done. It was not tacked on to a primordially secular nature by manipulative kings and priests but was natural to humanity.'[2] The concept of God was in fact the product of man's creative imagination. As Armstrong explains: 'The idea of God formed in one generation by one set of human beings could be meaningless in another… Consequently there is not one unchanging idea contained in the word "God" but the word contains a whole spectrum of meanings.'[3]

From the earliest times mankind has sought to discover how the world – both the earth and the heavenly bodies – came into existence and his place in it. He has used his powers of reasoning to devise philosophies and scientific principles that would explain the laws of nature and govern the behaviour of societies. Hand in hand with such philosophies was a belief in spirits and gods who were thought to exercise supernatural powers and provide protection to their adherents, thus giving rise to the subsequent study of theology. The whole course of Western history has been characterised by an uneasy intellectual compromise between philosophy and theology in which the steady expansion of scientific knowledge has played an increasingly important rôle in endeavouring to discover the foundations of reality.

In the Western world our modern idea of philosophy effectively began in Greece in the sixth century BC and notably with the rise of the Athenian Empire. Here the names of Pythagoras (580–500 BC), Socrates (d. 399 BC) and his disciple Plato (428/7–347 BC) are pre-eminent. Pythagoras, possibly influenced by ideas from India, considered that the human soul was a fallen deity incarcerated in the body and doomed to a perpetual cycle of birth and re-birth (c.f. re-incarnation in Buddhism and Hinduism). Thus he believed in the transmigration of souls (indeed, he fancied that he could remember one of his earlier incarnations – that he had been a certain Euphorbos, son of Panthous, a Homeric hero). Much of Plato's works has fortunately survived, and his *Phaedo* recounts the death of Socrates and his belief in immortality. Socrates was tried on a trumped-up charge of not worshipping the State gods[4] and of corrupting the young; he was found guilty, and was condemned to death in 399 BC at about the age of seventy. He was however remarkably unmoved by the imminent threat of death (which he considered to be the separation of soul and body), and believed that 'in the first place I am going to other gods who are wise and good (of which I am as certain as I can be of any such matters) and secondly (though I am not so sure of this last) to men departed, better than those whom I leave behind…'. In Socrates's view the good go to heaven after death and the bad to hell. While modern philosophers are critical of much of Socrates's philosophical reasoning, there can be no denying that he was a wise and good man and was effectively a martyr for his beliefs. Interestingly, with his belief in immortality he foreshadowed doctrines later to be appropriated by the Christians. 'For Plato, true reality lay in a transcendent world of unchanging, perfect, abstract Ideas, or Forms, a domain of mathematical relationships and fixed geometrical structures. This was the realm of pure being, inaccessible to the senses'.[5] But humanity dwelt in another world, namely a universe of material objects. Plato invented two gods to have dominion over each of these worlds. Over the world of Forms was 'the Good', eternal and immutable, beyond space and time. Over the material world was 'the Demiurge' who had the task of fashioning matter into an ordered state. Plato taught that the souls of men were immortal and came to them at birth from elsewhere (the doctrine of *anamnesis*), and indeed had existed since the Creation. This idea was regarded by later Christian authorities as heretical, but the belief lasted through to the poetry of the Romantics in the eighteenth century and is exemplified by Wordsworth's Ode: 'Intimations of Immortality from Recollections of Early Childhood':

> 'Our birth is but a sleep and a forgetting:
> The Soul that rises with us, our life's star,

Hath had elsewhere its setting,
And cometh from afar:
Not in entire forgetfulness,
And not in utter nakedness,
But trailing clouds of glory do we come
From God, who is our home:
Heaven lies about us in our infancy.'

The philosopher Aristotle (384–322 BC), a pupil of Plato, likewise believed in God (whom he termed the 'Unmoved Mover') – a God that should be loved by mankind but who, because of his perceived nature as 'pure thought', cannot reciprocate that love. He rejected Plato's concept of timeless Forms, and conceived the material world to be a living organism 'infused with purpose, and drawn towards its goal by final causes. Living things were ascribed souls to guide them...'.[6] Wisdom (*sophia*) was for him the highest of all human virtues. It does not however appear that Aristotle believed in personal immortality. Zeno (342–270 BC) of Citium, the founder of Stoicism, held that God is the soul of the world and that each mortal contains a share of the Divine Fire. The Stoics believed that at the end of the present age everything would be dissolved in fire, and that the life of the universe would begin again as formerly (a theory known as *palingenesia*). Later Stoics such as Posidonius (*c.*135–*c.*51 BC) and Seneca (*c.*55 BC–*c.*40 AD) had considerable influence on the doctrines of the early Christian Fathers. Marcus Tullius Cicero (106–43 BC), the Roman statesman, orator, and man of letters, in his essay *On the Nature of the Gods* stated 'It is clearly due to nature that all people of all races conceive of the gods in none other but human form... if the human figure is superior to the form of all living things, and a god is a living thing, then a god surely has the most beautiful form of all... But this form is not really corporeal, but merely resembles a human body: it does not have blood, merely the semblance of blood.' The concept would be revived by several later thinkers, such as Marcion (*c.*150), who held that Jesus was a 'phantasm' or manifestation of God who had the *appearance* only of human flesh – a position known as 'Docetism'.

The last of the great philosophers of antiquity was Plotinus (204–270 AD), the founder of Neoplatonism (a synthesis of elements from the philosophies of Plato, Aristotle, Pythagoras and the Stoicism of Zeno), many of those metaphysical theories were adopted by Christian theologians in the latter years of the Roman empire (e.g. the Platonic argument that the soul is immortal because ideas are eternal; the identification of Christ with the *Logos* or 'reason'; and his conception of a *philosophical* 'Trinity' of 'The One', 'Spirit' and 'Soul'). Plotinus's view on memory is instructive: 'Memory is concerned with our life in time, whereas our best and truest life is in eternity. Therefore, as the soul grows towards eternal life, it will remember less and less: friends, children, wife, will be gradually forgotten; ultimately, we shall know nothing of the things of this world, but only contemplate the intellectual realm. There will be no memory of personality, which, in contemplative vision, is unaware of itself.'[7]

Contemporary with Plotinus was the Christian philosopher Origen (185–254), who lived in Alexandria, then a centre not only of commerce but also of scholarship at its university. Origen was a brilliant scholar and wrote many books. His principal work was *De Principiis* in which he argues that, like Plato, the souls of men come to them at birth from elsewhere, and that all men (and even devils!) will be saved at the last. These and other of his theories were later considered to be heresies. Another of his works was a book entitled *Against Celsus* whose own book – now lost – had argued that the Christian theory of resurrection was identical to *metempsychosis* or transmigration or reincarnation of souls – a belief held widely by philosophers (e.g. Plato) and also held by the Orphic cult. In his refutation of Celsus's views Origen displays the 'twofold argument for belief which is characteristic of Christian philosophy. On the one hand, pure reason, rightly exercised, suffices to establish the essentials of the Christian faith, more especially God, immortality, and free will. But on the other hand the Scriptures prove not only these bare essentials, but much more; and the divine inspiration of the Scriptures is proved by the fact that the prophets foretold the coming of the Messiah, by the miracles, and by the beneficent effects of belief on the lives of the faithful.'[8]

Christianity had many competitors in its early years, and the irony is that the first Christians were accused of being 'atheists' by their pagan rivals because they refused to acknowledge the cult of the Roman emperor and his claim to be worshipped as a god.[9] The Romans were extremely tolerant in matters of religion: the state demanded religious observance but the individual could choose (within limits) whom he worshipped. The only cults proscribed in the early period of the empire were those, like Druidism, whose practices (such as human sacrifice) were deemed contrary to civilised behaviour, or which were held to be subversive (as was Christianity in its early years). This is well illustrated by the younger Pliny's letter to the emperor Trajan:

'I have never been present at an examination of Christians. Consequently, I do not know the nature or the extent of the punishments usually meted out to them, nor the grounds for starting an investigation and how far it should be pressed... For the moment this is the line I have taken with all persons brought before me on the charge of being Christians. I have asked them in person if they are Christians, and if they admit it, I repeat the question a second and third time, with a warning of the punishment awaiting them. If they persist, I order them to be led away for execution; for, whatever the nature of their admission, I am convinced that their stubbornness and unshakeable obstinacy ought not to go unpunished. There have been others similarly fanatical who are Roman citizens... Now that I have begun to deal with this problem, as so often happens, the charges are becoming more widespread and increasing in variety. An anonymous pamphlet has been circulated which contains the names of accused persons... Amongst these I considered that I should dismiss any who denied that they were or ever had been Christians when they had repeated after me a formula of invocation to the gods and had made offerings of wine and incense to your statue (which I had ordered to be brought into court for this purpose along with the image of the gods), and furthermore had reviled the name of Christ: none of which things, I understand, any genuine Christian can be induced to do. Others... first admitted the charge and then denied it... This made me decide that it was all the more necessary to extract the truth by torture from two slave-women, whom they call deaconesses. I found nothing but a degenerate sort of cult carried to extravagant lengths. I have therefore postponed any further examination and hastened to consult you. The question seems to me to be worthy of your consideration, especially in view of the number of persons endangered; for a great many individuals of every age and class, both men and women, are being brought to trial, and this is likely to continue. It is not only the towns, but villages and rural districts too which are infected through contact with this wretched cult. I think though that it is still possible for it to be checked and directed to better ends, for there is no doubt that people have begun to throng the temples which had been almost deserted for a long time; the sacred rites which had been allowed to lapse are being performed again, and flesh of sacrificial victims is on sale everywhere. It is easy to infer from this that a great many people could be reformed if they were given an opportunity to repent.'[10]

Trajan replied:
'You have followed the right course of procedure, my dear Pliny, in your examination of the cases of persons charged with being Christians, for it is impossible to lay down a general rule to a fixed formula. These people must not be hunted out; if they are brought before you and the charge against them is proved, they must be punished, but in the case of anyone who denies that he is a Christian, and makes it clear that he is not by offering prayers to our gods, he is to be pardoned as a result of his repentance... But pamphlets circulated anonymously must play no part in any accusation. They create the worst sort of precedent and are quite out of keeping with the spirit of our age.'[11]

The point was that all 'political societies' were at that time forbidden, and the Roman authorities believed that Christian communities were potentially seditious groups (and indeed that they had been responsible for the burning of Rome in the emperor Nero's reign). The numbers attending gatherings of other cults, such as those of Bacchus and Mithras, were also closely controlled to avoid politically subversive meetings. It is clear that it was the political, rather than the religious aspects of Christianity that the Romans feared, and historians now recognise that Jesus's trial before the Roman prefect Pontius Pilate must have been on grounds of sedition rather than blasphemy and that he may have been arrested with the seditious group known as the 'Zealots'. The Roman attitude was essentially one of believing in a contract between the gods and the individual state: if the correct rituals were observed, the gods would offer their protection. 'The old Roman worship was businesslike and utilitarian. The gods were partners in a contract with their worshippers, and the ritual was characterised by all the hard and literal formalism of the legal system of Rome.'[12] Thus an answered prayer, where a vow had previously been made by an individual, would often be followed by the erection of an altar to the deity concerned, bearing an inscription which referred to 'a vow fulfilled'. In this the Roman attitude towards religion was quite different from our own. As Jon Davies points out: 'the whole pressure of Roman religion was to impose the supremacy of the imperial cult as the principle of order in the seemingly endless profusion of cults, native and foreign, new and old, which characterised the Ancient Near East and the other lands of the Empire.'[13] The ethical element in religion was totally absent: questions as to what was morally right were for philosophers to answer; before embarking on any public business the will of the gods was sought by divination through the interpretation of certain signs. The pagan function of sacrifice (usually of a bull or calf) played a large part in securing the favour of the gods. This was a common practice amongst primitive peoples worldwide where sacrifices – often of human beings (for example, in the Aztec empire of central America) – were necessary to appease the gods and thereby ensure the blessings of nature (rain and sunshine). Personal religious practices centred on the *Lares* or household gods (said to have been 'the souls of men admitted to the company of the gods'), to whom a shrine would be dedicated within each house (sometimes containing busts of decreased members of the family). Family burials always took place outside a town, and the richer citizens often had elaborate tombs.[14] The pantheon of Roman state religions resembled the Olympian gods of Greek mythology some of whom were assimilated into it (e.g. the Roman god Jupiter was equated with the Greek Zeus, Venus with Aphrodite, Diana with Artemis, Neptune with Poseidon).

However, the two Greek deities Apollo and Dionysus (or Bacchus) retained their Greek names. To Plutarch, the genius of Greco-Roman religion lay in its ability to absorb the gods of other lands. In the case of Egyptian gods he emphasised that 'Isis and the gods related to her belong to all men and are known to them... There is nothing wrong with this if in the first place they preserve the gods as our common heritage, and do not make them the peculiar property of the Egyptians.'[15]

By the beginning of Augustus's reign the effects of a century of civil war had produced a sharp moral and religious decline in society. Writers such as Virgil and Horace urged a return to the old virtues of public duty and religious observance which had inspired their fellow countrymen during the early years of the Republic and Virgil's emphasis on the subordination of men's actions to the will of God was later seen by some as foreshadowing the coming of Christianity. Thus the poet Virgil (70–19 BC) in *The Georgics* writes:

> '...For God, they say,
> Pervades all things, the earth and sea and sky.
> From Him the flocks and herds, and man and beast,
> Each have the thin-spun stream of life at birth;
> To Him all things return, at last dissolved:
> There is no place for death...'[16]

And it was Christianity which was to succeed the ossified religions of the Roman Empire, and to which the classical Greek philosophical theories of Plato and Aristotle later became attached.

In return for the Roman emperor Constantine's favours, and specifically his famous so-called Edict of Milan in 313 which legalized Christianity, the fourth-century Christian leaders were prepared to concede to the emperor the Messianic achievement which Jesus Christ had manifestly failed to deliver, and to acknowledge his priest-king status under the patronage of Sol Invictus or 'God the Father' of their faith. Indeed, Eusebius, bishop of Caesarea (*c.*264–340), addressing Constantine in the following politically obsequious terms: '...most God-fearing sovereign, to whom alone of those who have yet been here since the start of time has the Universal All-ruling God Himself given power to purify human life' comes perilously close to denying the very existence of Christ.

Religious conservatism was perhaps the most difficult obstacle for the new religion to overcome, and we have it on good authority that at the end of the fourth century the majority of the Roman Senate had shown little sympathy towards it. For them and for many of their countrymen *Roma Dea*, the idealised genius of the Latin race, was the object of their real devotion:

'Imbedded in law, language, literature, the deepest instincts of the people, her ancient worship seemed inseparable from the very identity of Rome. The true Roman, even though his religious faith might not be very deep or warm, inherited the most ancient belief of his race that the gods of a city were sharers in all its fortunes... The complete and literal acceptance of the Christian faith seemed to mean a refusal to perform the duties of citizens or soldiers, a scornful abandonment of the old traditions of culture, even a loss of faith in the mission of Rome.'[17]

This was very much the view of the emperor Julian (361–3), known as 'the Apostate', who personally renounced Christianity and while not persecuting its adherents nevertheless stripped the church of many of its privileges and openly encouraged the old state religion.

It is clear that in its early years Christianity had to compromise and adapt in order to survive. Indeed its success against its rivals reveals an extraordinarily astute sense of what was required to appeal to contemporary popular religious imagination, and how this could be met by borrowing accepted myths and rituals from other cults. One of its rivals of long standing was the worship of Cybele, the Phrygian '*Magna Mater*' or 'Mother of the Gods', which had been adopted by Rome in 204 BC and had achieved considerable support in parts of the Roman Empire. It can hardly be coincidental that the death and resurrection of Christ as related in the New Testament contains precisely identical symbolism to the death and resurrection at the spring equinox of the Phrygian Attis, a youthful tree-spirit or vegetation god and consort of Cybele. He, too, was said to have been born miraculously of a virgin (a not uncommon attribute of divinity in primitive societies,[18] and often accompanied by the simultaneous rising of a star); his effigy was annually buried in a sepulchre with great mourning and lamentation; he also was held to have risen from the dead as a testimony that his disciples would triumph over the grave; and his day of resurrection – the third day – was an occasion for great celebration (the Festival of Hilaria, held on 25 March). Furthermore, the worshippers of Attis had mystical initiation ceremonies which included a sacramental meal and baptism in the blood of a bull which ensured that the novitiate 'had been born again to eternal life and had washed away his sins in the blood of the bull'.[19] These ceremonies were carried out 'at the sanctuary of the Phrygian goddess on the Vatican Hill, at or near the spot where the great basilica of St Peter's now stands; for many inscriptions relating to the rites were found when the church was being enlarged in 1608 and 1609'.[20] According to a fourth century Christian writer, supporters of the Phrygian 'Mother Goddess' cult bitterly attacked the Christians for having copied the death and resurrection of Attis in their new religion.[21] Alone of all other religious of the Roman empire Christians totally rejected animal sacrifices, and their willingness to perform sacrifice came to be used as a key test when interrogated during periods of Christian persecution.[22] The cult of the Syrian Adonis (meaning 'Lord') was in many ways similar to that of the Phrygian Attis, and the celebration of his death and resurrection was widely observed in Syria and the West about the time of the birth of Christ.[23] Likewise worship of the Egyptian god Osiris and his sister-wife Isis attracted many adherents. According to Frazer the worship of Isis 'was one of the most popular at Rome and throughout the empire'. With the future of the empire visibly disintegrating and various religions competing for adherents, it is not surprising that 'the serene figure of Isis with her spiritual calm, her gracious promise of immortality, should have appealed to many like a star in a stormy sky, and should have roused in their hearts a rapture of devotion not unlike that which was paid in the Middle Ages to the Virgin Mary. Indeed, her stately ritual, with its shorn and tonsured priests, its matins and vespers, its tinkling music, its baptism and aspersions in holy water, its solemn processions, its jewelled images of the Mother of God, presented many points of similarity to the pomps and ceremonies of Catholicism. The resemblance need not be purely accidental. Ancient Egypt may have contributed its share to the gorgeous symbolism of the Catholic Church as well as to the pale abstraction of her theology. Certainly in art the figure of Isis suckling the infant Horus is so like that of the Madonna and Child that it has sometimes received the adoration of ignorant Christians'.[24] The worship of Bacchus (or Dionysus) was also popular and 'offered an intense and often ecstatic communion with the deity involving an initiation ceremony...' There was 'mass participation by males and females in ceremonies that involved music, dancing, and the consumption of wine'.[25] A detailed description of Bacchic practices was written by Livy, involving magic, fraud, and immorality and a senatorial decree was passed in 186 BC regulating its organisation and activities.[26]

For the new religion of Christianity to be successful amongst the wide diversity of people within the Roman Empire Jesus Christ had to be no less a god incarnate than his rivals such as Attis, Adonis or Osiris, all of whom were believed to have died and to have been re-born in the spring, and the Christian festival of Easter (so named by Bede in the early eighth century as being derived from the pagan Scandinavian Eostre, goddess of the dawn, whose festival was celebrated at the spring equinox) appears to have been deliberately made to coincide with the spring rites of these contemporary cults. It was at Easter that ordinary people were allowed to participate in the Eucharist and partake of bread and wine (the only other occasions when this was allowed was at Christmas and Whitsun).

There were thus numerous cults familiar to early Christians – e.g. those of Adonis, Attis, Isis, Dionysus – which practised the ritual re-enactment of the death and re-birth of the god, associated with a variety of fertility rites. As Dr Tom Wright points out: 'These multifarious and sophisticated cults enacted the god's death and resurrection as a *metaphor*, whose concrete referent was the cycle of seed-time and harvest, of human reproduction and fertility... when Christians spoke of the resurrection of Jesus they did not suppose it was something that happened every year, with the sowing of seed and the harvesting of crops... It is of course quite possible that, when people in the wider world heard what the early Christians were saying, they attempted to fit the strange message into the worldview of cults they already knew.'[27] But even if Jesus's resurrection was not an annual event, like that of a cult god, other attributes – such as virgin births, stars in the east presaging such births – could be incorporated by the early Christians into their 'new' religion to lend it credibility amongst contemporaries.

It has long been recognised that, according to the principles of homeopathic magic, primitive man regarded the eating of the flesh and drinking of the blood of his enemies as a means of acquiring their attributes (e.g. strength, skill or courage). In like manner the consumption of the physical attributes of a vegetation god like Adonis or Attis – that is bread from corn and wine from the grape – would be tantamount to consuming the real body and blood of the god and thereby sharing in the god's attributes and powers. The drinking of wine at Dionysian festivals was for this reason regarded as a solemn sacrament. By the same symbolism the Christian Eucharist, in which bread and wine are consumed, would have been the most readily comprehensible sacrament to adherents of the early Christian Church. Here again, then, we have another plausible example of the pagan stock on to which a Christian ritual was grafted. After making an impassioned defence of the Christian incarnation doctrine in a recent book Canon Michael Green had to admit that 'what is perfectly true is that, given their faith in the incarnate Lord, the early Christians used (sometimes rather unwisely) such partial parallels and analogies as they could find in the mythology of the pagans they were seeking to evangelise.'[28] The 'star in the east', the 'Virgin Birth', the death and resurrection on the third day, and the sacramental meals are obvious parallels.

Another cult contemporary with Christianity was that of Orpheanism, derived from the teaching of a certain Orpheus, a priest and philosopher as well as a musician. Orphics believed in the transmigration of souls; that the soul would be rewarded or condemned in the future life depending on its behaviour in this life. Gnosticism (see below), a title which embraced a number of differing sects or individuals, broadly rejected the then current

Jewish claim to be the 'Chosen People; and one of their sects (the followers of Cerinthus) maintained that Jesus was a mere man, and that the spirit of God descended upon him when he was baptised and abandoned him during the Passion (which they based upon Jesus's outcry: 'My God, my God, why hast thou forsaken me?'). This doctrine was adopted by Muhammad who recognised Jesus as a prophet but not the divine Son of God, and this has since become the orthodox view of Islam.

Gnosticism,[29] as a system of belief, was one of the most widespread and popular ways of thinking. Its name derives from the Greek word 'gnosis' meaning 'knowing through observation or experience', such knowledge implying insight into, and comprehension of, spiritual truths, and above all the awareness of the presence within certain people of a spark of divinity implanted by God. Thus people have immortal souls which are temporarily imprisoned in this world of matter, and are desperate to return to the divine realm from which they came. As Professor Bart D. Ehrman explains, gnostics claimed to know secrets that can bring salvation: 'for gnostics, a person is saved not by having faith in Christ or by doing good works. Rather, a person is saved by knowing the truth – the truth about the world we live in, about who the true God is, and especially about who we ourselves are. In other words, this is largely self-knowledge.'[30]

Gnostic beliefs may be traced back to at least the sixth century BC, and partly derive from Zoroastrianism and partly from the cult of Dionysus and its offshoot Orpheanism (see above). What is important to realise is that there were many sects and much diversity of belief amongst people who were termed gnostics.[31] As the late Professor Gilbert Murray pointed out: 'The Gnostics are still commonly thought of as a body of Christian heretics. In reality there were Gnostic sects scattered over the Hellenistic world before Christianity as well as after. They must have been established in Antioch and probably in Tarsus well before the days of Paul or Apollos. Their Saviour, like the Jewish Messiah, was established in men's minds before the Saviour of the Christians.'[32] Gnostics recognised one transcendent God from whom descended a series of lesser Gods or Aeons one of whom, Sophia, caused a cosmic catastrophe by recklessly creating another God – the so-called 'Demiurge' – who was the creator of the material cosmos (a concept derived from Plato) and was equated with Yahweh (YHWH) or Jehovah (in Elizabethan English), the Hebrew God revealed to Moses in the uncompromisingly arrogant statement: 'No god was formed before me, nor will be after me. I am Yahweh, there is no other saviour but me' (Isaiah 45:21).

How do gnostics learn the secret knowledge required for salvation? They need a revelation from above, and in Christian gnostic belief the one who comes from above to reveal this knowledge is Jesus Christ. Some gnostics believed that Jesus was an aeon from the world above and was not in reality a man of flesh and blood but rather he was a divine phantasm who had the appearance of human flesh (a teaching known as 'Docetism'), whose major exponent was the philosopher Marcion (see below). Others (such as Cerinthus) considered him to be a real man who received divinity at his baptism (when the Spirit descended upon him), which enabled him to deliver his teachings and to perform miracles, but which left him prior to his crucifixion (hence his cry 'My God, my God, why has thou forsaken me?'). Thus the gnostic apocryphal Gospel of Peter relates that Jesus's cry on the cross was: 'My power, O power, you have left me', while the gnostic Gospel of Philip states ' 'My God, my God, why O Lord have you forsaken me?' For it was on the cross that he said these words, for it was there that he was divided.'[33]

One of the best known gnostics who was a contemporary of the early Christians was Marcion (c.85–c.160), a ship-owner or mariner from Sinope, whose followers were known as Marcionites. They began as Christians but later became gnostic, and their sect was one of the earliest 'heresies' to rival Christianity. As Michael Goulder explains: 'The Samaritan Christians were a powerful section of the first-century church, and... their movement grew into Christian Gnosticism in the second, and this movement presented a challenge to Galilean Christianity everywhere.'[34] Marcion is thought to have been one of the early Christian bishops (his father was Bishop of Sinope in Pontus). As a teacher in Rome he was the first person to attempt to put together a canon of Scripture, and proposed a collection of 11 books (containing many letters written by Paul and a version of Luke's gospel). He summoned a council of church leaders in Rome and put his proposals to them. They were not impressed and excommunicated him (144) after he had allegedly threatened to divide the Church: 'to cause within her a division which will last forever'! He went on to found a church of his own – teaching that there were two gods – 'one the stern, lawgiving, creator God of the Old Testament, and the other the good, merciful God of the New Testament'. He rejected the incarnation of Jesus, maintaining that he was merely a 'manifestation' of the Father or 'good' God rather than God incarnate (i.e. the standpoint of a Docetist). He believed celibacy to be in keeping with Jesus's teaching, and while welcoming anyone to his church they could not become full members if they were married. Over a doorway of a house in a Syrian village, which had formerly been the site of a Marcionite meeting house or church, was inscribed in Latin the date 1 October AD 318, the church being dedicated to 'The Lord and Saviour Jesus, the Good' – i.e. Chrestos not Christos, 'one perfected, the holy one, the saint',[35] as distinct from 'Christos' which is the Greek for the Hebrew Messiah or anointed one (an attribution denied by Marcionites). Marcion's teaching laid great stress on asceticism and self-discipline, and had a profound effect on Manichaeism (which later absorbed it). It had churches in Rome, Palestine, Egypt, Syria and elsewhere in the Near East and these lasted until the eighth century. From an orthodox point of view Marcion's theology was attacked by Tertullian from the year 207 onwards, who alleged that Marcion's 'good' God 'had more in common with the God of Greek philosophy than the God of the Bible'. It is interesting that on a visit to Rome St Polycarp met the heretic Marcion, who called on him to recognise him, 'to which Polycarp replied: 'I recognise, I recognise, the first-born of Satan'![36]

As we shall see later on, the discovery of scrolls near Nag Hammadi in Egypt provided a great deal of information about gnostic beliefs, which we know to have been forcefully condemned by Irenaeus (c.130–200), bishop of Lyon, in his great refutation *Against Heresies*. Despite this religious condemnation gnosticism did not perish at the hands of orthodox Christians. It simply went underground. Professor Keith Hopkins believes that 'the sheer virtuosity of their inventions induced more conservative Christians to sharpen the boundaries of orthodoxy. Conservative Christian traditionalists insisted more rigorously on the uniqueness of the single ever-existent Creator and his single human/divine son Jesus. In contrast to the esoteric, mutually conflicting and unverifiable inventions of the gnostics, conservative Christians also increasingly insisted on a fixed canon of sacred texts, on the bodily resurrection of a historical Jesus, and on the traditions of a 'known' apostolic succession.'[37] And as Elaine Pagels has written in her book *The Gnostic Gospels* (1980): 'Had Christianity remained multiform [i.e. had it continued to include a variety of gnostic communities in addition to the orthodox community], it might well have disappeared from history, along with dozens of rival religious cults of antiquity. I believe that we owe the survival of Christian tradition to the organisational and theological structure that the emerging church developed. Anyone as powerfully attracted to Christianity as I am will regard that as a major achievement.'[38] It was indeed due to the political acumen of the orthodox churchmen in the early years of Christian history who realised the absolute necessity of crushing the insidious gnostic movement that Christianity was able to survive. Indeed, as we have seen earlier, Eusebius, bishop of Caesarea (*c.*264–340), in order to win the support of the emperor Constantine, felt constrained to acknowledge the priest-king status of the emperor under the patronage of Sol Invictus (or 'God the Father' of his faith).

After studying the Nag Hammadi scrolls, scholars are generally of the opinion that 'Gnostics were mostly individual believers or members of cliques within Christian congregations. Beyond a set of core beliefs, they had no agreed universal doctrine and there were many different published versions.'[39] The devout martyr St Polycarp (*c.*69–155), bishop of Smyrna, who had been a disciple of St John, is reported to have been horrified by the gnostic heretics he encountered in his old age. Eusebius recalled that he would exclaim 'O good god! For what times hast thou kept me that I should endure such things!'[40] When once at Ephesus he recalled that the Apostle John went to the baths and, finding the early gnostic Cerinthus there, rushed out, saying 'Let us flee, lest even the bath-house fall in, for within is Cerinthus, the enemy of the truth.'[41] Polycarp lived to the age of 86, when he suffered martyrdom in Rome (?155).[42]

Another of the early Church apologists was Justin of Caesarea (*c*.100–*c*.165) who was finally martyred for his faith. He was an early student of Stoicism, and in his two *apologiae* (*c*.150 and *c*.155) he argued that Christians were in fact following Plato in his belief in a single and all-powerful God. He maintained that Jesus was the incarnation of the Stoic idea of the *logos* or divine reason which had been present in the world throughout history and had been the inspiration of both Greeks and Hebrews.

Mani (216–276), an Iranian visionary and a former member of a heretical Christian sect known as the Elchasaites, believed he encountered his spiritual self or 'twin', which is now 'a recognised psychological aspect of the journey towards Truth'.[43] He was surprisingly arrogant and considered himself to be on a par with spiritual leaders such as the Buddha, Zoroaster and Jesus. He sought to found a universal religion which would replace all the other contemporary systems of belief. Life for Manichaeans was an illusion – nothing is real, and the world is evil. He taught that a class of persons, the Elect, should live a life of self-denial and they would return to Paradise, while the rest would be reincarnated. Interestingly, St Augustine (354–430) was an auditor in the Manichaean church, before joining the Catholic church, and he subsequently wrote a number of treatises demolishing Manichaean beliefs.

There are still gnostic societies and churches in existence today (e.g. the Gnostic Society in America), and as Bernard Simon explains: 'The Gnostic Jesus, far from dying as an atonement for the sins of the world, an act that many might think was pointless, actually descended from the spiritual realm in order to make information available that was necessary both for self-perfection and for the perfection of the whole human race.'[44] There is surely a parallel here with the quest for Buddhist 'enlightenment'.

The popular cult of Mithraism, called after the Indo-Iranian god Mithra (who was a minor deity in the Zoroastrian pantheon under Ahura-Mazda), was widely known throughout the Roman world from *c*.100. The cult was only open to men, and its devotees met in small sanctuaries or temples for a ritual meal. The cult had grades of initiation, involved sun worship, taught the immortality of the soul, a future judgement, and the resurrection of the dead, and was very popular with the Roman army (a temple to Mithra may still be seen on the Roman Wall in Northumberland). Its initiation ceremony, known to Romans as the *taurobolium*, involved the initiate drinking the blood of a sacred bull or, alternatively, drinking a chalice of wine as a symbolic representation of blood. In respect of its belief in sun worship (and in some Mithraeae there were figures of Sol and Mithra shaking hands over a burning altar) Mithraism was considered to be complementary to the Roman state religion, Sol Invictus. A representation of Mithra slaying a bull seems to be a standard feature of all Mithraic sanctuaries.[45] Both Mithraism and Christianity were tolerated by the emperor Constantine who was disposed to regard the deified Jesus as an earthly manifestation of Sol Invictus, and his eclectic outlook thus allowed him to build a Christian church at the same time as raising statues to Sol Invictus (in his own likeness) and to Cybele the 'Mother Goddess'. The Council of Nicaea, meeting under his presidency in 325 to discuss Christian dogma and organisation, decided by a reassuring vote (218 in favour with two against) that Jesus was in fact a god and not a mortal prophet (and, from the emperor's point of view, could therefore be more easily accommodated with the state religion).

A relic of the Church's struggle with the cults of Sol Invictus and Mithraism (which had an alarming ability to absorb other cults and whose shrines are believed to have been attacked by Christians in the fourth century) lies in the Christian festival of Christmas. The 25th December, being then (as reckoned by the Julian calendar) the date of the winter solstice, was celebrated by both the state cult of Sol Invictus and also by that of Mithras as the festival of Natalis Invictus (the birth of the unvanquished sun) representing also the birthday of Osiris (or Aion, as he later became known). For centuries Egyptians were accustomed to watch for the appearance of the star Sirius on the horizon, for this event foretold the birth of Osiris and the rising of the waters of the river Nile. Now the Egyptian Christians were accustomed to celebrate the birth of Christ on 6th January, but according to a Syrian Christian Scriptor Syrus, writing in the late fourth century: 'It was a custom of the pagans to celebrate on the …twenty–fifth December the birthday of the Sun, at which they kindled lights in token of festivity. In these solemnities and revelries the Christians also took part. Accordingly when the doctors of the Church perceived that the Christians had a leaning to this festival, they took counsel and resolved that the true Nativity should be solemnised on that day' and the festival of the Epiphany on the sixth of January.[46] This change of date for the celebration of Christ's birth was first attested in a Roman calendar of 334.[47] Thus Christ's nativity was made coincident with the start of the traditional festivals by which for thousands of years primitive societies had celebrated the re-birth of the sun, and whose imminent birth was signalled by the appearance of the star Sirius. He thereby assumed the place of Mithra as Sol Invictus, or, in Christian prophetic parlance, the 'Sun of righteousness', and effectively became for many the latest in a series of sun gods known by different names in many parts of the ancient world. The aureole of light which crowned the head of the sun god was soon transmuted into the Christian halo. The 'twelve days of Christmas', ending with the feast of Epiphany (6th January), coincided with the Roman festivals known as the Saturnalia (starting on 17th December) and the Kalendae (from 1–3 January) which were carnivals of merry-making and licence. Since holly was the emblem of the Roman Saturnalia, and ivy was associated with the Dionysiac winter solstice revelries in Greece, it is hardly surprising to find that the holly and the ivy adorned the homes of early Christians at Christmas, one of many pleasantly pagan traditions which has persisted to this day. By a similar process of transmutation, the festival of the Assumption of the Virgin succeeded the festival of Diana; that of St John the Baptist the pagan Midsummer festival; and that of All Saints the old pagan festival known as Samhain. As Frazer concluded: 'Taken together, the coincidences of the Christian with the heathen festivals are too close and too numerous to be accidental. They mark the compromise which the Church in the hour of its triumph was compelled to make with its vanquished yet still dangerous rivals.

The inflexible Protestantism of the primitive missionaries, with their fiery denunciations of heathendom, had been exchanged for the supple policy, the easy tolerance, the comprehensive charity of shrewd ecclesiastics, who clearly perceived that if Christianity was to conquer the world it could do so only by relaxing the too rigid principles of its Founder, by widening a little the narrow gate which leads to salvation.'[48] This 'easy tolerance', which enabled the fourth century Roman to attend a Christian Service in the morning and sacrifice to his *lares familiares* in the afternoon; which allowed the Saxon Raedwald, King of East Anglia, to retain in his church not only a Christian altar but an altar to his heathen gods, may be recognised even today – some two thousand years later – in (for example) central America, where pagan shrines surrounded by lighted candles are sometimes to be found within the very walls of Christian churches. These various cults continued to attract adherents until the Roman emperors became Christian, at which point they disappeared underground.

The acceptance of Christianity by the emperor Constantine in *c*.313, and its consequent legalisation, was a seminal event for the new religion. From being a cult of social outcasts, persecuted on all sides, it had instantly become a religion of the entire Roman empire and thousands of conversions resulted. In 331 Constantine wrote to Eusebius, bishop of Caesarea, requesting him to have fifty Bibles produced at imperial expense for the major churches he was building (e.g. the basilica of St Peter on the Vatican Hill). This gave rise to the founding of Christian scriptoria in many urban areas. Copies of the scriptures thus began to be made from the fourth century onwards, and much of this work was carried out by monks working in monasteries who would be employed to copy sacred texts. By the fourth century members of the Roman senatorial aristocracy had begun to decline the office of official priesthoods – those who were responsible for overseeing the pagan rituals, ceremonies and sacrifices – and the Christian emperor Gratian (375–383) was the first to reject the office of *pontifex maximus*. Later emperors followed Gratian's example, and the title was eventually taken over by the Christian pope! From the time of Constantine onwards Christian emperors issued a series of regulations against traditional contemporary pagan cults.

Theodosius, for example, banned divinations and traditional sacrifices.

One of the first tasks of the early Church was to formulate a canon of 'approved' Scriptures, which would provide accurate guidance on Jesus's teaching and life. This was no easy task. One of the surprising, but universal, traits of religious men is the tenacious way in which they express their views and their seeming intransigence. And there were many Christian religious groups in the second century which had determined views about the nature of Jesus and what texts should be included in the new Scriptures. Some Christians believed that Jesus was both divine and human, i.e. God and man; others, that he was completely divine; some felt that Jesus was entirely mortal but adopted by God to be his son but was not himself divine. All these people wanted to have their say. In the early years of the second century we know that Marcion (see above), who had docetic leanings, proposed a canon of 11 books, but that this was turned down and after a disagreeable confrontation with his colleagues (144) he was excommunicated.

Another attempt was made by Tatian in c.150 who composed a 'harmony' of the four later authorised gospels and (possibly) of an apocryphal gospel which was used by the early Church in Syria until the fifth century, but this was similarly turned down. It is clear that after much bad-tempered disputation one group – the proto-orthodox group in which Irenaeus, bishop of Lyon, played the leading part – won the day and decided which texts should constitute the new canon. The first group of texts to be included as authoritative were the four Gospels – known to contemporaries as the 'memoirs of the apostles'. Thus Justin Martyr (100–165), writing about a church service in Rome, states 'On the day called Sunday, all who live in cities or in the country gather together to one place, and the memoirs of the apostles or the writings of the prophets are read, as long as time permits; then, when the reader has ceased, the president verbally instructs, and exhorts to the imitation of these good things... (1 Apol. 67).'[49] Later, the names of the authors were attached to their 'memoirs' to form the Gospels of Matthew, Mark, Luke[50] and John. But Bishop Irenaeus insisted that there should be only *one* 'gospel' as such in a fourfold written form, i.e. *one* gospel according to Matthew, Mark, Luke and John. Apart from these four books there were included the Acts of the Apostles, the Epistles of Paul, James, Peter, John, Jude, and finally the Revelation of St John – in all 27 books which were to comprise the New Testament. But what biblical scholars find of particular interest is the alterations made to the earliest texts of 'approved' writings, and the interpolations made in them, in order to exclude any heretical passages or nuances. It is clear that the proto-orthodox authorities censored the manuscripts of the Apostles so as to remove any words that might be interpreted as supporting any heretical beliefs, and added other words or phrases if necessary.[51] The first official mention of this new canon occurs in a pastoral letter from Athanasius, bishop of Alexandria in the year 367 when all 27 books are listed.

The 'disappointed' groups of Christians whose views on the texts for inclusion in the canon had been rejected did not however give up, but their beliefs on the nature of Jesus were pronounced heretical. We have already noted that Marcion and his supporters continued to keep together as a sect and began to build their own churches. The Jewish Ebionite party, to which Jesus's family had belonged, remained active. What happened to all the texts which had been rejected from the canon of Scriptures? These provide a fascinating corpus of documents – the so-called 'apocryphal gospels' – and have been studied in great detail by biblical scholars. To name just a few, there were: Gospels of Judas, Philip, Peter and Thomas; Epistles of Barnabas and Peter; and Apocalypses of Peter and Paul.[52] Some of the most interesting texts have in fact been re-discovered, after being lost for centuries, for example the Gospel of Peter,[53] containing an account of Jesus's trial, crucifixion and resurrection (which, because of its 'docetic' (i.e. heretical) nature, is known to have been proscribed by bishop Serapion in the second century). Scholars believe that this was not written by St Peter (who was executed c.64) but dates from the second century. The so-called Gospel of Thomas (allegedly written by Jesus's twin brother Didymus Judas Thomas) was found in 1945 amongst the buried Nag Hammadi scrolls in Upper Egypt. It contains 114 sayings of Jesus, but the real author is unknown. It dates from the second century.[54] Finally, one of the most intriguing of any documents discovered is the Acts of Paul, a collection of Paul's missionary activities which includes the Acts of Thecla, a female disciple of Paul, who was once widely revered as a martyr. This document was apparently forged by a presbyter in Asia Minor in the late second century.[55]

Despite Bishop Irenaeus's great work *Against Heresies* there was a constant emergence of heretical ideas amongst Christians. One of the most insidious was the Arian heresy. Arius (*c.*250–336) was a priest living in Alexandria who believed that Jesus, although created by the Father, was in fact wholly mortal (and not therefore *consubstantial* or of the same substance as the Father), but was an inspired teacher. The orthodox view of the Church was that the Father and the Son were equal and of the same substance but were distinct Persons. This was one of the matters brought up for discussion at the Council of Nicaea (325), but Arius's view was not finally declared to be heretical until the Council of Constantinople in 381. Interestingly, Arianism continued to attract support in Western Europe for many years after, and elements of Arian belief were to be found as late as the thirteenth century amongst the tenets of the Cathars, against whom in 1208 Pope Innocent III launched the 'Albigensian Crusade'.[56] Other influential 'heretics' included Priscillian (*c.*340–386), bishop of Avila, who had a large following in north-west Spain and who was in fact executed in 386 (the first person to be executed for heresy in the Church) and Nestorius (d. 451), patriarch of Constantinople, who was excommunicated and exiled to Egypt in 435.

The Nestorian controversy was interesting. It concerned the Incarnation, and the relationship between Jesus's divinity and his humanity. Nestorius was patriarch of Constantinople and he held that there were two Persons in Jesus, one human and one divine, and for this reason he objected to the Virgin Mary being called *Theotokos* or 'Mother of God' since she could only be the mother of the human person (whereas the divine person, who was in fact God, could have no mother). Or were there two natures in one Person – which was the view of St Cyril, patriarch of Alexandria? The Council of Ephesus, meeting in 431, decided in favour of Cyril and Nestorius was declared a heretic and exiled to Egypt (435) where he became the founder of the 'Nestorian' sect which had adherents throughout Syria and as far away as India and China. In 449 another Council held at Ephesus decided that Jesus had only one *nature* (as propounded by the Monophysites), but in 451 a further Council held at Chalcedon ruled that Jesus existed in *two* natures, one human and one divine, and thereafter this became the orthodox Christian doctrine of the Incarnation. It may seem surprising to us today that such esoteric doctrinal matters roused such fierce antagonisms between the contending parties, but this was frequently the case as we can see from the famous English Synod of Whitby in 663–4 when there was a contest between the Celtic and Roman Churches over the date on which the festival of Easter should be held and on the style of the monastic tonsure!

The continuing strength and resilience of heretical opinion is illustrated by Procopius (*c.*499–565) in *The Secret History* where he refers to the many heresies then prevalent within the Empire – Montanism,[57] Sabbatarianism, Manichaeism, for example – and goes on to state that 'the churches of these heretics, as they are called, especially those who professed the doctrines of Arius, possessed unheard-of riches...'[58] Even allowing for Procopius's exaggeration of the wealth of these churches (which the Emperor Justinian expropriated) this passage clearly indicates that the numerous 'heretical' sects had long been tolerated and some – especially the Arians – had become immensely wealthy by the mid-sixth century AD.

Another source of Christian heresies was the *Panarion* of Epiphanius, bishop of Salamis in Cyprus, written in the mid-370s, in which he listed some 60 heresies which were regarded as being unorthodox. Being himself a Nicene, therefore orthodox, member of the Church, anyone who subscribed to 'subordinationism' (i.e. that Jesus was subordinate to the Father) was condemned. This included the great fourth-century missionary Ulfilas, who converted the Goths to Christianity in the 340s and who translated the Bible into Gothic. The Alexandrian theologian Origen (185–254), one of the most brilliant intellectuals of his time, described by no less a man than St Jerome as 'an immortal genius', was similarly condemned for his subordinationism, his belief in the pre-existence of souls and his denial of bodily resurrection. He maintained that the Son was distinct from the Father, who used him as a mediator between himself and the material world. Jesus was therefore subordinate to the Father who placed him within a human body for his earthly mission. Although Origen's views were eventually condemned as heretical at the Council of Constantinople in 553 a number of his works survived, to be championed by Erasmus in the sixteenth century. As Charles Freeman argues: 'What attracted Erasmus to Origen was his belief in free will and reason. Origen's belief that one should be curious, sceptical and confident of the possibilities of human creativity appealed to Renaissance humanists. Erasmus saw Origen's approach to theology as far superior to the narrow pessimism of Augustine, who had openly derided what he called 'the disease of curiosity' and portrayed humanity as sunk in sin.'[59]

Ironically, the early church historian Socrates Scholasticus (b. *c*.379) of Constantinople is said to have remarked that 'controversy and conflict are the very stuff of church history, and that if the Church were suddenly to be at peace, there would be nothing for [the historian] to record.'! The development of early church theology is indeed fraught with endless disputes, bickerings and rivalries between cantankerous bishops (often leading to violence amongst their supporters and enemies). It is regrettable that the current controversy between Churches in the Anglican Communion over the questions of the ordination of women bishops and homosexual priests and bishops (matters which might be thought to have but marginal relevance to the gospel the Church professes to preach) continues this tradition of undignified behaviour, and is hardly likely to enhance its standing in the wider world.

The Jewish religion, from which Christianity sprang, was a 'Religion of the Book' – that is, it had its own 'Scriptures'. As a Jew Jesus was brought up in the tradition of the Jewish faith and as a rabbi he was familiar with the Law of Moses and other Jewish writings, and with their relationship to the Jewish God Yahweh. The Jewish faith was founded on the belief that the Jews were a small group whom God loves and that they were therefore the 'Chosen People'. For the Jews the Mosaic Law was all-important and its provisions – covering such diverse subjects as circumcision, abstinence from eating pork and other 'unclean' meats, observance of the Sabbath and of religious rituals, the prohibition of marriage with gentiles – had to be strictly observed. In their early history the Hebrews exiled to Egypt worshipped various gods (e.g. the Babylonian god Tammuz) but were eventually persuaded that they should worship only one god, Yahweh, who was held to be all-powerful. From then on the Hebrew religion became monotheistic. The Hebrew Scriptures contained the epic story of the tribulations of the Jewish people (their exodus from Egypt followed by 40 years in the wilderness before arriving in the 'promised land') and the admonitions of many of their prophets (such as Jeremiah, Ezekiel and the two Isaiahs). Now the Seleucid King Antiochus II embarked on a policy of Hellenizing all his territories c.175 BC, but this was strongly opposed by a Jewish party known as the Hasidim who rebelled under their leader Judas Maccabaeus who re-captured Jerusalem. Because of the rigidity of the Law, St Paul – who was himself a well-educated Jewish Pharisee – realised that he would have to disregard some of its deeply-entrenched provisions especially those concerning circumcision, ceremony and ritual, or there would be little chance of his being able to convert the Greek-speaking 'Gentiles' amongst whom most of his missionary work was undertaken. Because the Alexandrian Jews had become Hellenized they soon began to forget the Hebrew tongue and Ptolemy Philadelphus (285–246 BC) ordered a Greek translation of the Old Testament for the library at Alexandria. He commissioned seventy scholars for this work, which was referred to thereafter as the Septuagint (or LXX). Improved by Origen (185–254) in the third century it was not however until St Jerome's Vulgate was written that a definitive Latin text appeared.

It will therefore be appreciated that the Christian religion as developed from the time of its founder incorporated several strands of discrete thought. First, there was the historic Jewish background – with its concept of the 'Chosen People' (which for Christians became the 'Elect') and their historical development since the Creation under the direct tutelage of God. Secondly, the importance of Mosaic Law, which was the foundation of the Jewish religion under their God Yahweh, but from which

Christians soon broke free and placed prime emphasis on the imperative to love God and one's neighbours. Thirdly, the Jewish belief in the Messiah, who would be a descendant of the House of David, and whose arrival would bring them victory over their enemies on earth, but for Christians the Messiah was none other than the historical Jesus, identified as the *Logos* (or true explanation of the nature of the universe) of Greek philosophers, and whose kingdom would be in heaven. Lastly, the concept of the Kingdom of Heaven where the virtuous would enjoy the fruits of their behaviour in this world while the wicked would be condemned to an eternity of torment. Judaism's belief in 'the Last Things', or the sequel to death, appears to have been influenced from a very early date by the Zoroastrian faith (founded by the Iranian prophet Zarathustra (Zoroaster) (*c.*600 BC)) which introduced the idea of a 'Last Judgement' in which all human beings (both those alive and those already dead) would be judged by a judge deputizing for the 'good' god Ahura Mazda (supporters of whom were to fight for the good against the 'wicked' god Angra Mainyush). This came about because the Jews of Palestine were part of the Babylonian Empire which was later annexed to the First Persian Empire which in turn was succeeded by the Greek Ptolemaic monarchy (323 BC) and then by the Seleucid monarchy (198 BC), whose king Antiochus IV Epiphanes began to persecute the Jews in Palestine in 168 BC. Up until that period the Jews had believed that the dead were consigned at death to Sheol. Thereafter they began to adopt the Zoroastrian belief in bodily resurrection of the dead and a forthcoming Day of Judgement. This belief came to be held by the Pharisee sect who believed in immortality, bodily resurrection and a Last Judgement with the righteous going to Heaven and the wicked to Hell. The Sadducees sect, on the other hand, who regarded the Torah alone as their spiritual authority, rejected the Pharisees' belief. But after the Roman occupation (*c.*70 AD) of Jerusalem the Sadducees disappeared leaving the religious belief of Pharisaic Judaism as the 'orthodox' religion. Hence the Zoroastrian concept of 'the Last Things' – viz. the survival of the souls of the dead, a future bodily resurrection of the dead, and a Last Judgement – became imported into the orthodox religious doctrines of Judaism and of its two daughter religions, Christianity and Islam. St Paul, for example, maintained that the resurrection of Jesus provided a guarantee of the future resurrection of all Christians (1 Cor. 15: 12–17). While the Zoroastrians expected the world order to last for a further several thousand years, the first generation of Christians supposed that the arrival of the Kingdom of God and of the Last Judgement were imminent. Although it had not materialised during the following six hundred years the Prophet Muhammad nevertheless still believed in the imminent arrival of the Kingdom and of the Last Judgement. The dramatic account contained in the Book of Revelation lasted in the popular imagination up to the time of Dante's *Divina Commedia* in the early fourteenth century.[60] It may be noted that the Egyptians – in parallel with the Zoroastrians of Persia – also believed in the concept of judgement after death by Osiris their god of the dead. The righteous were thought to go to Kentamentiu, a paradise on earth, similar to the Greek idea of Elysium (from which it may in fact have been derived). It may be noted that contemporary followers of Judaism and Islam recognise Jesus as a prophet, but *not* as the divine 'Son of God'.

The fact that Jewish scriptures had foretold the coming of the Messiah but that when Jesus appeared the Jews failed to recognize him as such, caused antipathy between early Christians and Jews which led eventually to pronounced anti-Semitism in the Christian countries of Western Europe.[61] Today's secular state of Israel, founded in 1948, is regarded by Jews as the restoration of their homeland which they had lost under Roman occupation following the Jewish Revolt in 132 AD.[62]

As Christianity spread, a form of Church government became necessary and especially after Roman emperors from Constantine onwards embraced the faith. In the beginning, local leaders were elected to take charge of new Christian communities. Rules were formulated covering their communal life and ritual practices. One of the earliest surviving documents which contains a form of Service to be held by communities is known as the *Didache* or *The Teaching of the Apostles* and dates from *c*.100 AD. Bishops were the first administrators of Christian dioceses and were elected by popular vote. Bishops of large towns, financed by the offerings of the faithful, became important figures and of equal status to secular administrators. They were often given judicial powers and the responsibility for overseeing poor relief (e.g. corn and oil). Like secular magistrates they also possessed the power to free slaves. As a result of exercising their secular powers bishops became immensely wealthy. The Roman historian Ammianus Marcellinus (c.330–390) recorded that the bishops of Rome 'enriched by the gifts of matrons, ride in carriages, dress splendidly and outdo kings in the lavishness of their table', and it was said that the Bishop of Rome's income was equal to all that of his other clergy put together.[63] It was the beginning of the increasing worldliness of the papacy which was only finally to be checked at the Reformation. In the early years the plums of spiritual office could hardly be resisted, and 'almost every vacant bishopric gave rise to murder and intimidation as rival candidates fought for the position'.[64] Hardly the behaviour expected of responsible spiritual dignitaries! When there were doctrinal dissensions the emperor might summon all the bishops to an ecumenical conference, such as that at Nicaea (325) which laid the foundations for the Nicene Creed (finalised in 381) which became the touchstone of Christian orthodox belief until the present day.

From the death of Jesus Christ until the end of the Roman Empire in 476 there lived three men who between them were responsible for laying the foundation of the doctrines of the Christian Church. St Ambrose (c.339–397), bishop of Milan, was a man of good education and son of a Roman official who had turned his back on a legal career to devote his energies to the service of the Church. He had to deal with Roman emperors such as Gratian and Theodosius with great tact and diplomacy and with aristocratic senators many of whom were still pagans. Although no theologian he wrote for the young emperor Gratian a treatise on the Nicene faith (which was in fact derided by St Jerome!) and gradually impressed upon the emperors their duty of service towards Almighty God while emphasising the independence of the Church from the State in all matters concerning religion. Ambrose was essentially a statesman, while his contemporary St Jerome (c.342–420) was a cantankerous and quarrelsome ascetic who is remembered for his Latin translation of the Scriptures from Hebrew, Aramaic and Greek manuscripts which became known as the Vulgate, and which was the first major book to be printed (1450–6) by Johannes Gutenberg (1400–1468) on his new printing press and which still remains the official Roman Catholic version of the Bible. Jerome's many letters have survived and vividly express the deep concern felt by contemporary Romans at the fall of the Empire and the triumph of the barbarous Goths, Huns and Vandals. The third great Christian was St Augustine (354–430), a man of towering reputation whose *Confessions* describe his early dissipated life, his brief association with the Manichaeans, and his eventual conversion to the service of the Church, having been baptised by St Ambrose in Milan, and going on to be chosen as bishop of Hippo, near Carthage (*c.*396) where he remained until his death. Augustine's most memorable work however was his *City of God*, written shortly after the sack of Rome by the Goths in 410 (which the pagans attributed to the abandonment of the ancient gods) and which was to remain of fundamental importance throughout the Middle Ages. Its essential thesis is to contrast the 'city' of this world with that of the 'city of God' (which is the home of the 'Elect'). While he asserts that knowledge of God can only be sought through Jesus Christ he nevertheless invokes the support of the ancient philosophers such as Plato to defend the power of reason to argue with those who denied the validity of the Christian revelation. Augustine was remarkable in that he 'stressed the importance of respecting the conclusion of the sciences in relation to biblical exegesis... and therefore urged that biblical interpretation should take due account of what could reasonably be regarded as established facts'.[65] Augustine claimed that there will be two resurrections – that of the soul at death, and that of the body at the Last Judgement (when those condemned will burn eternally in hell). Augustine is clear that the State must remain separate from the Church and subservient in all matters of faith. This practice has been maintained ever since, although in medieval times the Roman Emperor and Pope were often in conflict. Augustine followed St Paul in believing in predestination: those who are saved by God's grace – provided they have been baptised – are those whom God has predestined to salvation, i.e. the 'Elect'. It was this gloomy view – based on Augustine's concept of 'original sin' – which imbued the medieval church with an aura of the sinfulness of mankind, with hell and the damnation of souls being a constant theme in church frescos, carvings and paintings. One cannot avoid the conclusion that Augustine's view of predestination is supremely unethical. It implies the predestination of all humans, before birth, to either Heaven or Hell, and nothing he or she does in this life – whether good or evil – can alter the preordained verdict of God! Augustine also spent much effort in combating the Pelagian heresy. Pelagius, a cultivated Welsh priest, 'believed in free will, questioned the doctrine of original sin, and thought that, when men act virtuously, it is by reason of their own moral effort. If they act rightly, and are orthodox they go to heaven as a reward of their virtues'.[66] These views did not however accord with Augustine's belief in original sin and of God's grace in choosing the 'Elect' to go to heaven. Pelagius's views were therefore deemed heretical.

Yet the towering figures of Ambrose, Jerome and Augustine might well have failed in their objective of establishing the 'orthodox' faith for their new religion had not Irenaeus (and others like Justin Martyr) already taken a remarkably robust attitude towards 'heresies'. It must be remembered that in the first and second centuries there were many competing religious cults or 'mystery religions' and all were trying to become the 'universal' religion in the Near East. Gnosticism was perhaps the most difficult to counter (as we learn from Irenaeus's condemnation of it), but there were others equally dangerous, such as Manichaeism and the Marcionites which were no less of a threat. And centuries later we find Pope Innocent III leading a crusade against the contemporary heresy of the Albigensians (who did not believe, inter alia, in bodily resurrection) in 1209.

In the century after St Augustine's death there were several interesting religious figures. One was Boethius (c.475–524), a senator serving under the Gothic emperor Theodoric who, believing that there was a plot against his life by members of his government, had Boethius imprisoned and later executed. While awaiting execution this remarkable man – like Socrates similarly under sentence of death – wrote his *Consolations of Philosophy* (524), a deeply philosophical work but imbued with Christian insights ('the substance of God consisteth in nothing else but in goodness…'). Another figure of exceptional interest was the writer known as Pseudo-Dionysius who was probably a Syrian monk writing anonymously about 500 AD (and whose name was later taken from Denys the Areopagite who was converted by St Paul). Denys took great trouble to conceal his real identity, but his influence was such that Thomas Aquinas quoted him no less than 1700 times! As Professor John Hick recalls: 'Denys is famous for his insistence upon the absolute and unqualified ineffability of God… God is utterly transcendent, totally ineffable, indescribable and incapable of being conceptualised by the human mind…" He is in fact 'out of the reach of every rational process.'[67] Nevertheless Denys asserts that the ineffable God is self-revealed in the Bible: 'the Word of God makes use of poetic imagery' and truth is made known to us 'by way of representative symbols'.[68] It is therefore apparent that for him the language of revelation is metaphorical or mythological. Denys is imbued with the Neoplatonist conception of the universe as a divine emanation: 'everything in some way partakes of the providence flowing out of this transcendent Deity which is the originator of all that is'.[69] Furthermore, he maintains that we as spiritual beings are 'sparks of divinity' which have fallen into the material world and our aim should be to strive to ascend again towards reunion with the unknowable God. There is an obvious contradiction in Denys's theology. As Hick points out 'Denys was… deeply implicated in this contradiction that, on the one hand, the transcendent Godhead lies beyond both being and knowledge and yet, on the other hand, that we know that it is a divine Trinity, one person of whom became incarnate as Jesus of Nazareth'.[70] Thus he writes often of 'the ultimate Transcendent as the divine Trinity who has acted self-revealingly in the scriptures', but also sometimes 'speaks of the transcendent Godhead as beyond even divinity'.[71] There is a parallel here with the Sethian Gnostic view that 'there is not just one God but many gods and where the creator of this world is not the true God but an inferior deity, who is not the Father of all and is certainly not almighty'.[72] Professor Hick wrote that 'Denys' affirmation of the transcategorical nature of ultimate reality, of the metaphorical character of human language about that reality, and of the practical function of that language in promoting spiritual growth, even though they may

not cohere with everything else in his writings, expresses the basic
elements of modern religious pluralism.'[73]

During the period of constant warfare throughout Europe it
was the Church which became the depository of the culture of the
now-collapsed Roman Empire. Two names stand out in the
history of the Church during the sixth century. The first is that of
St Benedict (c.480–c.547), an Italian of an aristocratic family who
became an ascetic and went on to found the celebrated monastic
community at Monte Casino for whose inmates he drew up a set
of rules which later became known as the Rule of St Benedict.
This became the prototype for the governance of most subsequent
monastic orders throughout Europe. He was, incidentally, the
twin of St Scholastica, foundress of the Benedictine nuns. St
Gregory the Great (c.540–604), the scion of a wealthy and noble
Italian family, had begun as an administrator and by 573 had
become prefect of the City of Rome. But he decided to devote
his life to religion and, having given away all his wealth, became a
Benedictine monk. However, Pope Pelagius II sent him as his
envoy to Constantinople, where he lived between 579 and 585.
After Pelagius's death Gregory became Pope (590–604). It was
then a time of political turmoil; heresy was rife and simony
amongst church leaders endemic. But owing to his personal
qualities and authority Gregory was soon accepted as having
jurisdiction outside his own diocese, and his *Book of Pastoral
Rule* – with its spiritual and practical advice to bishops – became
an essential guide (and was even translated by King Alfred into
Anglo-Saxon). Many of his letters have survived and display the
extraordinary range of his proffered advice. One interesting
instruction from Gregory was that pagan temples in England were
not to be demolished, but the idols within them were to be
destroyed and the temples then consecrated as Christian churches.
It was Gregory who in 597 sent Augustine and 40 missionaries to
England to convert the Angles, Saxons and Jutes, Augustine
becoming the first Archbishop of Canterbury. But this was not
however the first occasion on which Christianity was introduced
to Britain. Missionaries had already reached Wales and Ireland via
Brittany in the fourth century, and the Celtic church established a
monastic tradition which spread to Northumbria. A clash between

the new Roman and old Celtic Churches took place at the Synod of Whitby in 663–4.

Apart from Christianity the major monotheistic religion is of course Islam.[74] Muhammad (b. 570), a member of the Meccan tribe of Quraysh, believed in *al-Lah* (Allah) the chief of the pantheon of deities worshipped by other Arabs. However, in the year 610 he experienced an extraordinary revelation in which the archangel Gabriel appeared to him and commanded him to 'recite'. After protesting his inability he found himself beginning to recite the words of an unknown scripture, which came to be known as the *Qur'an* ('the recitation'). Over a period of twenty-three years, the scriptures were revealed to him, line by line, and verse by verse, as he entered into a state of trance. Afterwards he would read the revelation aloud, and others would then write it down. The definitive edition of the Qur'an dates from 651. The Qur'an is basically a reflection upon various themes and contained a powerful message of the absolute supremacy of God (or Allah) over all created beings, a future resurrection and divine Judgement, and the hope of Paradise for all believers. As Karen Armstrong explains: 'There were no obligatory doctrines about God: indeed, the Qur'an is highly suspicious of theological speculation, dismissing it as *zanna*, self-indulgent guess-work about things that nobody can possible know or prove. The Christian doctrines of the Incarnation and the Trinity seemed prime examples of *zanna* and, not surprisingly, the Muslims found these notions blasphemous. Instead, as in Judaism, God was experienced as a moral imperative'.[75] Muhammad never asked Jews or Christians to convert to his religion of *al-Lah*, and the Qur'an did not see its revelation to Muhammad 'as cancelling out the messages and insights of previous prophets but instead it stressed the continuity of the religious experience of mankind'.[76] It is therefore a simple monotheism, devoid of such complications as the Christian Incarnation and the doctrine of the Trinity. Nor of course did Muhammad claim to be divine but rather a mortal prophet. The *Hadiths*, a series of stories based on the sayings of Muhammad (recorded some 250 years after his death by non-Arabs) and how he conducted his life, are also important for Muslims. Unfortunately, some of these have been fabricated by ultra-conservative and extremist sects such as the Wahhabi and Deobandi, and are responsible for the oppressive attitudes towards women, religious intolerance and jihad which have given Islam a bad name and are not faithful to the original teachings of the faith. From Mecca Muhammad is held to have made a miraculous night journey, or Isra, to the Temple Mount in Jerusalem where the Dome of the Rock now stands. And the Lailatul Miraj – the Night of the Ascent – following his night journey, or Isra, is now commemorated by the Muslim festival of the *Isra and the Miraj.* This underlines the sacredness of Jerusalem to Muslims and the obligation on every believer to pray five times a day. For it was at the Temple Mount that Muhammad was believed to have been greeted by Abraham, Moses, Jesus and other prophets, whom he led in prayer. After which Muhammad and Gabriel ascended the seven heavens to the Throne of God.

Following a tribal dispute life became difficult for Muhammad and his followers in Mecca, and in 622 some seventy Muslim families migrated to the settlement of Yathrib (or Medina, as it came to be known), a move termed the *hegira,* from which date Muslims date the foundation of their era (AH). Muhammad himself died ten years later. Thereafter, the period of Arab conquests began, but in the West the Arab expansion was defeated by the Frankish leader Charles Martel at the battle of Tours in 732. However, by the fifteenth and sixteenth centuries three great empires had been established, that of the Ottoman Turks in Asia Minor and Eastern Europe, that of the Safavids in Iran, and that of the Moghuls in India. Each achieved a high degree of cultural pre-eminence similar in many respects to that of the Italian Renaissance. Islam became divided into two sects, the Sunni and the Shiah, a political rather than a doctrinal division which led to unfortunate repercussions in later years. There is no supreme hierarchical authority in Islam which has power to lay down an authoritative ruling on matters of faith, but Muslims are expected to observe the Shariah, the corpus of medieval (man-made) Islamic Holy Law. And holy men such as ulama, imams and ayatollahs are accorded great respect and have considerable influence upon their followers. This lack of supreme doctrinal authority has given rise in recent years to Islamic extremism in which – in the reported words of Dr Ali Goman, the Grand Mufti of Egypt, 'each and every person's unqualified opinion is considered a fatwa'. He deemed it essential for Muslim jurists and muftis to reflect on how Islamic law is applied in the present age and to answer the challenge of holding fast to an authentic, moderate and tolerant Islam 'to stand in the face of those who would use our religion for their own agendas'.[77]

The vast extent of the former Arab empire encouraged a thriving commerce and Muslim countries such as Iran produced some fine artists, poets (e.g. Omar Kayyám (c.1050–c.1123) and Jalal ad-Din Rumi (1207–1273) a mystic and lyrical poet who wrote a long epic on the Sufi mystical doctrine) and philosophers (e.g. Avicenna or Ibn Sina (980–1027) and Mulla Sadra (1571–1640)).

The patriarchs of Constantinople, although willing to be subservient to the emperors were not disposed to acknowledge the suzerainty of the popes and from the year 1054 began the effective separation of the Eastern and Western Churches. In the West Pepin, successor of the Merovingian kings, granted to Pope Stephen III the town of Ravenna and a large area of territory in Italy. His son Charlemagne occupied Rome and confirmed his father's donation to the Pope and was himself crowned by the Pope as Emperor in Rome on Christmas Day, 800 AD. Later, a forged document – known as the 'Donation of Constantine' – purported not only to confirm Pepin's grant but also to bestow on the Pope the old city of Rome and its western territories. This document provided the territorial basis of future papal power, and helped to ensure the superiority of Rome over other centres of Christian authority, such as Alexandria. Shortly afterwards the papacy fell under the influence of the Roman aristocracy, and a series of depraved men were appointed to the throne of St Peter.

By the eleventh century it became clear that the Church was in need of reform. It had grown up haphazardly against the background of warring states and difficult relationships with various secular powers that had overrun Europe. The clergy – however humble and ignorant their background – claimed certain powers over the laity. The most significant was the position of priests with regard to transubstantiation: the priest was believed to have the power in the Eucharist to transform the wafer and the wine offered to communicants into the real body and blood of Jesus Christ. From 1079 this became orthodox Church doctrine. Moreover, a priest had important powers over the laity with regard to their future life. Correct performance of the 'last rites' (or *Extreme Unction*) by a priest would ensure that a person ultimately went to heaven, but before that he would have to spend a period in Purgatory, and a priest could shorten this period by saying special masses for his soul – after an appropriate payment had been made. Because of the growing worldliness of the Church, simony – the acquisition of clerical preferment by payment rather than merit – was rife. Thus it became customary for the king to sell bishoprics and for a bishop in turn to earn money from ordinations within his diocese. Lack of clerical celibacy was another cause of potential moral scandal. Most parish priests were married, and it was possible for them to pass on church property to their sons if they in turn became priests. Furthermore monastic houses had by this period become lax both in discipline and morals. Above all the papacy was in one of its periods of scandal. Benedict IX, for instance, was said to have been only 12 years old when 'elected' pope in 1032. His debauchery was such that he decided to resign the papacy and marry. Whereupon he sold the office to his godfather who became Pope Gregory VI, but the latter was subsequently deposed by the Emperor Henry III on the grounds of simony. One of the most powerful popes in the latter part of the eleventh century was Hildebrand, who took the title of Gregory VII (1073–85). He did his best to enforce clerical celibacy and laid down that the Eucharist celebrated by married clergy was invalid. He is best remembered, however, for his lasting struggle with the Emperor Henry IV over the investiture of bishops.

The eleventh century produced two ecclesiastics of great philosophical and theological eminence: Lanfranc of Bec (appointed Archbishop of Canterbury in 1070) and St Anselm, also from the monastery of Bec, who was appointed Archbishop of Canterbury in 1093. Anselm is remembered for attempting to prove the existence of God by force of reason (a concept which dated from the philosophy of Origen in the third century), and much of his philosophy was derived ultimately from Plato and his theory of ideas. Of twelfth-century scholars one of the most notorious was Peter Abélard (1079–1142), mainly on account of his association with Héloise (the story of which was one of the best loved of medieval romances). He was a skilled dialectician and teacher and was condemned (1121) for an unorthodox book on the Trinity. In terms of theology it is instructive to note St Bernard's (largely unjust) accusation against him: 'He asserted that Abélard treats the Trinity like an Arian, grace like a Pelagian, and the Person of Christ like a Nestorian; and he proves himself a heathen in sweating to prove Plato a Christian; and further, that he destroys the merit of the Christian faith by maintaining that God can be completely understood by human reason.'[78] As Bertrand Russell pointed out, the last charge was untrue, but it was Abélard's unfortunate habit of criticising influential contemporaries that landed him on more than one occasion with the charge of heresy. It was Abélard, incidentally, who first coined the term 'theology' to describe a systematic exposition of Christian doctrine.

The thirteenth century produced several great personalities in Europe. Pope Innocent III (1198–1216) was conscious of the high calling of his office and was determined to assert his spiritual supremacy over the nations of the West. King John of England tried to oppose him but was ultimately obliged to offer his kingdom to Innocent and to receive it back as a papal fief. He took decisive action to root out heresy and instigated the Crusade (1209) against the Albigensians[79] in the south of France. He attempted to reform the Church and codified the Canon Law. At his request the Emperor Otto was deposed in favour of Frederick, the young king of Sicily, who became the Emperor Frederick II (1194–1250). The latter became the most formidable of emperors – fluent in six languages, highly intelligent and cultured, and known as 'Stupor mundi' by his fearful admirers. He finally agreed to papal pressure to go on Crusade, but being naturally on good terms with the Muhammadans (whose culture he admired) he induced them to restore Jerusalem to him. His political ambitions, however, made him many enemies amongst local rulers, including the popes (who attempted to depose him).

Two saints – St Francis (1181/2–1226) and St Dominic (*c*.1170–1221) – played a significant part in the development of the Church at this time. Francis of Assisi, when a young man, gave up all his worldly wealth and, with a group of like-minded friends, took a vow of poverty and devoted the rest of his life to preaching the Gospel. He founded the Order of Friars Minor (OFM), usually known as the Franciscans. His followers initially had no buildings of their own nor any churches, and were expected to beg their bread. The contrast with the lax existence of those who lived a monastic life was plain to all, and Pope Innocent III validated the new order, but persuaded them to relax their views to the extent of building their own houses. Unhappily, the purity and selflessness of Francis and his followers disappeared after his death and the order became no less corrupt than the monastic orders and many Franciscans subsequently became instruments of the Inquisition. One of the most distinguished Franciscans was St Bonaventure (1221–1274), a man of great learning who wrote a commentary on the *Sentences of Peter Lombard*, which explained the doctrines of the Christian faith. St Dominic (*c*.1170–1221) of Castile, also pledged to a life of poverty, founded his order in 1215, the Order of Preachers (OP), now commonly known as Dominicans, and devoted his life to preaching, and was especially concerned with the suppression of heresy, taking part in the Albigensian Crusade. Later Dominicans were prominent in the activities and cruelties of the Inquisition. The order did however have a constructive side in its encouragement of learning; they founded a school of theology at Oxford, and many were distinguished scholars – the great St Thomas Aquinas was a Dominican.

Thomas Aquinas (1225/6–1274) has the reputation of being the greatest of medieval philosophers and acceptance of his philosophy and theological doctrines now form an essential element of Catholic orthodoxy. He became a Dominican and studied in Cologne and Paris, and became the leading proponent of Aristotelian philosophy (which he preferred to that of Plato). His most influential work was the *Summa Theologia*e in which he sought to establish the truth of the Christian religion by reasoned argument. In this he maintained that reason can demonstrate the existence of God (although not necessarily of his nature) and the immortality of the soul, but not the Trinity, the Incarnation, or the Last Judgement. He maintained there are three ways of knowing God: 'by reason, by revelation, and by intuition of things previously known only by revelation'. But Aquinas was concerned how the timeless, ineffable, immutable, abstract Platonic God could be reconciled with the 'time-dependent physical universe, and the God of popular religion'.[80] This problem has been addressed by both Nelson Pike and by John O'Donnell,[81] but it has proved to be a stumbling block for the Church. Importantly, Aquinas stated that the sacraments were valid even when dispensed by sinful priests, to answer the doubts of many of the laity who feared that priests living in sin could not properly administer the sacraments. The Church felt bound therefore to assure the laity that a priest's sins did not incapacitate him from performing his sacramental duties. The same excuse was no doubt made for the revolting excesses of some of the sixteenth century Italian popes! Aquinas was a firm believer in Aristotelian philosophy and attempted to show how this can be adapted to Christian dogma. Aquinas's views have been succinctly described by Professor Alister McGrath as follows: 'God is the cause of all things. Yet God's causality operates in a number of ways. While God must be considered capable of doing certain things directly, God delegates causal efficacy to the created order. For Aquinas, this notion of secondary causality must be considered as an extension of, not an alternative to, the primary causality of God himself. Events within the created order can exist in complex relationships, without in any way denying their ultimate dependency upon God as final cause.'[82] Although he has earned a great reputation as a philosopher, Russell pointed out that 'There is little of the true philosophic spirit in Aquinas. He does not, like the Platonic Socrates, set out to follow wherever the argument may lead. He is not engaged in an enquiry, the result of which it is impossible to know in advance. Before he begins to philosophize, he already knows the truth; it is declared in the Catholic faith. If he can find apparently rational arguments for some parts of the faith, so much the better; if he cannot he need only fall back on revelation. The finding of arguments for a conclusion given in advance is not philosophy, but special pleading.'[83]

By the end of the thirteenth century it is possible to perceive the culmination of a synthesis of classical Greek philosophical theories (especially those of Plato and Aristotle), the influence of oriental mystical beliefs ('the dying and resurrected god, the sacramental eating of what is purported to be the flesh of the god, the second birth into a new life through some ceremony analogous to baptism')[84], and the rise of an institutional priesthood with political power, into what eventually became the westernised institution of the Christian Church. The Church had inherited from the Jews the concept of a monotheism based on a book of sacred scripture, although it rejected some Jewish ritual and adherence to the Mosaic Law. In its organisation the Church had learnt from Roman administrative methods, and papal power and wealth slowly grew through the abilities of men like Gregory the Great, Innocent III and Boniface VIII. But the power of the papacy began to decline and the Great Schism (1378–1414) – with two rival popes in Rome and Avignon – detracted from its status and influence as an institution (the schism being finally resolved by the Council of Constance in 1414).

By this date the corruption of the Church and widespread clerical abuses were plain for all to see, and one of the most prominent church reformers before the European Reformation was an Englishman, John Wycliffe (c.1329–1384). Wycliffe was an Oxford theologian and popular teacher. His anti-papal views gained him the support of the noblemen and citizens of London, but his proposals for the secular control of the clergy antagonised the bishops who summoned him to appear before the archbishop in St Paul's in 1377. The Pope published bulls demanding that he should be imprisoned. The election of an antipope gave Wycliffe the chance to condemn the whole fabric of the Church, which he declared would be better without pope or prelates. He went on to condemn the clerical power of absolution, confessions, penances and indulgences. He then organised a body of itinerant preachers, known as his 'poor priests' or Lollards, to spread his ideas throughout the country and set about the enormous task of completing a translation of the Bible from Latin into English so that the common people might have direct access to the teachings of Holy Scripture, and Wycliffite Bibles began to appear in the 1380s. But his fatal mistake was to deny the doctrine of transubstantiation, 'which he called a deceit and a blasphemous folly'. In 1382 Archbishop Courtenay condemned Wycliffe's opinions and his followers were arrested and compelled to recant. He withdrew to his benefice at Lutterworth from where he continued his work, and his doctrines passed to Bohemia (the country of King Richard II's wife) where the reformer John Huss (c.1369–1415) became one of his disciples. In 1415, thirty years after his death, as a result of a decision at the Council of Constance, forty-five articles from his writings were condemned as heretical, and his bones were ordered to be dug up, burned and thrown into the river Swift – a sentence executed in 1428. The unfortunate John Huss was condemned for heresy by the Council, refused to recant, and was burned on 6 July, 1415, leading to the bloody Hussite wars against the empire. But Wycliffe's influence persisted for many years amongst the clergy of England, and during the Reformation not all priests were happy with the doctrine of their Church, which the conservative Henry VIII had refused to modify. We find that a certain Richard Jordan, a fellow of the collegiate church of All Saints, Derby, at its dissolution was accused during Mary's reign of heresy, 'having said that the "Mass was the most abomination that ever was said" and having denied transubstantiation, the clerical tonsure and chrism at baptism before his parishioners.'[85]

Renaissance scholars were for the most part disgusted by the wickedness of contemporary popes even if they were employed by them. Guicciardini wrote (1529) 'No man is more disgusted than I am with the ambition, the avarice, and the profligacy of the priests, not only because each of these vices is hateful in itself, but because each and all of them are most unbecoming in those who declare themselves to be men in special relations with God, and also because they are vices so opposed to one another, that they can only co-exist in very singular natures. Nevertheless, my position at the Court of several Popes forced me to desire their greatness for the sake of my own interest. But, had it not been for this, I should have loved Martin Luther as myself, not in order to free myself from the laws which Christianity, as generally understood and explained, lays upon us, but in order to see this swarm of scoundrels… put back into their proper place, so that they may be forced to live either without vices or without power.'[86] The shameless political ambition, nepotism and immoral lives of medieval popes such as Sixtus IV (1471–84) and Alexander VI (1492–1503) (the father of the notorious Cesare Borgia whose family's pursuit of dynastic ends, where murder, treachery and immorality became the everyday activities of the Vatican, have been fully recorded) are a stark reminder of the depths to which the head of the Western Christian Church could sink. Renaissance humanists could not themselves initiate a reform movement because of their close ties with the Church, and it was left to the Protestant Reformation movement to reject the authority of the Pope and the discontinuation of the financial tribute paid into the papal Treasury. Moreover Protestant reformers claimed the right to exercise critical reasoning in the interpretation of the scriptures, rather than accepting the authority of the Church.

Martin Luther (1483–1546) in Germany, John Calvin (1509–1564) in Geneva and Huldrych Zwingli (1484–1531) in Zurich, the most prominent sixteenth-century reformers, sought to make radical changes in hitherto accepted orthodox beliefs. Luther, for example, maintained that Scripture and Faith alone were the foundations of the Christian religion, and that the Church as an institution was unnecessary for salvation. His proposed 'new' doctrine was that of 'justification by faith' – essentially a Pauline concept – emphasising that mankind was powerless to save himself and only God could ensure the establishment of a proper and lasting relationship between a sinner and his God. His view was that 'faith was a leap in the dark towards a reality that had to be taken on trust.'[87] Luther subscribed to the orthodox doctrines of the Trinity and the Incarnation and was suspicious of intellectual speculation about God's nature and doubted if it was possible to 'prove' the existence of God. The reformers expressed disbelief in the concept of Purgatory from which the souls of the dead could be delivered by means of special masses, for which payment was demanded – a massive contributor to papal revenues. Luther supported the idea that Protestant sovereigns should be head of the

Church in their own countries (and in England both Henry VIII and Elizabeth made this claim). John Calvin's doctrine of predestination removed the fate of souls after death from any lucrative control by the priesthood. Calvin, who (with the other reformers) had hoped ultimately to be able to re-join a reformed Catholic Church, subscribed to many orthodox beliefs and was intolerant and indeed brutal towards 'heretics'. Thus after Michael Servetus, the Spanish theologian, was executed in 1553 for his denial of the concept of the Trinity, he admitted in a letter dated 1561 that 'such monsters should be exterminated, as I have exterminated Michael Servetus the Spaniard'. Intolerance is so often the handmaid of reform. 'Calvinism' had a profound influence on religion in the Western world. Calvin's ideas were an inspiration for the Puritan revolution in England under Oliver Cromwell in 1645 and his condemnation of the veneration of the saints (in order to propitiate an angry God). This, regrettably, led to the destruction of many ecclesiastical works of art. During the Middle Ages religious imagery was an important aid to the ignorant parish peasantry and acted as a stimulus to personal devotion. Throughout the Western world stained glass, sculpture (religious and secular) and frescoed walls in parish churches helped to inculcate a sense of the divine presence at Church Services. Calvin however insisted that there should be no portrayals of God in human form, following the biblical commandment in Exodus (20: 4–5) forbidding the making of graven images, since he felt that all such artistic representations were a distraction from preaching (which for Protestants was the over-riding priority). As a result, many stained glass windows and sculptures in churches were wantonly destroyed or defaced during the seventeenth century, and wall frescoes whitewashed over (many of which thus survived and were later restored). The Puritan revolution gave rise to an extraordinary outbreak of religious fervour. Many humble people believed in the imminent arrival of the Apocalypse. One such sect, the Quakers, founded by George Fox (1624–1691) and James Naylor (1616–1660), preached that every person could achieve salvation here on earth. Fox himself preached pacifism, non-violence and a radical egalitarianism for his Society of Friends,[88] which has lasted until the present day as a sect without a hierarchy and devoid of theological doctrines and set forms of liturgy. They devote themselves to world-wide peace and the relief of poverty and hunger.

The Protestant Reformation had a devastating effect on the Roman Catholic Church, largely brought upon itself by its worldly greed, its political and social ambitions, and by abuse of its spiritual duties. The invention of the moveable type printing press by Johannes Gutenberg c.1450 provided a ready means of disseminating information to the public eager to learn more about the shortcomings of the Church and so be able to obtain authoritative religious texts (for example, William Tyndale's New Testament in English was published in 1526). The financial effect on the papacy was dire, as sovereign states became head of their respective Churches and traditional payment to the papacy ceased. In France, views were divided on the Reformers' claims and supporters on each side soon became embroiled with politics and this led to the savage French wars of religion which were to ruin the country for a generation. In England, Henry VIII, a typical Renaissance prince (being a gifted scholar, an accomplished poet and musician) who was a devout Christian, objected to Luther's doctrinal attack on the Sacraments. He was moved to issue a reply (with the ready assistance of Sir Thomas More) which earned for him the gratitude of the Pope and the title 'Defender of the Faith' (which Protestant English sovereigns have curiously retained to this day, as may be seen on the English coinage where the inscription round the head of the Queen runs (in part) 'Elizabeth D.G. Reg F.D.'). While the Reformers' new ideas were subject to intensive debate amongst scholars in Cambridge, Henry became increasingly impatient with the papacy for not sanctioning an annulment of his marriage to his wife Katherine of Aragon. He dismissed his religious advisor Cardinal Thomas Wolsey and began an assault on the clergy who were obliged to acknowledge him as 'Singular Protector, only and supreme Lord, and, as far as the law of Christ allows, even Supreme Head of the Church in England.' Henry then promoted legislation severing the ties binding England to the Roman *curia*. Appeals to Rome were forbidden by law, and it became clear that the King had become supreme head of both Church and State. The papacy suffered financially in a number of ways: the first-fruits of benefices as well as annual tithes on all clerical incomes, which had previously been paid to the Holy See, yielded a revenue to the King of some £50,000 a year. The suppression and spoliation of the monasteries in England followed shortly. In terms of doctrine, Henry published in 1539 his *Act of Six Articles* which laid down what people had to believe on the six most contentious matters of the day: 'To deny transubstantiation was to incur the death penalty. Communion in one kind for the laity, the celibacy of the clergy, the permanence of religious vows, the benefit of private Masses, and the use of auricular confession were all commended; to repudiate any of them was to become liable to loss of property and liberty for the first offence, and to death for the second.'[89] Although the death penalty was subsequently removed from all offences except the denial of transubstantiation, this 'bloody whip with six strings' was a blow to the Protestant reformers, and showed how conservative the King was in matters of doctrine by turning back the clock to before Wycliffe's denunciation of transubstantiation as 'a deceit and blasphemous folly'.

The Catholic Church felt bound to respond to this series of attacks both on its spiritual and temporal authority. Martin Luther was excommunicated and condemned for heresy. In 1545 it summoned a general Council of Trent (which in fact lasted for more than 18 years) and a Counter Reformation was planned. It brought about a renewal of the Catholic Church. Amongst those who took the lead were Pope Pius V, who did much to reform clerical abuses and to unify the Sacred Liturgy for the Western Church, as well as St Charles Borromeo, St Teresa of Avila and St Philip Neri. But perhaps the best known of the Counter Reformers was St Ignatius de Loyala (1491–1556), the founder of the Society of Jesus (SJ) in 1534. Loyola's *Spiritual Exercises*, designed for his early Jesuits, were intended as a course of religious self-examination as part of a thirty-day retreat under a spiritual director. The Jesuits were fanatically disciplined; they concentrated on the education of the young, realising that this was how lasting influence could be achieved (and their example has been assiduously followed by the Roman Catholic Church ever since), but their main object was to combat heresy and they urged all

Catholic sovereigns to persecute heretics and to re-introduce the former Inquisition (the Roman Catholic tribunal for the suppression of heresy, renowned for its cruelty). In many respects the Jesuits were similar to the Puritans, experiencing God as a dynamic force which imbued them with confidence and energy to travel the world (for example, the Puritans set sail for New England while the Jesuits travelled to India, China and Japan, and in China they discovered Confucian philosophy as a result of which Confucius's *Analects* were translated into Latin). The Jesuits are still a powerful force in the Roman Catholic Church, numbering today some 19,200 members (the largest and most influential order in the Church) and running two educational institutions in Rome – the Pontifical Gregorian University and the Biblical Institute. The effects of theological rivalry and religious wars in Europe were to disillusion many people and turn the more intelligent to secular learning, especially in the fields of science and mathematics which were to flourish during the seventeenth century.

Sir Isaac Newton (1642–1727), one of the greatest scientists and mathematicians of this new age, believed God to be eternal and infinite and to be everywhere present. For him the regularity of planetary motions was proof of divine design. As he wrote to his friend Richard Bentley, Dean of St Paul's, 'Gravity may put ye planets into motion but without ye divine power it could never put them into such a Circulating motion as they have about ye Sun, and therefore, for this as well as other reasons, I am compelled to ascribe ye frame of this System to an intelligent Agent.'[90] But Newton did not believe in the concept of the Holy Trinity which he said 'had been foisted on the Church by Athanasius in a specious bid for pagan converts... the doctrines of the Trinity and the Incarnation were spurious.' The long arm of the Church had already reached out to the great astronomer Galileo Galilei (1564–1642) who had asserted that the earth rotated round the sun, and he was condemned by the Inquisition for such a nonscriptural theory in 1633 and obliged to recant. But in Protestant countries the heliocentric theory was adopted by men of science, and in 1991 the Vatican finally admitted that the Church had been wrong in condemning him. Before his death

Newton likened himself to a child picking up a few shells on the seashore while the great ocean of truth lay undiscovered before him.

René Descartes (1596–1650), often referred to by the Latin name 'Cartesius', was the most brilliant rationalist philosopher and mathematician of the seventeenth century scientific revolution. His essential philosophy was to subject everything to the power of reason. Apart from speculating on earlier metaphysical, scientific and mathematical problems, he conceived the idea of God as the absolutely Perfect Being – leading to what was held to be the 'ontological argument' for the existence of God (who would exist as a matter of logical necessity). This argument (previously advanced by Anselm) was, and is, regarded by philosophers as unsound, but contemporaries also drew attention to the problem of evil, suffering and pain as being inimical to an all-powerful, beneficent god and a demonstration of the imperfection of the created world. This line of questioning stimulated doubt about many of the tenets of the Christian faith and encouraged the spread of atheism. Many began to feel that atheism liberated humanity from false notions of supernatural powers and the advances of science seemed to entertain the possibility that science could one day explain the mechanisms and origin of the universe. And the English dislike of domestic religious conflict was exemplified in the philosopher John Locke's *Letter Concerning Toleration* (1689) arguing for freedom of conscience and religious expression.

The philosopher G. W. Leibniz (1646–1716) is important for – in Russell's words – having 'brought into their final form the metaphysical proofs of God's existence. These had a long history: they begin with Aristotle, or even with Plato; they are formalized by the scholastics, and one of them, the ontological argument, was invented by St Anselm. This argument, though rejected by St Thomas, was revived by Descartes. Leibniz, whose logical skill was supreme, stated the argument better than it had ever been stated before.'[91] Immanuel Kant (1724–1804) – one of the most influential of modern philosophers – claimed in his *Critique of Pure Reason* to have demolished the metaphysical arguments of earlier philosophers (holding 'that as a matter of logic we cannot reason from the conditions of the empirical world to the conditions of a transcendent super-empirical reality'). According to Kant, all previous arguments in favour of the existence of God failed, although he had great respect for the so-called 'argument from design' which (he contended) allowed for the existence of an *architect* of the world rather than a *creator*. However Kant invented a new moral argument for the existence of God, based partly on the proposition that there would be no concept of right or wrong unless God existed.[92]

The French philosopher Voltaire (1694–1778) was a Deist, and believed in the 'divinity of reason'. He believed in a supreme being who had falsely been taken over by 'religions' – and specifically by the French Roman Catholic Church whose corruption and immorality he mercilessly condemned in his satirical publication *Candide* (1759). Yet it is clear that he had little time for atheism as such whose attraction he felt was the result of the corruption of Christian institutions. Voltaire was one of the principal players in the movement which would come to be known as the 'Enlightenment', whose members did not reject the idea of God but rather the doctrines which the Church had invented about him. The spread of atheism received strong support during the French Revolution, and since the Roman Catholic Church was one of the three pillars of the *ancien régime*, it was one of the chief targets of the revolutionaries (some 30,000 clergy fleeing the country). In England, William Godwin (1756–1836) followed Voltaire in believing in the supremacy of reason where God had no place, and his major political work was *An Enquiry Concerning Political Justice* (1793) in which he envisaged the rule of law being replaced by the rule of reason. But the Romantic poets, who were amongst those who turned against God, criticised the 'cold' view of nature without imagination or emotion. For them nature inspired thoughts of the transcendent, of beauty and mystery. For William Hazlitt the new movement represented 'reason without passion'. For William Wordsworth natural beauty inspired thoughts of transcendence, which were destroyed by the aridity of 'the meddling intellect' with its doctrinal theories. John Keats wrote of the 'vulgar superstition of the conventional churches'. Percy Bysshe Shelley became a vigorous critic of the Church's concept of God, maintaining that 'the existence of God cannot be proved and is ultimately a matter of faith'.[93] For William Blake the Christian God had been used 'to alienate men and women from their humanity', repressing their 'sexuality, liberty and spontaneous joy' and he rebelled against the oppressive attitudes of the Church. Friedrich Schleiermacher (1768–1834), an exact contemporary of Godwin, was regarded as one of the most important theologians of his time and was much influenced by the Romantic movement with its emphasis on experience, feeling and imagination. In his book *The Christian Faith* he defined religious experience as the consciousness of being absolutely dependent on God, and sought to counter the Romantics' view of religion as mere superstition. In his view man cannot be imagined 'without the capacity for religion'. The French philosopher Denis Diderot (1713–1784) did not regard the existence or not of God as important (although he nevertheless believed that reason could prove God's existence). He maintained that there was no need for a Creator God: nothing but matter existed and matter had its own laws which were responsible for the apparent 'design' of the universe which we imagine we can see. Similarly, Paul Heinrich Dietrich Baron d'Holbach (1723–1789) argued that there was no supernatural alternative to nature which was 'but an immense chain of causes and effects which necessarily flow from one another'. Karen Armstrong sums up his views as follows: 'To believe in a God was dishonest and a denial of our true experience. It was also an act of despair. Religion created gods because people could not find any other explanation to console them for the tragedy of life in the world. They turned to the imaginary comforts of religion and philosophy in an attempt to establish some illusory sense of control, trying to propitiate an 'agency' they imagine lurking behind the scenes to ward off terror and disaster. Aristotle had been wrong: philosophy was not the result of a noble desire for knowledge but of the craven longing to avoid pain. The cradle of religion, therefore, was ignorance and fear and a mature, enlightened man must climb out of it.'[94] This theme would be followed by Feuerbach in the next century (see below).

Alongside the rationalism of the Enlightenment there emerged a new type of Christianity of which the Wesley brothers were paramount examples. Thus John Wesley (1703–1791), a devoted Christian, experienced a 'revelation' that he had been 'born again' and had received a commission from God to preach a 'new' religion – throwing aside traditional doctrinal complexities such as the mystery of the Trinity in favour of a simple heartfelt faith. He maintained that religion was not a matter of orthodox doctrine 'in the head' but rather a 'light in the heart'. Thereafter, he travelled up and down the country preaching in the open air to the working classes and farm labourers, and attracted an immense following whose members became known as Methodists. They became numerous in newly-industrialised areas and had a great following in the nineteenth century amongst the coalminers who were housed in new villages where the Church of England never penetrated. In 1790, shortly before Wesley died, the Methodists in Britain numbered 57,000, and by 1890 the number had increased to 726,000.

An original theory was propounded by the atheist Auguste Comte (1798–1857) in his book *Cours de philosophie positive* which appeared in an English translation in 1853. In Professor Alister McGrath's words Comte had argued 'that the development of human thought passes through three distinct stages: the theological, the metaphysical, and the scientific. In the first phase, humanity believed that it was legitimate to seek the ultimate causes of events, and located those causes in super-human personal beings known as gods. A clear progression from animism through polytheism to monotheism can be discovered within this phase of thought. In the second stage, personal deities are transformed into metaphysical abstractions, leading to the notion of God being displaced by essentially natural categories. In the third, scientific (or 'positivist') phase, a more mature outlook develops, in which the human mind comes to concern itself purely with observed facts and not with the unobservable inner essences of things. According to Comte's account Western culture had passed the threshold between the second and third phases, and was about to enter a purely scientific mode of thinking. There was no way back to earlier ways of thinking. History had passed its verdict, and there was no appeal. Who could resist the laws of inexorable historical progress?'[95]

Doubts about the historical accuracy of the New Testament were voiced as early as the eighteenth century by the German philosopher Herman Reimarus (1694–1768). The idea of a supernatural redeemer did not accord with Enlightenment rationalism, whereas a simple mortal teacher did. Reimarus rejected miracles and the historical reliability of the Gospel accounts of Jesus's resurrection. He argued that Jesus proclaimed the forthcoming arrival of the Kingdom of God, but this (as for all contemporary Jews) was to be a *political* kingdom here on earth. Jesus saw himself as the leader of a political uprising, as the Messiah. The Romans realised this and in due course had him put to death. But his disciples determined to found a new religion in Jesus's name and proclaimed him as a *spiritual* Messiah. It was thus vital for them to steal Jesus's body from the tomb in order to validate their new faith. This theory led to Albert Schweitzer's study *The Quest of the Historical Jesus* (1906) which raised further critical questions about the historical accuracy of the Gospel narratives. What those enquiries demonstrated was that 'the doctrines of orthodox Christianity must have developed at a time later than the historical Jesus and his apostles, later even than our earliest Christian writings.'[96] Moreover, Reimarus had 'pointed out that in the Gospels Jesus never claimed that he had come to atone for the sins of mankind. That idea, which had become central to Western Christendom, could only be traced back to St Paul, the true founder of Christianity. We should not revere Jesus as God, therefore, but as a teacher of a 'remarkable, simple, exalted and practical religion.'[97] The philosopher Wilhelm Hegel (1770–1831) put forward the idea of a Spirit 'which was the life-force of the world' in place of the conventional deity, and he regarded reason and philosophy as superior to religion. By contrast, his contemporary Artur Schopenhauer (1789–1860) asserted that there was no Spirit, no God and no Reason in the world, but only an instinctive desire for life. And everything in the world is an illusion, only the arts and a spirit of compassion could give mankind a measure of comfort in this life.

Another German scholar F. C. Baur (1792–1860) devoted much effort to examining the historical reliability of the New Testament, while his namesake Walter Baur (1877–1960) studied the theological conflicts in the early years of the Church in his important book *Orthodoxy and Heresy in Earliest Christianity* (1934). All these studies only served to demonstrate the extreme diversity of beliefs in the early Church and the lengths to which each party would go to try to promote its own beliefs (through forged documents, polemical tracts and falsified writings then in circulation). It is hardly an edifying spectacle. Emile Durkheim (1858–1917), one of the foremost students of the social aspects of religion, maintained that religion is a 'unified system of beliefs and practices relative to sacred things... which unite into one single moral community called a church, those who adhere to them.' In his view religions are both social and moral phenomena.[98]

Karl Marx (1818–1883), Ludwig Feuerbach (1804–1872) and Sigmund Freud (1856–1939) were the intellectual giants of the nineteenth century atheistic movement. Feuerbach's publication *The Essence of Christianity* (1841) sought to show that God was a human creation invented as a consolation and distraction from the sorrows of the world. In his view 'God is merely the hypostatised and objectified essence of the human imagination'. Marx was the inventor of the 'materialist conception of history'. Material needs, he argued, determine the way in which people live and think. Moreover, the concept of God 'is a human attempt to cope with the harshness of material life and the pains resulting from social and economic deprivation.'[99] In his view, 'religion in general, and Christianity in particular, are direct outcomes of unjust social conditions'.[100] Essentially, in Marx's view, 'religion is a comfort that enables people to tolerate their economic alienation', and 'religion is the sigh of the oppressed creature, the heart of a heartless world, just as it is the spirit of a spiritless situation. It is the *opium* of the people.'[101] For Marx, therefore, belief in God is an illusion. The author well remembers being told by a tourist guide in Russia as late as the 1970s that 'religion is the opium of the people'! Nevertheless it is mildly ironic that Bertrand Russell of all people should say of Marx that he 'retained a cosmic optimism which only theism could justify.'[102] Sigmund Freud was an admirer of Feuerbach's philosophy, and he claimed only to have added 'some psychological foundation to the criticisms of my great predecessors'. Thus Freud's theory was that 'religion is an illusion and it derives its strength from the fact that it falls in with our instinctual desires.' In his view 'God is to be seen as a wish fulfilment, arising from repressed, unconscious infantile longings for protection and security.'[103] He went on to develop the science of psychoanalysis which sought to explain that illusions arise from within the human unconscious in order to give expression to its deeply-felt yearnings. His clinical successes earned for him considerable fame, and his views on religion were highly popular in America. The popularity of the anti-religious theories of Feuerbach, Marx and Freud rested on the belief that they were scientific in character, and that 'belief in God widely seen as a construct of the consolation-seeking human mind, which would evaporate with further scientific advance.'[104] Intellectuals therefore began to question the hitherto accepted dogmas of religion and look to the advances of scientific discovery as the key to the new age. The title of J. W. Draper's book *History of the Conflict between Religion and Science* (1874) and A. D. White's *History of the Warfare of Science with Theology in Christendom* (1876) give a flavour of the intellectual debate after the appearance of Charles Darwin's *Origin of Species* (1859) (for which see Chapter 4 (i)).

The novelist George Eliot (or Mary Ann Evans, 1819–1880), brought up as an evangelical Christian, is an extremely interesting example of someone who rejected this type of faith because she felt that 'the quality of a person's faith was now judged by doctrinal correctness rather than a love for Christ.'[105] In a letter to her father she affirms that she regards the Jewish and Christian scriptures as 'histories consisting of mingled truth and fiction'. But she was clearly influenced by a recent book by Charles Hennell entitled *An Inquiry concerning the Origin of Christianity* (1838) in which he maintained that 'Jesus Christ was a religious teacher with aspirations to reclaim the throne of David. Having failed in this effort, he suffered martyrdom. Nicodemus and Joseph of Arimathea removed his body as a precautionary measure. The early church mistakenly interpreted the empty tomb as evidence of a resurrection, and thus initiated a relentlessly inflationary understanding of Jesus's identity that transformed him from a Jewish teacher to the Son of God incarnate.'[106] Yet he goes on to say that 'Christianity thus regarded as a system of elevated thought and feeling will not be injured by being freed from those fables, and those views of local or temporary interest, which hung around its origin.'[107] Eliot then proceeded to translate David Friedrich Strauss's *The Life of Jesus Critically Examined* (1835) with its rationalist criticism of orthodox Christianity in which 'Christians came to believe when there was no objective historical basis for their faith'. Acknowledging that the Resurrection was the fundamental article of the Christian faith (after all, St Paul had said so) 'Strauss concluded that religion was ultimately an expression of the human mind's ability to generate myths in the first place, and then to interpret them as truths revealed by God.'[108] Eliot believed that 'the moral aspects of faith could... be maintained without the metaphysical basis of Christianity. We can be good without God.'[109] This is precisely the theme echoed in Richard Holloway's recent book *Godless Morality: Keeping Religion out of Ethics* (1999). On the other hand, Friedrich Nietzsche (1844–1900) took the view that you cannot separate Christian faith from Christian morals: 'Christianity is a system, a *whole* view of things thought out together.'[110] And, as Richard Holloway pointed out, Nietzsche's critique of Christianity 'was that it inculcated a slave morality of obedience to authority and denial of the life-force, in contrast to the heroic ethic of struggle and overcoming'.[111] Nietzsche maintained that Western culture no longer had faith in the plausibility of God. It was, as Professor McGrath explains: 'one of the great ideas of nineteenth-century materialism: that human beings create divinities out of their deepest longings and aspirations.'[112] By the early nineteenth century the Church of England was in an unhappy state: worldly, irreligious and unspiritual. The incumbents of many parishes were absentees, their duties being carried out by poorly paid curates, and the spiritual well-being of parishioners was plainly neglected. However, a new spiritual revival in the Church began with John Keble's famous Assize Sermon in Oxford in 1833 which heralded the start of what was to be known as 'The Oxford Movement' for Church reform.

This sought to revive the genuine *catholic* (as distinct from the *Roman* Catholic) tenets of seventeenth-century Anglicanism, and the leading light in this movement was John Henry Newman (1801–1890), a fellow of Oriel College, Oxford. Newman and his friends wrote a series of pamphlets called *Tracts for the Times*, aimed largely at the clergy, and he himself preached a series of sermons in St Mary's, Oxford, proclaiming their message. However, in the last of the Tracts to be published, Tract 90, Newman claimed that the 39 Articles of the Church of England (to which all clergymen had to subscribe) denied the objective presence of Christ in the sacrament of the Eucharist – the doctrine of transubstantiation – and this led to a considerable scandal which obliged Newman to resign his cure, whereupon he was received into the Roman Catholic Church (1845). He was later created a Cardinal (1878). The Oxford Movement developed into Anglo-Catholicism, which led to the building of many beautiful new churches in the high Gothick style by architects such as A. W. N. Pugin and Sir Gilbert Scott, and medieval-style church sculpture, furnishings and stained glass by Morris and Co and artists such as Sir Edward Burne-Jones. This revival of medieval church pageantry and liturgy led in turn to an increase in church attendance during the Victorian period and was well suited to the confident ebullience of society. Yet it was not to last, and towards the end of the nineteenth century in Britain the overall decline in faith continued. But it was not only in Britain that this was evident. In Russia the great novelist Fyodor Dostoyevsky in his *The Brothers Karamazov* (1880) railed against God and the Christian Church through the character of the Grand Inquisitor, and Russian liberals thought that atheism would secure their freedom from the oppression of the Church, political tyranny and other ills of society. The closing years of the Victorian era witnessed both the advance of atheistic ideas but at the same time a certain sadness at the passing of the old faith. This is beautifully expressed in Matthew Arnold's poem *On Dover Beach*:

> 'The Sea of Faith
> Was once, too, at the full, and round earth's shore
> Lay like the folds of a bright girdle furl'd.
> But now I only hear

2272

Its melancholy, long, withdrawing roar;
Retreating, to the breath
Of the night-wind, down the vast edges drear
And naked shingles of the world.'

In the twentieth century philosophers continued to speculate about religion and faith. Ludwig Wittgenstein (1889–1951) regarded religion as a 'family concept' and was doubtful about the 'truth' of some of its ideas. Carl Gustav Jung (1875–1961) 'sought to explain religious beliefs and experience in terms of influences from the subconscious minds', and he believed in the real existence of a psychic realm – although its precise status is unclear. While Freud considered religion to be an illusion, Jung regarded himself as an empiricist and would not commit himself to believing whether God existed or not.[113] Yet at the end of his life he is recorded as saying: 'All that I have learned has led me step by step to an unshakeable conviction of the existence of God.'[114] J. N. Findlay claimed that he could 'disprove' the existence of God;[115] that our conception of God should be 'one whose non-existence is *inconceivable*', and that such a conception would make no sense.[116] John Leslie considers God to be an ethical principle, and that his theory – 'extreme axiarchism' – can explain the existence and nature of the universe.[117]

Post-World War II culture in Britain was understandably reactionary. As Professor Alister McGrath describes it: 'For the trendy young things of the 1960s, God was an outmoded idea that belonged to the past – or, even worse, to their parents' generation. Reaction against God was the hallmark of a right-thinking and intelligent young person.'[118] In Europe there was a new Marxist resurgence; the May 1968 student riots in Paris, joined by some 10 million French workers, reminded people of the era of the *ancien régime* in 1789. There were also protests at Columbia University in New York and elsewhere. Philosophers added to the gloom. Jean-Paul Sartre (1905–1980), the leading Existentialist philosopher, acknowledged that faith in God had now evaporated, and 'insisted that even if God existed, it was still necessary to reject him since the idea of God negates our freedom... we must see human beings as liberty incarnate.'[119] Sir Alfred Ayer (1910–1991), the most distinguished member of the school of Logical Positivists, queried whether it was sensible to believe in God. Statements describing God are often meaningless. 'Theism is so confused and the sentences in which 'God' appears so incoherent and so incapable of verifiability or falsifiability that to speak of belief or unbelief, faith or unfaith, is logically impossible.'[120] But as Karen Armstrong points out, 'like poetry or music, religion is not amenable to this kind of discourse and verification.'[121] Paul Van Buren, in his *The Secular Meaning of the Gospel* (1963) believed that we must do without God and hold on to Jesus of Nazareth. The Gospel was 'the good news of a free man who has set other men free.' Jesus of Nazareth was the liberator, 'the man who defines what it means to be a man'.[122] Paul Tillich (1886–1965) agreed with Nietzsche that the personal God of traditional Western theism would have to be dispensed with. Yet he believed that some form of 'religion' was necessary to assuage the ever-present anxieties of mankind. Conventional prayer to God 'was a contradiction, since it attempted to speak to somebody to whom speech was impossible.' Tillich coined the definition of God as 'the ground of our being' or 'ultimate concern'. This is a similar concept to the belief of the Victorian artist George Frederic Watts (1817–1904) when he stated: 'If I were ever to make a symbol of the Deity, it would be as a great vesture into which everything that exists is woven'. The well-known Jesuit Pierre Teilhard de Chardin (1881–1955), a palaeontologist, saw the process of evolution of species as a divine force which propelled the universe from matter to spirit to personality and finally to God, who was immanent and incarnate in the world. This 'world theology' was in tune with the view of the philosopher A. N. Whitehead (1861–1947) who had little time for the concept of an other-worldly God, but rather believed in God 'sharing in the world's suffering'. The late Professor Arnold Toynbee recalled of this period: 'The remarkable features of this current change of outlook was a decrease in mental assurance, a consequent relaxation of dogmatism, and an accompanying expansion of the mental spectrum. The mental assurance that was now diminishing had been founded in the past on one or other of two beliefs: a belief in the infallibility of utterances or scriptures that were held to be the word of God, and a belief in the infallibility of the logic of the human reason at the conscious level of the human psyche.' Post-rationalist enquirers, he maintained, now follow experience, wherever this may lead, as their predecessors followed, respectively, revelation and reason. Psychic experience... leads to glimpses of possible reality that logical reasoning might find itself constrained to reject as being illusions.'[123]

Bishop John Robinson's book *Honest to God* (1963), which called for a redefinition of the conventional image of God, became a best-seller. 'What looks like being required of us... is a radically new mould, or *meta-morphosis*, of Christian belief and practice... And the first thing we must be ready to let go is our image of God himself.'[124] In fact, Robinson did not claim to be saying anything very new or radical. He had been impressed by Rudolf Bultmann's essay on the 'New Testament and Mythology', in which he had pointed out that the New Testament writers had used 'mythological' language to describe the incarnation, ascent and descent, miraculous intervention, etc. and that it was now time to 'demythologize' the whole question of God 'out there'. He pointed to the failure of theologians to communicate the insights of modern thinking stemming from the discoveries of the natural sciences and the claims of psychology. Bishop Robinson's book was immediately attacked by the traditional conservative Church hierarchy led by the Archbishop of Canterbury, Dr Michael Ramsey. Robinson was marginalized by the Church and resigned his suffragan bishopric of Woolwich and returned to Cambridge to teach until his death in 1983. His diagnosis of the problem facing the Church and of the need to develop a 'worldly holiness' fell on deaf ears, but was recently revived by Bishop John Shelby Spong, a former Episcopal bishop of Newark, USA, in his book *A New Christianity for a New World* (2002). In this he maintains that the primary task of the Christian Church today 'is that of separating the extraneous from the essential, the timeless God-experience from the time-warped God-explanations of the past'. The Church must 'develop new visions, prepare new models, chart new solutions'. His proposals are further discussed in Chapter 7 below.

Dr Don Cupitt, a former Anglican priest whose views have now shifted towards atheism, finds himself much influenced by

Buddhism which he believes is more suited to today's society than the tenets of the Christian Church. Buddhism teaches that there is no one way to enlightenment. Faith must be for each individual to decide, and in his view the Church's monopoly regarding salvation is now over: it will change into a 'de-mythologised' religion, that is to say humanism, with human – rather than God-centred morals. The former theology of judgement, repentance and salvation is being abandoned in favour of spirituality and humanism. Cupitt sees Jesus as a supremely wise rabbi whose followers invented his return following his crucifixion. He vigorously condemns the blind faith of fundamentalists, but sees the Bible as a continuing influence for good and believes that it is possible to have a religious view of life within a secular culture. Cupitt does not believe in an afterlife and sees God not as a real divine force but rather a human creation or a spiritual ideal.[125]

In America the popular cry in the 1960s was 'God is dead' and the local best-selling book was Harvey Fox's *The Secular City* contrasting the rural beginnings of the Christian faith with contemporary life in the cities of America. By contrast, in the post-revolutionary society of Russia, where Marxist-Leninist political theory had scorned religion as 'the opium of the people', it was to be expected that the people would take the advice of their communist and atheist masters. On the contrary, Christianity refused to die and remained the core spiritual belief of a large part of the population. Indeed, under the leadership of Patriarch Alexei II (d. 2008) more than 20,000 churches were built or restored in Russia, while some two-thirds of Russia's 142 million people now profess to being Christians. In Britain, from the 1960s for the next twenty or so years, there emerged what came to be known as the 'Charismatic' movement (derived from the Greek word *charismata*, meaning 'gifts' or 'spiritual gifts') whose supporters believed they could re-discover and make use of the power of the Holy Spirit as demonstrated on the Day of Pentecost. Thus young people began to meet together, away from a church environment, armed only with a Bible and – frequently – a guitar. Everyone was encouraged to participate – in Bible quotations, discussions, spontaneous songs and disco-like dancing. This developed into attempts at 'prophecy' (in Old testament-style declamation), 'speaking in tongues' (as at Pentecost), healing by the 'laying on of hands', shouting, clapping and fainting, and these experiences of being 'born again' could be followed by baptism in a ritual of full immersion. In many cases this behaviour appeared similar to the rituals and trance-like devotions of animist ceremonies and were regarded with suspicion by other Christian branches. With the political Cold War then at its height, and the possibility of nuclear oblivion for mankind, there was a sense of 'an imminent apocalypse, the return of Christ, the definitive moment in the cosmic battle between good and evil...'[126] In the early 1980s the Charismatics gradually merged with the Evangelical movement. In fact, the term 'evangelical' is of sixteenth-century origin, and referred to writers who wished to revert to biblical beliefs and practices. It is now 'used widely to refer to a transdenominational trend in theology and spirituality, which lays particular emphasis upon the place of Scripture in the Christian life'.[127] Evangelicals maintain that every human being is 'corrupted by sin' which incurs 'divine wrath and judgement' but that salvation for the human race has been achieved through the 'atoning sacrifice of Christ on the cross'. Nevertheless, for the individual salvation can only be achieved by repentance from sin and through faith in Christ. Evangelicals believe (like Charismatics) in extempore prayer and preaching, in healing, exorcism, and in dramatic 'speaking in tongues'. They are also devoted to the written word of God, and some even carry Bibles with them everywhere.

Undoubtedly a lot of interest has been shown in the latest craze for charismatic religious experience, and in particular the phenomenon known as 'speaking in tongues' or *glossalia*. Followers believe that this is the spirit of God taking possession of them. Scientific tests organised by the University of Pennsylvania have been carried out on volunteers while they have been 'speaking in tongues' – usually an incomprehensible babble, and it has been found that the front and parietal lobes of the brain showed diminished activity while they were speaking. This signified that the subjects were not in control of the usual language centres of their brains. The psychological conclusion is that it would be a ludicrous jump in logic to take this as proof that speaking in tongues is a divine experience. Some people have the ability to slip into a trance quite easily, and it is similar to hypnosis. Theologians take the view that *glossalia* 'has less to do with the Holy Spirit and more to do with people's desire for a religious experience'. One practitioner of speaking in tongues described the experience as follows: 'You're aware of your surroundings, you're not really out of control, but you have no control over what's happening; you're just flowing. You're in a realm of peace and comfort and it's a fantastic feeling'.[128] For young people, in particular, Charismatic religion is not so much a dialogue with God as an experience of religious ecstasy to which you surrender – an experience shared with many devoted men and women throughout history. In fact, there is little difference from the taking of drugs for the same purpose. The new Charismatic movements in both Britain and America lay great emphasis on a perceived and dynamic 'religious experience' rather than on any traditional theology or church structure.

If the Anglican Pentecostal and Charismatic movements have given rise to a spiritual revival in parts of the world, there are parallel charismatic movements in the Roman Catholic Church. These are the fundamentalist, traditionalist groups, which flourished particularly during the papacy of John Paul II, such as Opus Dei, Neocatechumenate, and Charismatic Renewal, and which all have the approval of the Vatican. Not all these new missionary movements have been welcomed in the United Kingdom, the late Cardinal Basil Hume being wary of their 'fundamentalist' views, although his successor, Cardinal Cormac Murphy O'Connor, welcomed them as helping to invigorate the modern Church. Opus Dei's high profile in the worlds of politics, finance and the media is legendary, and the aim of all these groups is to promote, *inter alia*, conservative legislation concerning sexuality and procreation. All have been enthusiastically supported by Pope Benedict XVI. Yet the Vatican is itself wary about the increasing number of dubious miracles and 'private revelations' which have occurred in recent years which it considers poses a threat to the unity of the Church and some of which have warranted an 'exemplary pastoral response' from the Holy See.

The other branch of the Anglican Church is that of the traditional liberal Catholics, rational and opposed to the fundamentalism of some Evangelical sects, who promoted the *Alternative Service Book* (ASB) in 1980 to take the place of the 1662 *Book of Common Prayer*. This in turn was succeeded in 2000 by the book of *Common Worship* to mark the new millennium. The ordination of women to the priesthood in 1992 – a liberal Catholic policy but contrary to the practice of the Roman Catholic Church – gave rise to consternation in church circles and led to the departure of many Catholic-oriented priests from the Anglican Church. A total of 441 clergy received compensation (amounting to £27.5 million) of whom 260 joined the Roman Catholic Church (33 later returning to the fold). In 2009 the Church was stunned by the news that the Vatican proposed to issue an apostolic constitution which would allow Anglicans to enter full communion with the Roman Catholic Church while preserving elements of their own tradition (such as liturgical practice). Thus a new 'Anglican Ordinariate' is to be established to offer pastoral care to those defecting from the Anglican Communion. With the influx of many married priests into the Catholic fold, there is likely to be pressure on the Vatican to relax the normal requirement of clerical celibacy. After all, the Orthodox Church allows married priests (but not bishops), and if married priests were to be permitted it might prove to be one of the best recruiting agents to stem the diminishing numbers of Catholic priests worldwide. Whatever the consequences of Pope Benedict XVI's action, there can be no doubting that it will have a disastrous effect on the patient efforts of those organisations which have been working towards Christian unity. The liberal attitude of the Church of England towards the ordination of women was soon extended to the toleration of homosexual priests ('sexual orientation is not a bar to ordination in the Church of England').

Across the Atlantic there has also been a remarkable revival of interest in the practice, rather than the philosophy, of Christianity.[129] In the first place there are the American 'Evangelicals', who share a faith resting on a personal relationship with God and embrace both theological liberals and conservatives. The latter include a number of 'Fundamentalists' who have a pre-Enlightenment mindset and subscribe to a literal interpretation of the Bible in which modern principles of evolution and scientific dating techniques are rejected.[130] There is apparently a powerful correlation between fundamentalism and lack of education, which is hardly surprising. According to Susan Jacoby 'Fundamentalists represent a back-and-white value system. Because their beliefs matter so much more to them than religious indifference does to the religiously indifferent, they exert influence far out of proportion to their number.'[131] Parallel to the Charismatic movement in the UK has been the emergence in America of Pentecostalism whose adherents claim to undergo a direct experience of God (which itself derives from the Biblical account of the early apostles 'speaking in tongues' on the day of Pentecost). Known also by the familiar UK term 'charismatic', it has penetrated into the mainstream church across the world, including the Roman Catholic Church in regions like Brazil and Latin America. The attraction of charismatic churches is that they are socially more inclusive (appealing to marginalised and deprived communities), have no conventional 'prayer book' or traditional ecclesiastical hierarchy, and can adapt themselves to the cultural backgrounds of their adherents. The American Pentecostals incidentally began in Iowa as long ago as 1895 and thereafter spread rapidly. The largest contemporary group of Pentecostals is the 'Assemblies of God' with over 1 million members.[132] Professor McGrath describes it thus: 'In many ways Pentecostalism has become the new Marxism of the third world, displacing its secular rival for the affections and loyalty of the dispossessed.' He goes on to show that Pentecostalism is important 'for its sense of the immediacy of God's presence through the Holy Spirit' and that it repairs 'the felt loss of the presence of the divine in everyday life in the West.'[133] As Adrian Wooldridge and John Micklethwait point out in their recent book *God is Back: How the Global Rise of Faith is Changing the World* (2009), the recent rapid rise of evangelical religion in the United States is fundamentally changing that country. Its popularity is in stark contrast to the well-attested gentle decline in religious belief in the United Kingdom and parts of Europe that has been going on for the past half-century. One of the main reasons for this difference, according to its authors, is that most West European countries have effective state welfare systems, whereas the United States does not. The US Churches, which are extremely wealthy institutions, have moved in to try to match the gap in social care not catered for by the state. Evangelical revival in other countries – Latin America, Asia and Africa – mirrors the American model. Thus the authors suggest that there appears to be an inverse relationship between the generosity of the welfare state and the success of religion: 'the more generous the secular welfare state, the more it will "crowd out" religious-based charities and reduce the demand for religion in general.' As many developing countries are too poor to offer European countries' generous welfare provisions, religious organisations and charities which have offered to finance social programmes (such as schools) have proved immensely popular. Yet, interestingly, as Susan Jacoby reported (2008): 'people who belong to no Church made up the fastest-growing segment of the American population. In the 1980s, no more than 8% refused to identify a religious affiliation. This year, the Pew Forum on Religion & Public Life found that the ranks of the unchurched had doubled. Highly educated Americans are most likely to fall within a group ranging from atheists to those describing their religion as 'nothing in particular'.[134] The contrasting indifference to religion in Europe and the West is explained by Karen Armstrong in the following terms: 'one of the reasons why religion seems irrelevant today is that many of us no longer have the sense that we are surrounded by the unseen. Our scientific culture educates us to focus our attention on the physical and material world in front of us... one of its consequences, however, is that we have, as it were edited out the sense of the "spiritual" or the "holy" which pervades the lives of people in more traditional society at every level and which was once an essential component of our human experience of the world.'[135]

The high point of atheistic belief, which had originated with philosophers such as Descartes in the seventeenth century as a protest against the corruption and complacent arrogance of the Christian Church, had been reached by the end of the twentieth century, and, as we have just seen, has been followed by a remarkable revival of Christianity in the form of a Charismatic or Pentecostal Church. Part of the attraction of Pentecostalism, both in America and England, is its Gospel Music, which sprang out of folksy spiritual songs sung by oppressed slaves in the Caribbean and in the southern states of America. Some 10% of English churchgoers are black (44% in Inner London) and many of the Pentecostal Churches have accomplished choirs singing Gospel Music. One of the best-known groups is the London Community Gospel Choir. Some of the Pentecostal black majority Churches date back to the 1950s and 1960s from the time of the first post-war Caribbean immigrants, when the new arrivals found themselves cold-shouldered by the mainstream Church of England. Half of all Pentecostal churches in Britain are in London, and the movement includes many separate organisations and autonomous churches, of which the largest are the Assemblies of God and Elim Pentecostalism. The basis of all such groups is the Book of Revelation, with its stirring prophecies of the end of the world. They confidently offer their adherents an element of certainty in an uncertain world, in contrast to the equivocations of the more traditional branches of the Church arising from doctrinal doubts revealed in recent years by biblical scholarship.

The Methodist church has suffered severely since the arrival of Pentecostalism which has overtaken it in numbers of churchgoers. Having risen in number to 726,000 in 1890 their number declined to 425,000 a century later, and by 2004 had fallen to below 300,000, a decline paralleled in the mainstream churches. In 1969 and 1972 Methodists voted overwhelmingly for union with the Church of England, but the latter – surprisingly – turned the offer down. Since then, in parts of Britain, some Methodist churches have been growing – e.g. in London amongst congregations of Caribbean and West African origin. But the Methodists are unlikely to expand much further in Britain, although as a missionary movement from the nineteenth century onwards they are still represented in more than 80 countries.

At this point in time the historian has cause for reflection. There are few human traits so unedifying as intolerant spiritual prejudice, and especially prejudice in relation to religious beliefs. From the earliest times after Christianity became a religion, human prejudice ostensibly justifying even the smallest points of doctrine has had catastrophic consequences. It is not only the State, for reasons such as sedition, which has condemned to death Christians such as Jesus, but rather the Church itself has condemned innumerable so-called 'heretics' for their honestly held beliefs – from Arius (excommunicated in 325), Priscillian bishop of Avila (executed – yes, *executed* – in 386), Origen (condemned in 553 – long after his death – for his subordinationist views, and views on the pre-existence of souls and of bodily resurrection), Peter Abélard (excommunicated in 1121) and John Wycliffe (whose bones were ordered by the Vatican to be dug up and burnt in 1428 as a result of his 'heresy'), through to victims of the medieval Roman Catholic Inquisition, and the Church was also responsible for the disastrous European religious wars of the seventeenth century. It is a depressing record. Now, at the very moment when it is apparent to everyone that traditional Christianity is in decline (despite the emergence of the Pentecostalist movement), we have the spectacle of the Worldwide Anglican Church tearing itself apart over two relatively trivial matters of prejudice. In 1987 the English Church decided to allow women to be ordained deacon, and in 1992 the General Synod voted for the ordination of women to the priesthood. More recently, the Church has decided to permit the consecration of women bishops, subject to certain safeguards for parishes 'unable to accept' the ministry of women bishops. The latter move was vigorously opposed by Catholic-orientated Anglican bishops and priests, and by the Roman Catholic Church on the grounds that the English Church had no authority to permit such a momentous change on its own, for which there was no scriptural authority. The view of traditional churchmen that the status of women is intrinsically subordinate to that of men is however a position which clearly ignores the realities of the modern world. Contemporary scholars understand the Bible to be a patriarchal text and believe that 'in Christ there was neither male nor female and that women worked as 'co-workers' and 'co-apostles' in the early Church... Scripture is not able to provide certainty on this type of question.'[136]

The second matter concerned the consecration of homosexual priests as bishops (a practice which had already begun in the American Episcopal Church). This was opposed by many Anglican bishops on the ground that homosexual practice is incompatible with Scripture, and by the Roman Catholic Church on the ground that homosexuality is a 'disordered' condition (although the Catholic Church can hardly dare to claim that none of its 'celibate' priests are homosexual). The Lambeth Conference of the Worldwide Anglican Communion in 2008 (which the bishops of the Ugandan Province refused to attend) failed to resolve their differences on the question of homosexuality, and since that conference the House of Bishops of the Episcopal Church (TEC) in the United States has voted 'to allow in principle the appointment, to all orders of ministry, of persons in active same-sex relationships', thus in effect dividing them from the rest of the worldwide Anglican Communion and thereby creating a schism in the Anglican Church.

From an outsider's point of view both points of contention seem relatively trivial. Women have been involved in church work and mission for years, and it can only be unfounded prejudice and misogyny which seek to deprive them of the opportunity to enlarge their spiritual responsibilities. Homosexuality (no less than Lesbianism) is an entirely natural condition, affecting a small proportion of the total population (and comparable in this respect to left-handedness). Those subject to it are neither mentally sick nor morally depraved. Sexual orientation is morally neutral but can give rise to positive or negative patterns of behaviour. Those who object to homosexuality, including the Roman Catholic Church, and parts of the Anglican Communion, tend to present it as a moral choice – 'a deviation, an irregularity'. In fact, scientists recognise that homosexuality is a naturally-occurring behaviour in the animal kingdom and is documented in more than 450 species. In humans it is recognised in every known culture. Few gay men and women believe that they have *chosen* a way of life, and this is supported by science. Homosexual preferences 'are as much part normal human variation as traits such as height or intelligence, to which nature and nurture also both contribute.'[137] Many people consider that the disparaging references to homosexuality more than two thousand years ago in the Bible (two verses in Leviticus and two words and one paragraph quoted by St Paul) differ little from the frequent condemnations in Scripture of adultery, idol worship, perjury, drunkenness and other sins. Bishop Tom Wright, on the other hand, declares that 'Jesus's own stern denunciation of sexual immorality would certainly have carried, to his hearers, a clear implied rejection of all sexual behaviour outside heterosexual monogamy.' Michael Perham, Bishop of Gloucester, considers that 'although the last word has not been said, there is a vast amount of knowledge available to us, for instance about the nature of homosexuality, that our forebears simply could not know. It would be extraordinary if we dismissed that knowledge as irrelevant [138] in trying to establish a contemporary Christian ethic. So although Paul condemns homosexuality, Jesus never expressly mentions it, and his emphasis on love ('You should love your neighbour as yourself' (Mark 12, 30–1)) and compassion (e.g. for the woman 'taken in adultery' (John 8, 10–11)) suggests that he would have been unlikely to have shared Paul's uncompromising attitude. Although not susceptible to a statistic (any more than personal good works can be), most young people today do not regard sexual orientation as sinful or evil; they accept it as a fact of life for a minority of people, and consider it to be an injustice that such prejudice should be extended to gays and lesbians. Indeed they consider discrimination against people on the ground of their sexual orientation as equivalent to racial discrimination – which is not only immoral but criminal. Many would argue that there is much deeper love in a homosexual union that in many heterosexual marriages. Furthermore, gay priests are making a significant contribution to parish life. Christians are committed to love God and to love one another. Many people will recall the Lambeth Conference in 1998 when a large majority of bishops passed a resolution which condemned homosexuality as sinful. As Richard Holloway recalled: 'But it was the tone of the debate that was devastating. It was filled with a hateful glee that prompted one English bishop to liken it to a Nuremburg rally', and such 'blind prejudice and ugly hatred paraded in the name of Jesus' profoundly shocked him.[139] Karen Armstrong makes the point: 'Instead of quoting the Bible in order to denigrate homosexuals, liberals or women priests, we could recall Augustine's rule of faith: an exegete that must always seek the most charitable interpretation of a text... Instead of using a biblical passage to back up a bygone orthodoxy, modern hermeneutics could bear in mind that exegesis is a quest for something new… An exegesis based on the 'principle of charity' could be a spiritual discipline that is deeply needed in our torn and fragmented world.'[140] Not surprisingly, in view of their history, it is the Quakers who have become the first mainstream religious group to approve marriages for homosexuals. They have agreed 'to treat same-sex committed relationships in the same way as opposite-sex marriages, re-affirming our central insight that marriage is the Lord's work and we are but witnesses.' It is a tragedy that at a time of steadily diminishing numbers conservative members of the Anglican Church should scorn the advancement of women priests and gay men. It is little wonder that the general public looks on with cynical indifference.

Meanwhile, how in Britain are the numbers of Christian worshippers holding up? A 2001 census in Britain surprisingly indicated that some 71% of the population still thought of themselves as 'Christian',[141] although only some 15% of the population attended a conventional church.[142] Indeed, the increasing number of empty pews is symptomatic of a malaise affecting both Anglican and Roman Catholic Churches. For the latter, those attending Mass dropped by 40% between 1965 and 1991. More recently, Sunday Mass attendance has decreased still further from 1,703,800 in 1989 to 875,600 in 2005, a drop of 49%.[143] In a recent report entitled *The Future of the Catholic Church in Britain*, Tom Horwood stated: 'The Church in Britain is suffering from a terminal decline in membership, irregular commitment among the remnant, and, in the wake of persistent child abuse scandals, a leadership of bishops and priests that has toppled from its pedestal with a mighty crash.' He calls for more effective leadership from bishops and emphasised the need for 'straight-talking honesty'.[144] The sad fact that 60 reports of alleged child abuse were passed to the police in 2005 demonstrated the malaise of the Catholic Church in Britain. (And not only in Britain. In Ireland a Commission set up to Inquire into Child Abuse by Roman Catholic priests of The Christian Brothers, a male religious order established to run schools and residential homes for children in Canada, Australia and the UK, has reported (2009) that more than 800 individuals were responsible over the years for physical or sexual abuse of children in their care. The

Sisters of Mercy, who cared for the girls, also came in for much criticism. The government apparently turned a blind eye to what was going on. Hardly surprisingly in Dublin – the home of one million Catholics – only one priest was ordained in 2004). However, the Church can take some comfort from the fact that, during the past two years, the number of Roman Catholics in Britain has exceeded Anglicans for the first time since the Reformation – largely due to the influx of Catholic migrant workers to the UK from eastern Europe. By the end of 2006 the number of Pentecostal supporters had overtaken the Methodists and become the third most popular Church after the Anglicans and Roman Catholics. But there is now a real fear that both the Church of England and the Roman Catholic Church will shortly become financially unviable owing to declining church attendances and the ever-increasing expenses resulting from the upkeep of their buildings. The Church of England, for example, has 43 cathedrals and 16,000 parish churches to maintain. Although the Church Commissioners have funds valued at some £4.3 billion, the income from this is devoted to the support of cathedrals, bishops and the payment of clergy pensions. Despite the declining church attendance it is nevertheless encouraging to note that there appears to be some re-kindling of interest in religion – for example, there are more young people opting for religious studies at GCSE and A-level, and increasing numbers of students attending theological and Bible colleges. Indeed, applications to study theology and religion at British universities have been steadily rising in recent years despite the well-known doubts of some academics that theology has no place in a modern university as an academic discipline. However, the recent application of social sciences to religious studies has broadened the scope of the discipline and increased its attraction. And women priests may yet come to the rescue. Since the first women were ordained in 1994 about 4,000 have been priested, and over 3,000 are still active and represent about one-third of the total number of serving priests. It seems clear that women priests are likely to outnumber men within a few years, with a growing representation in the episcopacy. There are, however, many flourishing Anglican churches in the country, led by able and dedicated ministers, sometimes spurred on by new evangelistic ideas such as the 'Alpha' courses,[145] but there can be no disguising the overall decline in church attendance. This is discussed further in Chapter 7.

Yet in contrast to the decline in church attendance has gone a revival in the popularity of pilgrimages. More people than ever are now walking or cycling to such well-known shrines as Santiago de Compostela in northern Spain, to Lourdes in France, to Walsingham in Norfolk, and to the Isle of Iona, quite apart from the major pilgrimage attractions of Jerusalem and the Church of the Holy Sepulchre. Pilgrims enjoy the physical challenge – walking in wind, sun and rain, the experience of living together with a diverse group of fellow pilgrims, and the spiritual sensation of taking part in an act of religious devotion. So there are clear signs of a continuing desire for a spiritual experience.

Finally, an analysis published in *The Times* newspaper (31 October, 2007) recorded that 47% of all respondents believed in life after death (69% in the case of non-whites); 62% believed in the possession of souls; 43% of Christians believed in both heaven and hell (55% of non-whites); and 23% of all respondents believed in reincarnation (35% in the case of non-whites). These figures suggest that half the population still believes that we humans have spiritual souls and that there is some form of life after an earthly death. This surely confirms the widespread *instinct* amongst the general populace of a belief in the existence of the Transcendent, and once again provides an example of the incontrovertible fact that 'man is a religious creature'.

NOTES

[1]   Jonas, D. F., 1976, *Life, death, awareness, and concern: a progression*, in Toynbee *et al.*, 1976, 176
[2]   Armstrong, 1999, 3
[3]   Ibid., 4–5
[4]   Hence the Greek word *atheistos* or one who denies the Athenian state religion. The term *atheist* has therefore a long pedigree as meaning 'a denyer of God'
[5]   Davies, P., 1992, 35

[6] Ibid., 3, 6

[7] Russell, 1965, 296–7

[8] Ibid., 328

[9] As Valerie Warrior recounts: 'After the deification of Augustus, all but the most egregiously bad emperors, like Caligula (37–41 CE), Nero (54–68 CE) and Commodus (180–192), were deified. When he realised he was dying, the emperor Vespasian, noted for his wit, is reported to have said, 'O dear. I think I'm becoming a god' (Suetonius, *Vespasian* 23) (Warrior, 2006, 118)

[10] *Pliny: a self portrait in letters* (trans. and intro. by Betty Radice) (Folio Soc. edn., 1978), 241–2

[11] Ibid., 242–3

[12] Dill, S., *Roman Society in the Last Century of the Western Empire* (2nd edn., 1919), 75

[13] Davies, J., 1999, 140

[14] One of the more impressive survivals is the mausoleum of the Flavii family at Kasserine in Tunisia (Davies, J., 1999, 151, 221–4)

[15] Davies, J., 1999, 163–4

[16] Publius Virgilius Maro, *The Georgics* (trans. K. R. Mackenzie) (Folio Soc. edn., 1969), 76

[17] Dill, 1919, 10

[18] Thus Gilbert Murray notes that it is the saviour-gods of paganism who are often reputed to have been virgin-born (Wells, 1971, 30)

[19] Frazer, 1949, 347–56. An account of the ritual known as the Taurobolium (bull-slaying) in the cult of Magna Mater is given in Beard *et al.*, 2005, 160–2

[20] Ibid., 351–2

[21] Ibid., 361

[22] See, for example, the account of the interrogation and subsequent martyrdom of SS Perpetua and Felicitas in Beard *et al.*, 2005, 164–5

[23] It was recorded in Athens as early as 414 BC when the Athenian fleet was being fitted out for an expedition against Syracuse (Frazer, 1949, 336)

[24] Frazer, 1949, 383. A graphic account of a procession of Isis is given in Apuleius's work *Metamorphoses* (see Beard *et al.*, 2005, 134–6, 209–12). For an account of Osiris and Isis and the theology of ancient Egypt see Davies, J., 1999

[25] Warrior, 2006, 86–7

[26] Beard *et al.*, 2005, 288–292

[27] Wright, 2003, 80–1

[28] Green, 1977, 39

[29] A detailed account of the history of Gnosticism is given in Simon, 2004

[30] Kasser *et al.*, 2006, 84

[31] Simon, 2004, 27–31

[32] Ibid., 19

[33] Ehrman, 2006, 172–3

[34] Goulder, 1977, 67

[35] Simon, 2004, 95–99

[36] Staniforth and Louth, 1987, 115

[37] Simon, 2004, 180

[38] Ibid., 200–1

[39] Ibid., 128

[40] Staniforth and Louth, 1987, 115

[41] Ibid.

[42] A singular record has been found relating to the martyrdom of Polycarp – see Staniforth and Louth, 1987, 125–132

[43] Simon, 2004, 99–102

[44] Ibid., 210–11

[45] Beard *et al.*, 2005, 305–319. See also Davies, J., 1999, 40–6

[46] Hutton, 1996, 1. In Anglo-Saxon times the feast of the Nativity was described simply as 'midwinter', and the term 'Christmas' does not appear in literature until 1038 (Ibid., 6). It should be noted, however, that the Eastern Orthodox Church has retained the celebration of Christmas on 6th January and that of the New Year on 13th January

[47] Vermes, 2006, 10

[48] Frazer, 1949, 361

[49] Ehrman, 2006, 32

[50] Of Luke's Gospel Professor Ehrman says: 'In Luke 1: 1–4, for example, the author states that "many" predecessors had written an account of the things Jesus said and did, and that after reading them and consulting with "eyewitnesses and ministers of the word", he decided to produce his own account, one which he says is, in contrast to the others, "accurate". In other words, Luke had both written and oral sources for the events he narrates – he was not himself an observer of Jesus's earthly life. The same was probably true of the other Gospel writers as well' (Ehrman, 2006, 222 Note 17)

[51] See Ehrman, 2006, which gives a fascinating account of changes discovered in the texts of the New Testament and the reasons for them

[52] For a fascinating account of these 'other', and rejected, writings see Ehrman, 2003

[53] Ehrman, 2003, 13–28

[54] Ibid., 55

[55] Ibid., 33–5

[56] For the Arian heresy see p224 below

[57] Founded by a certain Montanus of Pepuza (a small and insignificant village in Phrygia), who regarded himself as a prophet. One of his more amusing prophecies was that the 'new Jerusalem' would descend from heaven to Pepuza 'where the Kingdom of God would arrive and Christ would then reign' (Ehrman, 2003, 150)

[58] Procopius, 53

[59] Freeman, 2008, 219 Note 11

[60] Toynbee, 1976, 25–28

[61] See, in this connection, Professor Ehrman's exposition of the subsequent conflict between Christians and Jews (Ehrman, 2006, 187–195)

[62] Since when the Jews have always harboured a revulsion for the Roman emperor Hadrian, who crushed the rebellion with great cruelty, re-built Jerusalem, and placed a statue of himself on Temple Mount (the most holy Jewish site), which was compounded by the later Islamic conquest and the building of the mosque of the Dome of the Rock

[63] Freeman, 2008, 66

[64] Ibid., 67

[65] McGrath, 2005, 70

[66] Russell, 1965, 361

[67] Hick, 2004, 86

[68] Ibid., 87–8

[69] Ibid., 89

[70] Ibid., 93

[71] Ibid.

[72] Kasser *et al.*, 2006, 103–4

[73] Hick, 2004, 94

[74] For a comprehensive account of the establishment and development of Islam see Armstrong, 1999, 155–197

[75] Armstrong, 1999, 167

[76] Ibid., 177

[77] Michael Binyon in *The Times*, 5 June, 2007

[78] Russell, 1965, 430

[79] The Albigensians, or Cathari, held doctrines which had come from the East via the Balkans and which were widely held in north Italy and the south of France. What united their believers was a disgust at the wealth and moral depravity of the clergy. Doctrinally they believed that for the virtuous there was no bodily resurrection, and that the souls of the wicked would transmigrate into the bodies of animals (for which reason they were vegetarians). They believed in the literal truth of the New Testament and considered the Old Testament Jehovah to have been a wicked spirit (this is reminiscent of earlier Gnostic thought). Other contemporary heresies included the Armenian Paulicians (who rejected infant baptism, the Trinity and the concept of purgatory and followed the teaching of St Paul in rejecting Jewish elements in Christianity) and the Waldenses (who lived a life of virtue and poverty). The efforts of various popes to root out heresies led to Pope Gregory IX founding the organisation known as the Inquisition in 1233. This body was largely staffed by Dominicans and Franciscans, and perpetrated the savage torture and burning of those believed to be guilty of heresy.

[80] Davies, P., 1992, 37

[81] See Nelson Pike, 1970, *God and Timelessness*, 3 and John O'Donnell, 1983, *Trinity and Temporality*, 46

[82] McGrath, 2005, 58–9

[83] Russell, 1965, 453–4

[84] Ibid., 466

[85] Clark, R., 'Lists of Derbyshire Clergymen 1558–1662', in Derbyshire Archaeological Journal, 126 (2006), 175

[86] Jacob Burckhardt, *The Civilisation of the Renaissance in Italy* (trans. S. G. C. Middlemore), Phaidon Press, 1945, 286

[87] Armstrong, 1999, 320

[88] Ibid., 366

[89] Mackie, 1952, 426–7; Bettenson, 1946, 328–9

[90] Armstrong, 1999, 348

[91] Russell, 1965, 566

[92] For a study of Kant's views on religion see Ward, 2004, 188–191

[93] See McGrath, 2004, 122–7 for a full exposition of Shelley's atheistic views

[94] Armstrong, 1999, 395

[95] McGrath, 2004, 60

[96] Ehrman, 2003, 170

[97] Armstrong, 1999, 353

[98] See Ward, 2004, 55–62

[99] McGrath, 2004, 63

[100] Ibid., 64

[101] Ibid., 65–6

[102] Russell, 1965, 754

[103] McGrath, 2004, 68–76

[104] Ibid., 77

[105] Ibid., 128

[106] Ibid., 129

[107] Ibid.

[108] Ibid., 130

[109] Ibid., 131

[110] Ibid., 132

[111] Holloway, 1999, 19

[112] McGrath, 2004, 43

[113] See Ward, 2004, 92–6

[114] Hardy, 1979, 56

[115] See *Mind* 57 (1948), 176–183

[116] See Smart and Haldane, 2003, 205–7

[117] John Leslie, *Value and Existence* (Oxford, Basil Blackwell, 1979). A critique of Leslie's theory is given in Smart and Haldane, 2003, 26–32

[118] McGrath, 2004, 155

[119] Armstrong, 1999, 433

[120] Ibid., 434

[121] Ibid.

[122] Ibid., 436

[123] Toynbee, 1976, 35

[124] Robinson, 1971, 122–141

[125] See Cupitt, 1980

[126] For a vivid personal account of the happenings during this 'charismatic' period see Hampson, 2006, 66–93

[127] McGrath, 2007a, 80–81. In his article *Pursuing Truth and Unity: why Evangelicals should remain in the Church of England*, in Chartres, C. (ed.), 2006, the Revd John Stott defines the Evangelical position. Essentially, they believe in the Incarnation (if the Church were officially to repudiate the Incarnation, Stott says, 'the only possible course would be to secede'); in the supremacy of Scripture for salvation and the justification of sinners 'by grace alone, in Christ alone, through faith alone'; and in the liturgy of the Church (to safeguard uniformity of doctrine). He recalls that the movement contains different strands (for example, reformed and charismatic)

and 'is as much a coalition as a party'. 'We claim no infallibility', he says, 'and may be mistaken on certain points. We are open to have our minds changed if Scripture can be shown to require it'

[128] For a discussion of Charismatic experiences see Carol Midgley and Ruth Gledhill in *The Times, 19 December, 2006*

[129] Religious belief in the United States of America is divided between a large number of diverse sects. This has arisen because of repeated schisms over details of their respective faiths. The largest sect is that of the Pentecostalists (embracing, *inter alia*, the Assemblies of God), followed by that of the Holiness Movement (comprising no less than 61 separate bodies) and, thirdly, by that of the Baptists (divided between the American Baptist Churches and the Southern Baptist Convention). In fourth place are the Adventists, whose members believe in the imminence of the Second Coming of Jesus. This has caused problems for many prophets of this event. William Miller, for example, declared that the Second Coming would take place between 21 March, 1843 and 21 March, 1844, and as a result many thousands of believers sold all their property and waited to embark for heaven. As with Jesus's own prediction the end failed to arrive. Miller humbly admitted his error. One of his followers, however, a certain Samuel S. Snow, re-adjusted Miller's calculation and announced that the millennium date should be 22 October, 1844. This date – referred to by believers as the 'Great Disappointment' – similarly produced no millennium. Yet there are still many groups – especially the Seventh-Day Adventist Church – who await an imminent Advent. Another prophet, Charles Taze Russell, took up the challenge and re-worked Miller's date calculations predicting that, after a 'dawn period' between 1874–1914, the millennium would finally arrive in 1914. His followers were known as Jehovah's Witnesses and in 1879 Russell and his supporters began to publish a weekly journal *Watch Tower* which is still delivered door-to-door every week. The outbreak of World War I was seen as the harbinger of the apocalypse which Russell then declared would arrive in 1918. Once again the apocalypse failed to arrive, but Russell himself had died in 1916 so was never personally disillusioned. Not surprisingly, his supporters were obliged to 're-interpret' his scheme of events by suggesting that Jesus had in fact begun a period of 'invisible rule' in 1914 which soon will end! Russell's supporters have splintered a number of times, but the main body of Jehovah's Witnesses numbers over 1 million outside the United States (Stark and Bainbridge, 1985, 138–143)

[130] The original Fundamentalist Movement dates from *c.* 1890; it has since split into several sects of which the 'Independent Fundamental Churches of America', founded in 1922, is the largest (Stark and Bainbridge, 1985, 142)

[131] Susan Jacoby, *The Times*, 31 October, 2008

[132] Stark and Bainbridge, 1985, 138

[133] Ibid., 197

[134] Susan Jacoby, *The Times*, 31 October, 2008

[135] Armstrong, 1999, 10

[136] Armstrong, K., *The Times*, 22 September, 2007

[137] Mark Henderson, *The Times*, 24 December, 2008

[138] Perham, 2010, 65

[139] Holloway, 2001, ix-xi

[140] Armstrong, K., *The Times*, 22 September, 2007

[141] This compares with a figure of 93% for Americans in the U.S.A. (Collins, 2007, 4)

[142] Heald, 2000. A survey of the beliefs of 2,200 people undertaken (2007) for John Humphrys by You Gov shows that 22% believed 'in a personal God who created the world and hears my prayers', 26% believed 'in something' but I'm not sure what', 10% said 'I'm really not sure what I believe and I don't give it much thought', while 16% declared themselves to be atheists ('the whole notion of a supernatural God is nonsense'). Of attendance at a place of worship, 62% attended only 'for special occasions such as weddings or funerals', while 18% said they never attended. Only 4% attended once a week. Humphrys contends that 'organised religion is in a state of near terminal decline' (Humphrys, 2007, 112–19)

[143] Christian Research English Church Census, 2005

[144] Quoted by Ruth Gledhill, *The Times*, 4 July, 2006

[145] 'Alpha' courses were designed by the Revd. Charles Marnham as 'a way of introducing newcomers to the basic principles of the Christian faith'. It has been particularly effective for 18–35 year-olds. See Gumbel, N., 'Alpha Plus', in Chartres, C. (ed.), 2006, 89–98

(ii)   Reflections on past history

From the point of view of Christian theism we may recognise a number of significant strands of thought and development arising from the foregoing historical and theological resumé. In the first place, thinking people have from the earliest times sought to explain the meaning of life, the laws of nature, and the supernatural world with its feared powers over the destiny of humanity. Mankind is, instinctively, a *religious* creature and has always believed in the reality of a God or gods to be feared and therefore worshipped in the hope and expectation of divine protection. Philosophers from Plato to St Thomas Aquinas, and from Aquinas to a range of modern philosophers, have proposed theories concerning mankind's relationship to supernatural beings or gods outside this world, the existence of a human 'soul', of life after death, the question of free will, and many other philosophical and religious problems. The pre-Christian Stoics maintained that God was the soul of the world, and that each mortal had a share of the Divine Fire. Plato thought that the souls of humankind came to them at birth from elsewhere, and his metaphysical ideas of a world of perfect, abstract Ideas or Forms had a profound influence on the theology of St Paul and of the early Church Fathers. Moreover, the Neoplatonist Plotinus was the first to identify Jesus with the *Logos* or 'reason', as he also conceived of a *philosophical* 'Trinity' of 'The One', 'Spirit' and 'Soul'. What is manifestly evident is that from its earliest days Christian theology owed a considerable debt to pre-Christian classical philosophers such as Plato and Aristotle.

Secondly, it is abundantly clear that, in its early years, the new religion of Christianity had many competitors – especially the cult of Cybele, the Phrygian 'Magna Mater' (adopted by Rome in 204 BC) and her consort Attis, the cult of the Syrian Adonis, the cults of Orpheanism, Manichaeism and Marcionism, and especially the popular cult of Mithraism. From these cults the early Christians borrowed myths and rituals – for example, the Virgin Mother and the Immaculate Conception, Jesus's death and resurrection on the third day, the sacraments of Baptism and the Eucharist, and the immortality of the soul. From Judaism – although ultimately from Zoroastrianism – came the Christian belief in bodily resurrection and a Last Judgement (which had supplanted the ancient Jewish belief in a shadowy underworld known as Sheol). Moreover, the dates of Christian festivals were deliberately altered to coincide with those of the cults of Sol Invictus and Mithraism. The Christians celebrated the birth of Jesus on 6 January, but since the state cult of Sol Invictus and the followers of Mithras celebrated the festival of Natalis Invictus (also the birthday of the Egyptian god Osiris, preceded by the rising of the star Sirius) on 25 December, the Western Christian Church decided to mark the Nativity of Christ on that day. Likewise, the festival of the Assumption of the Virgin Mary succeeded the festival of Diana, that of St John the Baptist the pagan Midsummer festival, and that of All Saints the former pagan festival of Samhain. Thus Christian church sacraments, such as Baptism and the Eucharist, as well as the dates of its major festivals were all based on pagan precedents, while the concepts of bodily resurrection and the Last Judgement came from its Judaic origins.

Thirdly, while it is clear that the disciples of Jesus were ordinary, simple men with no pretence to scholarship or theology moving about in small groups attempting to convert local communities to their new faith, through their examples of healing and exorcism, it became necessary — and especially after Roman emperors from Constantine onwards embraced their faith — for a form of 'church' government to be set up and Christian doctrines formulated which would act as a guarantor of its unity and orthodoxy.[1] This institutionalisation of the church was not achieved overnight, and this phase of historical development is characterised by prolonged and extraordinarily bitter disputes about the doctrines that should be established for the new Christian Church. These concerned matters such as the nature of Jesus, and the concept of the Holy Trinity, the concept of atonement and original sin, and the implications of the resurrection. Once these had been formulated by a small group of bishops (in particular, Irenaeus, bishop of Lyon and Justin Martyr) any attempt by 'outsiders' to question their doctrinal decisions was met by vigorous accusations of 'heresy' and the guilty party would be excommunicated. Bishop Irenaeus's great 5-volume work *Against Heresies* demonstrates the extent and nature of these 'alternative' views by other scholars and theologians. Views of men like the scholar Origen (whose ideas were later to be championed by Erasmus) and the Alexandrian priest Arius were dismissed at ecclesiastical councils (but the popularity of Arius's thesis was such that 'Arianism' survived into medieval times).

From then on the whole tone of Christianity altered and, instead of being a simple and unstructured faith – known originally to its followers as 'the Way of Jesus', the new Church started to become an increasingly powerful institution. Christian dioceses were then established under the leadership of bishops (elected by popular vote) who were financed by the offerings of the faithful. They often became important figures and many were given judicial powers by the State. So developed an ecclesiastical hierarchy with supporting administrations and courts. At the summit of the church hierarchy was the Bishop of Rome, later known as the Pope, who assumed the leadership of the Christian Church within the Roman Empire, while the Patriarch of Constantinople later became leader of the Eastern Orthodox Church. After the Church had steadily increased its temporal power and wealth, the notoriously corrupt, immoral and scandalous behaviour of some medieval popes sapped the authority and prestige of the papacy, and the public began to question the moral and spiritual authority of the Vatican Curia. Hence the Protestant Reformation movement spearheaded by Martin Luther, John Calvin and Huldrych Zwingli, and the subsequent sweeping away of many clerical abuses (such as the sale of Papal Indulgences). But the Catholic Church's doctrinal foundations were largely unaffected by the Reformation. The doctrine of the Holy Trinity has remained the bedrock of Catholic belief since it was finally confirmed as an orthodox doctrinal statement at the Council of Toledo in 675. The doctrine of Transubstantiation, a fundamental tenet of Catholic orthodoxy since it was formally defined by the Fourth Lateran Council in 1215, which was condemned by John Wycliffe and the Lollards but supported by King Henry VIII, also remains sacrosanct to this day. The Catholic doctrine of Purgatory has survived but with modification: it is no longer considered to be a 'place' but rather 'a spiritual state of the soul in which it's purified before entering heaven'. And of course the scandal of selling Masses to shorten the time that an individual had to remain in Purgatory has been removed. Catholics are somewhat coy about Hell, now no longer considered to be an abode of burning fire and brimstone to which those who were not among 'the Elect' were consigned, but rather a place of 'utter isolation as well as eternal torment' (whatever that may mean). The Reformation checked the spiritual abuses and unbridled wealth of the Roman Catholic Church since nations (such as England) ceased to pay clerical dues to the Holy See. The high point of the traditional Church had now been passed, and religious wars in Europe would in future alienate the increasingly intelligent laity still further. The Church as an institution had now begun its irreversible decline.

Lastly, the religious rivalries in Europe were to lead to the disillusionment of many people, and there was a movement towards secular learning especially in the fields of science and mathematics. The period of The Enlightenment now began to take hold of the intellectual centres of Europe. Descartes (d. 1650) stood out in Europe as the most brilliant rationalist philosopher and mathematician, and he also speculated on the nature of God. Leibniz (d. 1716) and Kant (d. 1804) also advanced theories of a transcendent reality, as did Voltaire (d. 1778), Schleiermacher (d. 1834) and Comte (d. 1857). As early as the eighteenth century the German philosopher Herman Reimarus (d. 1768) had insisted that Jesus was a mortal teacher and prophet rather than consubstantial with God. In his view it was essential for his supporters to steal his body from the tomb in order to validate their new 'religion'. Jesus had never claimed to be God or that he came to atone for the sins of the world (this idea originating with St Paul). This was later followed up by Albert Schweitzer (1906) who raised fresh doubts about the historical accuracy of the Gospel assertions about Jesus. He maintained that the doctrines of orthodox Christianity must have been developed at a time later than the historical Jesus and the Gospels. The nineteenth century saw an intensification of philosophical theories about the existence of God. Is God, after all, as Feuerbach (d. 1872) suggested, the hypostatised and objectified essence of the human imagination? Is God, according to Freud (d. 1939), merely a 'wish fulfilment'?

Increasingly, intellectuals began to question hitherto accepted religious dogmas and to look to the advance of science as a key to a new age. The publication of Charles Darwin's *Origin of Species* (1859) was of seminal importance in this debate, and led to sceptical views on religion by authors such as Draper, White, Hennell and Strauss. In the twentieth century theologians and philosophers continued to speculate about religion and faith; the reactionary post-World War II culture led to student riots in France and America (where the popular cry was 'God is dead'). In Russia, after the collapse of communism, Christianity amongst the people — long dormant during the years of repression — staged a strong recovery. In America there has been a startling revival of Christian belief in the form of Pentecostalism and in the popularity of 'charismatic' churches.

But the findings of biblical scholarship over the past century have severely weakened the hitherto accepted narratives of 'traditional' Christianity. It has now been established that many statements attributed to Jesus are later interpolations *ex post facto* in order to accord with Old Testament Messianic prophecies, and scholars increasingly question the decisions of the early bishops regarding Jesus's nature — especially his 'divinity' and his relationship to God, bearing in mind that Jesus never himself claimed to be regarded as divine, any more than he ever claimed that he had come to atone for the sins of mankind. These topics are discussed in later chapters.

In Britain, although in 2001 a census indicated that some 71% of the population still regarded themselves as 'Christians', only a fraction of respondents actually attended a conventional church. The ineluctable feature of religious belief in Britain today is the total indifference of a large proportion of the population to any form of structured religious worship.

NOTE

[1]   The word 'church' is derived from the Greek word *ekklēsia* which originally meant an assembly of citizens, and would have been used to represent the messianic community established by Jesus to spread his message as Messiah (Thiede, 2004, 70–1)

4. CRITICAL VIEWS OF CHRISTIAN THEISM

(i)   Philosophical arguments about God

(a)   The metaphysical case

Along with the revival of practical 'charismatic' Christianity, there has been a parallel and intensive philosophical contest between theists and atheists on the whole concept of God. At the root of the continuing debate lies the question whether the universe as we know it has been created or is a naturally occurring entity. Atheists maintain that the classical philosophical arguments for the existence of God cannot be sustained. The so-called 'Ontological Argument', advanced by both St Anselm and Descartes, and perfected by Leibniz, namely that God exists as a matter of logical necessity, is now considered by most philosophers to be unsound.[1] The 'Cosmological Argument' or the 'Argument from Contingency', advanced by St Thomas Aquinas, conceived God to be eternal (i.e. being altogether outside time), but Atheists argue that concepts of space-time do not require belief in a creator God, and that 'the universe has nothing beyond itself and so cannot be dependent on anything else'.[2]

The 'Design Argument', stemming from the beauty of the laws of nature and of the apparent 'fine tuning' of natural processes, which all argue for a world 'designer', is rejected by Atheists with scepticism. Thus Professor Dawkins considers that 'Darwinian evolution, specifically natural selection... shatters the illusion of design within the domain of biology, and teaches us to be suspicious of any kind of design hypothesis in physics and cosmology as well'.[3] As we have noted earlier, the philosopher Kant was impressed by the design argument and envisaged the possibility of an *architect* of the world (rather than a *creator*). John Stuart Mill, who rejected the cosmological and ontological arguments for God's existence, was likewise impressed by the argument from design, contending that 'there might well be an entity, less than omnipotent, which deserved the name of God'. He stated: 'In the present state of our knowledge the adaptations in Nature afford a large balance of probability in favour of creation by intelligence'. Yet he did not regard the evidence as 'rendering even probable the existence of an omnipotent and benevolent creator'.[4] However, perhaps the most compelling argument for premeditated design is to consider our very existence in the universe. Cosmologists inform us that the universe began with a 'big bang', an explosion occurring some 12–15 billion years ago resulting in an expanding universe of galaxies of which planet Earth is an insignificant part. This was the beginning of space-time for mankind. But the significant fact is that the form of this cosmic expansion was (in Processor Hick's words) 'determined by basic conditions which, if they had been even slightly different, would not have produced galaxies, including planets, including life, including us'. These conditions were needed 'if the universe as we know it, with ourselves as part of it, was to come about. In fact it looks as though our universe has been precisely designed to produce intelligent life'. Sir Martin Rees (the Astronomer Royal) 'does not himself believe in a creator God, but he does acknowledge the extraordinary series of coincidences that has been necessary to produce ourselves'.[5] The cosmologist Paul Davies reckoned that the odds against the formation of our cosmos were 'one followed by a thousand billion billion billion zeros, at least'! The incredible degree of fine-tuning of the various physical constants of the universe has been the subject of amazement for cosmologists like Professor Stephen Hawking, who writes: 'Why did the universe start out with so nearly the critical state of expansion that separates models that recollapse from those that go on expanding forever, that even now, 10 thousand million years later, it is still expanding at very nearly the critical rate? If the rate of expansion one second after the Big Bang had been smaller by even one part in 100 thousand million million, the universe would have recollapsed before it ever reached its present size'.[6] He adds: 'It would be very difficult to explain why the universe should have begun in just this way, except as the act of a God who intended to create beings like us'.[7] As Dr Francis Collins reflects: 'The existence of a universe as we know it rests upon a knife-edge of improbability'.[8] Professor Hick continues: 'on top of that we have the further improbability of the production within this universe of beings who can conceive of and worship God. Is it really credible, many ask, that such an enormously improbable occurrence as a universe containing spiritual beings should have happened purely by chance? Must it not have been deliberately designed?'[9] Sir Martin Rees conceives of multiple universes: 'the multiverse concept is already part of empiric science: we may already have intimations of other universes... In an infinite ensemble, the existence of some universes that are seemingly fine-turned to harbour life would occasion no surprise...'[10] Professor McGrath sums up the position as follows: 'the appearance of design can offer persuasion, not proof, concerning the role of divine creativity in the universe'.[11]

Lastly, the 'Argument from Religious Experience' is susceptible of so many explanations – based, for example, on emotion, credulity or illusion – that it can hardly be regarded as an *objective* warrant for belief.[12] Likewise the example of miracles, of which David Hume said that: 'a miracle can never be proved so as to be the foundation of a system of religion'.[13] As Professor Haldane has observed: 'some make much of the potential of personal religious experience but this is fraught with epistemological uncertainties, and notoriously liable to social and psychological eccentricity'.[14] A good-natured philosophical debate (surely a model of its kind, with no intemperate point-scoring which we have seen in more recent years) between Professors J. J. C. Smart and J. J. Haldane on the relative merits of atheism and theism is contained in their book *Atheism and Theism* (2003). This also examines some recent and contentious theories which have been propounded as to the nature of God (e.g. that God should in fact be regarded as 'an ethical principle'[15]), and more will doubtless follow. Older readers may also remember the historic debate on the existence of God between Bertrand Russell and Father F. C. Copleston, SJ in 1948.[16]

After Charles Darwin had published his *Origen of Species* (1859) there was much debate about its implications for traditional Christian beliefs. At a first glance Darwin's theory clashes with a literal acceptance of the Biblical account of the creation of the world in seven days, and with the beliefs of some Christian fundamentalists that the age of the earth is a mere 6,000 years. However, the non-literal interpretation of Genesis – i.e. that the whole world was *not* in fact created in a mere seven days – was accepted by orthodox Christians from as early as the time of St Augustine, and advances in the sciences of geology and archaeology have long since disproved the picturesque assertion of Archbishop James Ussher that the world was created on Saturday afternoon on 22 October, 4004 BC! Thus it was soon realised that the new theory was quite consistent with Christian theology. T. H. Huxley welcomed the rapprochement between the Church and the new scientific theory of evolution. He was 'profoundly irritated by those who dogmatised on matters of religion, whether positively or negatively. Science is, by definition, agnostic on matters of religion. And there, he argued, things should be left'.[17] And so far as his own views were concerned he stated: 'I have never been an Atheist in the sense of denying God. I think that generally (and more and more as I grow older), *but not always*, that an Agnostic would be the more correct description of my state of mind'.[18] Darwin (it should be noted), in his *The Descent of Man*, observed how 'a belief in all-pervading spiritual agencies seems to be universal'. He himself abandoned Christianity in favour of theism, but later abandoned theism in favour of agnosticism. Yet, as John Cornwell has pointed out: 'for all his latter-day scepticism, at no time did Darwin suggest, in his private writings or in public, that religious belief was incompatible with the scientific imagination; nor did he judge religionists to be contemptible or dangerous'.[19]

Today it is not unusual for gifted intellectuals, in their younger years, to be so dazzled by the exciting advances of scientific discovery that they dismiss 'religion' as medieval superstition and 'irrelevant' to real life, and the concept of God as infantile delusion explained by Freudian psychoanalysis (which we have described earlier). Most usually grow out of it. Not so, however, in the case of Professor Richard Dawkins, author (*inter alia*) of the best-selling books *The Selfish Gene* (1976), *The Blind Watchmaker* (1986) and *The God Delusion* (2006) who has popularised neo-

Darwinism as an alternative to creationism and speculated on how life might have originated without recourse to a deity of any kind. Dawkins maintains that 'slow, gradual, cumulative natural selection is the ultimate explanation for our existence',[20] and urges that 'the present lack of a definitely accepted account of the origin of life should certainly not be taken as a stumbling block for the whole Darwinian world view'.[21] The Darwinian theory of evolution is nowadays not in question, but for Professor Alister McGrath 'the real issue for me is how Dawkins proceeds from a Darwinian theory of evolution to a confident atheistic world-view, which he preaches with messianic zeal and unassailable certainty'.[22] He continues: 'In that Dawkins sees Darwinism as a worldview, rather than a biological theory, he has no hesitation in taking his argument far beyond the bounds of the purely biological'.[23] Yet 'Darwinism neither proves nor disproves the existence of God... If the great debate about God were to be determined solely on Darwinian grounds, the outcome is agnosticism – a principled, scrupulous insistence that the evidence is insufficient to allow a safe verdict to be reached. This does not suit Dawkins at all. His efforts to force an atheist conclusion upon a Darwinian description of the world are the least convincing, not to mention the least attractive, aspects of his writings.'[24] Professor McGrath's book *Dawkins' God* (2005) is a masterly critique of Dawkins's expressed views, and as a scientist himself McGrath has highlighted the intellectual superficiality and blind prejudice of Dawkins's polemical attacks on Christian theism.[25] The distinguished philosopher Professor Sir Anthony Kenny has demonstrated how evolutionists like Richard Dawkins have misunderstood 'the nature of theistic argument.' He points out that 'it is wrong to suggest, as is often done, that Darwin disproved the existence of God. For all Darwin showed, the whole machinery of natural selection may have been part of a Creator's design for the universe... Natural selection and intelligent design are not incompatible with each other...'.[26] Professor Keith Ward has also noted Dawkins's 'systematic mockery and demonising of competing views, which are always presented in the most naïve light'.[27] It is interesting to note that, in his latest book *The God Delusion* (2006), Dawkins totally ignores the many trenchant critical points raised by McGrath in his book. This is hardly surprising, since Dawkins appears more concerned with ridiculing religion (believed in by 'dyed-in-the-wool faith-heads') than in rigorous objective scholarship.

Stephen Jay Gould (1941–2002), a former atheist teacher at Harvard University, contended that 'any suggestion that Darwinian theory of evolution is *necessarily* atheistic goes way beyond the competency of the natural sciences, and strays into territory where the scientific method cannot be applied. If it is applied, it is *mis*applied'.[28] In other words, there are limits to the scientific method, a point made recently by both Sir Peter Medawar and by Sir Martin Rees (President of the Royal Society).[29] Thus Rees declares 'The pre-eminent mystery is why anything exists at all. What breathes life into the equations of physics, and actualized them in a real cosmos? Such questions lie beyond science, however: they are the province of philosophers and theologians.'[30] A point endorsed by John Cornwell who states: 'while science explores the material universe, it is only a partial description of a reality, from which consciousness, value, and purpose are missing'.[31] For most unbiased scientists and scholars, therefore, the widespread assumption that we have to choose between a scientific and a religious understanding of the universe is fundamentally mistaken.

In addition to Alister McGrath's critiques, Andrew Wilson (in his book *Deluded by Dawkins* (2007) has analysed Dawkins's arguments against God, highlighted those that are unsubstantiated assertions, truisms or irrelevant and/or facetious, and singles out eight salient points with which Christians may be expected to disagree. An altogether different style of riposte to Richard Dawkins's views is John Cornwell's *Darwin's Angel: a Seraphic Response to The God Delusion* (2007), which reveals the shallowness of many of Dawkins's arguments. Cornwell chides Dawkins on his inability to appreciate the nature of faith; his confusion between scientific and religious areas of thought; his ignorance of the history of philosophical speculation about the possibility of God and its effects; his confusion of terminology (e.g. between 'creationism' and the 'doctrine of creation' and the definitions of 'supernatural' and 'fundamentalism'); and the paucity of his sources ('your book is as innocent of heavy scholarship as it is full of false modesty. I note that the author most often cited (both in the bibliography and in the text) is yourself – your own works, your own sayings, thought experiments, speculations, conversations with experts, and favourable opinions of your works by others... I loved your admission that Mrs Dawkins consented to read out loud to you *The God Delusion* in its 400-page entirety; not once but *twice*. How many professors could boast publicly of such uxorious devotion'.[32]) He concludes that 'science cannot encompass the multi-dimensional symbols of religion, which by their nature must resist explanation and control'.[33]

Professor Sir Anthony Kenny, a former Roman Catholic priest, who subsequently became Master of Balliol College, Oxford and President of the British Academy, asked himself the question: is it *rational* to believe that God exists? To be rational we must ask: is it defensible by argument? Kenny considers the traditional arguments unsatisfactory and therefore is unconvinced about the reasonableness of theistic belief and concludes that he can only therefore be an agnostic on the question of the existence of God.[34] Yet elsewhere he has asserted: 'I don't think that as an agnostic one wants to jettison a whole religious tradition that has offered so much to literature and art and philosophy... one could take the traditional statements about God and the history of salvation not as a literal narrative but as forms of poetry'.

The last scholar we shall consider whose views on the existence of God should command universal respect is Dr Francis S. Collins, the distinguished head of the Human Genome Project in the USA and one of the world's leading scientists. Dr Collins has explained in his book *The Language of God* (2007) how he began life as an atheist and gradually developed a firm Christian faith, and clearly demonstrating how the scientific and spiritual world-views can be reconciled. In 2001 Dr Collins' team had just completed the first draft of the human genome – the hereditary code of life containing within it the instructions for building a human being – and this momentous event was announced by President Clinton who included in his speech the passage: 'Today we are learning the language in which God created life. We are gaining ever more awe for the complexity, the beauty, and the wonder of God's most divine and sacred gift'. As Dr Collins himself described the feat: 'We have caught the first glimpse of our own instruction book, previously known only to God'.[35] No doubt Professor Richard Dawkins and other atheists regard Dr Collins's beliefs as pure fantasy! Collins himself comments: 'Dawkins is a master of setting up a straw man, and then dismantling it with great relish. In fact, it is hard to escape the conclusion that such repeated mischaracterisations of faith betray a vitriolic personal agenda, rather than a reliance on the rational arguments that Dawkins so cherishes in the scientific realm... The major and inescapable flaw of Dawkins's claim that science demands atheism is that it goes beyond the evidence. If God is outside of nature, then science can neither prove nor disprove His existence. Atheism itself must therefore be considered a form of blind faith, in that it adopts a belief system that cannot be defended on the basis of pure reason'.[36] One of the most impressive books in recent years has been written by a distinguished scientist Professor Edgar Andrews. In his *Who Made God?* (2009) Andrews highlights with expertise and humour some of the inaccuracies and absurdities of many of Richard Dawkins' pretensions and those of 'new atheism'. He illustrates how traditional Christian theology is in no way compromised by the advances of science, and aims in his book to 'explore how the biblical hypothesis of God provides a comprehensible, intellectually consistent and spiritually satisfying view of being that encompasses man's experience of life, the universe and everything'. By now everyone is able to recognise the arrogant, intellectually-defective and vitriolic nature of Professor Dawkins's diatribes against religious believers − 'faith-heads' he scathingly calls them. It is significant that John Humphrys's BBC Radio 4 series *Humphrys In Search of God* elicited a large response from the public. 'Most of the letters, the vast majority, were written by sympathetic intelligent people who have given their faith (or lack of it) a great deal of thought over the years and wanted to share their views and their experience. Some were deeply moving...' Many of his correspondents 'found comfort in their faith and no one has the right to ridicule them for it. If their faith helped them through those dark days, their grief and suffering, we have no right to mock. For many it did all that and often much more. It is still helping them. For some, it is their lives. They simply cannot imagine living without God. Dawkins and company may find this risible. They may scoff or even sneer. But if they do they should be ashamed of themselves. Believers have every right to be treated with respect.[37]

In the realms of metaphysics we may recall Professor Stephen Hawking's reflection on a hoped-for time when a unified mathematical theory of everything is discovered, when he wrote: 'Then we shall all, philosophers, scientists, and just ordinary people, be able to take part in the discussion of the question of why it is that we and the universe exist. If we find the answer to that, it would be the ultimate triumph of human reason – for then we would know the mind of God'.[38] We may reasonably wonder whether mathematics, along with the structure of DNA, is another 'language of God'. Let Professor Alister McGrath have the last word: 'The debate between atheism and religious belief has gone on for centuries, and just about every aspect of it has been explored to the point when even philosophers seem bored with it. The outcome is a stalemate. Nobody can prove God's existence, and nobody can disprove it'.[39] The latest twist in this long saga is the recent setting-up of a new research project at the University of Oxford designed to discover *why* people believe in God, and whether this is a natural instinctive endowment or has arisen as a by-product of evolution. It will wisely *not* be concerned with the question of whether or not God exists!

Interestingly, a survey of religious views of scientists in 1996 showed that 40% had active religious beliefs, 40% had none (and can thus legitimately be regarded as atheists), and 20% were agnostic.[40] Not to be outdone, Professor Dawkins informs us about the religious opinions of Fellows of the Royal Society (of which Dawkins himself is one) according to a survey about to be published. Of those Fellows who responded to this survey 'the overwhelming majority of FRS, like the overwhelming majority of US Academicians, are atheists'.[41] But Dawkins is baffled by 'the polar opposition between the religiosity of the American public at large and the atheism of the intellectual elite'. Thus 93% of Americans profess some form of belief in God, while only about 40% of biologists, physicists, and mathematicians were believers'.[42]

In Britain a survey in the year 2000 recorded just 8% of the population as 'convinced atheists'.[43]

(b)   Theological arguments

Apart from metaphysical proofs (which have been the subject of unending philosophical argument for centuries) theists argue that there are other reasons – such as revelation and spiritual reflection – which may be adduced to support their belief in the 'truth' of God and his continuing involvement in today's world. Thus St John claimed to reveal (John 1: 1–14) that the 'Word' or *logos* of Greek philosophers – that is, the explanation of all things – was born into this world in the person of Jesus so that he might act as teacher and reveal God to mankind. Moreover, St Paul claimed that:

'What can be known about God is plain to [men] for God has shown it to them. Ever since the creation of the world his invisible nature, namely his eternal power and deity, has been clearly perceived in the things that have been made.'

(Romans 1: 19–20)

The implication of this remark, according to Professor Haldane, is that Paul 'is asserting that even those who do not already have an idea of God are in a position to determine that God exists simply by reflecting on the material order'.[44] Thus the great spiritual figures of history, such as St Augustine, have been inspired by an intense conviction of the divine purpose of life. The real problem is that, in philosophical reasoning, it is seldom possible to arrive at watertight conclusions. This point had been well understood by T. H. Huxley who in 1869 had coined the term 'agnostic' 'to designate someone who recognised that the great questions of life lay beyond demonstration'.[45] As Professor McGrath points out: 'It is increasingly recognised that philosophical argument about the existence of God has ground to a halt. The matter lies beyond rational proof, and is ultimately a matter of faith, in the sense of judgements made in the absence of sufficient evidence'.[46]

Among the most compelling recent expositions of the Christian religion in today's world are two works by Professor Keith Ward: *God, Chance and Necessity* (1996), and *God, Faith*

& the New Millennium (1998). Professor Ward points out that almost all the great classical philosophers 'saw the origin of the universe as lying in a transcendent reality. They had different specific ideas of this reality, and different ways of approaching it, but that the universe is not self-explanatory and that it requires some explanation beyond itself was something they accepted as fairly obvious'.[47] He takes issue with the materialist views of eminent scientists such as Professor Richard Dawkins and Professor Peter Atkins who 'have published books that openly deride religious beliefs, and claim the authority of their own scientific work for their attacks. Their claims are seriously misplaced. Their properly scientific work has no particular relevance to the truth or falsity of most religious claims'. [48] Ward contends that the theory of Darwinian natural selection does not provide 'a completely adequate explanation of all the mysteries of evolution',[49] but that the theist belief in a cosmic mind of immense wisdom creating a system with purpose and intelligence does provide a sufficient answer. Furthermore the development of consciousness 'is the refutation of materialism. It presents one with facts no materialist account could ever explain, in principle. Yet the whole history of evolution seems superbly well designed to lead to the existence of consciousness'.[50] Finally, Professor Ward believes that 'the hypothesis of God is a simple and elegant one, and explains the cosmos as intended to realise the goal of generating a self-aware and self-directing physical reality, or a community of such realities, capable of conscious relation to their creator. God provides the basis of an all–embracing cosmic purposive explanation...'[51]

Dr Francis S. Collins, the distinguished American scientist, states categorically: 'In my view, there is no conflict in being a rigorous scientist and a person who believes in a God who takes a personal interest in each one of us. Science's domain is to explore nature. God's domain is in the spiritual world, a realm not possible to explore with the tools and language of science. It must be examined with the heart, the mind, and the soul – and the mind must find a way to embrace both realms.[52]

In his critique of the opinions of atheists such as Richard Dawkins and Christopher Hitchens (whom he comically refers to as 'Ditchkins'!), Professor Terry Eagleton says that 'Dawkins makes an error of genre, or category mistake, about the kind of thing Christian belief is... he also has an old-fashioned scientistic notion of what constitutes evidence. Life for Dawkins would seem to divide neatly down the middle between things you can prove beyond all doubt, and blind faith. He fails to see that all the most interesting stuff goes on in neither of these places. Christopher Hitchens makes much the same crass error...'[53] In his view 'it would greatly enhance Ditchkins's moral integrity and intellectual honesty to intersperse his mildly monomaniac diatribe on the subject of religion with the odd glancing allusion to, say, the work in alleviating human suffering which Christianity and other faiths have carried on for centuries among the wretched of the earth, or their efforts in the cause of global peace, or the readiness some religious types have shown to lay down their lives for their fellows...'[54] The Catholic Church, it may be added, maintains that the incarnation of God in Jesus Christ and the foundation of a Church through his disciples has provided the ultimate demonstration of the existence of the deity. The Church also claims that the Pope and his successors has been granted the power of doctrinal infallibility. Belief in the incarnation of God in Jesus Christ and the claim of papal infallibility are now seriously open to question.

If, like Professor Ward, you have faith and imagination it is not difficult to construct a cosmological scenario where Christians believe in a *purposive* creation with anthropomorphic qualities, where God 'cares for beauty and truthful understanding', where human beings 'learn to co-operate with the divine creative Spirit', in a 'world in which wisdom, creativity and friendship can be celebrated and enjoyed',[55] and where 'the creator wills to limit and express the divine nature in such a way that it can establish a personal relation, not unlike that of human love, with some of its creatures...'[56] And indeed a consummation of the cosmos 'in which it becomes an expression of perfect beauty, without conflict or defect, fully expressive of the divine nature as love, shaped by communities of love which share in the expression of the divine love'.[57] Yet in the end Professor Ward is bound to admit that although the process of evolution could have been designed by a benevolent God 'it must be accepted that it could all have happened by chance',[58] and that 'it is impossible either to prove or disprove the activity of God as a selective cause in the process of evolution'.[59] He concludes that: 'contrary to what has sometimes been said, there is some sort of "natural fit" between the scientific worldview and mainstream Christian beliefs, which does make Christian faith a plausible, though not provable, religious view in a scientific age'.[60]

The same kind of optimistic, imaginative scenario has been voiced by Dr Tom Wright, bishop of Durham, who maintains that God intends 'to put the whole creation to rights. Earth and heaven are made to overlap with one another, not fitfully, mysteriously and partially as they do at the moment, but completely, gloriously and utterly. 'The earth shall be filled with the glory of God as the waters cover the sea…' The great drama will end, not with 'saved souls' being snatched up into heaven, away from the wicked earth and the mortal bodies which have dragged them down into sin, but with the New Jerusalem coming down from heaven to earth, so that 'the dwelling of God is with humans' (Revelation 21: 3)'.[61] And in God's new world Jesus will be the central figure.

In the end, as Professor McGrath contends: 'the things that really matter in life often lie beyond demonstrative proof. Nobody is going to be able to settle the question of the existence of God with complete certainty. It's simply not in the same category as whether the earth is flat, or whether DNA takes the form of a double helix'.[62]

Yet here is a paradox. If, under Professor Ward's benign vision of cosmological evolution, the Christian God is predicated as omnipotent, omniscient, compassionate and merciful, whose very essence is the spirit of love for his creatures, how can we explain away the problem of evil, pain and suffering, the unending and seemingly endemic process of wars which have characterised the history of 'civilisation' from the earliest times? Indeed, it has been well said that 'the great paradox of religion is that it can be used to create peace and love or to justify violence and hatred'. The problem of evil, according to the *Oxford Companion to Philosophy*, is 'the most powerful objection to traditional theism'.

The standard reply by churchmen is that moral evil results from the misuse of free will with which we have been endowed by God, and as Professor Haldane has observed: 'that although God is responsible for everything we do he is not the author of moral evil, and that it is incompatible with the good that he *has* authored in creating rational animals that he should then override their decisions whenever these are morally wrong'.[63] Professor Ward explains that the answer lies in the 'fallacy of omnipotence'. God is assumed to have unlimited power and could therefore if he wished create a world with little or no suffering. But in fact God is constrained to 'choose from among a set of necessarily given possibles. In this sense, God's choice is not entirely free'.[64] He continues: 'To put it bluntly, God could not create *us* in a better universe, or a universe with fewer possibilities of suffering in it'.[65] This is but one example of a theodicy (a theory 'to justify the ways of God to men'), and the problem has given rise to much debate amongst theologians.[66]

This is certainly one of the most controversial aspects of the Christian religion. John Humphrys in his book *In God We Doubt* (2007) questioned faith leaders on it. The Archbishop of Canterbury, Dr Rowan Williams, when asked by Humphrys how a living God could allow the suffering of (for example) a mother watching her child dying of cancer, responded initially 'We don't quite know why', and went on to suggest that there was 'hope of healing… in God's time, maybe within this world and maybe not…'[67] Similarly, Michael Perham, Bishop of Gloucester, in his book *Glory in our Midst* (2005), commenting on the Indian Ocean tsunami in 2004 states: '…the world witnessed an extreme example of one of those acts of nature that inevitably cause people to question the kind of God in which they believe. Nearly 300,000 around the Indian Ocean died in a few moments through the savagery of an earthquake and a tidal wave.' He continues: 'Where was God in the tsunami? people were asking. There is, of course, no easy answer… Part of me, like many before me, even in the scriptures, wants to rail against God… And, though there have to be other, more complex answers as well, I believe we need to say in response to the question, "Where was God in the tsunami?", that he was and is in the helpless, the powerless, the vulnerable, the humble and the suffering, who were overwhelmed by the flood'.[68] And now, more recently, we have witnessed the horrific earthquake in Haiti which has devastated most of the capital city of Port-au-Prince and killed more than 220,000 people. This is clearly a most uncomfortable dilemma for the Church. Perhaps the most plausible explanation is to divide the problem of evil and suffering into two categories. The first category is a matter of 'moral evil', where tragedies occur as the result of human beings' behaviour towards each other – e.g. as a result of wars and of personal crimes against each other (such as the Nazi extermination camps for the Jews). These cannot be laid at God's door: they are the result of our own wilful actions: the consequence of free will. The second category, that of 'physical evil', covers natural disasters – e.g. earthquakes, volcanic eruptions, tsunamis, floods and famines. These essentially are the consequences of the evolutionary development of the universe which can occur at any time and without warning. It can hardly be expected that God would intervene to prevent such periodic consequences of his own creation. Yet it emphasises the contrast between the reality of unanticipated suffering and the Christian belief in the ever-present compassion of God towards his created beings. It is also important to record that one of the consequences of disasters and suffering is to bring about the opportunities for spiritual growth through suffering – a theodicy recognised by the world's great faiths (e.g. the Buddha's Four Noble Truths begin with an allusion to 'Life is suffering'). This, paradoxically, has been a source of great comfort to many.

Whatever the true explanation of evil and natural disasters one can readily appreciate the argument – contrary to Professor Ward's idealistic cosmic consummation of the universe, without conflict or defects – that if sinful mankind persists with wrongdoing it may be a sufficient reason for God to close the book on human history, in the colourful biblical words:

'Just as the weeds are gathered and bound with fire, so will it be at the close of the age. The Son of Man will send his angels, and they will gather out of his kingdom all causes of sin and all evildoers, and throw them into the furnace of fire; there men will weep and gnash their teeth. Then the righteous will shine like the sun in the kingdom of their Father...'

(Matthew 13: 40–4)

And of course although the early Christians were expecting the *Parousia* or 'Second Coming' within a few years, a mere 2,000 years later may still not be sufficient to establish the degree of evil required to give rise to the dreaded Apocalypse. Indeed, we may with luck be able to postpone this event until the law of entropy brings our space-time universe to an end.[69] That would surely be a poetic ending to the history of our universe, and, if we believe in the Stoic *palingenesia*, the whole process may begin again in another universe – perhaps anticipating Sir Roger Penrose's theory of *aeonic* cyclic cosmology.[70] Finally, it may be worth reflecting that some 900 years ago the brilliant Muslim philosopher Abu Hamid al-Ghazzali (1058–1111) was convinced that it was 'absolutely impossible to prove God's existence beyond reasonable doubt. The reality that we call 'God' lay outside the realm of sense perception and logical thought'.[71]

Since the period of The Enlightenment from the end of the seventeenth century astronomers, mathematicians and scientists such as Copernicus, Galileo, Kepler, Newton, Boyle, Einstein, Crick and Hawking have gradually discovered many of the fundamental laws by which our universe is governed. Such discoveries will no doubt continue to be made in the future thereby adding further to our knowledge of the world in which we live. Some scientists believe that, in due time, all the laws of physics will be combined into a single mathematical formula: in other words, it may be possible to discover a 'Theory of Everything' that will serve to unify all the laws of nature. At the end of his celebrated work *A Brief History of Time* (1988) Professor Stephen Hawking concluded:

'If we do discover a complete theory, it should in time be understandable in broad principle by everyone, not just a few scientists. Then we shall all, philosophers, scientists, and just ordinary people, be able to take part in the discussion of why it is that we and the universe exist. If we find the answer to that, it would be the ultimate triumph of human reason – for then we would truly know the mind of God'.[72]

According to John Humphrys, Hawking told him that he had considered cutting out the last sentence. However, he was glad that he didn't because, if he had, the sales of the book might have been halved because of those last four words! Believers of course seized on the idea that this brilliant professor, thought to be an atheist, was now entertaining the concept of God. However, when Humphrys questioned Hawking the position became rather different. 'What I meant when I said we would know the mind of God, was that if you discovered the complete set of laws, and understood why the universe existed, we would be in the position of God. We are making progress towards that goal, but we still have some way to go'.[73] Pressed further, Hawking continued: 'One could define God as the embodiment of the laws of nature. However, this is not what most people would think of as God. They mean a human-like being, with whom one can have a personal relationship. When you look at the vast size of the universe, and how insignificant and accidental human life is in it, that seems most implausible'. Alas, Stephen Hawking does not believe 'in anything remotely resembling the personal God of the monotheistic faiths. His 'God', if you can call him that, is the embodiment of the laws of nature. That's pretty much what Albert Einstein thought'.[74] And in his latest book, *The Grand Design* (2010), Hawking had shied away from his earlier flirtation with the concept of God, maintaining that modern physics requires no such assumption since physical laws are sufficient for the universe to have come into existence spontaneously. Sir Roger Penrose has also entered the lists with his latest book, *Cycles of Time* (2010), in which he suggests that the existence of our universe may be cyclical, consisting of a series of *aeons* each culminating in a 'big bang' which is itself the start of a new universe. Again, the concept of God is not involved in this model. These theories contrast with the belief of the Archbishop of Canterbury, Dr Rowan Williams. When asked by John Humphrys whether he *knew* that there is a God or *believed* it, Williams replied: 'I don't know that there is God or a God in the simple sense that I can tick that off as an item I'm familiar with. Believing is a matter of being committed to the reality of God: the knowledge that comes, that grows if you like, through a relationship. I believe I commit myself. I accept what God gives me... Grow in that relationship and you grow in a kind of certainty or anchorage in the belief. Knowledge? Well, yes – of a certain kind – but not acquaintance with a particular fact or a particular state of affairs. It's the knowledge that comes from relation and takes time'.[75] Michael Perham, Bishop of Gloucester, writes of his relationship to God in the following terms: 'God is not a person... but he is personal in the sense that we can have a relationship with him... Of course it remains a mind-blowing truth that God can know the unique you or call you by your name, hold you individually in his heart. I can't begin to understand that, but I can sense it, and experience it... Prayer is where I experience God and know myself to have a personal relationship with him.[76]

Finally, Professor Paul Davies maintains that a complete understanding of the existence and properties of the universe 'lies outside the usual categories of rational human thought' and believes that 'the search for a closed logical scheme that provides a complete and self-consistent explanation for everything is doomed to failure'.[77] Yet even if the search for a scientific 'proof' of the existence of God may be doomed to failure, we have nevertheless discovered intimations of an extra-terrestrial reality whose implications we shall examine in the following section.

NOTES

[1]   This is discussed at length in Smart and Haldane, 2003, and in Peterson *et al.*, 2003, 79–83. Unsurprisingly, Professor Richard Dawkins ridicules it (Dawkins, 2006, 80–3)

[2]   Smart and Haldane, 2003, 37; Peterson *et al.*, 2003, 83–91; Dawkins, 2006, 77–8

3   Dawkins, 2006, 118
4   Kenny, 2006, 51
5   Hick, 2004, 27
6   Hawking, 1988, 138
7   Ibid., 144
8   Collins, 2007, 73
9   Hick, 2004, 5, 27
10 Ibid., 28
11 McGrath, 2007, 8. For a discussion of the 'Design Argument' see Peterson *et al.*, 2003, 95–8
12 See Dawkins, 2006, 87–92
13 Smart and Haldane, 2003, 52
14 Ibid., 147
15 Stemming, according to John Leslie, from Neo-Platonism. He has there put forward a theory of 'extreme axiarchism' which he contends explains the existence and nature of the universe. See Smart and Haldane, 2003, 26–32
16 See Russell, 2005, 125–152
17 McGrath, 2005, 75–6
18 Ibid., 76
19 Cornwell, 2007, 13
20 Dawkins, R., *The Blind Watchmaker* (Penguin Books, 1991 edn.), 318. Bishop Hugh Montefiore's book *The Probability of God* is dismissed by Dawkins as being based on what he terms the 'Argument from Personal Incredulity' – see pp. 37–41. Dawkins himself claims to be 'a *de facto* atheist. I cannot know for certain but I think God is very improbable, and I live my life on the assumption that he is not there' (Dawkins, 2006, 50–1)
21 Dawkins, 1991, 166
22 McGrath, 2005, 10
23 Ibid., 51
24 Ibid., 92
25 Ibid., 10–14. Another product of what some might call a warped mind is Dawkins's theory that the idea of God is like a cultural virus of the mind, i.e. a malignant infection that can be transmitted like an epidemic! A development of his 'meme' concept (already dismissed by critics) this whole idea – according to Professor McGrath – 'founders on the rocks of the absence of experimental evidence, the subjectivity of Dawkins's personal value judgements implicated in assessing what is 'good' and 'bad', and the circularity of self-referentiality' (Ibid., 135–6)

26 Kenny, 1992, 113–4; 2006, 27–8

27 Ward, 1996, 99

28 McGrath, 2005, 80. Naturally such a view is hotly contested by Richard Dawkins who hastens to add that 'Gould, by the way, was not an impartial agnostic but strongly inclined towards *de facto* atheism'! (Dawkins, 2006, 55–61)

29 McGrath, 2007b, 14, 17–18

30 Quoted in Cornwell, 2007, 153

31 Ibid., 61

32 Cornwell, 2007, 29–30

33 Ibid., 45

34 Kenny, 1992, 58. His view is that 'Reflection in later years has made me more rather than less doubtful about the possibility of the existence of anything to which one can seriously attribute the predicates out of which the traditional notion of Godhead is constructed' (Kenny, 2006, 9)

35 Collins, 2007, 2

36 Ibid., 164–5

37 Humphrys, 2007, 198–201

38 Hawking, 1988, 175

39 McGrath, 2005, 92. A comprehensive discussion of the compatibility of religion and science is given in Peterson *et al.*, 2003, 246, 262

40 Ibid., 111

41 Dawkins, 2006, 102

42 Collins, 2007, 4

43 Heald, 2000

44 Smart and Haldane, 2003, 127

45 McGrath, 2004, 93–4

46 Ibid., 179

47 Ward, 1996, 7

48 Ibid., 11

49 Ibid., 73

50 Ibid., 148

51 Ibid., 190

52 Collins, 2007, 6

53 Eagleton, 2009, 6–7

54 Ibid., 97–8

55 Ward, 1998, 28

56 Ibid., 29

57 Ibid., 30

58 Ibid., 121

[59] Ibid., 122

[60] Ibid., 11

[61] Wright, 2006, 185

[62] McGrath, 2005, 96

[63] Smart and Haldane, 2003, 141

[64] Ward, 1998, 94

[65] Ibid., 95

[66] The problem of evil is discussed at length in Peterson *et al.*, 2003, 128–149. God's power of intervention in relation to 'miracles' raises some similarly disturbing questions as to why he can apparently be observed to intervene in certain tragic cases and clearly not in others (Ibid., 189–190). Furthermore, if, as St Thomas Aquinas maintained, happiness was one of God's names (Radcliffe, 2005, 55), it is all the more extraordinary that he is seen to be powerless when *natural* disasters strike his created world

[67] Humphrys, 2007, 140–142

[68] Perham, 2005, 72

[69] It is a sobering thought that our galaxy is hurtling at 300,000 mph towards Andromeda, which in some 2 billion years time is likely to absorb us!

[70] Penrose, 2010, 147

[71] Armstrong, 1999, 221

[72] Hawking, 1998, 175

[73] Humphrys, 2007, 54

[74] Ibid., 54–5

[75] Ibid., 68–9

[76] Perham, 2010, 14

[77] Davies, P., 1992, 225–6

(ii)   Transcendent Reality

Having demonstrated that neither the existence nor the non-existence of God can be proved by methods of current scientific analysis, and that different criteria of evidence and argumentation must be found to explain the creation and purpose of the universe, where can the questing individual now turn?

As has presciently been pointed out by Karen Armstrong: 'Throughout history, men and women have experienced a dimension of the spirit that seems to transcend the mundane world. Indeed, it is an arresting characteristic of the human mind to be able to conceive concepts that go beyond it in this way. However we choose to interpret it, this human experience of transcendence has been a fact of life... All the major religions, however, would agree that it is impossible to describe this transcendence in normal conceptual language. Monotheists have called this transcendence "God" but they have hedged this around with important provisos...'[1] We are thus at once confronted with the limitations of language. Theologians have recognised the 'apophatic' nature of God, that is 'the impossibility of speaking about him in anything but inadequate terms' (either analogically or metaphorically). As Susan Howatch has expressed it: 'All religious thought is symbolic in that it attempts to bridge the gap between the describable and the inexpressible, but that doesn't mean it's untrue. Quite the reverse'.[2] What we want to define, but cannot because we don't know its parameters (since it is outside the scope of human conceptual systems) is 'something' ineffable, or, metaphorically, what Johannes Tillich called 'the ground of our being'. We can only attempt to describe it in familiar terms like 'God', 'the Divine', 'the Infinite', 'the Ultimate Reality', 'the Transcendent', who/which is omnipotent and omniscient and altogether outside time.[3] We cannot know if this 'something' is personal or non-personal, but long-established tradition based on scriptural accounts has attributed to it a divine 'personality' – e.g. the 'God' of Jewish and Christian scripture, the 'al-Lah' (*rahman hahim*) of the Qur'an or the Vishnu and Shiva of Hinduism. Bishop John Shelby Spong asks rhetorically: 'Can I experience God without being able to define God? Is there anything to the sense of transcendence; is there an experience of otherness that is not a delusion born out of fear?... Is there a reality that we agree to call by the name of *God* whose face may be hidden but whose effects I can see?[4] In order to avoid prejudicing the essence of the 'Ultimate Reality', and to remove the connotations which the term 'God' has for some people, perhaps the best term for us to use would be 'the Transcendent' – implying something which can be apprehended 'existing apart from, and not subject to the limitations of the material universe'. It can perhaps best be likened to something operating through a spiritual 'internet'. The responses of the many different religions to the Transcendent will naturally differ because of their different cultural backgrounds. In the Christian tradition 'God' is regarded as 'a supreme Person, a self-existent subject of infinite goodness and power, who enters into a relationship with us comparable with that of one human personality with another. The theist is concerned to argue the existence of such a Being as the creator and most sufficient explanation of the world as we know it.'[5] But is this supposed personal relationship correct? Is it not explained, rather, by D. F. Strauss's theory (which we have discussed earlier) that religion is ultimately 'an expression of the human mind's ability to generate myths in the first place, and then to interpret these as truths revealed by God'? T. H. Huxley regarded religion as a necessity of the human spirit, which in practice would allow either for a self-generated 'God' (as Strauss proposed) or for an independent but real divinity. There is also a danger that the man-made theistic image of God, fostered by organised religion to increase hierarchical power over its adherents, may disguise the reality of a transcendent God (or Ultimate Reality), and that the development of liturgical worship has led to popular idolatry. Have we (for example) exchanged the idolatry of the Blessed Virgin Mary and of the Saints as a partial substitute for the *real* God?

Leaving aside the Christian belief in a 'personal' God who is continually involved in today's world, are there further dimensions of the Transcendent beyond the physical? Professor John Hick has suggested that there is in fact a 'non-anthropomorphic conception of the ultimately Real that has always been present within the mystical strands of the great traditions', and that 'we are all linked at a deep unconscious level in a universal network in which our thoughts, and even more our emotions, are all the time affecting others, and others are in turn affecting us'.[6] He points to feelings for the Transcendent when he contemplates the beauties of the natural world and the human arts which engender within us a link 'between our own spiritual nature and a greater spiritual reality around and beyond us'. The poet William Wordsworth found himself groping for something he sensed but could barely explain in his poem 'Lines composed near Tintern Abbey':

> 'And I have felt
> A presence that disturbs me with the joy
> Of elevated thoughts; a sense sublime
> Of something far more deeply interfused,
> Whose dwelling is the light of setting suns,
> And the round ocean and the living air,
> And the blue sky, and in the mind of man:
> A motion and a spirit, that impels
> All thinking things, all objects of all thought,
> And rolls through all things.'

The late Bertrand Russell, the pre-eminent philosopher of his time, found himself unable to become a Christian because of his dislike for doctrines and behaviour of the Christian Church hierarchy whose creeds he felt were unbelievable to any rational person. Yet his agnostic views contrasted with his emotional and 'religious' impulses: 'I have always ardently desired to find some justification for the emotions inspired by certain things that seem to stand outside human life and to deserve feelings of awe. And so my instincts go with the humanists, but my emotions violently rebel. In this respect the 'consolations of philosophy' are not for me'.[7] Indeed his daughter, Katharine Tait, wrote that 'He was by temperament a profoundly religious man'. Russell's 'things that seem to stand outside human life and to deserve feelings of awe' reinforces the experience of many others who would not subscribe to being Christians yet are conscious nevertheless of a transcendent world beyond our present existence. Gerald Priestland, for example, admitted to having had flashes of 'religious experience' – sometimes of an aesthetic nature ('a few bars of music, a phrase of poetry, the first impact of a painting') which have given him 'a split-second glimpse of eternity, of reality, in a nutshell'. On other occasions he is aware of a verbal message, not immediately clear in itself but later turning out to be of crucial importance.[8]

Hick also sees powerful 'signals of transcendence' in the lives of saintly people who have undergone a transformation from natural self-centredness to live in harmony with 'the transcendent, the Holy, the Divine, the Ultimate'. He believes there is an aspect of us that is 'in tune' with the Transcendent which is sometimes referred to as 'the image of God'[9] within us or as the 'divine spark' mentioned by Plotinus, Pseudo-Dionysius and other Christian mystics. As Geoffrey Parrinder reminds us: 'Plotinus welded Platonic and other mystical ideas into a coherent whole and his essays are among the classics of mysticism. Plotinus taught the union (*enosis*) of the soul with the divine one, which is the Good and the source of all existence and values'.[10] Similarly, Pseudo-Dionysius writes of the 'union' of the soul with God out of the gradual 'divinization' (*theosis*) of man'.[11] Those sensitive to the Transcendent have seen visions of angels, deities and prophets – e.g. Dame Julian of Norwich (*c.*1342–1416) with her visions of Christ, or Teresa of Avila (1515–1582) with her erotic encounter with a beautiful angel. Similar experiences are recorded by Islamic and Hindu mystics. Muslims developed their own mystical tradition, practised from the eighth century by the Sufis who may in turn have been influenced by the Christian ascetics of the Near East. They sought to experience God in the same way as Muhammad when he received his revelations. They practised fasting, vigils and chanting and members of the Mawlawiyyah Sufi order – known in the West as the 'whirling dervishes' – founded by Jalal ad-Din Rumi (1207–1273) were accustomed to spin round and round in order to put themselves into a trance so as to achieve a mystical experience.[12] The Jews within the Islamic empire were influenced by the mystical practices they observed and some, known as Kabbalists (from Kabbalah, or 'inherited tradition'), attempted to distinguish between the essence of God and the 'God' observed in creation and revelation (an essentially Gnostic and Neoplatonic distinction). Their best known text was called *The Zohar* ('The Book of Splendour') written *c.*1275 by the Spanish mystic Moses of Leon,[13] which seeks to uncover the true essence of God and the meaning of life. Its critical thesis is that God is a source of infinite, pure spiritual light, with every human being containing sparks of divinity within themselves, and with the goal of becoming closer to the divine source. Historically, Kabbalah was not studied until the student had reached the age of forty, and had gained experience in life, but recently it has become something of a popular cult with the rich and famous. As was well appreciated both by St Thomas Aquinas and the fourteenth-century Sufi Al-Junayd the nature of awareness of the divine depends on the religious traditions of the person who experiences it.[14]

Turning to modern times we see an example in the life of Mohandas Gandhi (1869–1948), known in his lifetime as Mahatma ('great soul') Gandhi, with his campaign of non-violence and profound spiritual vision. Gandhi believed that God is not a 'Person', 'but is beyond the personal/impersonal distinction as the ultimate reality underlying all things'.[15] Gandhi believed that there is a divine element in each of us and spent his life trying to transform Indian society and to educate the masses. Most significantly, Gandhi shared the ancient Hindu assumption that 'religions are different roads converging at the same point. What does it matter that we take different roads so long as we reach the same goal? I believe in the fundamental truths of all great religions of the world. I believe they are all God given... No one faith is perfect. All faiths are equally clear to their respective votaries'.[16]

From prehistoric days, there appears to have been an innate awareness of the 'sacred' in the human mind. Anthropologists note signs of religious concern in the earliest manifestations of human behaviour, e.g. the care devoted to the burial of their dead where numerous examples occur of grave goods such as food, flint artefacts, drinking bowls and weapons. These imply belief in some form of afterlife, and they are clearly linked to early primitive rituals. Moreover, there was a widespread belief that unseen spirits inhabited the sky, forests, rivers and trees, and these had to be worshipped and their protection sought. The prime purpose of superstitious rituals and magic was one of self-protection from unknown enemies, and the pagan practice of eating the body (corn) and drinking the blood (wine) of a deity, as a means of 'communion' with the powerful unseen, was an instinctive belief of primitive man which ultimately carried over into the Christian ritual of the Eucharist.

From the idea of numerous spirits who had to be placated, through to the classical pantheons of Greece and Rome, comes – after many centuries – the more restricted concept of all-powerful 'God' to whom worship was due. Such an entity was described as 'the Divine', 'the Holy', 'the Eternal' and 'the Infinite', but a distinction may be recognised between a personal 'God' and a parallel non-personal transcendent power with which certain mystics have believed themselves to have been associated. Thus mysticism has been defined as 'the experience of union either with God or with an ultimate non-personal reality'.[17] Pseudo-Dionysius (c.500 AD) speaks of the mystic goal as 'to be at one with God'. Meister Eckhart (c.1260–1327) says that God 'is light and when the divine light pours into the soul, the soul is united with God'. The mystic Catherine of Siena (1347–1380) exhibited a desperate anxiety to be at one with God, and wrote an extraordinary work entitled *The Dialogue* in which she sought to display how God's grace and mercy may be discovered. Her mystical experiences were combined with a practical mission to minister to the sick and suffering and to care for the poor. In 1370 she experienced a 'mystical death' during which for four hours she experienced an ecstatic union with God while seeming to the outside world to be dead. Her book is in the form of a dialogue between herself and God on matters such as divine providence, prayer and obedience. She quotes God as saying: 'I also want you to look at the bridge of my only-begotten Son and see its greatness. That is, that by it the earth of your humanity is joined to the greatness of the Deity, for it reaches from heaven to earth. I say then that this bridge constitutes the union which I have made with man'.[18] Amusingly, and truthfully, she says in a passage 'Eternal Father! Forgive my ignorance that makes me presume to chatter to you'! The anchorite and mystic Julian of Norwich (c.1342–1416) saw visions of Christ and wrote of the love of God and of asking 'reverently of our Lover whatever we will… we can never cease wanting and longing until we possess him in fullness of joy…'[19] St Teresa of Avila (1515–1582) also saw visions and experienced raptures, claiming to pass beyond such states 'into the peace of union with God'.[20]

Three centuries after the mystics of the fourteenth and fifteenth centuries there was another outburst of mystical devotional writing, often in verse and by both clergymen and the laity. John Donne (1573–1631), Dean of St Paul's, the layman Francis Quarles (1592–1644), George Herbert (1593–1633) (a country parson) and Henry Vaughan (1622–1644) (a doctor) were notable mystical writers. Thus Henry Vaughan, in his poem *Beyond the Veil*, wrote:

> 'And yet, as angels in some brighter dreams
> Call to the soul when man doth sleep,
> So some strange thoughts transcend our wonted themes,
> And into glory peep'

But perhaps the most memorable was the seventeenth-century clergyman Thomas Traherne who believed in the 'unity of all beings, in and with God', and produced 'some of the finest and most diverse expressions of mystical thought' in both poems and prose.[21]

John Hick notes that historically a distinction has been drawn between the 'unknowable Godhead' (*Gottheit, deitas*) and the 'Known God of the Bible' (*Gottdeus*) which was first seriously adumbrated by Pseudo-Dionysius (*c.*500 AD)[22] and mentioned by Meister Eckhart (*c.*1260–1327) in which the latter speaks of 'the unknown God above all gods'. He makes the clear distinction that 'whereas the God of the Bible is personal and triune, and acts within human history, this cannot be said of the Godhead: 'God acts. The Godhead does not'. This is similar to the pan-Indian distinction between 'God in God's-self' and 'God in relation to the creation'.[23] Thus the theistic God which man has invented from his earliest years as a means of re-assurance and comfort to counter his ills and fears is *not* the same as Tillich's God who is the 'ground of our being' or the Ultimate Transcendent Reality. The pagan Olympian and other Near Eastern gods, no less than the personal and triune 'God of the Bible' or the many gods of the Hindu pantheism, were theist gods and on a lower plane than Ultimate Reality or Brahman or the unnamed and unknowable

Jewish godhead. There are surely echoes here of pre-Christian gnostic belief in one transcendent god from whom descended a series of lesser gods. It is re-assuring to note that all the great religions bear witness to a cosmic optimism which will succeed our present pessimistic predicament.[24]

What distinguishes humankind from the animal world is its endowment of consciousness. All living creatures are born with a sense of instinct (largely for self-preservation), but the conscience of humankind gives it the ability to distinguish between right and wrong, the instinctive recognition of an underlying moral law. The concept of right and wrong, according to Dr Francis Collins, 'appears to be universal among all members of the human species (though its application may result in wildly different outcomes). It thus seems to be a phenomenon approaching that of a law, like the law of gravitation or of special relativity'.[25] From the voice of conscience stems the impulse to altruism, expressed in *agape* or selfless love, exemplified in the lives of such well-known figures as Catherine of Siena or Mother Teresa. Consciousness also gives humankind the ability to communicate by language, to reason, and above all the powers of imagination from which springs the inspiration of the creative arts and the recognition of transcendence. In Professor Ward's view: 'humans have a strong moral sense, which leads them to think of morality as objective and demanding, and a strong aesthetic sense, which leads them to think of beauty in sound, colour and words, as conveying intimations of objective value. Many of the wisest and most morally heroic people have a strong sense of the presence of God, or a transcendent reality of ultimate value'.[26]

Most neuroscientists have concluded that the nature and status of consciousness is a sheer mystery. Professor Roger Penrose says: 'conscious actions and conscious perceptions – and, in particular, the conscious phenomenon of understanding – will find no proper explanation within the present-day picture of the material universe, but require our going outside this conventional framework to a new physical picture... whose mathematical structure is very largely unknown'.[27] The doubts of so many eminent neuroscientists 'reflect the fact that consciousness/brain identity is not a genuine scientific hypothesis. For it is not capable of empirical confirmation or falsification'. Professor Hick concludes: 'So we are left with the mysterious but undeniable fact of consciousness as a non-physical reality, a reality which we have to assume is capable of free self-determining activity'.[28] As the psychologist William James pointed out: 'our normal waking consciousness... is but one special type of consciousness, whilst all about it, parted from it by the flimsiest of screens, there lie potential forms of consciousness entirely different'.[29] Altered states of conscience can be induced by (for example) drugs, and these have for centuries been used to enhance religious worship (in India and Mexico, for example). Music and dancing can evoke a sense of transcendence, no less than colourful liturgies of Catholic, Orthodox and high Anglican Services − 'enhanced by uplifting music, splashes of golden, purple and green vestments, candles, incense, tinkling bells, archaic language and solemn hieratic processions'.[30] This is not a new experience, for it was the same two thousand years ago in the rituals of the pagan cults of Cybele, 'Mother of the Gods' and the Egyptian goddess Isis (see page 24 above). The transformation of the lives of mystics and saints suggests a consciousness of transcendence and 'aspects of the universe that fall outside our natural framework of thought'. Since we utilise only about 5% of our brains, there are clearly endless possibilities concerning our states of consciousness, and Professor Eric Kandel has declared: 'the last frontier of the biological sciences − their ultimate challenge − is to understand the biological basis of consciousness and the mental processes by which we perceive, act, learn and remember'.[31]

Throughout recorded history there have been cases of spontaneous 'spiritual' experiences, of which St Paul's 'conversion' (probably in an epileptic fit) in a blaze of 'light from heaven' on the road to Damascus is perhaps the most memorable. From medieval times we find many examples of visions. As we have seen earlier, the anchorite Julian of Norwich (c.1342–1416) believed she saw visions of Christ. Catherine of Siena (1347–80) believed that she conversed regularly with God, while both the mystic Nicholas of Cusa (1401–64) and St Teresa of Avila (1515–82) believed themselves to be in the presence of God, although neither could actually see him.[32] In the eighteenth century there were several well-documented instances of spontaneous revelation. Thus Colonel James Gardiner (d. 1745) experienced a 'blaze of light' falling upon a book he was reading and when he looked up he saw a vision of Christ on the Cross; John Wesley, at 8.45 p.m. on 14 May, 1738, 'felt my heart strongly warmed. I felt I did trust in Christ, Christ alone, for salvation; and an assurance was given me, that he had taken *my* sins, even *mine*, and saved *me* from the law of sin and death'; William Huntingdon became suddenly aware of sin: 'I leapt up, with my eyes ready to start out of my head, my hair standing erect... and later had a vision of the Holy Ghost.[33]

It is significant that a number of eminent scientists have claimed to have had mystical experiences. Einstein, for example, averred that 'cosmic religious feeling' had inspired his reflections on the order and harmony of nature.[34] The science writer David Peat records a sense 'that all boundaries between ourselves and the outer world vanish, for what we are experiencing lies beyond all categories and attempts to be captured in logical thought'.[35] Revelatory experiences seem often to occur spontaneously. The astronomer Sir Fred Hoyle, for example, was driving north to Scotland one day and thinking about a 'quantum mechanical problem' when suddenly 'my awareness of the mathematics clarified, not a little, not even a lot, but as if a huge brilliant light had suddenly been switched on. How long did it take to become totally convinced that the problem was solved? Less than five seconds...'[36] Hoyle sensed that the organisation of the cosmos is controlled by a 'superintelligence' who guides its evolution through quantum processes... He believed that by acting at the quantum level this superintelligence can implant thoughts or ideas from the future, ready-made, into the human brain. This, he suggested, is the origin of both mathematic and musical inspiration.[37]

Sir Alister Hardy, a former professor of zoology at Oxford, founded the Religious Experience Research Unit in Oxford in 1969 and collected an enormous archive of personal stories submitted by members of the public which relate to spiritual experiences which they had undergone. Hardy believed that 'the main characteristic of man's religious and spiritual experiences are shown in his feelings for a transcendental reality which frequently manifest themselves in early childhood; a feeling that 'Someone Other' than the self can actually be sensed; a desire to formalize this presence into a deity and to have a private I-Thou relationship with it, communicating through prayer'.[38] This is the 'sense of presence' experienced by many – either within or outside the person concerned; their lives being influenced by 'a Power felt to be beyond the self... sustaining, encouraging, strengthening, guiding or compelling them'. He notes that for the great majority there is a strong feeling of a transcendental reality and that institutional religion plays little part in most of the accounts submitted. Thus it is 'this transcendental element that is fundamental: the feeling that there is a spiritual reality that *appears* to be beyond the conscious self with which the individual can have communion in one way or another...'[39] A passage in Alexander Solzhenitsyn's book *Cancer Ward* comes to mind:

'It was then it struck Oleg that Shulubin was not delirious, that he'd recognised him and was reminding him of their last conversation before the operation. He had said, 'Sometimes I feel quite distinctly that what is inside me is not all of me. There's something else, sublime, quite indestructible, some tiny fragment of the universal spirit. Don't you feel that?'[40]

It is significant that a sizeable number of respondents looked back at their childhood experiences and regarded them as of vital importance. One is reminded of Wordsworth's words:

'Our birth is but a sleep and a forgetting:
The Soul that rises with us, our life's Star,
Hath had elsewhere its setting,
And cometh from afar:
Not in entire forgetfulness;
And not in utter nakedness,
But trailing clouds of glory do we come
From God, who is our home:
Heaven lies about us in our infancy!'[41]

And in his *Confessions* St Augustine mused:

'...did my infancy succeed another age of mine that died before it? Was it that which I spent within my mother's womb? for of that I have heard somewhat, and have myself seen women with child? and what before that life again, O God my joy, was I any where or any body? For this have I none to tell me, neither father nor mother, nor experience of others, nor mine own memory. Dost Thou mock me for asking this...?[42]

While Henry Vaughan (1622–1695) in his poem *The Retreat* looks back at the mystery of his infancy:

> 'Happy those early days, when I
> Shined in my Angel-infancy!
> Before I understood this place
> Appointed for my second race,
> Or taught my soul to fancy aught
> But a white, celestial thought;
> When yet I had not walk'd above
> A mile or two from my first Love,
> And looking back, at that short space
> Could see a glimpse of His bright face;
> When on some gilded cloud or flower
> My gazing soul would dwell an hour,
> And in those weaker glories spy
> Some shadows of eternity;
>
> O how I long to travel back,
> And tread again that ancient track!
> That I might once more reach that plain,
> Where first I left my glorious train;
> From whence th' enlighten'd spirit sees
> That shady City of Palm trees!
> But ah! My soul with too much stay
> Is drunk, and staggers in the way: –
> Some men a forward motion love,
> But I by backward steps would move;
> And when the dust falls to the urn,
> In that state I came, return.'

Finally, if we look back to Anglo-Saxon monasticism we find the Venerable Bede (673–735) comparing the life of man to that of a sparrow which – from the driving rain and snow – enters into the warm hall of an Anglo-Saxon lord (where 'the fire is burning on the hearth in the middle of the hall and all inside is warm') and flies out again a moment later into the storm. 'So this life of man appears but for a moment; what follows or indeed what went before, we know not'. Again, the uncertainty of both a previous existence or a life to follow – although the message of Jesus would be to assert the reality of a future life in a heavenly kingdom.

Some of the subject-matter of reported subjective experiences are fascinating: the 'out-of-body' experiences in particular. Here the person concerned leaves their body – the 'discarded' body having every appearance of reality. 'It is this aspect of the phenomenon which has been held by some to support the belief that there is a so-called 'astral' non-material body which is an exact duplicate of the physical one, and further that it is this 'astral body' which leaves the physical body at death'.[43] In classical times, according to A. N. Wilson (when considering the Mithraic cult and its practices at the time of St Paul), 'journeys from our present earth-bound condition to a different plane of consciousness were possible in the religious traditions of both Jews and Gentiles, and Paul makes clear that their authenticity and reality as spiritual experiences are in no way invalidated by the suggestion that the initiate might not have journeyed to outer space in person in order to reach the 'third heaven'.[44] Numerous examples of telepathy have also been recorded – the supposed communication between one mind and another by means other than those of the physical sense organs. Hardy believed that '…both artists and musicians are *expressing the ineffable*. This tacit knowledge which comes to us through their skill and inspiration is on another level to that which comes to us through the spoken or written word. Artists and musicians have the remarkable gift of communicating *direct* to the spiritual level of those who are able to receive it.[45] Hardy's conclusion is that 'The spiritual nature of man is, I believe, being shown to be a reality. We now need a new biological philosophy which will recognise both this and the need to study consciousness as a fundamental attribute of life'.[46]

If one seeks to study the mystery of consciousness a starting point might be the most unusual experience which is related by Michal Levin in her book *The Pool of Memory* (1998). While working as a television reporter she took up meditation which, to her surprise and alarm, led her to a new world of the transcendent. At each session of meditation she felt she left her body, and moved into another world 'to join the Light'. Guided by a messenger from God, known to her as the Disciple, she is told that he comes from 'the world that watches the worlds'. She asks if there are other worlds and is told 'Yes, but you can not know now – after this life you will know'.[47] She confides to a friend 'I don't think it is my unconscious fantasising... I simply can't see what the source of it all is'. She continues: 'Throughout, I am very clear in my mind that what I do in the other world, what happens, what is said, is not the reality of everyday. It goes without saying that I accept the language and events as metaphor of some sort. But more, it seems to me that any relationship between events in my meditation and the everyday is purely speculative. Logically, I accept it could all be my fantasy. But I know with my heart that some, at very least, is not'.[48] In her meditation she encounters 'the Christ figure' and 'I take to praying to the Christ specifically, as well as to God, my version of the Creative force behind life'.[49] Later, she relates: 'Behind the Christ... is the Golden Buddha. The Buddha explains that he and Christ are from the same source, that there is no difference. That Christ's will and the Buddha's will are the same. Then I link hands with the Christ and the Buddha and there is a tremendous sensation of energy flow. Together, we go to work in the darkness of a dark place, establishing Light'.[50] Towards the end of her sessions of meditation she believes that God speaks to her: 'Beloved, now it is time for you to go. I have high expectations of you, as do others who are with you. Persevere. Remember you are a voice for us on earth'.[51] She concludes that 'I am intimately connected to God and the presences I have encountered in the "other" world, which is also this reality. It is hard to say if I am part of them, or they are part of me. Questions of why, how and what does it mean surface from time to time. I let them be. Easily'.[52] Significantly, when urged on one occasion to speak out by a medium, she involuntarily declares:

'I have known the other side, the unused side of the brain, like the darker side of the moon. Or perhaps I have travelled beyond the brain. Into space, to another domain, one without location on the four co-ordinates. Known nothing and everything of myself and others too. Learnt to experience and love God and man in all guises...'[53] As a result of her extraordinary other-worldly experience Michal Levin has become a much sought-after healer, Intuitive and teacher. The reference to 'the other side, the unused side of the brain' suggests that the large area of the brain whose purpose is at present a mystery to neurologists has the potential to link consciousness to other areas of the transcendent: an exciting prospect.

Twenty years earlier (1976) Rosalind Heywood recalled her psychic experiences of extrasensory perception (ESP). She describes instances of 'contact with sparks of consciousness, which seem to exist outside the physical world as it is perceived via the senses... ranging from telepathy between the living to an apparent awareness of the invisible, yet purposeful, presence of my recently departed friends – and, on a few occasions, even beyond'.[54] Some interesting points emerge from these accounts. In the case of making contact with an old friend, lately deceased, he conveyed the message 'that he had been entirely mistaken in expecting extinction at death. On the contrary, he had had scope, freedom and opportunity beyond his wildest dreams. The surprise was not merely on being alive but on this magnificent expansion of opportunity'.[55] Asking for evidence of this wonderful life her friend replied to the effect 'I cannot give you evidence. You have no concepts for these conditions. I can only give you poetic images'. Whereupon she was aware of 'an immense pair of white wings flying in a limitless blue sky'. Mrs Heywood commented: 'Nobody has any concepts for conditions which differ in *kind* from those conveyed through the senses, for one reason because the senses, as Professor H. H. Price has pointed out, reveal only those elements in our surroundings which make for physical survival'.[56] She concludes: 'If these apparent contacts are not illusory, can one guess at a possible process? May the right hemisphere of the brain, which, as Professor Ornstein wrote, is largely associated with intuition and artistry, provide a misty trail between the conscious self and the deeper and vaster subliminal world? And can there be anything in my feeling that the subliminal world passes without a break into other aspects of being? Such an idea fits in with the sense of the numinous evoked by natural beauty and art – especially by music, the art of pure relationships'.[57] After speculating about the relationship of her experiences to the possible nature of life after death, she concludes with a quotation from a poem by the early Greek philosopher Xenophanes (*fl.* 540–500 BC), translated by Karl Popper:

> The gods did not reveal from the beginning
> All things to us, but in the course of time
> Through seeking we may learn to know things better.
> But as for certain truth, no man has known it,
> Nor shall we know it, neither of the gods
> Nor yet of all the things of which I speak.
> For even if by chance he were to utter
> The final truth, he would himself not know it;
> For all is but a woven web of guesses.'[58]

Professor Arnold Toynbee's view (to which we referred in Chapter 3(i) is undoubtedly correct when he said that 'psychic experience… leads to glimpses of possible reality that logical reasoning might find itself constrained to reject as being illusions'.

Sensitivity to the Transcendent also includes a class of experiences by people approaching or on the verge of death. A remarkable account of such other-worldly contacts is given in the recent book by Peter and Elizabeth Fenwick entitled *The Art of Dying* (2008) in which the authors have listed hundreds of personal experiences. These include end-of-life and near-death experiences compiled from interviews with many nurses and carers at hospitals and hospices who have had first-hand knowledge of patients approaching death. End-of-life cases include visions (not related in any way to pathology or drugs) which convince patients that they have only a limited time left because they are shortly going to be collected or taken away on a journey – indeed, in one case a man seemed to be talking to someone just before he died and said: 'right, I am ready now. You can get my coat'.[59] Others have warned relatives not to visit them the following day as they would not be there. In many instances patients appear to be visited by dead relatives and friends who may then disappear and return later to lead them away into 'the light', whereupon they die. Extraordinarily, the patient may have a three-way conversation with other-worldly visitors and relatives by their bedside – although the latter cannot see the former! Most of their experiences tend to be accompanied by a bright light and a palpable sensation of love and compassion. There are instances – as in the case of cardiac arrest when they may be clinically dead – where a person feels as though they have left their body on a cord and look down on it from above watching the resuscitation process. Often dying patients believe themselves to be entering a dark tunnel and travelling towards a pinpoint of light which grows larger as they approach it. They may then arrive at a barrier beyond which may be seen dead relatives or friends who may indicate that they must go back, that it is not yet time for them to come through and join them. They then get pulled back by the cord attached to their physical body. Interestingly, there is a reference to this cord in the Old Testament passage: 'man goeth to his long home, and the mourners go about the streets: *Or ever the silver cord be loosed*, or the golden bowl be broken,… Thus shall the dust return unto God who gave it' (Ecclesiastes 12: 5–7). Hospital and hospice staff report that terminally ill patients seem to have some control over the moment of their departure, thus some will cling on until a special relative arrives to say good-bye. Visiting apparitions are nearly always seen as welcoming and the dying person responds with joy. Thus in one account: 'suddenly my Gran sat up in bed and smiled. She said, 'I'm going now and here's Dad and George come to meet me'. She then died with this big smile on her face'.[60] A singularly interesting case occurred some thirty years ago when an ex-First World War soldier was dying of cancer: 'He was too ill to contribute much to the conversation… when he suddenly leaned forward and stared across the room. He became very animated and looked very happy as he began to talk to people he could obviously see but we couldn't; he was calling them each by name and asking how they were and how wonderful it was to see them again. It became apparent from what he was saying they were some of the men who had served with him at the Somme and died there. There was a look of wonderment on his face and he forgot his pain'.[61] There are many accounts of some white 'form' or 'shape' seen leaving a body – usually from the mouth, chest or through the head – at the point of death, which many have interpreted as being the 'soul' or 'spirit' finally leaving the body. Those who have had out-of-body experiences talk of leaving and re-entering the body through the top of their head (this is also a common theme in Buddhist literature).[62]

Evidence gathered by the Fenwicks suggests that 'consciousness is not limited to the brain but is spread out and links together in a very real way those who have close and loving relationships'; that 'the view of the universe which we normally perceive in our everyday state of consciousness may be a very limited one'; that 'this transcendent universe appears to those who see it to be full of love and light, and, strangely, just one thing that we are all part of and are not separate from'; that 'as death approaches we enter into a highly charged spiritual arena, an area of intense personal meaning, which reflects the insight of the transcendent reality of love, peace and light as described by those who have had transcendent or mystical experiences. Sometimes spiritual presences appear to those who are able to see them, and have been reported to be composed of light'; and that sometimes, at the moment of death, 'people appear, usually dead relatives whose sole purpose seems to be to accompany the dead person on a journey from this reality to elsewhere'; that 'the 'visits' of the dying at their moment of death to someone they are emotionally close to, seemingly to say a final goodbye or reassure them that 'everything is all right' only seem explicable in terms of an extension of consciousness'.

The Fenwicks conclude their book with the words: 'The evidence points to the fact that we are more than brain function, more than just a speck in creation, and that something, whether we regard it as soul or consciousness, will continue in some form or another, making its journey to 'Elsewhere'. It suggests that when we enter the light we are coming home, that we do indeed touch the inner reaches of a universe that is composed of universal love. This is the territory of the dying'.[63]

A former Archdeacon writing of near-death experiences suggests that such experiences 'are going to provide for many people the real proof that there is a life after death. Or maybe it's going to prove that we are all capable of fooling ourselves, and that there is something archetypal in the human being that when it's faced with death presents a kind of fantasy scenario which tells him that he's not going to be snuffed out'. In his view 'we are never in this life going to get proof, all we're going to get is pointers'.

Another subject occasionally raised in connection with the Transcendent is that of angels. Angels are part of the rich mythological tapestry of the Bible and of the Qur'an. If you are of an imaginative turn of mind it is easy to believe in angels, just as many people readily believed in the fairies of the fake photographs a century ago. Angels mostly appear at moments of great importance in the narratives of the Abrahamic faiths to emphasise their significance – e.g. at the nativity of Jesus, beside the empty tomb in which Jesus had been interred, and when the prophet Muhammad was instructed to recite the words of God which became the Qur'an. According to a fourth-century AD source these heavenly beings are divided into three hierarchies each of three orders. Most are of human form, seemingly beautiful and androgynous, and with wings, often associated with dazzling light, and appear to act as 'messengers' of God (the name angel being derived from the Greek word *angelos*, meaning a messenger). Of the highest grade are the archangels, like Michael (the warrior angel) and Gabriel (who appeared to the prophet Daniel, to Mary (mother of Jesus) and to Muhammad). Angels feature in the apocryphal books of the Bible, e.g. the apocryphal book of Enoch (dating from the second or first century BC and which enumerates no fewer than seven archangels – Uriel, Raphael, Raguel, Michael, Sariel, Gabriel and Jerahmeel). In addition to angels and archangels there are apparently a class of Cherubim (associated with guarding the Garden of Eden and the Jewish 'Ark of the Covenant', and with judgemental matters) and of Seraphim (which, uniquely, have no less than six wings and seem to be mostly concerned with attendance on, and praise of God). The concept of 'guardian angels' has become part of the comforting folklore of Christianity in the hope of protection from unknown powers and natural disasters. Jane Williams tells us that 'many, many people are sure that they have been saved from road accidents or other kinds of fatal errors by the direct intervention of an angel... In the past, the majority of people who met an angel were religious believers, but encounters with angels do not seem to have diminished in our increasingly secularized Western world'.[64] In the seventeenth century belief in angels was common, as we may recall from Henry Vaughan's poem:

> 'And yet, as angels in some brighter dreams
> Call to the soul when man doth sleep,
> So some strange thoughts transcend our wonted themes,
> And into glory peep.'

The author is not aware of any recent comprehensive study of angelic experiences comparable to that of Sir Alister Hardy's investigation into religious experiences (to which we have referred above).

About one third of the population of Britain, America and Australia report having experiences of 'a powerful spiritual force that seemed to lift you out of yourself'.[65] It is thus relatively common for people who have no particular identity with any religious faith to experience – out of the blue – a sensation that can only be described as 'transcendental' or, as they often describe it, an experience of the reality of God. They say they 'have found God'. It is an instantaneous revelation, often quite unexpected, and consequently one of shock. It can surely only be confirmation of the closeness of the barrier between this life and the next – a veil which can be penetrated in certain undefined circumstances. Professor Ward remarks: 'This suggests that there is a capacity for spiritual apprehension, varying quite widely in degree, which does not correlate with any other specific personality type, and which is spread widely throughout the human race.'[66] Professor Paul Davies has an open mind about mystical experiences, but considers that they may 'provide the only route beyond the limits to which science and philosophy can take us, the only possible path to the Ultimate'.[67]

It is evident that one of the aspects of consciousness is its susceptibility to hitherto unexplained and undefined spiritual influences – indeed, a new spiritual dimension of which some people, over the years, have become vividly aware, and from which it derives inspiration, whether imaginative, religious, artistic or musical. The degree to which an individual is 'attuned' to this spiritual dimension will determine his or her sympathy with and ability in any of these fields (and, as John Cornwell puts it, religion 'is as much a product of the imagination as art, poetry, and music'[68]). Conscience allows human beings to realise their true potential and to be able to understand the elegant and beautiful structures of the universe and of nature. They in turn are inspired to emulate beauty and harmony in their lives. It may seem strange that mathematicians and physicists often refer to the 'elegance' of their equations and laws of nature, as if these are in some sense works of art. 'The belief that the underlying order of the world can be expressed in mathematical form lies at the very heart of science, and is rarely questioned'.[69] Professor Roger Penrose believes that 'mathematical truth is something that goes beyond mere formalism... there often does appear to be some profound reality about these mathematical concepts, going quite beyond the deliberations of any particular mathematician. It is as though human thought is, instead, being guided towards some eternal external truth – a truth which has a reality of its own, and which is revealed only partially to any one of us'.[70] He also sees an analogy between mathematics and inspired works of art: 'It is a feeling not uncommon amongst artists, that in their greatest works they are revealing external truths which have some kind of prior ethereal existence... I cannot help feeling that, with mathematics, the case for believing in some kind of etherial, eternal existence... is a good deal stronger'.[71] Professor Paul Davies states that: 'It is widely believed among scientists that beauty is a reliable guide to truth, and many advances in theoretical physics have been made by the theorist demanding mathematical elegance of a new theory'.[72] Matters of aesthetics are of course necessarily subjective, yet Davies notes how 'many distinguished scientists have expressed the feeling that their inspiration has come from some sort of mental contact with a Platonic realm of mathematical and aesthetic forms'.[73] Great artists have clearly received inspiration to paint the classical myths of antiquity (e.g. Titian's *Diana and Acteon*), the significant events in Christian history such as the Nativity and the Crucifixion, no less than aspects of human life such as love, fear or sacrifice, and the beauties of nature in all its variety. Likewise illustrious composers have been inspired by Christian themes such as the Passion, the Crucifixion and the Messiah, as well as by liturgical Solemn Masses. There is an undoubted link between individuals and the spiritual 'internet' which gives them − to a greater or lesser degree − the ability to appreciate the arts. Thus the harmonies of music literally strike a chord with many people and resonate within their whole being. Giants of sacred music such as Bach, Handel and Palestrina have the ability to transport their hearers into a transcendental spiritual ecstasy beyond words, which perfectly matches the subject-matter of their religious themes. Likewise the recent passion for poetry derives from an appreciation of its rhythm, incantation and powers of emotional expression. Such feelings produce a sensation of being 'at one' with the Transcendent. As Bishop Tom Wright puts it: 'The arts are not the pretty but irrelevant bits around the border of reality. They are highways into the centre of a reality which cannot be glimpsed, let alone grasped, any other way'.[74] Inspiration, through the mediation of the conscience, is evident throughout history. As John Polkinghorne argues: 'The whole range of subjective expression, from perceiving a patch of pink, to being enthralled by a performance of the Mass in B Minor, and on to the mystic's encounter with the ineffable reality of the One, all these truly human experiences, are at the center of our encounter with reality…'.[75]

Canon Michael Austin has made an interesting contribution to this subject in his book *Explorations in Art, Theology and Imagination* (2005). He recounts that the 'moments of vision' which are given to all true artists are − according to the late Kenneth Clark − 'moments of intensified physical perception'. He suggests that 'if we take seriously what artists and religious believers say there is little difference of substance between aesthetic and religious experience'.[76] Moreover, he asks 'And what is this transcendence of which men and women claim to have a vision? Is it a revelation of God or (without the religious coding) an awareness of 'the beyond' or is it nothing more than a heightened state of physical perception, as Kenneth Clark argues and some contemporary neuroscientists are suggesting? Whatever it is and however they speak of it artists seem to possess this sense of 'the beyond'.[77] To my mind this is an indication of the ability of artists and religious devotees to access the 'spiritual internet' from which they can derive both inspiration and enlightenment.

Through the mediation of the conscience it is claimed that the Holy Spirit continues to receive prayers and to inspire charitable and magnanimous works of human kind, no less than facilitating the spiritual enlightenment of priests of religious faiths throughout the world (indeed a continuation of the Pentecostal powers entrusted to the Christian apostles). The concept of the Holy Trinity which was laid down at the Eleventh Council of Toledo in 675 was a *human* attempt to subsume the historic person of Jesus into the Godhead (however defined) and to leave open a channel of communication between the Godhead and the universe through the Holy Spirit. All references thereafter to the 'Holy Spirit' (or 'Ghost') confirm this practical link between the two. For those 'attuned' to the transcendent – saints, mystics, members of cenobitic orders, priests – their mental processes have been energized by 'messages' (directly or instinctively felt) and visions from this spiritual source and, to a greater or lesser extent, it has applied also to the laity in the practice of their faith, charitable works and artistic inspiration, as well as to those who are susceptible to other-worldly or end-of-life experiences. Theologically, the concept of the Holy Trinity is fraught with difficulties (as we have discussed elsewhere), but it was the best that clerics could devise in the seventh century AD! After Jesus was crucified, and *irrespective* of whether the New Testament story of his resurrection is 'true' or not, we may reasonably surmise that the only channel for communication left open between God and the world was through the Transcendental 'internet'. The prime example of this was the story of Pentecost, when 'tongues of fire' descended upon the disciples and they were apparently filled with the Holy Spirit and began to 'speak in other tongues'.

In practice, the concept of the Holy Spirit has been of great practical use to Christianity. Priestland recounts that 'as Hans Küng complains, when theologians do not know how to justify a particular dogma, they appeal to the Holy Spirit. When fanatics do not know how to authenticate their whims, they invoke the Holy Spirit. The Holy Spirit is called in to the authority of unconvincing statements of faith, and is made a substitute for credibility and objective discussion. I have even heard the Holy Spirit given the credit for successfully whipped votes in the General Synod of the Church of England...' He recalls Bishop John V. Taylor's comment: 'My own attempt to understand the Holy Spirit has convinced me He is active in precisely those experiences that are very common – experiences of recognition, sudden insight, an influx of awareness when you wake up and become alive to something...'[78]

How, it may be asked, can we humans deliberately make contact with the Transcendent? Peter and Elizabeth Fenwick inform us that 'people who meditate regularly say that they enter a band of consciousness composed of light, the primary qualities of which are of bliss, compassion and universal love'.[79] This is similar to Michal Levin's experience (see above) after she took up meditation when she felt that she left her body and moved into another world 'to join the Light'. Meditation and entering into a trance (as in the case of many mystics and religious practitioners), as well as the taking of drugs (used as an aid to religious worship in India and Mexico), appear therefore to provide one answer, but – as with neuroscience in general – on this we are as yet largely ignorant.

Few will deny that there have always been – and still are – 'saintly' men and women of religion. They have all felt, in one degree or another, a direct link with God and/or Jesus, and have been inspired through the mechanism of the transcendental spiritual 'internet'. Some have claimed to speak directly to God or to Jesus. But what is surprising is that *none* have elicited from their 'conversations' any details of the next life, to which we are all bound. Ask a churchman and he/she will immediately refer to the passage in John 14: 2 'in my Father's house are many mansions: if it were not so, I would have told you. I go to prepare a place for you'. But it is singular, and disturbing, that the only information about the next life comes, not from churchmen (as one might have expected), but from messages passed to people during transcendental trances. In this book the most revealing is the message passed to Rosalind Heywood (1976) (see above) who received a message from an old (and lately deceased) friend about the wonderful new life in which he found himself. Mrs Heywood pointed out that no one has any concepts for conditions which differ in *kind* from those conveyed through the senses which, as Professor Price confirmed, reveal only those elements in our surroundings which made for physical survival. There are doubtless many more examples of the kind of experience recounted by Mrs Heywood. It is clear therefore that our mental equipment in the present world is manifestly not designed to be able to understand the concepts which apply in the world to come. So the *details* of the next world are likely to remain a mystery to us.

To conclude our study of Transcendent Reality perhaps the position may be summarized as follows: consciousness is a non-physical reality capable of free self-determining activity which may enable us to enter into a spiritual dimension receptive to the Transcendent in its multiplicity of different aspects – from the religious, to the cultural, and finally to the ability to communicate with those who have passed over into a new life. This, surely, is the answer to the question posed in the opening paragraph of this section. We cannot scientifically *prove* the existence of God, nor can we otherwise explain the creation and purpose of the universe, yet through the medium of our consciousness some of us may be able to engage with the many facets of the Transcendent by 'logging-on' to the mysteries of the spiritual 'internet'. And if we reflect upon the accounts of those who have personally experienced 'contact' with another world, we may expect to find ourselves transformed, after death, into a hitherto unimagined existence infused by light, love and compassion and accompanied by a freedom and opportunity of a nature conceptually unimaginable to our worldly senses. If these glimpses of the next world are genuine, and not a psychic illusion, it is an exciting prospect!

NOTES

[1]   Armstrong, 1999, 6
[2]   Quoted in Thiede, 2004, 73
[3]   For a discussion of the Divine Attributes see Peterson *et al.*, 2003, 58–72
[4]   Spong, 2002, 64
[5]   Robinson, 1971, 48
[6]   Hick, 2004, 30
[7]   Russell, 2005, xii–xiii
[8]   Priestland, 1981, 45–6
[9]   Not the physical anatomy so much as the 'mind' of God, through which the Holy Spirit continues to influence events in the temporal world
[10] Parrinder, 1976, 9
[11] Ibid., 10
[12] For an account of Sufism see Parrinder, 1976, 128–140
[13] For a full discussion of Islamic and Jewish mystical tradition see Armstrong, 1999, 259–290
[14] Hick, 2004, 47–9
[15] Ibid., 197
[16] Ibid., 210
[17] Hick, 2004, 30
[18] Corrigen, 2007, 33
[19] Hume, 2002, 106
[20] Parrinder, 1976, 169–170
[21] Ibid., 155–8
[22] Who may have taken the idea from Marcion who believed in a 'stern, lawgiving, creator God of the Old Testament, and the other the good, merciful God of the New Testament'
[23] Hick, 2004, 95, 99–100
[24] This is described in detail by Hick, 2004, 62–79
[25] Collins, 2007, 23
[26] Ward, 2004, 72
[27] Hick, 2004, 32
[28] Ibid., 33–4
[29] Ibid., 106

[30] Ibid., 106–7

[31] Quoted in Humphrys, 2007, 241–2

[32] For an analysis of types of religious experience see Peterson *et al.*, 2003, 16–35

[33] See Hague, W., 2007, *William Wilberforce*, 78–9

[34] Davies, P., 1992, 227

[35] Ibid.

[36] Ibid., 228–9

[37] Ibid., 229

[38] Hardy, 1979, 131

[39] Ibid., 132

[40] Solzhenitsyn, A., *Cancer Ward* (1968–9), Penguin edn., 1972, 517

[41] Wordsworth, W., *Ode on intimations of immortality from recollections of early childhood*

[42] *The Confessions of St Augustine*, Kegan Paul, Trench Trübner & Co. edn., 1900, Book 1, ch. 6, 10

[43] Hardy, 1979, 36

[44] Wilson, 1998, 78. The 'third heaven' is an allusion to the Ptolemaic cosmological system. Claudius Ptolemaus, or Ptolemy, devised a cosmological system in which the sun, planets and stars revolved round the earth (this system eventually being displaced by that of Copernicus (1473–1543)). In Ptolemy's system the space round the earth was divided into seven (sometimes eleven) successive spheres or 'heavens'. In the Mithraic cult, which flourished in Paul's Tarsus, each grade of initiate corresponded to one of the several planetary 'heavens'

[45] Hardy, 1979, 86

[46] Ibid., 142

[47] Levin, 1998, 45

[48] Ibid., 107

[49] Ibid., 111

[50] Ibid., 111–112

[51] Ibid., 197

[52] Ibid., 247

[53] Ibid., 257

[54] Heywood, 1976, 203–237

[55] Ibid., 216

[56] Ibid., 216–7

[57] Ibid., 218

[58] Ibid., 235

[59] Fenwick and Fenwick, 62

[60] Ibid., 32

[61] Ibid., 35

[62] Ibid., 160

[63] Ibid., 240–242

[64] Williams, J., 2006, 70. Her book – charmingly illustrated by Linda Baker Smith – would have been of greater historical value had she given examples of the 'many of the narratives of encounters with angels' which 'come from people who are not necessarily religious believers' (*op. cit.* 115). Nor does she include any bibliography of angelic studies. She reasonably concludes that 'the existence of angels, like the existence of God, cannot be proved or disproved. It will remain a matter of faith… But although there are all kinds of reasons for doubting angels, and although some descriptions of meetings with angels are probably no more than consolatory fictions, perhaps we could argue that the proof of the pudding is in the eating…' (*op. cit.* 116)

[65] Ward, 2004, 85

[66] Ibid., 86

[67] Davies, P., 1992, 232

[68] Cornwell, 2007, 44

[69] Davies, P., 1992, 140

[70] Ibid., 142

[71] Ibid., 143–4

[72] Ibid., 175

[73] Ibid., 176

[74] Wright, 2006, 201

[75] Quoted in Collins, 2007, 228–9

[76] Austin, 2005, 46

[77] Ibid., 106

[78] Priestland, 1981, 106–119

[79] Fenwick and Fenwick, 151

(iii) Jesus Christ and the New Testament

The religion known as Christianity originated in the person of Jesus, a Jew born in 7 BC in the village of Nazareth in Judaea, and later known by his disciples as 'Christ' (from the Greek word 'Christos' meaning 'Messiah' or 'the Anointed One of God'). The symbol of the *Chi-Rho* monogram (deriving from the Greek capitals *chi* (Greek X) and *rho* (Greek P), representing the beginning of the word *Christos*), which has been found on tombs dating from the first century AD, soon came to be regarded as the symbol of the new religion of Christianity. It is found frequently in the Christian catacombs in Rome, and has come to light in a number of places in Roman Britain − e.g. at the Roman villa at Hinton St Mary, Dorset, on the silver hoard found at Water Newton, Northamptonshire, and on the Risley Park lanx (a forged reconstruction of a genuine Romano-British silver dish) found in Derbyshire. Tourists will find it inscribed on gravestones and pillars of early Christian basilicas across the Roman Empire (e.g. amongst the spectacular ruins of the Libyan Roman town of Sabratha).

Jesus's personal qualities marked him out as a prophet in the long tradition of Hebrew prophets (such as Elijah and Isaiah), and his declared relationship to God (to whom he referred in familiar social parlance as 'my Father') and his teaching about the imminence of the coming of the Kingdom of God had a profound effect on contemporary society. As an inspired teacher, healer, and interpreter of mankind's relationship to God, he was regarded as the promised Jewish scriptural Messiah who would deliver the Jews from the bonds of the Roman Empire. He was therefore regarded with suspicion by the Roman authorities, and with jealousy by the Jewish priestly hierarchy, and was finally crucified for sedition in AD 30. His body was placed in a tomb, from which his supporters believed he was resurrected on the third day and passed into heaven.

Then the trouble began. As St Paul found, when preaching to Athenian congregations, many mocked and doubted such a tall story, but Jesus's disciples were convinced that his resurrection was a fact and it became central to their missionary message. Since contemporary society in the Near East had a wide choice of religions to follow – one of the religions of the Empire since 204 BC was that of Cybele, the 'Mother Goddess' and the cults of Mithras and Dionysus were highly popular – the early Christians had to devise a 'religion' which would challenge other contemporary cults. The result was a mythological narrative (comparable to the mythological origins of contemporary cults) of Jesus's upbringing: his supposed 'virginal birth' (in keeping with the promised Messiah of the Jewish race), turning him first into the Son of God, and finally into the role of God the Son, the Second Person of an artificial concept known as the Holy Trinity.

The Old Testament contains a wealth of splendid narratives (clearly partly mythical) with constant reference to the Jewish God and his attachment to the small tribes which later liked to refer to themselves as God's 'chosen people'. For them God was very real. Abraham is recorded as meeting God frequently; Jacob has a vision of a ladder between the earth and heaven with angels walking up and down it; Moses, leading his people out of slavery in Egypt, sees God going before him in a pillar of cloud by day and a pillar of fire at night. When they finally reach Mount Sinai God appears on the summit and hands over to Moses the tablets of the Law. When, finally, the Jews find themselves established in Jerusalem with David as their king, a temple was planned, which David's son Solomon built, which became the sanctuary for the whole nation where God was believed to reside ('For the Lord hath chosen Zion; he hath desired it for his habitation. This is my rest for ever: here will I dwell; for I have desired it' – Psalm 132: 13–14). Thus the Jews had the firm belief in God's immanence on earth as well as in heaven. The Old Testament had also prophesied the coming of the Jewish Messiah – descended (of course) from their great king David – who would free his people from their subjection to Rome (which dated from 63 BC) and bring God's peace and justice to the whole earth. This was the theology in which Jesus of Nazareth was brought up. He knew all the historic prophecies; he believed he had come to announce the arrival of the new kingdom of heaven on earth. Central to Jesus's message was his repeated proclamation of the imminent arrival of the Kingdom of God and his followers were therefore urged to dispose of all their earthly possessions. When, after Jesus's death and the death of his apostles and their contemporaries, it became clear to the later Church authority that the prophesied event showed no signs of any imminent realisation, its leaders had to devise another explanation. The *Parousia* or Second Coming was adjourned *sine die*. The 'arrival of the Kingdom of God' was identified with the establishment of the 'Church', while the 'reign of God' was deferred until the 'coming again' of Jesus and the anticipated 'final Judgement'.

To maintain a continuing link between the risen Jesus and his followers the early Church authorities focused on the so-called 'Last Supper' of Jesus with his disciples at which unleavened bread and four cups of wine would – in the Jewish Passover tradition – have been ritually blessed by the host and drunk by his guests. At this meal – which in fact took place the day *before* Passover – Jesus is reputed by Luke and Paul, but not by the other evangelists, to have instructed his disciples to eat bread (symbolising his body) and drink wine (symbolising his blood) thereafter in his memory – 'do this in remembrance of me' – and thereby was responsible for initiating what later became known as the 'Eucharist' which the later Church developed into the major sacrament of the 'Mass' or 'Holy Communion', a ritual which subsequently became a bond between Christians right up until the Reformation.[1] The Eucharist was intended to keep Jesus's memory alive in the memory of his believers and to provide a Church equivalent to popular contemporary pagan practices claiming to offer a means of communion between a deity and its adherents. Thus Paul and the evangelists would have been well aware of the various pagan cults then flourishing in the Near East and their sacrificial rituals designed to achieve communion between the 'god' and his adherents, and Paul himself was at Corinth (close to the seat of the Mysteries of Demeter at Eleusis) when he announced his supernatural 'revelation' about the initiation of the 'Last Supper' ritual. And celebration of the birth of Jesus was also deliberately changed from 6 January to 25 December so as to coincide with (and hopefully supplant) that of the pagan feast of Sol Invictus, Jesus thereby becoming the 'Sun of Righteousness'. Such were the desperate efforts by the early Christians to establish a new 'religion' that would be credible to contemporary pagan culture.

The early followers of Jesus struggled on in small groups, often persecuted by the Roman authorities, until in the early fourth century the Emperor Constantine decided to allow Christianity as one of the recognised state religions. From then on the Church became institutionalised as a partner of the State. Thereafter it became necessary to develop firm ideas about the intellectual foundations of their faith and their understanding of the nature of Jesus and his relationship to God. After serious debate and many disagreements formal doctrines were eventually elaborated and all heretical opinion suppressed (although not altogether successfully). Jesus's teaching and the narratives of his disciples were written down and suitably manipulated so as to accord with the new Church's agreed doctrines. The 27 books of the New Testament were then decided on. After the collapse of the Roman empire in 410 the Church as an institution was strong enough to be able to foster a degree of stability amongst warring tribes and to become an ally of the nascent political kingdoms that were beginning to emerge in Western Europe. This was to culminate in the solemn crowning by the Pope of the Emperor Charlemagne as Holy Roman Emperor in AD 800.

If, as the Roman Catholic Church asserts, it is the incarnation of God in Jesus Christ and the foundation of a Church through his disciples which have provided 'the ultimate demonstration of the existence of the deity', then we must examine the evidence for the life and teaching of Jesus. Most Christians believe in the general, but not the literal,[2] 'truth' of the Christian scriptures as embodied in the Holy Bible, and specifically those of the New Testament, but it is now realised that this does not necessarily require belief in a number of concepts and narratives contained therein which contemporary believers find it difficult to accept.[3] To accept unequivocally the veracity of some of the Gospel stories presents obvious difficulties. Professor J. J. C. Smart explains: 'the earliest Gospel to be written was that of St Mark and is dated by scholars to some 40 years after the crucifixion (i.e. c.70 AD). Matthew and Luke incorporated the gist of almost all of Mark into their Gospels (probably written between 80–85 AD), in which scholars have detected another hypothetical documentary source, called 'Q'.[4] Mark also would have depended on oral tradition. It is commonplace that oral tradition can lead to distortions and exaggerations as words are passed from one mouth to another. There were stories of virgin birth and resurrection elsewhere in the Middle East, neo-Platonic influences from Greek philosophy, and historians in ancient times were not as scrupulous about literal truth as are modern ones'.[5] St Paul's epistles, on the other hand, as part of his energetic missionary activity, were written in the '50s and '60s of the first century, and accounts of Paul's conversion (Acts 9: 2) reveal that Christians were at this early date known as followers of 'The Way'. Paul's epistles were undoubtedly written for contemporaries because of the reference to the early second coming of Jesus, and it is certain that his writings date from before the Gospels were written. John's Gospel was the last to be written, probably c.90–95. Over all the records that have come down to us from the time of Jesus's life there hangs a shadow that cannot now be ignored. This is the fact that during the past century many distinguished biblical scholars have reached the uncomfortable conclusion that a number of narrative texts which had customarily been regarded as sacrosanct had been subjected to interpolation and revision by early Church authorities for doctrinal and political reasons. These will be discussed in due course.

Despite periodic attempts to prove that Jesus never existed, there is in fact convincing evidence of his life.[6] The Roman historian Tacitus (b. c.56) recalls that the great fire in Rome in 64 AD was blamed on the Christians by the emperor Nero to divert the accusation that he himself was responsible for starting it. Tacitus records in his *Annals* that 'they got their name from Christ, who was executed by sentence of the procurator Pontius Pilate in the reign of Tiberius. The pernicious superstition, suppressed for the moment, broke out again, not only throughout Judaea, the birthplace of the plague, but also in the city of Rome' (*Annals* 15: 44). Tacitus was a friend of Pliny the Younger, governor of Bithynia from 111–113 AD, and one of Pliny's letters (see page 20) written to the emperor Trajan in c.111 recounts how he dealt with Christians brought before him, and mentioned that Christians 'sing an antiphonal hymn to Christ as a god...' In Gaius Suetonius's life (c.120 AD) of the emperor Claudius he writes that Claudius expelled the Jews from Rome in 49 AD because they were being encouraged to riot at the instigation of *Chrestos* – possibly a misspelling of Christus or Christ. Suetonius regarded the Christian religion as a *superstitio nova et prava*. In the second century Lucian of Samosata writes that Christians worshipped 'that great man who was crucified in Palestine because he introduced this new cult into the world'. The Jewish historian Josephus (37–c.100), who became a supporter of Roman rule, records the stoning in 62 AD of James 'the brother of Jesus the so-called Messiah'. Elsewhere he refers to 'Jesus, a wise man... one who did surprising deeds, a teacher... on the accusation of our leading men Pilate condemned him to the cross, but those who had loved him from the first did not cease to do so... And to this day the tribe of Christians, named after him, has not died out'.[7] Surprisingly, the Jewish philosopher Philo of Alexandria, although mentioning the Essenes, says nothing of Jesus or his followers. Nor does the historian Justus of Tiberias (writing c.80 AD). References to Jesus in rabbinical literature occur in the Talmud from the early second century onwards.[8]

Jesus is now thought to have been born in 7 BC and to have been crucified in 30 AD.[9] What is known of the circumstances of his birth?

NOTES

[1] See McGrath, 2007, 433–440

[2] Certain Christian Fundamentalist sects do in fact believe in the literal 'truth' of the Bible

[3] The Old Testament, on the other hand, the Bible of the Jewish faith, is dominated by the God Yahweh (whom the atheist Professor Richard Dawkins delights to describe as 'arguably the most unpleasant character in all fiction: jealous and proud of it; a petty, unjust, unforgiving control-freak; a vindictive blood-thirsty ethnic cleanser; a misogynistic, homophobic, racist, infanticidal, genocidal, filicidal, pestilential, megalomaniacal, sadomachistic, capriciously malevolent bully' (Dawkins, 2006, 31). Likewise he gleefully tabulates the Old Testament offences meriting the death penalty (Ibid., 248). The Old Testament itself can best be regarded as a

collection of Jewish chronicles and folktales, handed down through the generations, embodying the movements, travails, rules of law (supposedly handed down by God to Moses), prophetic utterances, and behaviour of those who came to be regarded as God's 'chosen people'. Modern theologians now interpret much of the patently absurd parts of the Old Testament either symbolically or allegorically, but certainly not literally. The birth of Jesus was regarded as fulfilling the prophecies about a Jewish Messiah, but Jesus turned out not to be the militant Messiah whom the Jews hoped would free them from the Roman Empire and usher in a period of universal peace. Thereafter the Jews retreated into a claustrophobic sect concentrating on their Mosaic law and traditional customs

[4] For a discussion of the 'Q' document see Spong, J S, 2002, 84–6. The alleged source 'Q' is dismissed by the late Professor Carsten Thiede as a fiction (see Thiede, 2004, 123). He also believed that Matthew's Gospel was written as early as 66 AD, which would have implied that the author would have had personal contact with Jesus and it would therefore have represented a text recording the events of history rather than a piece of 'folklore' (see *Eyewitness to Jesus*, 1996, by Carsten Thiede and Matthew d'Ancona)

[5] Smart and Haldane, 2003, 57

[6] See Stanton, 2002, 143–152

[7] Ibid., 148–150. For a commentary on the authenticity of Josephus's references to James and Jesus see Wells, 1971, 190–6

[8] See Wells, 1971, 197–203

[9] Thiede, 2004, 143 Note 10. As the late Professor Thiede points out, the confusion over Jesus's date of birth arose because of the erroneous calendar reform of Dionysius Exiguus (*c.*478–535 AD) on behalf of Pope John I (Ibid.)

(a)   The birth of Jesus

It is an uncomfortable fact that the Nativity scene conjured up in most people's imaginations today bears little relation to historical accuracy and, in Professor Geza Vermes's words: 'mostly derives from man's hopeful and creative religious imagination'.[1] The Nativity is mentioned in only two Gospels, those of Matthew and Luke; neither are derived from one another; and both appear to be later additions to the main Gospel narratives and whose purpose 'seems to be the creation of a prologue, enveloping the newborn Jesus with an aura of marvel and enigma (mysterious conception, wonderful star, angelic messengers and revelatory dreams)'.[2] For historians one of the central features of the Nativity story is the virginal conception of Jesus and its implications (which Mark had clearly never heard of!). In Matthew's Gospel (1: 18) Mary was 'found with child of the Holy Spirit', and her offspring was to be called 'Emmanuel' or 'God with us' as predicted in Isaiah's prophecy (Matt. 1: 23). Luke refers to a *virgin* called Mary learning that she will conceive 'of the Holy Spirit' and that her offspring shall be called 'the Son of God' (Luke 1: 35). The idea of a child being conceived with no normal male contribution was totally unknown in biblical or post-biblical Jewish tradition (although quite common in the pagan world[3]), and Joseph, Mary's husband, was not unnaturally extremely concerned when he heard of this impending event. What is the 'truth' of the two Gospel accounts of Jesus's miraculous conception?

Biblical scholars now realise that the attribution of virginity to Mary is based on an accidental mistranslation from Hebrew to Greek in the passage in Isaiah 7: 14. Isaiah's prophecy runs: 'Behold a *virgin* shall conceive and bear a son, and his name shall be *Emmanuel* (which means, God with us)'. The Hebrew version of Isaiah 7: 14 does not refer to a *virgin*, or a *betulah* in Hebrew, but to an *almah*, that is to say, 'a young woman', a term which does not necessarily imply virginity. Nor is there any suggestion elsewhere in the Hebrew Isaiah that the person alluded to was still a virgin or that the forthcoming conception is to be miraculous in any way. The significance of the Hebrew passage lay in the name 'Emmanuel' which means 'God with us', and suggests its bearer would bring divine protection to his country. The Greek

Septuagint translator, however, translated the word 'almah' in the prophecy as 'parthenos', which usually carried the connotation 'virgin' in Greek. In Professor Vermes's words: 'The 'Greek' Matthew or the Semitic Matthew's Greek editor tumbled on this loose translation, and adopted it. This godsend enabled him to present to his Greek-speaking readers the conception of Jesus as unique and towering above all the other miraculous conceptions of the Old Testament. There is an incontrovertible proof that a substantial proportion of the intended audience of the final text of Matthew consisted of Greeks, who had no knowledge of Hebrew. In Matthew 1: 23 the Hebrew name 'Emmanuel' in the Isaiah citation is furnished with a translation to explain that it means 'God with us'. As one may guess, the original Hebrew Isaiah includes no such interpretation, but more important, it also lacks from its Greek rendering in the Septuagint. The Diaspora Jews for whom the Septuagint was produced were expected to know what Emmanuel signified. The Greek gloss in Matthew's quotation, 'which means, God with us', is manifestly the evangelist's own creation for the benefit of his non-Jewish Greek readers. So applied to Mary, the Isaiah prophecy, as worded in Greek, was intended to convey to the Greek-speaking public of Matthew's infancy narrative that 'Jesus – Emmanuel' or 'the Messiah – Son of God' would be conceived of the Holy Spirit and miraculously produced by Mary *as* a virgin'. Thus 'the virginal conception is a historicised extrapolation of the words of the Septuagint, proffered to and understood by a Hellenic Gentile-Christian audience of the Gospel of Matthew. The birth story of Jesus, told in Aramaic or Hebrew and quoting Isaiah in Hebrew, could never have given rise to such an interpretation. But in Greek, combined with the literal exegesis of the name 'Emmanuel = God with us', it became the source out of which arose the concept of the divine Son of a virgin mother. It must be reiterated, even though this may be *ad nauseam*, that such a development was possible only in a Greek-speaking Hellenistic cultural environment'.[4] It was only a short step, against the classical background of Graeco-Roman mythology and legends relating to the divine origin of eminent figures in the past for the idea to evolve 'via Paul, John and the philosophising Greek Church Fathers into the deification of Jesus,

Son of the God-bearing (*Theotokos*) Virgin'.[5] It may be noted that St Paul makes no mention of Jesus having had a miraculous virginal birth, while in John's gospel there is a reference to 'Jesus of Nazareth, the son of Joseph' (John 1: 45) and another to '...Jesus, the son of Joseph...' (John 6: 42) which show that St John had little time for the virgin-birth story. And even Luke contradicts himself. Thus after Jesus had been born Joseph and Mary, according to custom, went up to the Temple at Jerusalem so that Mary could be 'purified', offering a sacrifice of two turtle-doves. In Luke's account of this episode he refers to the 'parents of Jesus' meeting the elderly Simeon (Luke 2: 27) and later refers to 'his parents' going every year to Jerusalem (Luke 2: 41) – apparently having forgotten about the 'virginal conception' about which he had written in the previous chapter!

That Matthew's virginal conception was addressed essentially to *Hellenistic* Gentile Christians may be deduced from the teachings of the Jewish Christian sect known as the Ebionites. According to both bishop Irenaeus and the historian Eusebius 'the Ebionites rejected the doctrine of the virgin birth'. Eusebius makes plain that for them 'Jesus was "the child of a normal union between a man and Mary"' (*Ecclestiastical History* 3: 27)... He further explained that in order to bolster their teaching and pull the rug out from under the feet of Christian orthodoxy, the Ebionites championed the Greek version of Theodotion and Aquila as more correct than the Septuagint, and substituted for the *parthenos* (virgin) of the Septuagint the term *neanis* (young woman) in their rendering of Isaiah 7: 14 (*ibid.* 3: 21). In their view, the proof of the unreliability of the Septuagint sounded the death knell of Matthew's and the Christian Church's doctrine of the virginal conception'.[6] After all, since members of Jesus's family were Ebionites, and his brother James was their leader, it is hardly likely that they would not know what they were talking about! And, of course, because of the concept of the virgin birth it was necessary for the editor(s) of Matthew's Gospel to revise the genealogical table to avoid the implication that Jesus was descended from David *through Joseph*.[7] But unfortunately not all sources could be amended. For example, some Greek manuscripts and the Old Latin translation of Matthew 1: 16 refer to 'Joseph to whom the virgin Mary was betrothed, *begot* Jesus who was called Christ'.[8] One of the oldest documents, an early Syriac version of Matthew found by two intrepid Scottish ladies in the library of the monastery of St Catherine on Mount Sinai, refers to 'Joseph to whom was betrothed the virgin Mary, *begot* Jesus'. These and other examples, according to Professor Vermes: 'concur in making crystal clear who the father is meant to be and revealing what must have been the Semitic original subjacent to Matthew 1: 16'.[9]

As to Jesus's birth, Dr David Jenkins in his book *The Calling of a Cuckoo* (2002) has this to say:

'The birth narratives are far more about the obedience of Mary and Joseph in response to the unique graciousness of God than about Mary's physical virginity. The resurrection narratives are far more about encounters and namings and joyful recognitions than about the empty tomb. Miracles are gifts rather than guarantees, given to faith and perceived by faith, and they always involve a mysterious collaboration and convergence between the intervening power of God and human responses of faith, obedience and activity… We are always wanting to pin God down by getting things cut and dried and decisive'.[10]

This is an explanation hardly likely to mean much to an individual seeking answers *in plain English* to matters of major Christian theological importance! Records clearly show that Joseph was in fact described as the father of Jesus, and the latter's birth was not, as Dr Jenkins suggests, the result of a 'divine transformation of Mary's chromosomes and genes'![11]

For the Catholic Church the virginal conception is a matter of dogma and forms an essential part of its teaching. This has been an insurmountable barrier for Catholic scholars in pursuit of the truth, as is ruefully noted by Professor Vermes.[12] As the late Rudolph Bultmann (one of the greatest New Testament scholars of his time) pointed out: 'the original Semitic report of Matthew's Infancy Gospel contained nothing about the virgin birth… and it was first added to the Gospel account in the course of its transformation in Hellenism'. More recently, E. P. Sanders has 'asserted without the slightest hesitation that the birth narratives are 'the clearest cases of invention' in the Gospels'.[13] Apart from the explanation of the attribution of virginity to Mary, there were further Roman Catholic dogmas about her which strain the bounds of credulity. After proclaiming Mary's miraculous virginal conception followed by the birth of her son Jesus, the Church later declared her to be a 'permanent virgin', which meant that the parentage of Jesus's known brothers and sisters had to be explained away. She was then declared to be a 'postpartum virgin' (implying that Jesus had been delivered as a baby without rupturing the sacred hymen). Later, when scientific knowledge discovered that women could transmit genetic codes to their children, she was declared to have been immaculately conceived so that she would not have been able to pass on the 'sin of Adam' to her son (who was of course without sin)![14] And finally, 'at the very dawn of the space age', Mary was declared by the Church (1950) – appropriately enough – to have been bodily 'assumed' into heaven.[15] The authority of the Church guaranteed the infallible limits of the received faith, and as late as the nineteenth century the Pope was declared to be 'infallible' in matters of faith.

Luke dates the birth of Jesus to the time of a census ordered by the emperor Augustus when Quirinius was governor of Syria and Herod king of Judaea. However, Herod reigned between 37 BC and 4 AD and Quirinius was never governor of Syria during this period. And the only known census, according to the historian Josephus, was in 6 AD. So Luke's account is historically incorrect. Modern biblical scholars have however deduced that Jesus's birth took place in 7 BC.

The inescapable conclusion for the dispassionate historian must be that:

1. Jesus was born in a natural way, the son of Joseph and Mary, in the year 7 BC.

2. The legend of the 'virginal birth' was composed as an introductory supplement by the early editor(s) of the original Gospels of Matthew and Luke (which otherwise begin with the appearance in AD 29 of Jesus, then in his thirties, from nowhere).

3. The legend was designed to demonstrate that the biblical prophecy in Isaiah 7: 14 had in fact been realised. Not only did

Mary thereafter become the Mother of God (whose celebration has now quietly taken the place of the former feast of the circumcision of Jesus, now for obvious reasons deemed to be inappropriate), but it turned the Jewish baby Jesus first into the promised Messiah, then into the Son of God, and finally into the position of God the Son, the Second Person of the Holy Trinity. As Professor Vermes pointed out: 'By the early years of the second century Gentile Christians had become accustomed to consider Jesus not just as a metaphorical Son of God, but as a divine person'.[16] His mother, Mary, was in due course to be dogmatically elevated to different degrees of virginity, and finally declared to have been bodily 'assumed' into heaven.

4. Changes in the early Greek texts of Matthew included the upgrading of the three *magoi* ('magi' or magicians), a despised group of men who were originally astrologers or Zoroastrian priests, to wise men or Kings.[17] They have since received the names of Caspar, Melchior and Balthazar, whose imagined relics were found and eventually taken to Cologne (and their gifts of gold, frankincense and myrrh being regarded as symbolic of kingship, prayer and burial). As Archbishop Rowan Williams has pointed out: 'Matthew's Gospel doesn't tell us there were three of them, doesn't tell us they were kings, doesn't tell us where they came from. It says they are astrologers, wise men, priests from somewhere outside the Roman Empire, that's all we're really told'. Anything else was legend.[18] Legendary features such as the appearance of the mysterious star follow the popular belief (attested by Pliny the Elder) that appearances of a bright star heralded the birth of a great man (for example, before the birth of Octavian, the future Roman emperor, in 63 BC). Moreover, the appearance of the star Sirius was believed to foretell the birth of the god Osiris and the rising of the waters of the river Nile. And furthermore, the historians Suetonius and Tacitus 'allude to a rumour which was going round in the Eastern empire announcing that a ruler of the world would arise from Judaea. The Jews, engaged in war against Rome, took advantage of the prophecy and interpreted it as applying to one of their compatriots, the coming King Messiah'.[19] As well as other

legendary features, including the appearance of angels and dreams, even the charming image of the ox and ass round the Nativity crib turn out to have been borrowed from Isaiah (1: 3)![20]

5. The birth of Jesus – originally celebrated on 6 January – was altered to 25 December so as to coincide with the winter solstice which was the traditional birthday of the sun god in Egypt, Persia and elsewhere, in the hope of attracting converts to the new Christian religion.

6. Although the historian may rightly discount the Nativity story of Mary's 'virginal conception' through the agency of the Holy Spirit, and explain how many of the details of the traditional Nativity scene have arisen, this is not to deny the unique, historical person of Jesus, his special relationship to God, and the message which he preached to the world.

NOTES

[1] Vermes, 2006, 5. In his book Professor Vermes has examined in great detail the circumstances of the Nativity as related in the Gospels of Matthew and Luke

[2] Ibid., 163

[3] Thus Professor Wells records that: 'the idea that important personages are Virgin-born was widespread and derived from much older cults' (Wells, 1971, 30)

[4] Vermes, 2006, 69–70

[5] Ibid., 70–71

[6] Ibid., 71–72

[7] Ibid., 33. Luke's genealogy was likewise amended to record that Joseph was the 'supposed' father of Jesus (Ibid., 40–41)

[8] Ibid., 33–4

[9] Ibid.

[10] Jenkins, 2002, 180

[11] Ibid., 177–8

[12] Vermes, 2006, 18–22. The late Raymond Brown, a noted Catholic scholar, in his book *The Birth of the Messiah* (1973), surveyed the

biblical evidence for the attribution of virginity to Mary but does not appear to have realised that this originally arose because of a mistranslation from Hebrew to Greek of a passage in Isaiah. His conclusion was 'that the totality of the *scientifically controllable* evidence leaves an unresolved problem' (Brown, 1973, 66–7). Unfortunately, Brown is unduly influenced by the Catholic Church's 'unanimity in regarding the historicity of the virginal concept as unquestionable' and his palpable fear of the 'danger that the discussion might imperil a traditional formulation of faith that has served Christianity well' (Ibid., 22, 67). Scholars should be concerned that the Roman Catholic censorship of all research findings which throw doubt on orthodox doctrines inevitably gives rise to ludicrous equivocation on the part of some scholarly Catholics. We may recall the fate of Hans Küng, a noted Roman Catholic professor of theology in the university of Tübingen, who dared to raise questions about matters of Roman Catholic orthodoxy and was accordingly removed from his position as a Catholic theologian. The distinguished philosopher Anthony Kenny confirms that 'for a true believer there can never be a question of examining conflicting evidence with a view to possible revision of one's commitment to the articles of faith' (Kenny, 1992, 49). As a former Roman Catholic priest he ought to know, and it is a sad reflection on the neurotic Catholic attitude towards historical 'truth'.

[13] Vermes, 2006, 22

[14] Contrary to general belief that the doctrine of 'Immaculate Conception' follows from the Annunciation to Mary by the Archangel Gabriel, Roman Catholics understand that it means that 'from the first moment of *her* conception in the womb of her mother, St Ann, Mary was kept free from original sin by the power of divine grace. So the Immaculate Conception is about Mary's conception in her mother's womb' (Trigilio and Brighenti, 2003, 263). This doctrine was defined *ex cathedra* by Pope Pius IX in 1854. To believe it, it is of course necessary to believe in the theory of 'original sin' – one of St Augustine's more questionable and disputed theories!

[15] For these dogmatic pronouncements on Mary see Spong, 2002, 110–112

[16] Vermes, 2006, 81

[17] Ibid., 109–114

[18] *The Times*, 20 December, 2007

[19] Vermes, 2006, 108–9

[20] And now – horror of horrors! – moves are afoot to remove the crib scene and to take the infant Jesus to be born in Joseph's house!

(b)   The life of Jesus

At this period much of the Middle East was divided into provinces of the Roman Empire, with main roads and harbours which facilitated the transfer of goods and the transmission of ideas, such as religions. Christianity reached Rome very early and spread quickly – e.g. to Britain soon after the Claudian invasion of 43 AD. The Coptic tribes of Egypt were perhaps the earliest Christians outside Jewish territories. Alexandria at this time contained the largest Jewish community anywhere outside Palestine. The late Professor Carsten Peter Thiede has noted the remarkable facility for languages by even the humblest member of society at this period, and he notes that Jesus spoke Hebrew, Aramaic and Greek.

We know singularly little about the life of Jesus of Nazareth apart from the circumstances of his birth (embellished as they are by a host of colourful myths) and those of his death. There is no extant record of his childhood or of his early professional career. Professor Thiede considered that Joseph was a respected builder and that Mary had a well-off father and no brothers. Both Joseph and Mary were in fact descended from David, so that the Davidic prophecy foretelling the coming of Jesus the Messiah would have applied even if Joseph was not Jesus's father.[1] He also thought that Joseph and Jesus probably worked as builders on the re-building of the capital of Galilee, Sepphoris (Zippori) after its destruction in 4 BC by the Romans after a regional uprising.[2] Thiede has also noted the influence of local theatres and acting techniques displayed in some of Jesus's sermons and the sites where he chose to deliver them. In the cosmopolitan world of the Middle East the plays of classical authors such as Aeschylus, Sophocles and Euripides, as well as works of the contemporary Jewish playwright Ezekiel 'the Tragedian', would have been performed at Sepphoris and Caesarea. Jesus, for example, frequently used the word 'hypocrite' when describing his opponents. The original Greek word was *hypokritēs*, which meant an 'actor' – so that the people he so described were pretending to be something different from their true natures.[3]

Jesus had four brothers: James, Judas (his twin brother known as Didymus Judas Thomas), Joses or Joseph, and Simon, along with several sisters. He was not apparently on very good terms with his family, and, as he ruefully reflected, 'a prophet is not without honour, except in his own country, and among his own kin, and in his own house'. The earliest narratives of Jesus's life are to be found in the New Testament Gospels.[4] These were originally anonymous (thus when recalling what took place at church services Justin Martyr referred simply to the reading of 'the memoirs of the apostles') but in the second century came to be called by the names of Jesus's disciples (Matthew and John) and of two companions of the apostles (Mark, the companion of Peter, and Luke, the companion of Paul).[5] In the first chapter of his Gospel Luke refers to the fact that 'many have undertaken to draw up an account of the things which have been fulfilled among us', but none of these early sources have survived. Yet it is a disturbing and inexplicable fact that the earliest narratives of Jesus's life cover a period of only some 50 days. What of the rest of his life?

A number of other apocryphal 'gospels' were in circulation in the Near East at this period from which we might hope to discover something about Jesus's early life. Just before the Dead Sea Scrolls came to light another significant discovery was made near Nag Hammadi in Egypt which comprised a number of hitherto unknown writings. These included an anonymous Gospel of Truth, and gospels of several of Jesus's disciples such as Philip and Thomas (the latter containing 114 sayings of Jesus). But the most remarkable discovery from an early Christian point of view was the so-called 'Gospel of Judas', discovered in the 1970s in Middle Egypt and forming part of a codex now known as Codex Tchacos. This codex is a Coptic translation of a text originally composed in Greek and written probably between 140–160 AD. It is of significance in that Irenaeus, bishop of Lugdunum (Lyon), refers to this gospel in his work *Against Heresies* which he wrote about the year 180. The Gospel of Judas is a remarkable – even if incomplete – text.[6] Judas Iscariot (believed to signify 'the man from the village of Kerioth in Judaea', or, if you prefer a more melodramatic origin, Father Timothy Radcliffe tells us his name signified 'dagger man' or 'assassin'[7]) has always had the reputation as the one disciple who betrayed Jesus, and biblical accounts suggest either that he took his own life or met his death by an act of God after this dastardly act. In the Gospel of Judas, by contrast, Judas is depicted as Jesus' most intimate companion and friend who understands precisely who Jesus really is, and the only disciple to whom Jesus passes on the secret revelation that can lead mankind to salvation, and that he will himself attain salvation. Since he knows the 'truth' Judas is able to perform the greatest service for Jesus by handing him over to the civil authorities to be executed in order that the divine spirit within Jesus may be liberated from his material body. Thus in the gospel Jesus says: 'But you will exceed all of them [i.e. the other disciples]. For you will sacrifice the man that clothes me'.[8] One of the most interesting sections of the gospel is the secret revelation which Jesus imparts to Judas alone. It is in fact a scenario from the theological beliefs of the Sethian Gnostics who maintained that 'there is not just one God but many gods and where the creator of this world is not the true God but an inferior deity, who is not the Father of all and is certainly not almighty',[9] a view diametrically opposed to the 'orthodox' Christian view of belief in 'God, the Father almighty, maker of heaven and earth…' (as in the Nicene Creed). Not surprisingly, Irenaeus condemned such ideas as rank heresy. The significance of Jesus's death, according to the Gospel of Judas, is not 'to give his life a ransom for many' (as in Mark 10: 45) but rather to escape from this world and the evil creator god of the Jews and return to the divine realm of the true God, who has never been involved with this world. Interestingly, the Gospel of Judas ends abruptly after his betrayal of Jesus and there is no reference to his subsequent crucifixion.

It was hoped that when the 'Dead Sea Scrolls' were discovered they might throw light on Jesus's religious and political affiliations. These remarkably interesting scrolls discovered in 1947 in caves near Qumran in Judaea containing, *inter alia*, copies of all the books of the Hebrew Scriptures were written between c.150 BC and 70 AD by a cenobitical Jewish religious community, members of the Essene sect. The community had been founded by a priest referred to as the Teacher of Righteousness, who had withdrawn to the Judaean desert to await the impending triumph of God over evil and darkness which presaged the end of time. Since the putative date for the occupation of the site overlaps the period of

Jesus's lifetime a variety of sensational speculations have been advanced including one which suggests that the Teacher of Righteousness was in fact Jesus. There was also a totally misleading claim that some manuscript fragments represented remains of St Mark's Gospel and other parts of the New Testament. In fact, no evidential link has been discovered between Jesus and the Qumran community, and the Essene sect is not explicitly mentioned either in the New Testament or in rabbinic literature. What happened to the Essene community at Qumran is unknown, but no one subsequently returned to retrieve their buried library.[10]

Jesus's first adult public appearance was his baptism by John the Baptist, the prophet who called his compatriots to repentance, a theme echoed by Jesus's own proclamation: 'repent, for the Kingdom of Heaven is at hand'. For John he had the highest respect, and when he embarked on his own ministry he set out to continue John's work in the countryside of Galilee. John the Baptist is a figure of considerable interest and not a little mystery. He is a prophetic figure who baptises in water but whose main task is to bear witness to Jesus as the 'Son of God', and two of John's early followers, Andrew and his brother Simon Peter, both subsequently became disciples of Jesus. There is some confusion amongst the evangelists' accounts as to whether Jesus *needed* to be baptised by John, but Jesus eventually agrees.[11] Jesus's public ministry centred on charismatic healing and exorcism – notably, the expelling of evil spirits and the curing of the sick, the working of 'miracles', and general preaching about the imminence of the advent of the Kingdom of God. It should be borne in mind that Jesus attributed illness and sin to the influence of evil spirits and regarded healing, exorcism and forgiveness of sins as synonymous. The Jewish historian Flavius Josephus, writing shortly before AD 100, called Jesus a 'performer of astonishing deeds'. And yet it is remarkable that there are no stories of Jesus performing miracles anywhere in the writings of St Paul. Jesus was a great exponent of teaching in parables (a literary form used both in the Bible and in rabbinic writings) of which some 46 were recorded in the Synoptic Gospels. Clearly Jesus was an inspired ethical teacher, but the gospel accounts of his behaviour are full of contradictions and incompatibilities. For example, we are all familiar with his injunction to 'love our neighbour as ourselves'. Yet he denounces the scribes and Pharisees – calling them hypocrites, serpents and vipers (Mat. 23: 29, 33). He urges tolerance, yet any towns disbelieving his prophetic claims will be severely punished at the day of judgement, as will those who personally disbelieve him. He urges avoidance of anger, yet his Galilean temper is often displayed (e.g. Mark 3: 5). Jesus emphasised that his message was strictly for 'the lost sheep of the house of Israel' (Matthew 15: 24) and forbade his disciples to approach Gentiles ('go not into any way of the Gentiles, and enter not into any city of the Samaritans' (Matthew 10: 5)), implying that in his view citizenship of the Kingdom of God was reserved for Jews alone. Yet elsewhere we may note that in an account of the *risen* Christ he is said to have charged his disciples to evangelize the whole world ('go ye therefore, and make disciples of all the nations, baptising them into the name of the Father and of the Son and of the Holy Ghost; teaching them to observe all things whatsoever I commanded you' (Matthew 28: 19–20)). This is clearly a later interpolation, for Jesus would have had no knowledge of the concept of the Holy Trinity! Professor Vermes has examined all the evidence and concludes: 'Disturbing though this may sound to the uninformed, the order to proclaim the good news of salvation to all the nations must be struck out from the list of the authentic sayings of Jesus'.[12] After Jesus's death the relative lack of success of the Christian Church of Peter and of James (the brothers of Jesus) compared with Paul's striking achievements amongst the Gentiles of Asia Minor (whom he endeavoured to release from the constraints of traditional Judaism) confirmed the necessity of opening up the Christian message to the world at large. The reversal of Jesus's policy became vital for the future success of Christianity, and later Church authorities seemingly interpolated appropriate wording into various texts to give the impression that the world-wide mission was in fact Jesus's original intention. It does not require much imagination to guess that the touching prophecy of the aged Simeon when the child Jesus was brought to the Temple by his parents – that Jesus would be 'a light to lighten the Gentiles and to be the glory of his people Israel' – must have been an interpolation made in Pauline days to take account, and give the appearance of verisimilitude of the reversal of Jesus's deliberate instructions that only the Jewish people were to be partakers of the heavenly kingdom! In fact, it was the First Apostolic Council in Jerusalem in c.49/50 AD which decided on the new policy (Paul naturally being in favour and Peter against).

Jesus's close disciples were mostly uneducated Galilean fishermen whom he chose to spread the good news of the heavenly kingdom and instructed in charismatic healing and exorcism. Thus after Jesus had appointed a further seventy disciples they joyously reported, after they had returned home, 'Lord, even the devils are subject unto us through thy name' (Luke 10: 17). And even rabbinic literature records that an early Jewish-Christian, one Jacob of Kfar Sama, offered to heal the sick 'in the name of Jesus'.[13] It is necessary to understand the importance of magic, healing and exorcism at this period. Pliny denounced magic as 'detestable, vain and idle'. But it was immensely popular. A certain Simon known as 'the Magus' from Samaria had been proclaimed as divine on account of his magical powers. He arrived in Rome during the reign of Claudius. However, he was denounced by Simon Peter but is recorded as having offered money to receive the 'superior' power or 'magic' of the Holy Spirit which Simon Peter possessed (hence, incidentally, the origin of the medieval term 'simony' which denoted purchasing an office in the Church).[14] The common belief at this period was that illness was caused by 'demons', in whose existence virtually everyone believed, and Jesus and his disciples specialised in casting out demons and restoring their victims to health. When Paul visited Ephesus, an important regional capital whose presiding deity, Artemis, was renowned for her magical powers and whose temple was regarded as one of the Seven Wonders of the Ancient World, he caused consternation by challenging the cult of magic practised by the Ephesians. A. N. Wilson reminds us that 'God wrought special miracles by the hands of Paul' (Acts 19: 11) and Paul regarded himself as someone in whom Jesus was active and alive. 'Paul was able to heal the sick and to drive out demons merely by touch, and the name of Jesus therefore came to be used by other magicians… Gradually it became known that the name of Jesus was the most powerful 'magic' of all.'[15]

Mark records that Jesus moved from Nazareth to the large fishing village of Capernaum on the Sea of Galilee. Jesus never referred to himself as 'Messiah' or as the 'Son of God', but rather as the 'Son of man' in order to emphasise his humanity (e.g. 'the Son of man hath power on earth to forgive sins' (Mark 2: 10)). Jesus championed the weak and despised, and those like tax collectors and harlots whom society shunned. He was especially fond of children because of their absolute faith in paternal goodwill. But for all his kindness and compassion he retained the short temper of his Galilean compatriots (on one occasion addressing Peter as 'Satan') and as Professor Vermes points out: 'Jesus was not exactly the gentle, sugary, meek and mild figure of pious Christian imagination'.[16] Being born a Jew Jesus's religious piety focused on the Torah, which he interpreted in his own special way, and he taught that everyone should follow the Mosaic rules until the arrival of God's Kingdom. The religious and moral attitudes required of his followers are described in the Beatitudes, laying down who would gain admittance to the Kingdom. Without ever attempting a detailed description of the Deity, Jesus's idea of God 'is mirrored in sayings, parables and prayers'; he is above all a caring God and a loving Father (a title frequently used by Jesus when referring to him: the 'fatherhood of God' being an old rabbinical tradition with which he would be familiar).

Central to Jesus's message was his repeated proclamation of the imminent arrival of the Kingdom of God (although never spelling out precisely what this meant[17]), yet he admitted that he was unable to tell the exact moment when this would occur. To this end it was necessary for seekers of the Kingdom to dispose of their possessions and to cut their ties of kinship. As Luke pointed out (Luke 10: 11), the disciples 'supposed that the Kingdom of God was immediately to appear', and indeed James and John had the effrontery to request that they might 'sit, one on thy right hand, and one on thy left hand, in thy glory' (Mark 10: 37). Jesus's insistence on the imminent arrival of the Kingdom was to prove an embarrassment to the later Church when it became clear that this had not occurred, and its leaders had to devise another explanation. In Professor Vermes's words: 'the date of the Second Coming was adjourned *sine die*, and the notion of the Kingdom metamorphosed into that of the church.[18] In brief, both the *Parousia* doctrine and the identification of the Kingdom of God with the church are later correctives added to the authentic teaching of Jesus'.[19]

According to A. N. Wilson, surveying Jesus's life from an historian's point of view, 'when we have looked at the evidence, it will seem at the very least highly unlikely that Jesus, a Galilean exorcist executed in *circa* the year 30, probably for sedition, had any ambitions to found a world religion. All the indications are that this charismatic leader and preacher limited his sphere of activities to rural and exclusively Jewish regions. For example, though he was probably born, and certainly operated, near the great Hellenistic city of Sepphoris in Galilee, we hear no mention of that city in the Gospels. We read only of a Jesus who chose to move about among the fishing-towns and agricultural communities of Galilee – hotbeds of political dissent against Rome, according to Josephus. ... Jesus would seem to have shared the views of many Jewish contemporaries that the world was about to come to an end and that God would redeem Israel and bring to pass a new era in which the rule of the Gentiles would be smitten and driven away. Since the end of ages was at hand, and the gospels record Jesus as predicting as much, it is hard to imagine why Jesus would have entertained the quite incompatible belief that several thousand years of human history stretched ahead in which a new 'religion' would be necessary. As far as the historical Jesus was concerned, it seems overwhelmingly likely that he did not think there was any future for the human race at all...'[20]

Thus in Professor Graham Stanton's words: 'Jesus certainly did not intend to found a new religion... Jesus believed that he had been sent by God as a prophet to declare authoritatively the will of God for his people'.[21]

Jesus's last days have been described by the evangelists Matthew, Mark, Luke and John. But as Professor Vermes warns us: 'the Synoptic Gospels in their present form consist of an adjusted, supplemented and corrected version, a thoroughly revised edition, of the original message of Jesus. The words, idioms and images which a first-century AD Galilean master addressed to his compatriots and co-religionists were rephrased in the Gospels to suit a totally different public, imbued with Hellenistic thought, in the Greek-speaking part of the Roman empire'.[22] Indeed, it is clear that biblical scholars cannot avoid the conclusion that the orthodox leaders of the early Christian Church *manipulated* (and I use the word deliberately) the texts of the apostolic writings, notably the Gospels, to suit their own doctrinal agenda.

The Jewish festival of Passover, celebrating God's deliverance of his people from Egyptian slavery, was the major event in the religious year, and every adult Jew was expected to celebrate Passover in Jerusalem. It is well known that Jesus and his twelve disciples went up to Jerusalem for this purpose.[23] But there is considerable confusion between the gospel writers and early Christians as to the details of their visit, which culminated in Jesus's arrest and subsequent crucifixion. Professor Geza Vermes has now examined all the surviving records in great detail and an interesting picture emerges for the first time. According to the chronology given by St John the arrest and crucifixion of Jesus took place *the day before Passover*, and this would have prevented him from partaking in a conventional paschal dinner that evening. And John's Gospel contains no report of a Passover meal shared by Jesus and his apostles. So the so-called 'Last Supper', if indeed it took place at all (and was not a carefully devised story created after the crucifixion by the early Church authorities), could only have been *not* a Jewish *seder* (or Passover) supper held on the eve of Passover, but rather a private communal meal which Jesus held with his twelve disciples on Wednesday, 14 Nisan, the day *before* the Jews conventionally celebrated the Passover.[24] Jesus is nevertheless reported as instructing his disciples to obtain and prepare the food required by Jewish religious tradition for the celebration of the *seder* meal. The main dish at a *seder* meal would have been roast lamb, accompanied by unleavened bread, and four cups of wine would have been ritually blessed and drunk.

What precisely happened at this so-called 'Last Supper'? The Synoptic evangelists report what has always been understood to be the institution of the 'Eucharist' – a commemoration of this 'Last Supper' (Mark 14: 12–21; Matthew 26: 17–25; Luke 22: 7–14, 21–3), but do not agree on the detail of the ceremony.[25] Thus neither Mark nor Matthew asserts that Jesus, after blessing the wine, ordered a continuous repetition of the ritual (i.e. a rite to be observed by his followers in perpetuity), yet Luke adds: 'This do in remembrance of me' (Luke 22: 19). In this statement Luke appears to be following St Paul who, in his first letter to the Corinthians (1 Corinthians 11: 24–5), written some fifteen to forty-five years prior to the Gospels, expressly claims that Jesus ordered the repetition of the ritual after both the bread and the cup – specifically intended to serve as a reminder of his death 'until he comes' (i.e. until the day of the *Parousia*, which Christians expected daily). Thus it is evident that at the time of Paul's letter the institution of the Eucharist was already an established custom in Corinth but was not being observed correctly. The 'eucharistic' words, or words of blessing, were pronounced over the cup 'after supper' (1 Corinthians 11: 25), which copies the customary benediction after the fourth and final cup of wine of the traditional *seder*.[26] Paul states that he had learnt of the Last Supper explicitly and expressly from Jesus himself by revelation: 'For I have received of the Lord that which also I delivered to you' (1 Corinthians 11: 23). Thus Professor Vermes concludes: 'it would be reasonable to assume that the eucharistic interpretation of what seems to have been the ordinary and repeated communal meal of the church comes from Paul, who is certainly the earliest witness of it. It would then follow that the later evidence of Mark, Matthew and Luke is likely to bear the mark of the influence of Paul… Therefore there are good reasons to consider Paul as the primary source of the Paschal interpretation of the institution of the Eucharist, a ritual which was to be reiterated 'in remembrance' of Jesus.[27] Indeed, Hyam Maccoby is in no doubt that Paul's declaration in his letter to the Corinthians makes it abundantly clear that '*Paul himself was the inventor and creator of the Eucharist*, both as an idea and as a Church institution'.[28] But he is equally clear that the ideas underlying the proposed sacrament – that of worshippers supposedly eating the body of Jesus and drinking his blood (as if he were a divine god) would have been repugnant to Jesus as a Jew. To contemporaries it would have been the equivalent of turning an ordinary Jewish meal into a pagan sacrament. It is also worth noting that Paul's term for the Eucharist was 'the Lord's Supper' (Greek *kuriakon deipnon*) which happens to be the same term used in contemporary mystery religions for their sacred meals. A coincidence? The early Church Fathers were embarrassed by this and soon substituted for it the appellation 'Eucharist' which has survived to this day. But the ritual still retained something of its primitive and magical association because it was believed that a miracle occurred every time it was celebrated by virtue of the belief that the sacrificial bread and wine were transformed into the *real* body and blood of Jesus.

Neither Mark nor Matthew mentioned Jesus's supposed command: 'This do in remembrance of me'. 'For them the dinner in question was a single, special event. It makes full sense without any sacrificial *Passover* colouring and without any link to the *death* of Jesus...'[29] It was, essentially, an *agape* meal, a communal meal where fellowship groups would meet 'to break bread' (meaning to 'initiate a meal in a ceremonious way: the host... makes a blessing over a loaf of bread and then breaks the loaf, giving a piece to each person present' – with no suggestion that it has any symbolic or mystical significance). It is not surprising however that Luke's account should have followed from that of St Paul, since Luke himself is supposed to have been one of Paul's followers. We should note that in some early codices of Luke's gospel there is a shorter account of the 'Last Supper' which omits verses 19b and 20, including Jesus's injunction 'this do in remembrance of me'. It would appear that Luke's (?) original version has therefore been expanded at a later date to accord more closely with Paul's account.[30] It is almost inconceivable that the evangelists Matthew and Mark should have omitted from their descriptions of the pre-*seder* meal any reference to the introduction of the Eucharist (which has since become the pre-eminent ritual of the Christian Church) *if Jesus had in fact issued any injunction to them all* on that occasion. Yet Luke (Luke 22: 19) alone adds – almost as an afterthought – the injunction 'This do in remembrance of me' after an earlier (and shorter) version of his account does not in fact mention it. In Professor Vermes's view: 'The variations in recording a saying of such crucial importance for the Christian church are indicative of a process of re-wording and re-editing. This is all the easier to understand if it is accepted that the Passover supper tradition is devoid of any historical basis'.[31] While it is impossible to judge the veracity of the biblical accounts of the 'Last Supper', it is hardly surprising that 'there is general consensus among New Testament interpreters that the narrative of the Last Supper, with its paucity of concrete details, was first and foremost written as a record of what the early church understood from the outset as the institution of a significant religious ritual, that of the Eucharist'.[32] Professor Vermes also makes the important point that 'all three evangelists refer to Jesus's vow of abstention from wine until the coming of the kingdom of God... with the implied meaning that he was not foreseeing his imminent death but was looking forward to the forthcoming completion of his divinely entrusted mission, the ushering in of God's everlasting reign'.[33] He goes on to say: 'It he had been aware of his impending demise, such a vow of abstemiousness would have been empty of meaning'[34] – indeed a gross deception of his disciples, *and in all the circumstances he considers that the so-called 'Last Supper' did* not *'contain the institution of the Eucharist'*.[35]

That this is the correct interpretation of the evidence is demonstrated by the following argument. If Jesus had himself instituted the Eucharist as a perpetual ritual, one would have expected that *all* his followers would have observed it – especially those present at the 'Last Supper'. Yet it is a fact that 'the Eucharist ceremony was not practised by Jesus's followers in Jerusalem, who were led by the disciples of Jesus himself, who would surely have known whether Jesus had given them this new foundation rite'.[36] In other words, the 'Jerusalem Church' did not observe it, but only those churches that had come under the influence of Paul. It was therefore Paul's creation – derived from a mystery religion – which was later 'incorporated as historical fact into the Gospels, in the accounts given there of the Last Supper, and thus has been accepted as historical fact...'[37]

Significantly, the *Didache* (see Section (c) below), dating from the latter half of the first century and containing a teaching manual for an early Christian community, makes no mention whatsoever of the 'Last Supper' ritual foretelling the death of Jesus and instituting a memorial of that event. It must therefore be concluded that the supposed institution of the Eucharist by Jesus related apparently only by Paul and later copied by his follower Luke (but not by the other evangelists), *must have been a later interpolation in the knowledge of Jesus's subsequent death.*[38] This interpolation must have occurred at an early date since it had become an accepted belief by the time of the 'Apostolic Fathers'.[39] After Justin Martyr (*c.*150) had described the ritual of the Christian Eucharist he made the highly significant statement: 'This very thing the evil demons imitated in the mysteries of Mithras, and commanded to be done. For, as you know, or can discover, bread and a cup of water are set out in the rites of initiation with the repetition of certain words'.[40] Thus Mithraic rites – widely practised years before Jesus was born – may well have caused the early Church authorities to adopt a comparable form of ritual which had become standard practice for Christians by the time of the Apostolic Fathers. Percy Gardner noted (1893) that Paul's assertion that he had received a supernatural revelation about the institution of the Lord's Supper 'appears to have taken place at Corinth… and almost within walking distance was Eleusis, the seat of the venerable Mysteries of Demeter… And the central point of the ceremonial at Eleusis appears to have been a sacred repast, of which the initiated partook, and by means of which they had communion with the gods. It is precisely in the manner of St Paul that he should long to turn a pagan ceremony to Christian use'.[41] *So either the Eleusinian or Mithraic pagan rites could be the prototype for the Christian Eucharist as devised – almost certainly – by Paul,* who claimed (1 Corinthians 11: 23) to have received it from Jesus by 'revelation' – a highly dubious reason (as historians and scholars are only too well aware) for believing it!

It may be noted that John, in his account of the Last Supper, does not mention the supposed Eucharistic instruction, but refers to the 'Eucharist idea' when Jesus was preaching in the synagogue at Capernaum on a different occasion. Here he declared: 'Except he eat the flesh of the Son of man, and drink his blood, ye have no life in you. Whoso eateth my flesh, drinketh my blood, hath eternal life' (John 6: 53–4). His disciples were baffled by such cryptic language ('From that time many of his disciples went back, and walked no more with him' (John 6: 66)).

In fact, the idea of the Eucharist has a long pagan ancestry. The practice of eating bread sacramentally as the body of a god was a well-known pagan practice. It derived originally from simple homeopathic magic whereby primitive man believed he could acquire the divine properties of the god concerned. It was, for example, a practice recorded of the Aztecs in Mexico who 'believed that by consecrating bread their priests could turn it into the very body of their god, so that all who thereupon partook of the consecrated bread entered into a mystic communion with the deity by receiving a portion of his divine substance into themselves.[42] This of course amounted to a belief in the doctrine of transubstantiation and it was also a recorded practice amongst the Aryans of ancient India. Thus primitive man, no less than later followers of Jesus, readily understood that to preserve cohesion and unity it was essential to have some mystical act in which all followers could participate. Such was the invention of the Eucharist for Christian believers which a shrewd man like Paul was quick to promote. It is worth pointing out that Tarsus, Paul's home town, was a centre of Mithraic worship (which we have discussed in Chapter 3 (i)) and its initiates either drank the blood of a sacred bull or a chalice of wine as a symbolic representation of blood. This ceremony, known to the Romans as the *taurobolium*, was believed to confer on the initiates strength and eternal life. And Paul, from an early age, would have watched the annual commemorations of Mithras and vegetation gods such as Attis, Adonis and Osiris, and realised the possibilities for Jesus of Nazareth to be publicised as another 'divine' saviour.

Let us look a little further into Paul's activities at this time. When *c.*49–50 AD, Paul was staying at Corinth, where he established a 'church', and was the guest of his friends Priscilla and Aquila, he and his followers would no doubt have celebrated the Lord's Supper. According to A. N. Wilson 'There is not even the suggestion by Paul that this tradition derives from anyone who was actually with Jesus on the night before he died. And the idea that a pious Jew such as Jesus would have spent his last evening on earth asking his disciples to drink a cup of blood, even symbolically, is unthinkable. It is possible that when the Jewish followers of the Way met together, they broke bread in remembrance of Jesus; it is even possible that his Last Supper with his disciples was a Passover meal. But it took the genius of Paul to put all these facts together and to focus religious attention on the Blessed Sacrament'.[43] Wilson continues: 'Without Paul, what would the Christian Eucharist have been? As far as we can judge from Acts, it was not practised at all by the Jerusalem 'church'. Christianity without it is hard to imagine... The pious will always link it with the Last Supper, and thereby enter into Paul's understanding of the sacrificial nature of the death of Jesus. Paul's invention of the Christian Eucharist, as an addition to the 'agape meal' or love-feast practised by all Christians, is of a piece with his understanding of the sacrificial nature of Christ's death, which he saw in the same light that the followers of Mithras saw the death of the sacrificial bull. This would have had a powerful appeal to the pagans of Corinth... But who can deny that the existence of the Eucharist, the Mass, the Lord's Supper has been of stupendous imaginative importance in the history of civilisation? ... For even if you can believe that Jesus 'instituted the Eucharist' in any meaningful sense of that phrase, it is hard to see how the Gentiles could ever have heard of it, given the intransigent attitude of Jesus's Jewish followers and friends – the Peter church'.[44]

We may note that the old pagan cults arose in essentially agricultural communities, and the appeasement of their gods ensured the well-being of their crops, the arrival of the rains and other necessities of life. They were then essentially vegetation gods. One of the Roman state religions was that of Cybele, 'Mother of the Gods', and her consort Attis. At the spring festival of Cybele at Rome on 22 March a pine tree was brought into the sanctuary of the god, an effigy (probably symbolising Attis) was tied to the tree and then 'mourned over and buried in a sepulchre. But when night had fallen a light shone in the darkness, the tomb was opened, the god had risen from the dead, and this was hailed by his disciples as a promise that they too would issue triumphant from the corruption of the grave'.[45] The Christian writer Firmicius Maternus 'who was himself an initiate of the mysteries of Attis or Adonis, has left an account of the ritual which makes it clear that the deliverance of the god brings immortality to the initiates'.[46] Christianity, it should be emphasised, originated in an environment where public and private ceremonies of this kind were a familiar part of everyday life. Common amongst these cults were various practices such as an initiation, including baptism, a sacrifice of some kind and subsequent common meal. Thus we may readily recognise the origin of the Christian Baptism and Eucharist.

Interestingly, the Dominican Father Timothy Radcliffe maintains that 'the links between sexuality and the Eucharist are deep in our tradition. The First Letter of St Paul to the Corinthians is principally about the Eucharist and sexuality... we can only understand our sexuality in the light of the Eucharist...'[47] Presumably, being a Roman Catholic Radcliffe embraces the doctrine of Transubstantiation – where it is believed that, after the Elements have been consecrated by a priest, the recipients partake of the *very body and blood of Christ*, and therefore for Catholics this sacrament may be (and perhaps is) regarded as a most intimate, erotic and orgasmic spiritual experience (especially for nuns).[48] In the Reformed Churches (such as the Church of England) the rejection of the doctrine of Transubstantiation converts the Eucharist into a simple, a-sexual memorial service for Jesus acted out by those of the community of faith.

Luther believed that the sacraments were meant to reassure Christians that they were truly members of the body of Christ and heirs to the Kingdom of God. In his treatise *The Blessed Secret of the Holy and True Body of Christ* (1519) Luther stated: 'To receive this sacrament in bread and wine then, is nothing else than to receive a sure sign of this fellowship and union with Christ and all the saints...' Zwingli, too, felt that the purpose of the sacraments is to demonstrate that an individual belongs to the community of faith, and the Eucharist 'represents a continuing public declaration of loyalty to the Church'. In Professor McGrath's words: 'The Eucharist is thus a memorial of the historical event leading to the establishment of the Christian church, and a public demonstration of the believer's allegiance to that church and its members'.[49] The emphasis, then, is that the Eucharist is a *memorial service* and has no supernatural connotation such as is assumed in the Roman Catholic doctrine of transubstantiation, which harks back to pagan practices of 'communion' with a primitive deity. As we have already observed (page 33-4), the early Church authorities were extremely astute in 'taking over' the dates of pagan festivals as a means of gaining recruits to their new religion. The copying of a contemporary pagan 'communion' ritual (probably by St Paul) was a further means of attracting followers such as Firmicius Maternus to the new Christian 'religion'. The subsequent importance of the Eucharistic ritual, the question of the 'Real Presence' of Jesus Christ and the doctrine of Transubstantiation (positively defined at the Council of Trent in 1551) are fully discussed by Professor McGrath in his definitive work on Christian theology.[50]

In this day and age, only if you are a person who believes in miracles – and indeed in *repeated* miracles – will you be able to believe in Transubstantiation. Most people will probably agree with John Wycliffe who described the doctrine as 'a deceit and a blasphemous folly', or, more charitably, as superstitious idolatry.

Gerald Priestland recalls that 'round the table of a Sabbath, Jewish families regularly celebrate what might appear to be a Eucharist, with the sharing of unleavened bread and wine. 'But it is not a sacrament', insisted Rabbi Gryn, 'the wine continues to be wine and the bread remains bread. And the message of our Passover meal is really about human liberty'. My Jewish friends continued to disbelieve that Jesus the Jew could have meant what Christians say He meant. Rabbi Blue insisted: 'The whole force of Judaism is to disassociate itself from mythological elements: they were the bane of the old Hebrew life. The idea of eating one's God and using blood in relation to wine would be enough to make a Jew faint, if he took the idea seriously'.[51] We may note that neither the Quakers nor members of the Salvation Army, with their respective exemplary records of charitable social service, see any need for the sacrament of the Eucharist. The reason why the Quakers abandoned the sacrament was that in their view, by the mid-seventeenth century, the sacraments had become 'an empty performance not reflecting any integrity of conduct'. They similarly abandoned the church sacraments of baptism, confirmation and marriage.[52]

Of the events leading up to Jesus's crucifixion we may note the evangelists' accounts of Jesus's conversation with his disciples on the road to Jerusalem when he told them 'Behold, we go up to Jerusalem; and the Son of man shall be delivered unto the chief priests, and unto the scribes; and they shall condemn him to death, and shall deliver him to the Gentiles: and they shall mock him, and shall scourge him, and shall spit upon him, and shall kill him: and the third day he shall rise again' (Mark 10: 33–4). This and similar passages by the other evangelists appear to emphasise Jesus's wish to 'describe the cross and the resurrection as divinely predestined events foretold by the prophets and by Jesus himself, even though this made the uncomprehending apostles, who all abandoned and betrayed their Master at the moment of his ordeal, look silly, cowardly and undignified'. These passages – e.g. Mark 10: 33–4 – are therefore considered by scholars to be later interpolations.[53] It is clear that these predictions of his crucifixion and resurrection had no effect on Jesus's disciples, as is evident from the fact that the apostles all ran away and Peter even denied that he had known Jesus. As Professor Vermes concludes: 'The whole series of forewarnings has the appearance of *vaticinium ex eventu*, a 'prophecy after the fact', introduced by the evangelists with later Christian generations in view. Members of the primitive church had to be persuaded that the totally unexpected and disconcerting events of the crucifixion and resurrection were in fact foreordained by God and were the fulfilment of the predictions made by Jesus and by the earlier prophetic visionaries of the Jewish people'.[54] The accounts of Jesus's passion are clearly adapted from Isaiah and from Psalm 22. Thus 'one must conclude that the predictions by Jesus of his death and resurrection and his reference to biblical prophecies about his suffering and glorification are inauthentic'.[55] Here, then, is another example of how subsequent interpolations appear to have been made to New Testament narratives in an attempt to demonstrate that the events described were prefigured in the Bible and consequently foreordained by God.

Having been accepted as a popular charismatic teacher in Galilee and in Jerusalem hailed as 'the prophet from Nazareth in Galilee', Jesus nevertheless upset the religious authorities in Jerusalem when he indignantly overturned the merchants' tables in the Temple and created something of an uproar. His Galilean temper had clearly got the better of him! The authorities feared lest this disorder might incite a riot and decided to hand Jesus over to the Roman authority as a potential revolutionary leader because of his popularity with the crowds. Jesus's trial before the Roman Pontius Pilate (the Prefect of Judaea) must have been on grounds of sedition, rather than blasphemy (which would have been tried in a Jewish court), and this suggests that Jesus was at least connected with the seditious group known as the 'Zealots' (of whom his disciple Simon was certainly a member) and the possibility that the two 'thieves' crucified with Jesus were in fact Zealots.[56] And it might be thought strange that Jesus's disciples in the Garden of Gethsemane were apparently armed. But Mark's Gospel, recounting these events, was written for *Roman* Christians, and he would clearly not have wished to associate Jesus overtly with any Jewish nationalist group during the then current war which led to the destruction of the Temple in Jerusalem by Titus in AD 70. This trial led swiftly to Jesus's death sentence by Pilate, whom we know from other sources to have been a cruel and ruthless administrator (although the Gospel sources try to portray him – no doubt for political reasons – as a *reasonable* man persuaded against his better judgement to pass a capital sentence on Jesus).

Later, after Jesus had been condemned to be crucified and had been on the cross for several hours he cried out 'Eloi, Eloi, lama sabachthani' – meaning 'My God, my God, why hast thou forsaken me?', which was the Aramaic of the opening of the Hebrew Psalm 22, and which Professor Vermes suggests signified 'the consternation of a man of faith at the sudden realisation that God would not come to his rescue, the exclamation is a piously inspired prayer of disbelief'.[57] It is also, significantly, the only occasion that Jesus does not refer to God as 'Father', which points to a distinct coolness in their relationship. Furthermore, some of the bystanders misunderstood what he said, evidently did not identify his cry as a quotation from a well-known psalm, and believed he was calling on the miracle-working prophet Elijah to come and deliver him.[58] This well-known cry of Jesus was cited in support of the belief of some early Christians that Jesus had received his divine powers at the moment of his baptism by John, but that these were taken from him at his crucifixion when he returned to the status of a mere mortal (a belief held by some Gnostics, such as Cerinthus).

It is hardly surprising that in its early years Christianity borrowed heavily from Judaism. From Yom Kippur, the Jewish Day of Atonement, was taken the Christian concept of the death of Jesus as a sacrifice offered to God as payment for our sins, although as long ago as the eighteenth century H. S. Reimarus had observed that Jesus had never claimed in the Gospels that he had come to atone for the sins of mankind and that that idea could only be traced back to St Paul. Early Christians also made great play with the idea of Jesus as 'the lamb of God' whose blood washes away the sins of the world. Likewise the Jewish Passover embodies another sacrificial lamb whose blood was smeared on the doorposts of Jewish homes so as to avoid their destruction by the angel of death. The sacrificial lamb thereafter consumed by Jews at the annual Passover feast was the origin of the Christian belief that the shedding of Jesus's blood on the cross as 'the lamb of God' overcame the power of death for believers and led to St Paul's exclamation that 'Christ, our paschal lamb, has been sacrificed' (1 Corinthians 5: 7). The interpretation of Jesus's death 'has resulted in a fetish in Christianity connected with the saving blood of Jesus'. Protestants have delighted in being 'washed in the blood' and 'saved by the blood' of Jesus. Catholics are meant to believe that they are literally eating Jesus's flesh and drinking his blood. This cannibalistic ritual is hardly consistent with life in the twenty-first century!

After studying the Gospel narratives and early records of the period the following conclusions emerge:

1. Early Church authorities were obliged to revise Jesus's conception of the imminent arrival of the Kingdom of God. This, they said, was in fact synonymous with the establishment of the Church, but the 'reign of God' was

deferred until the 'coming again' of Jesus and the 'final judgement'

2. There are clear signs of the early Church authorities interpolating passages into the narratives of the evangelists *ex post facto* to give the appearance that Jesus –

  (i) had agreed that his message of salvation should be preached to the Gentiles as well as to the Jews

  (ii) had foretold the details of his death and resurrection

  (iii) had instituted the ritual of the Eucharist.

NOTES

[1] Thiede, 2004, 17–19

[2] Ibid., 15

[3] Ibid., 22–32

[4] See Professor Graham Stanton's scholarly exposition of recent research into the many problems concerning the four evangelists' portrait of Jesus.

[5] Kasser *et al.*, 2006, 117

[6] The remarkable story of its discovery and subsequent history is told in Kasser *et al.*, 2006.

[7] Radcliffe, 2005, 32

[8] Kasser *et al.*, 2006, 43

[9] Ibid., 103–4

[10] The definitive story of the Dead Sea Scrolls may be found in Professor Geza Vermes's book *The Complete Dead Sea Scrolls in English* (Penguin Books, Revised edn.), 2004.

[11] See the most interesting discussion on John the Baptist in Stanton, 2002, 178–189

[12] Vermes, 2004a, 380

[13] Vermes, 2008, 160 Note 1

[14] Wilson, 1998, 106–7

[15] Ibid., 185

[16] Vermes, 2004a, 404

[17] For a discussion of this point see Stanton, 2002, 203–217

[18] As Professor Vermes recalls: 'Latin Christian theology identified the arrival of the Kingdom of God with the establishment of the church. The Gospels themselves provide no basis for this idea which was first

fully formulated in the time of St Augustine (354–430) (Vermes, 2005, 341). In other words, it became established from the fifth century that the forecast 'arrival of the Kingdom of God' was synonymous with the establishment of the Church, while the realisation of the 'reign of God' was deferred until the 'coming again' of Jesus and the anticipated 'final judgement'

[19] Vermes, 2004a, 385

[20] Wilson, 1998, 17–18

[21] Stanton, 2002, 296

[22] Vermes, 2004a, 372. See also Wells, 1971, 56–122

[23] 'I have desired to eat *this Passover* with you' (Luke 22: 15)

[24] Thus Professor Vermes recounts that it is 'remarkable that the Gospel of John contains no report of a Passover meal shared by Jesus with his apostles. This is no doubt due to the fact that according to the Fourth Gospel the arrest and crucifixion of Jesus took place the day before the feast, and consequently there could not be any question of Jesus partaking in a real paschal dinner. Moreover, John specifies that the Jewish dignitaries who handed over Jesus to Pilate refused to enter his palace, the *praetorium*, so as to remain ritually clean so that they 'might eat the passover'' (see John 18: 28) (Vermes, 2004a, 302)

[25] The term 'Eucharist' originally referred to the prayers spoken at a meal, and only later came to represent the whole sacramental celebration

[26] Vermes, 2004a, 303

[27] Ibid., 304–5

[28] Maccoby, 1986, 113

[29] Vermes, 2004a, 305–6

[30] For a discussion of the 'Last Supper' accounts in the gospels see Stanton, 2002, 274–9

[31] Vermes, 2004a, 306

[32] Ibid., 302

[33] Vermes, 2005, 37

[34] Ibid., 122

[35] Ibid., 115. Indeed, all Jesus did may be seen as reciting the customary Jewish blessings over the bread and wine (Vermes, 2004a, 306)

[36] Maccoby, 1986, 117

[37] Ibid., 118

[38] And with corresponding interpolations such as the words 'before I suffer' in Luke 22: 15 and the vivid predictions in Mark 10: 33–4

[39] Thus Justin Martyr, describing Christian worship in *c*.150, stated that: 'the Apostles in the memoirs made by them, which are called gospels, have thus narrated that the command was given; that Jesus took bread, gave thanks, and said 'This do ye in remembrance of me; this is my body'. And he took the cup likewise and said 'This is my blood', and gave it to them alone' (Bettenson, 1946, 94). Justin's statement is of course incorrect, since only *one* apostle, Luke, mentions Jesus's supposed 'command'

[40] Bettenson, 1946, 94

[41] Quoted in Wells, 1971, 272

[42] Frazer, 1949, 490

[43] Wilson, 1998, 165

[44] Ibid., 166

[45] Wells, 1971, 235

[46] Ibid. For pagan influence on Christianity see Professor J Leipoldt's *Von den Mysterien zur Kirche* (Hamburg, 1962)

[47] Radcliffe, 2005, 94

[48] One has in mind the desperate craving of the late Mother Teresa for union with Jesus. She was described as a woman 'totally, passionately, madly in love with Jesus' *(Mother Teresa: Come Be My Light)* (ed. Kolodiejchuk, B, 2007, 259)

[49] McGrath, 2007a, 428–430

[50] Ibid., 431–440

[51] Priestland, 1981, 175

[52] Ibid., 171

[53] Vermes, 2004a, 248; 2008, 81–6. Professor Vermes points out: 'As is well known, the chief method adopted by the spokesmen of the early church in order to prove their message about the Messiahship of Jesus was to show that his story was prefigured in the Bible and consequently was foreordained by God. The teachers of the Dead Sea sect used the same technique... In retrospect, a similar fulfilment exegesis was inserted by the evangelists into the Gospel narrative regarding Jesus's suffering, death and resurrection' (Vermes, 2004a, 387)

[54] Vermes, 2004a, 251

[55] Vermes, 2008, 86

[56] See Brandon, 1967

[57] Vermes, 2005, 122

[58] Ibid., 75

(c)   The death of Jesus and its aftermath

After Jesus had been taken down from the cross his entombment by Joseph of Arimathea and Nicodemus (only mentioned by John) is related in broadly similar terms by all the evangelists, except that Matthew adds ('no doubt with the hindsight of later Christian polemical considerations') that 'the Jewish leaders, fearful that the disciples of Jesus might steal his body and stage a fake fulfilment of his predicted resurrection from the dead, asked Pilate to keep the tomb under military observation.[1] A guard was provided – under the command of a centurion named Petronius, and a stone sealed with seven seals was put in position blocking the entrance.[2] Professor Vermes has deduced that Jesus, crucified on the eve of Passover (14 Nisan), died on Friday, 7 April, AD 30.

The Gospel narratives of Jesus's resurrection may or may not be taken at their face value.[3] Could it be that Jesus did not in fact 'rise from the dead' after three days and 'ascend into Heaven' (Mark 16: 6, 19)? The Jewish custom was for the dead to be buried initially in a tomb, and when – after some six months to two years – the flesh had decomposed completely the bones would be gathered together and buried finally in an ossuary (or bone casket). Since the flesh was symbolic of the sinfulness of the old body, it was only the dry bones which could therefore look forward to bodily resurrection at the end of time. Except for the Sadducees this was believed by all other Jews, and was based on the prophecies of Ezekiel (Ezekiel 37) and Isaiah (Isaiah 26: 19). Ossuaries were inscribed with the name of the dead person and were often artistically decorated with various designs. Thus Jesus could have been provisionally buried in a new family tomb belonging to Joseph of Arimathea, with the expectation of his bones later being placed in an ossuary inscribed (probably) with the name 'Jesus the Messiah'.[4] But – according to Biblical sources – the body apparently disappeared from the tomb within only a short time of its having been placed there in accordance with normal Jewish burial custom.

In 1980 a first century AD tomb discovered on a building site three miles from Temple Mount, Jerusalem, containing the ossuaries of a family, revealed an ossuary marked 'Jesus son of Joseph' and others marked 'Mary' and various names similar to those of members of Jesus's family. However, experts were unable to identify the Jesus of the ossuary because Jesus was at the time a very common name, as was Joseph, and there were no clear marks on the bones of this Jesus showing that he had been crucified. There was also an ossuary inscribed to 'Judah son of Jesus' which revived the old theory that Jesus was married to Mary Magdalene and that this Judah was their son. However, this is all speculation, and so far no irrefutable evidence has emerged identifying the physical remains of Jesus. If, however, an ossuary were to be discovered in the future marked with Jesus's name and showing incontrovertible evidence of crucifixion, this would result in a seismic shock for the Vatican, but for the many Christians who have doubted the well-rehearsed claims of the 'resurrection' it would strengthen their conviction (shared by millions of Muslims and members of other faiths) that Jesus was a mortal prophet who died and was buried like the rest of us.

There has been endless speculation about Jesus's resurrection. Clearly his supporters had to be convinced that he really had risen from the dead so that 'the scriptures would be fulfilled' (Luke 24: 44) (an endless Jewish refrain whenever Jesus is involved!). Furthermore, St Paul had made it clear in his epistle to the Corinthians that if Jesus had *not* risen from the dead their faith would be in vain:

'But if there is no resurrection of the dead, then Christ has not been raised; and if Christ has not been raised, then our preaching is in vain and your faith is in vain... If for this life only we have hoped then we are of all men most to be pitied.'

(1 Corinthians 15: 13–20)

We must remember, too, that to 'rise on the third day' was a conventional custom for contemporary pagan deities such as Attis (consort of Cybele, 'Mother of the Gods'), Adonis and other gods with whom contemporaries of Jesus would be familiar.[5] Jesus must clearly be no different if he was to be regarded as divine. But some of the men of Athens to whom Paul preached before the court of the Areopagus plainly did not believe him – 'And when they heard of the resurrection of the dead, some mocked...' (Acts 17: 32).

Whether he rose or not, and whether the evangelists' narratives of his meeting his disciples 'in the flesh' after his death are factually correct, are matters which are unlikely ever to be established with certainty. The early Church authorities maintained that Jesus had been raised from the dead on the basis of a 'vision' of St Peter (Jesus whom 'God raised up the third day, and showed him openly; Not to all the people, but unto witnesses chosen before of God, even to us, who did eat and drink with him after he rose from the dead' (Acts 10: 40–1)). But as Arnold Toynbee pointed out 'The scriptural accounts of Jesus's appearances after his resurrection are ambivalent. On the one hand, the physical reality of his reanimated body is emphasised. He eats food; he shows his wounds. On the other hand, he is elusive, like a ghost. He passes through doors that are closed and locked; he suddenly appears and suddenly vanishes. Though his reanimated body is corporeal, this body is not subject to those laws of physical nature that govern the movements of ordinary bodies in time-space'.[6] It may be significant that the post-resurrection appearances of Jesus occur only in the later gospels (e.g. John 20: 11–31).

All these resurrection stories could well be an interpolation (as with much else) by later 'authorities' to ensure that the story was seen to be 'in accordance with the scriptures'. And although Paul later declared that Jesus 'died in accordance with the scriptures' (1 Corinthians 15: 3), Professor Vermes points out that 'he did not give this as a message of the Lord, nor did he quote chapter and verse from the holy books to substantiate his claim'.[7] 'The greatest difficulty which in the subsequent decades faced the apostles and early Christian missionaries was how to explain to Jews and to Gentiles the death and resurrection of Jesus. It should be recalled that neither the death nor the resurrection of the Messiah formed part of the beliefs and expectations of the Jews in the first century AD. So the apostles and the evangelists endeavoured to account for this death and resurrection and make them plausible by asserting that Jesus had had full advance knowledge of them; that he conveyed this knowledge to his disciples, and that the subsequent events simply fulfilled his own predictions. As is well known, the chief method adopted by the spokesmen of the early church in order to prove their message about the Messiahship of Jesus was to show that his story was prefigured in the Bible and consequently was foreordained by God.[8] But none of the allusions to the fulfilment of the scriptures 'cites the biblical passages in which the death and resurrection of Jesus are supposed to have found their realization. Neither does Paul reproduce any quotation from the Holy Books to support the claim that 'Christ died for our sins *in accordance with the scriptures* (1 Corinthians 15: 3)".[9] And the parallel claim that Jesus had died for the 'sins of the whole world' was probably regarded as bizarre! As Professor Vermes concludes: 'In the light of the evidence cited and examined, the most likely verdict is that the apostles knew nothing in advance about the final stages of Jesus' career. In fact, *'Eloi, Eloi, lama sabachthani'* ('My God, my God, why has thou forsaken me?') understood in its obvious sense... suggests that until the moment of the crucifixion Jesus himself did not expect any interruption of his mission, and looked forward to participating himself in the ceremony of inauguration of the Kingdom of God.'[10] And in none of his parables does Jesus allude to his forthcoming resurrection.

The whole subject of the resurrection has given rise to continuous speculation amongst scholars and theologians. As Professor Wells points out: '...the only evidence for Jesus' return to life is from the contradictory gospel narratives which are confirmed neither by Paul nor by archaeology'.[11] P. W. Schmiedel observed that 'we cannot avoid the conclusion from the contradictions between the Gospels that *the writers of them were far removed from the event* they describe'.[12] Professor Vermes concludes that: 'When every argument has been considered and weighed, the only conclusion acceptable to the historian must be that the opinions of the orthodox, the liberal sympathizer and the critical agnostic alike – and even perhaps of the disciples themselves – are simply interpretations of the one disconcerting fact: namely that the women who set out to pay their last respects to Jesus found to their consternation, not a body, but an empty tomb'.[13] In other words, the *interpretation* of the accepted fact of the empty tomb – i.e. the only *plausible* explanation – is that Jesus had risen from the dead. Yet 'the most significant peculiarity of the resurrection stories is that they nowhere suggest that the rising of Jesus from the dead was expected by anyone', and that many details of the gospel accounts are quite irreconcilable or even contradictory.[14] Above all 'there are no *independent* witnesses from outside the circle of the followers of Jesus to corroborate these accounts.[15] And it is surely significant that nowhere in his correspondence does Paul refer to the burial of Jesus or to the discovery of the empty tomb or to the disappearance of Jesus's body. Thus Schmiedel notes that Paul is silent about such gospel details as the empty tomb, even though he had visited Jerusalem and would naturally have been anxious to glean all available evidence for the actuality of the resurrection, on which for him the whole truth of Christianity depended.[16] What was the reason for this quite extraordinary silence? Were these matters upon which there was some continuing sensitivity on the part of the apostles? Hardly surprisingly Professor Vermes is led to the conclusion that 'not even a credulous non-believer is likely to be persuaded by the various reports of his resurrection; they convince only the already converted. The same must be said about the visions. None of them satisfies the minimum requirements of a legal or scientific inquiry'.[17]

Moreover, a number of other scholars have residual doubts about the resurrection stories. They emphasise again that there is little if any independent objective evidence for the gospel accounts of the resurrection, and there are obvious inconsistencies between the gospel narratives.[18] Furthermore, it is entirely plausible that Jesus's body was in fact stolen or hidden by the disciples and that the Jewish authorities had insufficient evidence to publicise an objective refutation for lack of independent witnesses. Was there in fact any 'truth' in the story about the bribery of the guards and that Jesus's disciples did in fact steal his body from the tomb: 'this saying was spread abroad among the Jews, and continueth until this day' (Matthew 28: 15). Finally, scholars contend that 'the burden of proof clearly lies with those who believe Jesus to have risen from the dead' but the historical evidence is weak and 'there simply exists no valid historical basis for maintaining that the resurrection of Jesus is an established fact (or even a reasonable probability)'.[19] Bishop N. T. Wright, in his magisterial work *The Resurrection of the Son of God* (2003), has exhaustively examined the evidence for the empty tomb and the various meetings between mortal people and the 'resurrected' Jesus, as well as the texts of numerous non-canonical early Christian writings on the facts and interpretation of the resurrection. He concludes that 'the actual bodily resurrection of Jesus (not a mere resurrection, but a transforming revivification) clearly provides a *sufficient* condition of the tomb being empty and the "meetings" taking place. Nobody is likely to doubt that. Once grant that Jesus really was raised, and all the pieces of the historical jigsaw puzzle of early Christianity fall into place. My claim is stronger: that the bodily resurrection of Jesus provides a *necessary* condition for these things; in other words, that no other explanation could or would do. All the efforts to find alternative explanations fail, and they were bound to do so... Many will challenge this conclusion, for many different reasons. I do not claim that it constitutes a "proof" of the resurrection in terms of some neutral standpoint. It is, rather, a historical challenge to other explanations, other world views...' The challenge is: 'what alternative account can be offered which will explain the data just as well...?'[20] One point of emerging interest is that Dr Wright – after studying the writings of the Apostolic Fathers – says that in general they 'confirm that, for the vast majority of early Christians known to us, "resurrection" was the ultimate Christian hope, and was meant in a definite bodily sense; that this entailed some kind of intermediate state, itself glorious and blissful; and that the future resurrection was dependent on, and modelled on, that of Jesus himself'.[21]

Yet the fact remains that the Resurrection is still an unproven historical event, and the markedly inconsistent gospel reports of Jesus's physical appearances – that of 'a physically resuscitated, formerly dead body' – did not apparently appear until the ninth decade AD. Bishop John Shelby Spong is quite emphatic in his view:

'I do not believe that the experience Christians celebrate at Easter was the physical resurrection of the three-days-dead body of Jesus, nor do I believe that anyone literally talked with Jesus after the resurrection moment, gave him food, touched his resurrected flesh, or walked in any physical manner with his risen body. I find it interesting that all of the narratives that tell of such encounters occur only in the later gospels. I do not believe that Jesus's resurrection was marked in a literal way by an earthquake, an angelic pronouncement, or an empty tomb. I regard these things too as the legendary traditions of a maturing religious system'.[22]

As Professor Vermes says in his recent book *The Resurrection* (2008) the Resurrection is an unparalleled phenomenon in history: 'Two types of extreme reactions are possible: faith, or disbelief'. For 'faith wrapped in scholarship' he refers to Bishop Wright's book, but he aims in his own book 'to investigate what the authors of the New Testament actually say in their writings, and not what interpretative Church tradition attributed to them... Its aim is the construction of a tenable hypothesis, but ultimately it will be up to the readers to make up their minds'.[23]

In Professor Vermes's view there are four ways of explaining away the resurrection conundrum: 'one: the body was not found by the women because the guardian of the cemetery used the first opportunity to move the body of Jesus out of the grave that had been prepared for someone else. Two: in the darkness the women lost their way and went to a wrong tomb. Three: the Apostles stole the corpse as was alleged by the priestly leaders. (But since nobody expected Jesus to rise again, why should anybody fake his resurrection?). Four: Jesus was buried alive and survived'. Vermes considers that there is one phenomenon which may lead us out of the mass of conflicting and contradictory evidence. This was the effect on the Apostles themselves – 'the metamorphosis achieved by the inward experience of the Spirit'. The recollections of his teaching had a transforming effect: they felt their master was still alive in some spiritual dimension and in touch with them. For them *this* was the real 'resurrection'.[24]

As has been pointed out by Willy Obrist:

'In Church circles it is still like breaking taboo when one speaks of the Christian myths, although the historico-critical study of the Bible has shown how they have acquired their shape: how the belief that Jesus had been raised was based on a vision (!) on the part of Peter, how it was only after his death that the idea that Jesus was the Messiah began to spread in the original Palestinian community, where the Messiah was still understood as a human being. This research also showed that the idea of the Messiah

(Christos) as a heavenly being arose in the Jewish diaspora and only entered the Christian myth through the missionary activity of diaspora Jews; finally that the equation of this Christ (now seen as a heavenly being) with the Logos (an idea of Hellenistic provenance) as the consubstantial Son of the transcendent God was only formed in the womb of the Gentile-Christian communities. Comparative religious studies make it clear that this 'message about Jesus' was composed exclusively of mythological units such as occur in other cultures too: the consubstantial Son sent by the Father; the incarnation by virgin birth; the inconspicuous birth and wanderings of a divine being who brings mankind a new law and a new revelation; the element of suffering, death and resurrection, coupled with that of the redemptive, sacrificial death of the God, etc.'[25]

He goes on to relate how 'the evangelists went about historicising the Christian myth and projecting it on to the person of Jesus. Thus for example, 'Mark' created scenarios for the inherited corpus of words of Jesus, welding these together with stories which had come down separately, according to his own plan of space and time, into that 'Life of Jesus' which was regarded as a historical account for many generations; moreover, utterances of the Christian myth – most notably those of 'John' – have actually been put into the mouth of Jesus, to be subsequently believed as Jesus' own words. These issues are known to all enlightened theologians. They are careful to keep them quiet. In raising them here and 'calling a spade a spade' I am calling for truthfulness. For our aim is to find out what lies behind the rapid growth of indifference and how the Church ought to react'.[26] His words deserve to be studied.

The small Christian communities must have been traumatised by Jesus's death. Had all his missionary exertions and charismatic healing been a delusion? 'The greatest difficulty which in the subsequent decades faced the apostles and early Christian missionaries was how to explain to Jews and to Gentiles the death and resurrection of Jesus. It should be recalled that neither the death nor the resurrection of the Messiah formed part of the beliefs and expectations of the Jews in the first century AD. So the apostles and the evangelists endeavoured to account for this death and resurrection and make them acceptable by asserting that Jesus had full advance knowledge of them, that he conveyed this knowledge to his disciples, and that the subsequent events simply fulfilled his own predictions'.[27] Professor Vermes continues: 'In consequence Jesus' appropriate predictions were incorporated into the Gospel narratives. The interpolation was then accompanied by further adjustments to make the behaviour of the apostles look less perplexing'. The conclusion must be that 'the apostles knew nothing in advance about the final stages of Jesus' career'.[28] Jesus's followers nevertheless believed that he was still alive and present in some spiritual dimension: that the new transcendent, divine person was in fact identical with the historical figure of the past. But in what special dimension did he now exist? This has always been a difficult problem for the Church. Article IV of the 'Thirty-nine Articles' states: 'Christ did truly rise again from death, and take again his body, with flesh, bones, and all things appertaining to the perfection of Man's nature; wherewith he ascended into Heaven, and there sitteth, until he return to judge all Men at the last day'. This amounts to apotheosis, and it is clear from the Acts that from heaven he is believed to exercise his continued ministry, whether it be by sending the Holy Spirit to continue his mission or by appearing (for example) to Paul on the road to Damascus in a blinding flash. After the experience of Pentecost, when the Holy Spirit had descended on Jesus's disciples, it was the firm belief of his later followers that Jesus's spirit continued to reside within them and inspire them. This belief has filtered down through the centuries and ministers of the Church regard themselves as inheritors of God's Holy Spirit which inspires them in their task of evangelisation. As St Paul said to the Corinthians: 'Know ye not that ye are a temple of God, and that the Spirit of God dwelleth in you?' (1 Corinthians 3: 16). In the words of the late Professor C. F. D. Monk 'The Spirit implements in Christians the insights and the character and the activity belonging to Christ... To be filled with the Spirit is to be enabled to speak and act, as a witness to and representative of Christ... The Johannine farewell discourses speak of the Spirit as repeating the teaching and guidance of Jesus, and acting, like him, as a Paraclete or mediator between God and the disciples and as the disciples' representative in heaven'.[29] In

Professor John Hick's view: 'It is unlikely that Jesus came physically back to life after his crucifixion, that he walked round Galilee and Judea for forty days, and then ascended bodily into the sky; or (for this is likewise part of the Gospel story) that at the same time 'the tombs also were opened, and many bodies of the saints who had fallen asleep [i.e. had died] were raised, and coming out of the tombs after the resurrection they went into the holy city [Jerusalem] and appeared to many'. This part of the story is interesting because the writer does not hesitate to claim that the event was seen by many, in spite of the fact that if such an earth-shakingly extraordinary thing had indeed happened it would certainly have registered in the consciousness and records of the time. Yet it was possible for a Christian scribe, writing forty to fifty years after Jesus's death, to accept without question the miraculous stories that had developed within his community'.[30] Indeed, such stories – however incredulous – were to provide the foundation for the new religion of Christianity (the name, incidentally, first being used of the Jesus-movement in the Syrian city of Antioch) and entered into the canon of unquestioned belief. They make historians today deeply sceptical. It is however likely that the followers of Jesus were not so much concerned about the resurrection of their master as their belief in the imminent arrival of the *Parousia* (which they believed would happen in their lifetimes) which would ensure their personal entry into the kingdom of God after the final judgement.

The conventional story of Jesus's resurrection is perhaps the greatest of any recorded 'miracle'. Another such 'miracle' was the prophet Muhammad's 'ascension' in which he was given the opportunity to view all the features of heaven and hell. Miracles are clearly witnessed on great occasions of history. As the distinguished physicist and Anglican priest Canon John Polkinghorne argues: 'Miracles are not to be interpreted as divine acts against the laws of nature (for those laws are themselves expressions of God's will) but as more profound revelations of the character of the divine relationship to creation. To be credible, miracles must convey a deeper understanding than could have been obtained without them'.[31]

The twin pillars of the Christian faith are Jesus's birth and resurrection. We have discussed the former in Section 3 (a). Few people today should have any difficulty in believing in the existence of Jesus since it is well attested in historical records and remembered by the colourful and partly mythological story of Christmas. The resurrection is different, however, and most people – even Christians – find it hard to accept and are inclined to regard it as another myth contrived by the early Church authorities on the spurious grounds that 'the scripture had to be fulfilled', even if neither the death nor the resurrection of the Messiah formed part of the beliefs of the Jewish people. However, as Professor Wells pointed out: 'In antiquity, any number of saviour gods died that we might live, and rose again, some of them on the third day' (for example, both Osiris and Attis are held to have risen from the dead on the third day).[32] Even so, the revival of a corpse to non-Jewish people in the Graeco-Roman world was regarded 'at best a nice dream, but more generally as folly (*dementia*)'.[33] The Mesopotamian underworld, the Greek Hades and the Jewish Sheol were all regarded as the 'land of no return'. Thus when Paul preached 'the resurrection' in the Areopagus in Athens most of his philosophically educated listeners, Stoics and Epicureans, simply poked fun at his 'babbling' (Acts 17: 18, 32). Yet we should recall that by the time of the Hebrew Jeremiah the prophet could rejoice: 'Thy dead shall live, their corpses shall arise, O dwellers in the dust, awake and sing for joy' (Jeremiah 26: 19). The prophet Ezekiel had a mystical vision (Ezekiel 37: 1–14) of the dry bones of the people of Israel being revived by God, and Daniel had prophesied that '...at that time... many of them that sleep in the dust of the earth shall awake, some to everlasting life, and some to shame and everlasting contempt...' (Daniel 12: 1–2). As we have noted earlier, the idea of the resurrection of the dead and of a final judgement was ultimately derived from Zoroastrianism, and was later adopted by Jews, Christians and Muslims. Thus it had become part of orthodox Jewish belief by the time of Jesus and was common amongst the Pharisees (but not the Sadducees). And Paul was of course a Pharisee. 'But some will say, How are the dead raised? And with what manner of body do they come?' said Paul addressing the Corinthians. He answered:

200

'Behold, I tell you a mystery: we shall not all sleep, but we shall all be changed, in a moment, in the twinkling of an eye, at the last trump: for the trumpet shall sound, and the dead shall be raised incorruptible, and we shall be changed. For this corruptible must put on incorruption, and this mortal must put on immortality' (1 Corinthians 15: 51–53). So for Paul the resurrection of Jesus is to be seen as the beginning of the end of the world, with a general resurrection for everyone (just as well as unjust) occurring when Jesus returned to the earth in glory. But as Jesus had warned his disciples 'of that day or that hour knoweth no one, not even the angels in heaven... Take ye heed, watch and pray... watch therefore; for ye know not when the lord of the house cometh...' (Mark 13: 32–5). With the expectation of the Second Coming becoming less and less real over the centuries, Christians by the time of the Middle Ages had nonetheless continued to believe in a general resurrection and in a Last Judgement which had been vividly portrayed in the Book of Revelation and in numerous artistic representations in painting, sculptures and church frescos.

The interim conditions of the mortal between death and final judgement were the subject of much debate among early Christian theologians. As we have seen above, Dr Wright says that 'this entailed some kind of intermediate state, itself glorious and blissful'. This is hardly consistent with the important concept of Purgatory, prevalent among the Jews before the time of Jesus (see 2 Maccabees 12: 44–45) and thereafter forming part of Roman Catholic dogma to this day, to which the souls of the departed passed (unless they were of saintly character, when they were excused) so that they might undergo a process of purgation of their sins so as to purify them before going on to heaven. This was linked to the idea of 'two resurrections' – belief in the resurrection of the individual and the final general resurrection of all mankind (see Revelation 20: 6). For the former, a spell in Purgatory could be reduced by the prayers of the living, and the purchase of masses to be said for the souls of the departed, which was believed would reduce the time they had to spend in Purgatory, became a lucrative source of revenue for the Church, and an abuse which only ceased as a consequence of the Reformation. In medieval times Purgatory was regarded as being a fearsome place (vividly

described in Dante's dramatic imagination), but for Roman
Catholics today Purgatory is envisaged not as a place but as a
spiritual state in which the soul is purified before entering heaven.
Whether this can reasonably be described as 'glorious and blissful'
(as originally believed by Clement of Rome) must remain a matter
of judgement.

The sceptical writers of the Enlightenment period – e.g. G. E.
Lessing, D. F. Strauss and H. S. Reimarus – had little time for the
resurrection story as an objective event. For Strauss faith in the
resurrection was 'the outcome of exaggerated "recollection of the
personality of Jesus himself" ... A dead Jesus is thus transfigured
into an imaginary risen Christ – a *mythical* risen Christ ...'[34] For
him belief in the resurrection as an objective event was impossible.
Miracles don't occur. In Strauss's words: 'rarely has an incredible
fact been worse attested, and never has a badly attested fact been
intrinsically less credible'.[35] Reimarus maintained that Jesus's
disciples invented the idea of the resurrection 'in order to cover up
the embarrassment caused by his death'.[36] Rudolph Bultmann, as
well as denying miracles, regarded the resurrection as 'a mystical
event, pure and simple. It was "something" which happened in
the subjective experience of the disciples...'[37] Karl Barth was
sceptical about the value of the empty tomb in laying the
foundation for faith in the risen Christ, while Wolfhart
Pannenberg had an open mind but saw it as anticipating the
general resurrection at the end of time and the final revelation of
God.[38] In Christian theology the resurrection is regarded as
affirming the divinity of Jesus and of giving hope of eternal life.
Thus in John's gospel Jesus is recorded as saying: 'I came forth
from the Father, and am come into the world; again, I leave the
world, and go to the Father' (John 16: 28), while Paul believed
Jesus to be the Son of God through the resurrection (Romans 1:
4). Even if the Church were to abandon her belief in the Virginal
Conception and the Incarnation, she would be loath to abandon
her belief in the Resurrection (as Paul would have recognised).

Yet the resurrection story may – perhaps most realistically – be
seen as part of Christian mythology. We have explained elsewhere
the pagan background of the myth of the 'Immaculate
Conception', the 'Virgin Birth', and the borrowing of cult rituals

of 'initiation' (i.e. baptism) and 'communion' (i.e. the Eucharist). Contemporary belief was that deities died and rose again after three days. So Jesus must be seen to behave in a like manner if he was to be accepted as a divine being (as Christians maintained). While some – but not all – Jews were disposed to recognise Jesus as the promised Messiah of the Jewish faith, there was no scriptural tradition of a bodily resurrection on the Messiah's death. But contemporary Jews were mindful of the death of the prophet Elijah (was it not to Elijah that spectators of the crucifixion thought that Jesus was appealing?), how he was said to have been taken up to heaven by a whirlwind (and, indeed, six hundred years later the prophet Muhammad was to follow the same tradition and to *bodily* ascend 'the seven heavens' to the throne of God). Exceptional prophets were therefore expected to experience *bodily resurrection*, and Jesus must be no different. The safest way of ensuring this would have been to remove Jesus's body from the tomb, bury him elsewhere, and then proclaim his *bodily resurrection* in the style of the Hebrew prophet Elijah (his earlier identification as the Messiah having been quietly forgotten). Pagan precedents and the lessons of the Hebrew scripture may therefore be seen as explaining much of the subsequent mythological 'history' of Jesus's life and death.

During the following centuries – until the Roman emperor Constantine's so-called Edict of Milan in 313 – survival was the name of the game. Christian communities would have been kept together, and received encouragement, by means of the numerous epistles sent to them by Paul (who is believed to have been executed in *c*.65) and by the early Apostolic Fathers.[39] Paul, above all, was the undisputed leader of the early church movement. Indeed, as A. N. Wilson declares: 'The fact that the Gentile world adopted Christianity is owing almost solely to one man: Paul of Tarsus. Without Paul, it is highly unlikely that Christianity would ever have broken away from Judaism'. One of Paul's most important attributes was that he was a fluent Greek speaker and writer, and was therefore at home anywhere within the Roman Empire of which Palestine was then part. It was through him that Jewish religious beliefs were transmitted to the wider world. He therefore lived in an intellectual milieu far more cosmopolitan than that of the humble Aramaic-speaking Jesus of Nazareth. He claimed also to be a Roman citizen, which could well have resulted through his father's purchase in earlier years. He was physically small of stature, immensely energetic and boastful (and one who clearly enjoyed living dangerously), and he claimed also to be a Pharisaic legal rabbi. Paul appears first in the records as a member of the Temple police, employed by the high priest, *inter alia*, to stamp out the followers of the 'Way of Jesus' (whom he admitted to have violently persecuted). Paul's business was that of a tentmaker, in which he was clearly very successful and became a man of substance, travelling widely throughout the Roman Empire. However, after his dramatic 'conversion' on the road to Damascus in *c.*33 AD he changed from being a persecutor of the followers of 'the Way' and spent the rest of his life as a devoted disciple of Jesus. Paul had been shocked by the crucifixion but came to regard it as a moment of glory, and in a visionary metamorphosis declared 'I have been crucified with Christ; and it is no longer I who live, but it is Christ who lives in me'.[40] As A. N. Wilson declares: 'The genius of Paul and the collective genius of the early church', ... was to mythologise Jesus. Paul... had a richer language-store, a richer myth-experience than some of the other New Testament writers, whose mythologies were limited to Jewish liturgy or folk-tales... One is not saying that Paul crudely invented a new religion, but that he was able to draw out the mythological implications of an old religion, and the death of a particular practitioner of that religion, and to construct therefrom a myth with reverberations much wider than the confines of Palestinian Judaism'.[41] As Professor Vermes points out: 'it was the supreme doctrinal and organisational skill of St Paul that allowed nascent Christianity to grow into a viable and powerful resurrection-centred world religion'.[42] And as Professor Hick relates: 'The powerful memory of Jesus and his teaching continued to inspire many of his followers, who now constituted a small 'new religious movement' within diverse first-century Judaism. They fervently awaited the *Parousia* or Jesus' return in glory as God's agent instituting the kingdom on earth. But as this was delayed year after year the expectation faded, and Jesus was gradually transformed in their thinking from the prophet of a future historical salvation to the agent of a present inner salvation. His spirit within them, the spirit of his life and teachings, was objectified as the Holy Spirit, the third member of a divine Trinity. And the Jesus cult developed into the cult of the risen Christ, transfigured and deified. With this the Christian myth was born...'[43] But the establishment of Christianity in the fourth century as the religion of the empire, and the Church's institutionalization as partner of the state, changed its character. During this early period many Christians (and indeed non-Christians) began to develop their own ideas about their faith and their understanding of the nature of Jesus and his relationship to God. The need for fundamental changes of interpretation of Jesus's declared views subsequently gave rise to tensions among the leaders of the new Church and demonstrated the importance of agreeing a coherent doctrinal line and to denounce heretical opinions which differed from it. Being a Jew Jesus was brought up to accept the authority of the Septuagint (the first five books of what Christians later called the Old Testament) and attained a reputation as a rabbi and authoritative interpreter of these scriptures (often referred to as the Law of Moses). But his teaching broke away from the constraints of Jewish scriptures and Mosaic law, and centred on his 'Ten Commandments' and a series of parables and exhortations to a godly life in fear of God, with the promise of a new life after death in the kingdom of heaven. After Jesus' death his teachings and those of his disciples were written down and eventually became embodied into the 27 books of what became known as the New Testament (of which, surprisingly, only four are about Jesus: the rest are letters (dominated by Paul)). But there were many more writings which were deliberately left out — e.g. an Apocalypse of Peter and an Apocalypse of Paul, Gospels of Philip, Peter, two of Jesus's brother Judas Thomas, and one by Mary Magdalene. Which of these various writings were to be regarded as 'orthodox' and included in 'official' scriptures?

There appear to have been several groups of Christians competing to determine this important matter during the second and third centuries, one of which included Irenaeus (c.130–c.200), bishop of Lyon, and men such as Justin Martyr (c.100–c.165) and Tertullian (c.160–220). According to Professor Bart D Ehrman:

'This group became 'orthodox', and once it had sealed its victory over all its opponents, it rewrote the history of the engagement – claiming that it had always been the majority opinion of Christianity, that its view had always been the views of the apostolic churches and of the apostles, that its creed were rooted directly in the teachings of Jesus... What happened to all the other books, the ones that told a different version of the story and so had been left out of the proto-orthodox canon? Some of them were destroyed, but most were simply lost or crumbled with age. They were rarely, if ever, copied after a while, since their views had been deemed heretical. Only in small marginal groups within Christianity – a gnostic group here, a Jewish Christian group there – were these writings kept alive'.[44] And the Gospel of Judas is fascinating in that it totally upsets 'orthodox' beliefs. 'Judas alone, according to this hitherto lost view, knew the truth about Jesus. Jesus did not come from the creator of this world and was certainly not his son. He came from the realm of Barbelo to reveal the secret mysteries that could bring salvation. It was not his death that brought this salvation. His death simply released him from this evil material world'.[45] The theology propounded in the Gospel of Judas is clearly related to the 'Cainite' or 'Sethian'[46] gnostic sect, and the fact that it was condemned by Irenaeus shows it to have been flourishing prior to c.180 AD. In Sethian texts 'the immortal realm of Barbelo', from where Judas declares Jesus to have come, is 'the exalted realm of the divine beyond this world', which is associated with the divine figure of Barbelo (who is often equated with a divine 'Mother' figure in heaven).[47]

Early heresies, which have been described in Chapter 3 above, are of much interest in illustrating the variety of views on the nature of Jesus, and Bishop Irenaeus's great work *Libros Quinque Adversus Haereses* provides considerable information about them, as do fresh written sources discovered in recent years. They were all part of a vigorous intellectual debate on the merits of Christianity as a new religion. And as late as the fifth century intelligent laymen were questioning the whole basis of the new faith (which the Roman historian Tacitus had referred to as a 'pernicious superstition'). Thus Volusianus, a friend of St Augustine (354–430), 'lived in a circle which debated not only the old philosophical questions, but those doctrines of the Christian creed which preserved the greatest obstacle to the reason. At one of these gatherings the difficulties of the miraculous conception of Christ, and of the Incarnation of the omnipresent Ruler of the Universe in a single human form, subject to all the changes, wants, and limitations of humanity, were raised. And Volusianus, in a letter full of deferential admiration for Augustine's character and learning, asks for some light on these puzzling questions'.[48] Men like Q Aurelius Symmachus or Vettius Agorius Praetextatus were far too inured to the old pagan religious tradition of their distinguished ancestors to pay heed to a new faith which seemed to them so far removed from practical realities. As Symmachus said in a speech to the Emperor Theodosius: 'Each nation has its own gods and peculiar rites. The Great Mystery cannot be approached by one avenue alone... Leave us the symbol on which our oaths of allegiance have been sworn for so many generations. Leave us the system which has so long given prosperity to the state. A religion should be judged by its utility to the men who hold it...'[49] Despite this plea, and fortified by the arguments of St Ambrose, the emperor stood firm. And in 392 a law was passed forbidding the worship of the household gods and all other forms of pagan worship. Notwithstanding the 392 law there is a record of many aristocrats deserting the Christian faith and lapsing into pagan practices. The situation was made more difficult for the Church when Rome was sacked by Alaric in 410, when many people held that this was due to the state having abandoned the old gods in favour of Christianity. It was largely in answer to this that St Augustine wrote his great work *De Civitate Dei* (413–426), a vindication of the Christian Church which he portrayed as a new world order rising from the collapse of the old Roman Empire.

After the Gospels there are a number of early accounts of contemporary life written by the 'Apostolic Fathers'. If we read the testimony of some of these men there can be little doubt that, after his crucifixion, Jesus was believed by them to have appeared again in the flesh before ascending into heaven. These men – Clement of Rome (living *c.*96), Ignatius of Antioch (*c.*35–*c.*107) and Polycarp (*c.*69–*c.*155) of Smyrna – allow us (in Andrew Louth's words) 'some glimpse at least of the much less settled, and less defined, life of the early Church'. Indeed, these are the writings of 'those who had known the Apostles and were faithful to their teachings as opposed to the writings of the New Testament, the work of the Apostles themselves'.[50] The epistle of Clement of Rome (who was the fourth bishop of Rome[51]) to the Corinthians may be dated to *c*.96 and is a call for peace and harmony and 'a condemnation of strife, envy and jealousy'.[52] He displays a remarkable knowledge of the scriptures (his references are always to Paul's epistles and not to the gospels) and his argumentation is clearly influenced by Stoic philosophy. He refers to ministers as 'bishops' and 'deacons', although elsewhere he calls them 'presbyters'. We may note his strict orthodoxy: 'think, my dear friends, how the Lord offers us proof after proof that there is going to be a resurrection, of which He has made Jesus Christ the first-fruits by raising Him from the dead'.[53] Moreover 'when the Apostles had been given their instructions, and all their doubts had been set at rest by the resurrection of our Lord Jesus Christ from the dead, they set out in the full assurance of the Holy Spirit to proclaim the coming of God's kingdom'.[54] Interestingly, Clement refers to the deaths of Peter and Paul and that they have gone to their '*temporary* abode in a blessed, glorious and holy place' before their *final* resurrection'.[55]

Ignatius (*c*.35–*c*.107), the third bishop of Antioch, was condemned as a Christian and despatched to Rome to face martyrdom in the arena during the reign of the emperor Trajan (98–117). Seven letters from him, written on his way, have survived, in one of which – to the Christians of Rome – he begs them not to try to prevent his forthcoming ordeal to which he looks forward with passionate desire. The other six are largely concerned with combating heretical beliefs – particularly Docetism (whose followers believed that Jesus was not a real human being but a phantasm who had the appearance of human flesh) which was held by some gnostic sects. And he was the first to mention the virgin birth and name the mother of Jesus to combat the Docetist beliefs. He also considered that his martyrdom was part of the conflict between the powers of good and evil which presaged the end of the world, and his letters contain overtones of contemporary gnostic thought. He is the first to use the expression 'the Catholic Church' – which looks forward to the establishment in the second century of episcopal authority which was to be a guarantee of unity and orthodoxy. Like many early Christians he believed 'the end of all things is near. From now onwards, then, we must bear ourselves with humility, and tremble at God's patience…'.[56] In his letter to the Magnesians Ignatius condemns not only Docetism but Judaism which relies 'on forms and rules instead of on His grace'.[57] He boldly proclaims: 'To profess Jesus Christ while continuing to follow Jewish customs is an absurdity. The Christian faith does not look to Judaism, but Judaism looks to Christianity, in which every other race and tongue that confesses a belief in God has now been comprehended'.[58] He continues: 'I want you to be unshakably convinced of the Birth, the Passion, and the Resurrection which were the true and indisputable experiences of Jesus Christ, our Hope, in the days of Pontius Pilate's governorship. God grant that none of you may ever be turned aside from that Hope'.[59] In his letter to the Trallians he asserts:

'Close your ears, then, if anyone preaches to you without speaking of Jesus Christ. Christ was David's line. He was the son of Mary; He was verily and indeed born, and ate and drank; He was verily persecuted in the days of Pontius Pilate, and verily and indeed crucified, and gave up the ghost in the sight of all heaven and earth and the powers of the nether world. He was also verily raised up again from the dead, for His Father raised Him; and in Jesus Christ will His Father similarly raise us who believe in Him, since apart from Him there is no true life for us. It is asserted by some who deny God – in other words, who have no faith – that His sufferings were not genuine (though in fact it is themselves in whom there is nothing genuine). If this is so, then why am I now a prisoner? Why am I praying for a combat with the lions? For in that case, I am giving away my life for nothing; and all the things I have ever said about the Lord are untruths'.[60]

In his letter to the Philadelphians Ignatius warns them against the upsurge of Judaism in their community, and urges unity and obedience to their bishop (the office of which is now clearly recognisable): 'never to act in independence of the bishop, to keep your bodies as a temple of God, to cherish unity and shun divisions, and to be imitators of Jesus Christ as He was of His Father'.[61] To the Smyrnaeans he also inveighs against Docetic dangers and claims: 'For my own part, I know and believe that He was in actual human flesh, even after His resurrection. When He appeared to Peter and his companions, He said to them, 'Take hold of me; touch me, and see that I am no bodiless phantom'. And they touched Him then and there, and believed, for they had had contact with the flesh-and-blood reality of Him.[62] That was how they came by their contempt for death, and proved themselves superior to it. Moreover, He ate and drank with them after He was risen, like any natural man, though even then He and the Father were spiritually one'.[63] Ignatius also wrote an affectionate personal letter to Polycarp (c.69–155), bishop of Smyrna, who was to suffer martyrdom at the end of his life and an account of which has been preserved.[64] These letters were written a mere eighty years or so after the event, when contemporary memories would still be fresh and the likelihood of a gross deception as to Jesus's resurrection would be barely credible.

Amongst the early Christian writers was Barnabas (*post* 110) whose epistle 'reproves Christians who lean towards Judaism' and attempts to demonstrate that much in the Old Testament prefigures the arrival of Jesus. He does not appear to have been aware of any of the gospels.[65] Papias (c.140), bishop of Hierapolis in Phrygia, is the first writer to allude to the gospels of Matthew and Mark by name. His book entitled *The exegesis of the Lord's oracles* is now lost, but it was known to Bishop Irenaeus who said of him that he was 'a hearer of John and a companion of Polycarp'. From the fragments of his book that have survived it appears that it contained a wealth of detail about Jesus and his disciples.[66] Writing about the same time as Papias was Aristides (c.140), an Athenian philosopher and author of *Apology for Christianity*. This consists largely of a criticism of religions other than Christianity.[67] Justin Martyr (d. c.167) was the author of the *Dialogue with Trypho*. This contains considerable biographical information about Jesus, and, like Barnabas, attempts to show that the Old Testament contains many prophecies about Jesus and his mission. By his time written gospels were available, and (as we

have noted earlier) Justin referred in his first *Apology* to the
institution of the Eucharist as having been handed down by the
Apostles in their 'memoirs' (which are called gospels). Perhaps
most significantly Justin argued that 'with their doctrine of the
virgin birth of Jesus, of his passion and of his ascension, the
Christians were affirming nothing new as compared with what
'was alleged of the so-called sons of Zeus'.[68] In order to 'sell' the
new religion of Christianity it was necessary to persuade Greeks
and Romans alike that the Judaeo-Christian message was
'attractive to people trained in classical thought'. Thus St Paul,
when in Athens, addressed the philosophers of the Areopagus and
displayed his erudition by quoting the philosopher Aratus (Acts
17: 28), just as he could quote from the playwrights Euripides and
Aeschylus. He was later succeeded by two Christian masters of
Greek literature, namely, Clement of Alexandria (*c.*150–*c.*215)
and Origen (185–254). Clement of Alexandria, who may have
been a student of philosophy at Alexandria, believed that the God
of the philosophers was equivalent to the Christian God – calm
and serene – and that Jesus was the divine *logos* who had become
man, who by his example would show how mankind could attain
to the status of God. Irenaeus of Lyon taught a similar doctrine:
that Jesus had been the incarnate *logos* and had shown humanity
how to be a model for Christians to follow. Yet, as Karen
Armstrong points out: 'Clement's theology left crucial questions
unanswered. How could a mere man have been the Logos or
divine reason? What exactly did it mean to say that Jesus had been
divine? Was the Logos the same as the 'Son of God' and what did
this Jewish title mean in the Hellenic world? ... How could
Christians believe that he had been a divine being and yet, at the
same time, insist that there was only *one* God? Christians are
becoming increasingly aware of these problems during the third
century'.[69] When Clement left Alexandria in 202 for Jerusalem his
place was taken by his brilliant young pupil Origen – perhaps best
known for having taken, too literally, Jesus's remark that some
people had made themselves eunuchs for the sake of the Kingdom
of Heaven, and who in his youthful enthusiasm had therefore
castrated himself – developed a form of Christian Platonism. His
theology 'stressed the continuity of God with the world. His was a

spirituality of light, optimism and joy. Step by step, a Christian could ascend the chain of being until he reached God, his natural element and home'.[70] As Karen Armstrong has remarked: 'Origen's view of the divinity of Jesus and the salvation of humanity certainly did not conform to later official Christian teaching: he did not believe that we had been 'saved' by the death of Christ but that we ascended to God under our own steam'.[71] Origen is remembered for being the founder of the first Christian library at Caesarea Maritima (231) containing some 30,000 scrolls. Another figure in these early years was Plotinus (205–270) who had studied at Alexandria. 'Plotinus has been described as a watershed: he had absorbed the main currents of some 800 years of Greek speculation and transmitted it in a form which has continued to influence such crucial figures in our own century as T. S. Eliot and Henri Bergson... The ultimate reality was a primal unity, which Plotinus called the One. All things owe their existence to this potent reality'.[72]

The importance of these early philosophical speculators is that when Christian thinkers attempted to explain their own religious experiences, 'they turned naturally to the Neoplatonic Vision of Plotinus and his later pagan disciples'. The celebrated church historian Eusebius of Caesarea (265–340) who was advisor to the first Christian emperor Constantine in his *Preparation for the Gospel* demonstrated that 'pagan philosophy was basically nothing but a step (albeit an important step) towards the full truth revealed in Christ'.[73]

All contemporary Christian writing at this early period showed an intense awareness of the impending end of the world. Ignatius of Antioch was convinced that the end of all things was near, warned his readers to prepare themselves, and went cheerfully to his martyrdom. Indeed we now see martyrdom being actively sought as the fulfilment of a spiritual need; a mystic conviction that the martyrs' deaths were necessary and of supreme spiritual experience. Hence they all embraced their fate *with joy*. The so-called Epistle of Barnabas, written sometime after 110 AD, advises: 'let us be specially wary in these final days, for all our past years of faith will be no good to us if now, in these lawless times and in face of the many trials that lie ahead of us, we fail to offer such resistance as becomes God's children to the insidious infiltration of the Dark One'.[74]

One of the most interesting codices to be discovered at the end of the nineteenth century was the text of the document known as the *Didache* or *The Teaching of the Twelve Apostles*, which had been mentioned by the historian Eusebius (*c.*264–340) but had disappeared.[75] Divided into two parts, the first part describes the Two Ways (a choice of how to live) and the second part consists of a Church Manual (concerning the worship and discipline of an early Christian community). It may be dated to the latter half of the first century – earlier than much of the New Testament – and in the words of its editor Andrew Louth it represents 'a small and tantalising piece of evidence from a period of enormous importance for the history of early Christianity of which we are almost totally ignorant and driven to conjecture and hypothesis… it provides… a picture of the Church standing on the brink of the world to come, eager for the coming of its Saviour, to whom it looks with joy, and aware of the momentous decisions we make in the face of that coming, a decision between light and darkness, life and death'.[76] The Church Manual section contains some fascinating passages. One is an exhortation to be prepared for the impending end of the world: 'Be watchful over your life; never let your lamps go out or your loins be ungirt, but keep yourselves always in readiness, for you can never be sure of the hour when our Lord may be coming…'[77] It displays the extraordinary apprehension amongst contemporary Christians that the arrival of the Kingdom of God, constantly preached by Jesus, was imminent. The eucharistic prayers, *with no mention of the 'Last Supper' or of the Cross of Christ*, suggest that at that date the Eucharist was still a fellowship meal or *agape* (a love feast) at which one might satisfy one's appetite, before it was subsequently transmuted into a solemn ritual recalling the so-called 'Last Supper' and the death of Jesus.[78] Andrew Louth points out that the eucharistic thanksgiving prayers used are in fact 'Christianised forms of Jewish graces at table' – perhaps another indication of the very early date of the *Didache*,[79] *and demonstrating that the author had no conception of the agape being about to be superseded as a liturgical symbol of Jesus's death.* Had Jesus instructed his disciples to institute such a commemorative act, this would surely have been made clear in the *Didache*. As we have already seen, the supposed institution of the Eucharist by Jesus appears to have been a later insertion into two (only) of the original narratives of the 'Last Supper' in the knowledge of Jesus's subsequent death, and it became a ritual which in the medieval period was to cause serious doctrinal disputes.

According to Professor Wells the biographical information about Jesus 'increases steadily from Paul through Clement to Barnabas, Ignatius and Papias and finally to Justin. Yet there is no escaping the fact that Paul's epistles – recognised as having been written before the gospels – 'exhibit such complete ignorance of the events which were later recorded in the gospels as to suggest that these events were not known to Paul or whoever it was who wrote the epistles'. According to Wells the Pauline letters have no single allusion to the parents of Jesus; let alone to the virgin birth; they never refer to the place of his birth, never call him 'of Nazareth'. They never use the title 'Son of Man', so often used in the gospels to designate Jesus; and they mention none of the miracles he is supposed to have worked... They do not refer to his trial before a Roman official, nor do they say that his crucifixion took place at Jerusalem. They never mention John the Baptist, nor Judas, nor Peter's denial of Jesus'.[80] This is indeed an amazing fact, and according to Wells 'we can hardly resist the conclusion that the teachings and miracles of Jesus are myths. Had a historical Jesus really said and done the things narrated of him in the gospels, it is inconceivable that a man so placed as Paul should pass them over in silence'.[81] Even the so-called epistle of James (whose author is in fact unknown), written somewhat later than Paul, refers to the lamentable condition of the Church. He never refers to the gospels, nor to Jesus as the author of the moral precepts which he recommends. Indeed, he might never have heard of Jesus! Likewise in the first epistle general of Peter ('Peter, an apostle of Jesus Christ'). E. J. Goodspeed (1968) comments that the Christian 'delay in creating literary materials is hard to explain in the light of the literature produced by other Jewish groups, notably the community at Qumran... If there was a historical crucifixion in AD 30, it is remarkable that the earliest Christian literature, the

Pauline letters, did not follow until thirty years later (quite apart from the fact that these letters give no indication of the time or place of the crucifixion). If, however, there was no historical crucifixion, and the Pauline letters represent the beginnings of Christianity, then there is no delay to explain'.[82] The silence of pagan writers on Jesus and his achievement was embarrassing for early Christians, who made various attempts at forgeries under pagan names, the best known of which is a Latin correspondence between Seneca and Paul, first attested by St Jerome and held by both him and St Augustine to be genuine! It is now generally admitted to be a forgery written in Rome in the late fourth century.[83] Tertullian, writing from Carthage in 197, alleged that Pontius Pilate had written a report to the emperor Tiberius informing him of the miracles of Jesus and of his crucifixion and resurrection, and that Tiberius had placed the story before the senate recommending that Jesus be placed amongst the gods. This story was believed by the historian Eusebius and others, but no later historian believed it! Of Jesus's life Professor Wells is therefore drawn to conclude: 'What is decisive is the failure of the earliest writers to mention any concrete facts about him at all when these are supposed to have formed the historical facts later recorded in the gospels'.[84]

The intellectual basis which eventually formed the foundation of the new religion of Christianity was a compromise between Jewish and pagan beliefs. From orthodox Judaism came ('tho ultimately from Zoroastrianism) the concepts of resurrection and of a Last Judgement. Contemporary pagan belief centred on popular deities such as Attis, Tammuz, Adonis and Osiris dying annually and being resurrected for the salvation of their adherents. They all had their own initiation ceremonies and rituals by which their followers could achieve intimate communion with their god. Contemporary Jews were daily anticipating the arrival of a Messiah, prophesied in their scriptures, who would free their people from the yoke of the Roman empire and result in their salvation. The name Jesus means, in Hebrew, 'salvation' (Jeshovah), and Jesus of Nazareth appeared as a possible contender for this role. But he was not the only contender, for Paul refers to 'another Jesus': 'For if he that cometh preacheth another Jesus, whom we did not preach...' (2 Corinthians 11: 4). Indeed, there is a reference to a 'Christian' inciting a Jewish revolt in Rome in the time of Claudius. As Paul says: 'Christ was crucified as a sacrifice, and raised from the dead to give us new life' and he and others demonstrated how a popular suffering pagan god whose followers held secret rites to ensure their initiates of resurrection to a fuller life could be subsumed into a new Jewish religion based on their promised Messiah, whom Jesus was recognised as being. The Christians thereafter copied the well-recognised pagan practice of cult initiation ('baptism') and communion (the 'Eucharist') for the salvation of their adherents, and proceeded to alter the dates of their festivals to coincide with those of the pagan gods (e.g. the birth of Jesus was altered to 25 December, the winter solstice, which was the 'birthday' of the sun god). Gradually, the followers of pagan cults (e.g. Mithraism, the cults of Cybele and Attis, Osiris, the Roman household gods or *lares*) changed their allegiance, impressed both by the zeal of the early Christian martyrs and the promise of personal resurrection and participation in a future kingdom of heaven. The place of 'sacrifice' had played an important role in pagan and Roman cultures. The pagan practice of sacrifice was used primarily to secure the favour of the gods. At the time the Revelation of St John the Divine (or the Apocalypse) was written, it was a common belief amongst pagan cults in the Middle East (such as Mithraism) that the blood of a sacrificed animal conveyed new life to their initiates, as well as to Jews who believed in the efficacy of the shedding of blood as a means of placating God. It was not surprising therefore that the Apocalyptic portrayal of Jesus as a slaughtered lamb, who thereby redeemed the Elect with his blood, should have been widely disseminated amongst Christians. The need to record the events of Jesus's lifetime was soon appreciated by his followers but was undertaken piecemeal and unsystematically, so that even Paul – the greatest publicity agent for the new faith – was unaware of the details of Jesus's early life and teaching. The inconsistent and often contradictory gospel narratives were the inevitable result.

Professor Hick sums up the position as follows: 'the establishment of Christianity in the fourth century as the religion of the empire, and the church's institutionalization as partner of the state, changed its character. Through the long medieval period, the divine authority of Christ the King was mediated through the emperor as his civil representative on earth. The picture of Jesus as our brother and teacher was overlaid by the picture of Christ sitting on the throne of judgement, with the torments of hell as a terrible possibility for the disobedient'. [85] No wonder the faithful were apprehensive as they contemplated the fearsome frescos on the walls of their parish churches. With the collapse of the Empire in 410 the Church as an institution was able to foster a degree of political stability, and soon became an important ally of the nascent political kingdoms that began to emerge in Europe over the next several hundred years and was to culminate in the crowning of Charlemagne by the Pope as Holy Roman Emperor in 800 AD.

Certain conclusions may be drawn from a scholastic re-appraisal of the Gospel narratives and from early codices relating to the period of Jesus's life and the century following his death:

1. Early Church authorities interpolated passages into the narratives of the evangelists *ex post facto* to give the appearance that –

(i) the death and resurrection of Jesus was prefigured in the Bible and foreordained by God

(ii) Jesus was fully aware of his forthcoming death and resurrection, and conveyed this knowledge to his disciples

(iii) Jesus had died for our sins, indeed for the sins of 'the whole world'

(iv) Jesus had established a Church (*ekklesia*) of which Simon Peter nicknamed Cephas (from *kepha*, meaning 'rock') was to be the leader with the keys to open and lock the gates of the Kingdom of God.[86]

2. Early Church authorities from the time of St Paul until that of the early Christian fathers such as Irenaeus (*c*.130–*c*.200), Justin Martyr (*c*.100–*c*.165) and Tertullian (*c*.160–220), established the historical narratives, doctrines and rituals which were to become the orthodox canon for the Christian Church, as well as defining Jesus's relationship to God. Sources incompatible with the canon (e.g. the Gospel of Judas), or intellectual theories as to the nature

of Jesus (like Arianism, Gnosticism or Docetism) were declared to be heretical. The Western Orthodox Christian Creed was debated under the presidency of the Emperor Constantine at the Council of Nicaea in 325 and was finally approved at the Council of Constantinople in 381. It has remained unaltered ever since.[87] In 392 worship of the traditional Roman household gods and all other forms of pagan worship was forbidden by law. By the time Rome was sacked in 410 and a vindication of the Christian Church had been written by St Augustine in his *De Civitate Deo* (413–26), the Church as an institution had formally been established in the West.

NOTES

[1]   Vermes, 2005, 80

[2]   This information comes from the apocryphal Gospel of Peter (considered by scholars to have been a later forgery – see Ehrman, 2003, 19)

[3]   See the careful analysis of the gospel accounts, and that in the Acts of the Apostles, of the resurrection of Jesus in Vermes, 208, 94–120

[4]   Thiede, 2004, 80–5

[5]   The cult of Cybele and Attis had been adopted by Rome in 204 BC. The rites of Adonis were being celebrated as early as 414 BC in Athens (Frazer, 1949, 336). An inscribed tablet known as 'Gabriel's Vision of Revelation', which was recently found on the eastern bank of the Dead Sea, has been interpreted as referring to a Jewish Messiah killed by the Romans four years before the birth of Jesus rising from his grave three days after his death, thus providing yet another example of an important figure 'rising on the third day' which was subsequently adopted by Jesus's followers (*The Times*, 9 July, 2008, 35)

[6]   Toynbee, 1976, 14

[7]   Vermes, 2004a, 215

[8]   Ibid., 387

[9]   Ibid., 387–8

[10] Ibid., 388

[11] Wells, 1971, 46

[12] Ibid.

[13]   Vermes, 1973, 41

[14]   Vermes, 2008, 106–114 where he gives a detailed collation of such discrepancies.

[15]   Ibid., 112

[16]   Wells, 1971, 46 Note 1

[17]   Vermes, 2008, 142

[18]   See Vermes, 2008, 106–114

[19]   Peterson, *et al.*, 2003, 187

[20]   Wright, 2003, 717–8

[21]   Ibid., 494

[22]   Spong, 2002, 4–5

[23]   Vermes, 2008, 2

[24]   Vermes, G., *The Times*, 6 April, 2009

[25]   Obrist, 1983, 45

[26]   Ibid.,

[27]   Vermes, 2004a, 387

[28]   Ibid., 388

[29]   Moule, 1978, 104

[30]   Hick, 2004, 244–4

[31]   Polkinghorne, 1998, 93

[32]   Wells, 1971, 47

[33]   Vermes, 2008, 5

[34]   McGrath, 2007a, 320–1

[35]   Quoted in Vermes, 2008, 104–5

[36]   McGrath, 2007a, 311

[37]   Ibid., 322

[38]   Ibid., 325

[39]   Ignatius (*c.*35–*c.*107 AD), bishop of Antioch, Clement (liv. *c.* 98), bishop of Rome and Polycarp (d. 155), bishop of Smyrna

[40]   Wilson, 1998, 14, 70

[41]   Ibid., 72. There remains a dearth of information about Paul in certain major respects. It is known that Paul was at loggerheads with the Ebionites (who represented the mainstream 'Christian' viewpoint and whose leader was James, the brother of Jesus), and Hyam Maccoby has suggested that Paul – always assumed to be a Pharisaic Jew – may not have been born a Jew at all! Rather, he may have been a 'tormented adventurer, threading his way by guile through a series of stormy episodes, and setting up a form of religion that was his own individual creation' (see Wilson, 1998, 34–5; Maccoby, 1986, 182–3). And of course there is no historical record of Paul's death. As A. N. Wilson points out: 'there is no copper-

bottomed evidence that Peter even so much as visited Rome; and there is certainly no hard evidence that Paul died the death of a martyr. Nevertheless, for Roman Catholics Peter became the first Bishop of Rome and suffered a martyr's death by crucifixion in Rome. Likewise, *tradition* holds that Paul was later martyred, after a trial in Rome, and a tomb in the basilica of San Paolo fuori le mura contains a tomb inscribed 'Paolo Apostolo Mart.' (Wilson, 1998, 248–9)

[42] Vermes, 2008, 152

[43] Hick, 2004, 242

[44] Kasser *et al.*, 2006, 118–9

[45] Ibid., 120

[46] The classic text of this school of thought is the Secret Book of St John. See Kasser *et al.*, 2006, 139–146

[47] Ibid., 140–1. For Gnostic belief see page 28 above

[48] Dill, 1919, 14–15

[49] Ibid., 30–1

[50] Staniforth and Louth, 1987, 10

[51] The Roman Catholic belief that Peter was the first 'bishop' of Rome – before episcopacy had even been established in the new Church – is a myth that has grown over the years (for a refutation of this myth see Wells, 1971, 214–217, and Wilson, 1998, 107–111). There is more substance to the legend of Peter's martyrdom (29 June, 64) in Rome after his supposed arrival there in the reign of the emperor Claudius (Wilson, 1998, 108–109).

[52] Staniforth and Louth, 1987, 19; Wright, 2003, 481–4

[53] Staniforth and Louth, 1987, 33

[54] Ibid., 40

[55] Wright, 2003, 481–2

[56] Staniforth and Louth, 1987, 64

[57] Ibid., 73 and Note 6

[58] Ibid., 73

[59] Ibid.

[60] Ibid., 81

[61] Ibid., 95

[62] Interestingly, Jerome alleged that this quotation came from the apocryphal *Gospel according to the Hebrews* and not from a canonical gospel.

[63] Staniforth and Louth, 1987, 101–5, 110–112. See also Wright, 2003, 484–6

[64] Ibid., 101–5, 109–110, 125–135

[65] Wells, 1971, 174–7
[66] Ibid., 177–180
[67] Ibid., 180
[68] Ibid., 33
[69] Armstrong, 1999, 117
[70] Ibid., 118
[71] Ibid., 119
[72] Ibid., 120–1
[73] Thiede, 2004, 105–110
[74] Staniforth and Louth, 1987, 162
[75] Ibid., 189–199; Wright, 2003, 488–9
[76] Staniforth and Louth, 1987, 189
[77] Ibid., 197
[78] Ibid., 188, 194–5. See also Wells, 1971, 263–9, 277–8
[79] Staniforth and Louth, 1987, 194, 198 Note 5
[80] Wells, 1971, 131
[81] Ibid., 146
[82] Quoted in Wells, 1971, 304 Note 1
[83] Wells, 1971, 189
[84] Ibid., 184
[85] Hick, 2004, 242–3
[86] Thus Professor Vermes believes that the words of Jesus in Matthew 16: 17–19 'should be credited not to Jesus but to Matthew or his editor in AD 80 or later' (Vermes, 2004a, 362).
[87] Bettenson, 1946, 34–7

(d)   The nature of Jesus

To our contemporaries it may seem bizarre that a group of worldly clerics meeting in council should presume to take a vote on whether the remarkable rabbi and prophet named Jesus of Nazareth was in fact a god or not; that a later group of clerics should seek to define precisely his 'nature'; and finally another group of clerics should devise a new concept embracing Jesus and known as the Holy Trinity. Needless to say, Jesus knew nothing of these institutional decisions since they took place several hundred years after his death. The historian, on the other hand, will realise that the cultural milieu in which such extraordinary decisions were made was quite different from that of today. At the time Jesus was alive it was perfectly normal for Roman emperors to be deified (indeed, as he lay dying, the Emperor Vespasian (a noted wit) is said to have remarked ruefully 'O dear, I think I'm becoming a god') and the custom of deification of important figures lasted until recent times in the person of deified Japanese emperors.

Thus it was that rather more than 1,300 years ago the early Church authorities formulated one of the cardinal doctrines of the Catholic Church: that of the incarnation of God in the person of Jesus, leading to the concepts of Jesus being the 'Son' and of God being the 'Father',[1] and then introducing a third entity known as the 'Holy Ghost' (or 'Spirit'), making up the Trinity of 'Father, Son and Holy Ghost' (i.e. three beings comprising a single substance) to define the Christian theology of God in the universe. Let us briefly examine how this doctrine of incarnation came to be formulated.

From the earliest days of his ministry people were puzzled as to who Jesus really was. 'Whom do men say that I am?' Jesus asked. There were differing replies. Some said 'John the Baptist', some 'Elias' and others 'one of the prophets' (Mark 8: 27–8). 'But whom say ye that I am?' said Jesus. Peter replied 'Thou art the Christ' (Mark 8: 29). Jesus himself did not give them an answer, but simply 'charged them that they should tell no man of him'. Yet they knew he was closely related to God, the proclamation of whose kingdom in the imminent future was one of the constant themes of his mission as well as his frequent reference to his heavenly 'Father' in his preaching. After his death his family and close friends who belonged to a sect known as the Ebionites, whose leader was Jesus's brother James, continued to observe the Jewish laws and to worship in the Temple. According to A. N. Wilson 'the Ebionites did not believe that Jesus was a divine being, or that he had been born of a virgin – they were his brothers and sisters, who knew that he was a fully human being and that he was an observant and devout Jew. They thought of him as a great prophet, who had come to tell the Jews that the End of Days was at hand.[2] 'Even the Resurrection of Jesus is not, in their teaching, a sign of anything particularly special about Jesus: for in the Jewish teaching the rising of the dead is a sign of the beginning of the messianic age. Jesus is only the first to rise'.[3] The Ebionites largely disappeared after the destruction of the Temple in 70 AD, but some of their survivors clashed with the Gentile Christians 'who were preaching a quite different message – that Jesus was a Saviour-God who had condescended to visit the earth to redeem the Gentiles and abolish Judaism. This distortion of the original message of Jesus by the Gentile Church was something for which the Ebionites directly blamed Paul'.[4] It is clear that there was no love lost between the Christian 'Gentiles' under Paul and the Jewish Christians under Peter. It is equally clear that Jesus's early followers and family did *not* regard him as divine, but rather that he was a human prophet, and it was not until the early ecclesiastics began to formulate their ideas as to the *nature* of Jesus from the late second century onwards that they decided to declare him to be the equal of God (i.e. at Nicaea in 325 AD). Needless to say, Irenaeus was to denounce the Ebionites as heretics and as little different from the Jews.

During the centuries following Jesus's death, when Christian believers first started to organise themselves into congregations, the early Church leaders began to debate the details of what was to become doctrinal 'orthodoxy' for the new Church, and one of the first matters to be resolved was the exact 'nature' of Jesus and his relationship to God. Some churchmen, like Marcion (*c.*150), a highly influential thinker who claimed to be a follower of St Paul (in that he rejected some of the Jewish elements in the new Jesus-movement), considered Jesus to have been a 'phantasm' or manifestation of God who had the *appearance* only of human flesh (a position known as 'Docetism'). Of course at this early stage of the Church's existence 'orthodoxy' meant what was agreed by the dominant ecclesiastics at the time, and there was much disputing amongst themselves. The opinions of those whose views were not acceptable to the majority were therefore deemed to be 'heretical', and this gave rise to a number of heretical groups within the early Church. Marcion's view on the nature of Jesus was amongst those deemed unacceptable.[5] It was to combat the many persistent heresies amongst numbers of the early Church that in the second century Irenaeus (*c.*130–*c.*200), bishop of Lyon, wrote his great work *Libros Quinque Adversus Haereses.*

But heretical ideas continued to spring up. The great scholar Origen (185–254) of Alexandria was baffled by the nature of Jesus and wrote: 'Of all the marvellous and splendid things about him [Jesus], there is one that utterly transcends the capacity of our weak mortal intelligence to think of or understand, namely how this mighty power of the divine majesty, the very Word of the Father, and the very wisdom of God... can be believed to have existed within the compass of that man who appeared in Judaea...'[6] He held that Jesus was the equal of God by the *transference* of God's being, yet ultimately he was subordinate to God and was 'less than the Father'. Jesus was used as a mediator between God the Father and the material world. Those who held a similar view, which included the Libyan priest Arius (see below) and many other theologians, were known as 'subordinationists'. But to the orthodox churchman any notion of Jesus's subordination to God was unacceptable and Origen's view was condemned as heretical. Origen's predecessor, Clement of Alexandria, was strictly orthodox and therefore condemned the 'docetism' of people like Marcion who (as we have noted above) saw Jesus as a 'phantasm' and not a real man and that when he was on the cross he could feel no pain. Yet in writing about Jesus's nature Clement stated:

'But in the case of the Saviour, it would be ludicrous [to suppose] that the body, as a body, demanded the necessary aids in order for its duration. For he ate, not for the sake of the body, which was kept together by a holy energy, but in order that it might not enter into the minds of those who were with Him to entertain a different opinion of Him... He was... inaccessible to any movement of feeling – either pleasure or pain'.[7] Does this explain the apparently 'real' Jesus who talked and ate with his disciples after the resurrection?

About the year 319 Arius (c.250–336), a priest of Libyan origin living in Alexandria, contended that Jesus was not the equal of the Father – who was the supreme God and the ultimate source of everything – but was created by him (the attribution 'Son' being simply a metaphor frequently used in the ancient world). He was not therefore eternally co-existent with the Father, but was simply an inspired teacher. In short, Jesus was not himself divine, as claimed by the Church. However, the orthodox line by this date was that the Father and the Son were equal: Jesus *was* therefore God incarnate. Arius's view engendered a most ferocious debate throughout the Christian world.[8] Many of the clergy and laity in Egypt, Syria and Asia Minor supported him although his bishop, Alexander, did not, and in 321 a synod of bishops at Alexandria excommunicated him. He was nevertheless absolved by Eusebius, bishop of Nicomedia and in 323 a synod at Bithynia pronounced in his favour. To settle the matter, the emperor Constantine convened a Council at his palace at Nicaea in 325 which was attended by some 250 bishops. It should be emphasised that this gathering was attended by bishops from the Eastern empire, while the bishop of Rome was only represented by an observer.[9] Eusebius, bishop of Caesarea put forward a compromise formula for the Council's consideration which stated that Jesus was 'the Word of God, God from God, light from light, Son only begotten, first-begotten of all creation, begotten before all ages from the Father...' This would have accepted the full divinity of Jesus, but said nothing about his subordination to the Father. It was however felt necessary to add to the statement the word *homoousios* ('of the same substance') as the Father. This was contested by the supporters of Arius who refused to agree to the final statement. A general consensus was finally achieved, however, and Arius was excommunicated and exiled. The Nicaean statement was thereafter to form the basis of the 'Nicene Creed' which has survived in the Catholic, Orthodox and some

Protestant Churches today. Constantine himself had misgivings about the statement and in 327 personally received the exiled Arius and ordered that he be reinstated to his former position in Alexandria. But his bishop, Alexander, flatly refused to admit him.

After further years of bickering the emperor in 335 convened a synod in Jerusalem and Arius was re-admitted to the Church. At a fresh synod in 336, after Arius had apparently declared to the emperor his assent to the creed of Nicaea, Constantine ordered Bishop Alexander of Constantinople to admit the penitent Arius to communion.[10] As Dr Williams recounts: 'Arius may have been genuinely repentant; but it sounds as though he was, rather, struggling to find a peaceful compromise'.[11] The last hours of Arius's life were described by Athanasius: 'It was a Saturday when the emperor ordered Alexander to admit Arius (at the liturgy on the following day). Faced with this situation, Alexander... withdrew to the episcopal chapel (Hagia Eirene) and prayed that either he or Arius might die before morning. Arius meanwhile, smitten by 'the necessities of nature', retired to a public lavatory, and died, apparently from some kind of internal haemorrhage or rupture'.[12] Needless to say the story 'is not without its difficulties' and Dr Williams concludes: 'we have no reason to doubt that Arius' death was embarrassingly sudden, and that the Nicene party were able to ascribe it to the effect of their fervent intercession; but whether it occurred with quite the convenient timing (and in quite the symbolically appropriate manner) described by Athanasius must be less certain'.[13] It should be made clear that 'Arianism', as it came to be known, could not be described as 'a coherent system founded by a great figure and sustained by his disciples'. Rather was it a collective description of mainstream Catholics who did not subscribe to the Nicene position, and whose heterodoxy found a focus in the charismatic figure of Arius and the congregations who supported him. It was also bound up with the position of the Alexandrian church which was regarded 'as the very exemplar of traditional and revealed religion', and this accounts for the bitter feelings between Arius and his bishop, Alexander, who – in William's words – 'more closely resembled an archbishop or even a patriarch than any other prelate in Christendom',[14] and who was uncompromising towards his heterodox bishops. Nevertheless the Arian controversy continued after Arius's death in 336, and was not finally settled until the Council of Constantinople in 381 when Arius's views were declared heretical. This did not however extinguish the controversy, which was even revived in England during the eighteenth century!

The chief proponent of the Nicene formula at this date was of course Athanasius (c.246–373), bishop of Alexandria from 326, whom critics accused of failing 'to define the distinction between Father and Son with any clarity, or, indeed, how Jesus' divinity could co-exist with his humanity'. The debate about the status of Jesus rumbled on behind the scenes and revolved round the 'subordinationist' argument which maintained that Jesus was 'less than the Father' and not therefore *homoousios* as had been agreed at Nicaea. It was generally agreed that if Jesus had brought salvation to mankind by undergoing suffering on the cross then his divinity had to be of a lesser nature to that of God, who was above suffering. A group of bishops met at Sirmium in 357 and drew up a revised creed which made clear that the term *homoousin* should *not* be included because the concept 'is not included in the divine Scriptures, and it is beyond men's knowledge nor can anyone declare the birth of the Son... There is no uncertainty about the Father being greater; it cannot be doubted by anyone that the Father is greater in honour, in dignity, in glory, in majesty... And nobody is unaware that this is Catholic doctrine, that there are two persons of the Father and the Son, and that the Father is greater, and the Son is subjected in common with all the things which the Father subjected to him...'[15]

Constantine's son, Constantius, was sympathetic to the subordinationist case as set out in the Sirmium Creed, and was determined to reach a final settlement of the problem. He therefore summoned two councils to meet in 359 – one at Seleucia for the Eastern Greek-speaking bishops and the other at Ariminum for the Western Latin-speaking bishops. Constantius produced a draft creed for consideration, and after the familiar acrimonious debates a joint declaration was finally agreed which removed the word *ousia* (substance) from the text 'because it was naively inserted by the fathers [at Nicaea]... and because the scriptures do not contain it...'[16] In 361 Constantius died, having failed to obtain universal agreement to the Nicaean creed. Likewise, the efforts of the so-called Cappodocian Fathers (Basil, bishop of Caesarea, his brother Gregory of Nyssa, and Gregory of Nazianzus) were equally unsuccessful. It was left to the emperor Theodosius to deal with the matter, and he summoned a Council of the Eastern Greek-speaking bishops to meet at Constantinople in 381 in an attempt to impose uniformity on the warring factions and restore peace between the bickering bishops.[17] Prior to the council Gregory of Nazianzus had preached a series of outdoor sermons (known as his 'Theological Orations') supporting the original Nicene position, but there were many who argued for the subordinationist case. In January, 381, before the Council began, Theodosius issued instructions to his prefect of Illyricum (and probably others) to impose the Nicene faith throughout his province, and those priests who resisted were obliged to hand over their churches to the orthodox Nicene supporters. The Council began by noting and endorsing the instructions contained in the emperor's letter to his prefect, but then the presiding bishop, Meletius of Antioch, died and the council was thrown into confusion. Nevertheless there was eventual agreement on a revised text of the Nicene Creed[18] which ran as follows:

We believe in one God Father Almighty, maker of heaven and earth and all things, seen and unseen;

And in one Lord Jesus Christ the Son of God, the Only-begotten, begotten by his Father before all ages, Light of Light, true God from true God, begotten not made, consubstantial with the Father, through whom all things came into existence, who for us men and for our salvation came down from the heavens and became incarnate by the Holy Spirit and the Virgin Mary and became a man, and was crucified for us under Pontius Pilate and suffered and was buried and rose again on the third day in accordance with the Scriptures and ascended into the heavens and is seated at the right hand of the Father and will come again to judge the living and the dead, and there will be no end to his kingdom;

And in the Holy Spirit, the Lord and Life-Giver, who proceeds from the Father, who is worshipped and glorified together with the Father and the Son, who spoke through the prophets;

And in one holy, catholic and apostolic Church;

We confess one baptism for the forgiveness of sins;

We wait for the resurrection of the dead and the life of the coming age,

Amen.[19]

It may be noted that there was no statement 'endorsing a Trinity of three consubstantial persons. There was certainly no consensus on the nature of the Holy Spirit'. In practice therefore it was the *political* imposition of the Nicene faith by the emperor Theodosius which resulted in the Council endorsing it at Constantinople. In November, 392, Theodosius promulgated a law banning any activity associated with pagan rites, even in domestic shrines. Which meant that some pagan customs (e.g. lighting lamps before pagan shrines) simply re-appeared in a Christian guise. Even the Olympian Games, held every four years and dedicated to the god Zeus, were banned. However, within two years a change of policy in the West by the local prefect resulted in a revival of the ancient pagan cult of Rome, and temples and their rituals were restored. Theodosius considered this an affront and moved with an army into Italy where he defeated a local general, Arbogast, in September, 394, at the river Frigidus, near Aquileia (helped, it was believed, by the hand of God).[20]

In the fifth century a controversy again arose over the Incarnation. Nestorius, bishop of Constantinople, held that there were two Persons in Jesus, one human and one divine, and he objected to the practice of calling the Virgin Mary 'Mother of God' – since she could only be the mother of the *human* person (see page 38). As against this, Cyril (d. 444), bishop of Alexandria, took the view that there were two natures in one Person. A Council was summoned by the emperor Theodosius to meet at Ephesus in 431. The Western bishops arrived first 'and proceeded to lock the doors against latecomers and decided in hot haste for St Cyril, who presided'. As a result, Nestorius was condemned as a heretic, but his supporters – who became known as the Nestorian sect – had a large following in Syria and elsewhere in the East.

Nestorianism even became strong in India and China! In 449 another Council was summoned by Dioscorus, bishop of Alexandria, to meet at Ephesus and adjudicated in favour of the so-called Monophysite heresy which maintained that Jesus had only one nature. Yet in 451 the new emperor Marcian summoned a Council to meet at Chalcedon which reversed this decision, condemning the Monophysites and re-affirming that Jesus was hypostatically united in two natures, one human and one divine, which thereafter became the essential ingredient of orthodox Christian doctrine. In translation, what became known as the 'Formula of Chalcedon' ran as follows:

'Following therefore the holy Fathers, we confess one and the same one Lord Jesus Christ, and we all teach harmoniously [that he is] the same perfect in Godhead, the same perfect in manhood, truly God and truly man, the same of a reasonable soul and body; consubstantial with the Father in Godhead, and the same consubstantial with us in manhood, like us in all things except sin; begotten before the ages of the Father in Godhead, the same in the last days for us and for our salvation [born] of Mary the virgin *theotokos* in manhood, one and the same Christ, Son, Lord, unique; acknowledged in two natures without confusion, without change, without division, without separation – the difference of the two natures being by no means taken away because of the union, but rather the distinctive character of each nature being preserved, and [each] combining in one Person and *hypostasis* – not divided or separated into two Persons, but one and the same Son and only-begotten God, Word, Lord Jesus Christ ...'[21]

This formula was not entirely satisfactory because it remained unclear whether the two natures of Jesus had existed before the Incarnation, or whether the human nature was imparted to him at the moment of his birth. As Charles Freeman points out: 'It was hard to imagine how one being could combine human and divine natures without the divinity, especially as defined by Nicaea, not dominating the human. Again how could Jesus' humanity be of 'one substance' with the rest of humanity if he was also distinct from the rest of humanity in being unable to sin?'[22] Nevertheless the bishops accepted it and the emperor Marcian called on his army officers to swear allegiance to the new creed. But that was not the end of the story because a number of clergy in Egypt and Syria refused to accept the Chalcedon definition, much to the emperor's displeasure.

As Dr Frances Young reminds us, early doctrinal controversies were shaped not merely by the inherent quality of the arguments used, but by personalities and politics. Thus Cyril's attack on Nestorius 'is related to the political struggle between the ecclesiastical power-centres of Alexandria and Constantinople'.[23] Far from the definition of the incarnation being a simple matter of undisputed historical 'fact' on the evidence of New Testament sources, it took the early Church over 400 years finally to resolve the matter! Thus it took until the Council of Nicaea (325) for Jesus to be accepted as a god and not a mortal prophet (and even then the emperor Constantine regarded the deified Jesus as an earthly manifestation of Sol Invictus!). And it was not until the Council of Chalcedon (451) that the 'nature' of Jesus was finally resolved.

As late as the fourth century men of intellect such as St Augustine's friend Volusianus were still debating the merits of this new religion. Volusianus 'lived in a circle which debated not only the old philosophical questions, but those doctrines of the Christian creed which presented the greatest obstacles to the reason. At one of these gatherings the difficulties of the miraculous conception of Christ, and of the Incarnation of the omnipresent Ruler of the Universe in a single human form, subject to all the changes, wants, and limitations of humanity, was raised. And Volusianus, in a letter full of deferential admiration for Augustine's character and learning, asks for some light on these puzzling questions'.[24] While men like Q Aurelius Symmachus or Vettius Praetextatus were far too inured to the old pagan religious traditions of their distinguished ancestors to pay heed to a new faith which seemed to them so far removed from practical realities.[25] Despite pleas from Symmachus and others, and fortified by the arguments of St Ambrose, the emperor Theodosius stood firm, and in 392 a law was passed forbidding the worship of the household gods and all other forms of pagan worship. Notwithstanding the 392 law there is a record of many aristocrats deserting the Christian faith and lapsing into pagan practices. The situation was made more difficult for the Church when Rome was sacked by Alaric in 410, when many people held that this was due to the state having abandoned the old gods in favour of Christianity. It was largely in answer to this that St Augustine wrote his great work *De Civitate Dei*.

Now in order to make the new religion acceptable to potential Hellenistic converts, it had to be shown to be complementary to Greek philosophical thought. The intellectual thought of the classical world was steeped in neoplatonic ideas deriving from Platonic/Stoic theories of a universal god, immortality of the soul, and the pursuit of reason, knowledge and virtue. The quest for knowledge was one of the prime tenets of various Christian gnostic sects then flourishing in the Near East, and the Christian concept of the *Logos* (meaning 'reason' or 'word') in St John's Gospel was held by Clement of Alexandria (*c*.150–*c*.215) and other Christian Platonists to be synonymous with Jesus who was believed to transmit the word of God to the world ('In the beginning was the Word, and the Word was with God, and the Word was God... The Word became flesh and made his dwelling among us. We have seen his glory, the glory of the One and Only, who came from the Father, full of grace and truth'. John 1: 1, 14). Moreover, Justin Martyr (*c*.100–*c*.165), one of the group known as Christian Apologists (his major work being an *Apologia* for Christianity), was concerned to demonstrate that the philosophical Logos anticipated and heralded the arrival of the Christian Logos as the ultimate source of all human knowledge. He compared the doctrines of the virgin birth, the passion and the ascension of Jesus to 'what was alleged of the so-called sons of Zeus'. It was indeed a credulous age. While Origen (185–254), one of the most learned of the early Church Fathers and author of numerous books, developed the idea of the Christian Logos still further. He saw God as a spirituality of light, optimism and joy, with his devotees gradually ascending to the realm of God, their natural home.

The doctrine of the Trinity is difficult – indeed incomprehensible – for many. Only two verses in the whole New Testament can bear a Trinitarian interpretation (Matthew 28: 19

and Corinthians 13: 14). In his letter to the Corinthians (2 Corinthians 13: 14) St Paul signs off with the words 'the grace of our Lord Jesus Christ, and the love of God and the fellowship of the Holy Spirit be with you all'.[26] Now St Paul, well versed in contemporary Hellenistic ideas, would have been aware of the Neoplatonic 'Trinity' of 'The One', 'Spirit' and 'Soul', and would readily have introduced the 'word' or 'spirit' to complement his references to God as the 'Father' and Jesus as the 'Son'. Thus the linkage between the Father, the Son, and the Holy Spirit gradually developed into the Christian doctrine of the Holy Trinity. In fact, Trinitarian terminology may be said to have originated in the fertile mind of Tertullian (c.160–220) who coined the word *Trinitas* to describe the three persons of the 'Trinity'. He maintained that God is one in terms of power, but is manifested in three separate ways. He also introduced the word *persona* – literally meaning a 'mask', being used in the sense of an actor playing a part in a Roman drama. His Trinitarian concept was that God 'played three distinct yet related roles in the great drama of human redemption'.[27] He also conceived the three components of the Trinity as having the same 'substance' in order to emphasise the fundamental unity of the Godhead. As Charles Freeman points out: 'There had been no mention of the Trinity in the Nicene Creed. The assertion 'And I believe in the Holy Spirit' had been included, but nothing was said of the Spirit having any divine status or being related to Father and Son in any way'.[28] While Athanasius had been the leading advocate of the Nicene formula, he had also composed a creed of his own which became known as the 'Athanasian Creed'. This began as follows:

> And the Catholick Faith is this: That we worship one God in Trinity, and Trinity in Unity;
>
> Neither confounding the Persons; nor dividing the Substance.
>
> For there is one Person of the Father, another of the Son; and another of the Holy Ghost.
>
> But the Godhead of the Father, of the Son, and of the Holy Ghost, is all one: the Glory equal, the Majesty co-eternal.
>
> Such as the Father is, such is the Son; and such is the Holy Ghost.

The Father uncreate, the Sun uncreate: and the Holy Ghost uncreate.

The Father incomprehensible, the Son incomprehensible: and the Holy Ghost incomprehensible.[29]

This attempt to explain the nature of the Trinity was hardly likely to appeal to contemporary churchmen with their differing and defiantly-held theological views and it was virtually put aside until the seventh century. It was however revived and in the Church of England's *Book of Common Prayer* it was laid down that the Athanasian Creed was to be sung or said at Morning Prayer on thirteen specified feast days throughout the year. The definition of the precise relationship between the 'Spirit' and the Father and the Son was largely due to Basil (*c.*329–379) of Caesarea in his work *On the Holy Spirit* (375) who urged the divinity and co-equality of the Spirit with the Father and the Son. This proposition was not however seriously considered until after a century of argument and discussion during which at least two heretical views had been aired. The first heresy – later termed 'Modalism' – originated in the late second century when Noetus and Praxeas expressed the opinion that the proposals under discussion might result in the Trinity being turned into some form of 'Tritheism' – i.e. that the Trinity would consist of three equal, independent and autonomous entities, each of which was divine. The other heresy – Sabellianism – originated in the claim by a certain Sabellius that the one supreme God acts in different ways in different times throughout history. Thus Jesus appeared on earth as a temporary manifestation of God.[30] It will be recalled that the doctrine of the Trinity was one of the matters debated at the Council of Constantinople (381), but there was no mention in the revised Nicene Creed of a Trinity of three consubstantial entities or a definition of the Holy Spirit. Nevertheless the Trinity featured in the emperor Theodosius's imposition in 381 of the Nicene Creed in the Eastern empire.[31] That it was a commonly accepted doctrine at the turn of the century is suggested by the attribution of the well-known hymn –

> 'I bind unto myself today
> The strong name of the Trinity,

By invocation of the same,
The Three in One, and One in Three.'

to St Patrick (c.372–466). It was not however until the Eleventh Council of Toledo in 675 that the final orthodox statement of the doctrine of the Trinity was to be set out in the following terms:

'This is the way of speaking about the Holy Trinity as it has been handed down: it must not be spoken of or believed to be 'threefold' [triplex], but to be 'Trinity'. Nor can it properly be said that in the one God there is the Trinity: rather, the one God is the Trinity. In the relative names of the persons, the Father is related to the Son, the Son to the Father, and the Holy Spirit to both. While they are called three persons in view of their relations, we believe in one nature or substance. Although we profess three persons, we do not profess three substances, but one substance and three persons. For the Father is Father not with respect to Himself but to the Son, and the Son is Son not to Himself but in relation to the Father; and likewise the Holy Spirit is not referred to Himself but is related to the Father and the Son, inasmuch as He is called the Spirit of the Father and the Son. So when we use the word 'God', this does not express a relationship to another, as of the Father to the Son or of the Son to the Father or of the Holy Spirit to the Father and the Son, but 'God' refers to Himself only'.[32]

So the definition remained until the whole nature of the deity was re-opened by the brilliant philosopher Peter Abélard in the early twelfth century. Peter Abélard is known to history primarily because of his love affair with Héloise (leading to her pregnancy, marriage and her uncle's brutal revenge by arranging for Abélard's castration). Yet his fame rests on his intellectual powers as a logician, and the orthodox position on the Holy Trinity was a doctrine to which he could not subscribe. 'How could there be three divine persons, Father, Son and Holy Spirit, distinct from each other, each fully God, but without there being three Gods?' To solve the problem he wrote his Theologia, which was condemned and ordered to be burnt in 1121. He then became obsessed with finding another intellectual defence of the doctrine and produced a formula which stated that 'Although God the

Father is entirely the same essence as God the Son or God the Holy Spirit, there is one feature proper to God the Father insofar as he is Father, another to God the Son, and yet another to the Holy Spirit'. This was ignored by the authorities who were offended by his popularity with his student followers. Abélard's chief opponent was St Bernard of Clairvaux, a Cistercian monk and friend of Pope Innocent II, who was outraged that 'the Catholic Faith, the childbearing of the Virgin, the Sacrament of the Altar, the incomprehensible mystery [sic] of the Holy Trinity, are being discussed in the streets and the market places'. He compiled a list of Abélard's supposed heresies for the pope to consider at a synod at Sens, but without waiting for Abélard's defence he persuaded the attending bishops to condemn them, as a result of which the Pope excommunicated Abélard (16 July, 1141) a sentence which was lifted at the instigation of the Abbot of Cluny. Abélard's was the first voice to deplore the intellectual sterility of his age, which resulted in 'the fact that one is never allowed to investigate what should be believed among one's own people... People profess themselves to believe what they admit they cannot understand, as if faith consisted in uttering words rather than in mental understanding'.[33] Is this not precisely true today of parts of 'accepted' Church doctrine?

We should note that St Thomas Aquinas, the greatest medieval theologian, had to admit that the Trinity was a mystery beyond the power of human reason to comprehend, and yet the status of the Trinity has since remained an article of faith for Christians – although frequently challenged by scholars – indeed by the great scientist Isaac Newton, who sought to demolish the scriptural arguments for the Trinity but was forbidden by law from publishing his conclusions. Newton believed that the doctrine 'has been foisted on the Church by Athanasius in a specious bid for pagan converts (Athanasius, it will be recalled, formulated his own Creed which concentrated on the Trinity and to which all Catholics were later bound to subscribe). Arius had been right: Jesus Christ had certainly not been God and those passages of the New Testament that were used to 'prove the doctrines of the Trinity and the Incarnation were spurious...'[34]

As Professor Sir Anthony Kenny, the distinguished philosopher and former Roman Catholic priest, wryly comments: 'Some doctrines, no doubt, are very difficult to understand and some may indeed appear to the unbeliever to be unintelligible or self-contradictory. If the doctrines are genuinely unintelligible, then the attitude to them of the devout can hardly be called genuine belief; one cannot really believe nonsense, no matter how devotedly one tries'.[35] Here, surely, is the professional philosopher and former priest speaking in language that the lay person can understand! Kenny goes on: 'Philosophers spend much of their time exploring the coherence of suppositions which are at least as prima facie implausible as the doctrines of the Trinity or of Transubstantiation'.[36] He refers to the view of St Thomas Aquinas that 'If the belief of the simple believer is to be justified, there must be arguments for the existence of God, ...' As we have already seen (Chapter 4 (i)), it is now recognised that philosophically the existence of God cannot be proved. So the 'simple believer' is unlikely to be convinced of 'implausible' doctrines which have now become fossilized into the bedrock of the Church. Michael Perham, Bishop of Gloucester, on the other hand, dismisses (and therefore avoids) the widely held theological difficulties concerning the concept of the Holy Trinity ('for me it is extraordinary that people have made the Trinity difficult...'). He regards the Trinity as a mystery which 'is not the kind of mystery you need to solve. It is not one you have to explain...' For him the Trinity is a metaphor for love – about 'the Father loving the Son, the Son loving the Father, the Spirit that love that flows between them'.[37] Such a view does not appear to have been held by the early Christian Fathers who devised the formula, nor by theologians (like Abélard and Thomas Aquinas) who have wrestled with its meaning, but such an interpretation certainly makes life easier – even if it adds to the scepticism of critics!

Theologians and churchmen frequently use the expression 'by the grace of God' or 'by divine grace' in their everyday speech, as if this use of the term 'grace' were an unquestioned ex-cathedra assumption. Professor Kenny states: 'We may raise the question whether there is such a thing as divine grace, and if so what is its nature'. He continues: 'it may be claimed that there are certain beliefs which it is beyond the unaided power of reason to attain to, and which can be reached with the aid of grace. Any such beliefs are the mysteries of faith... What has been a near unanimous view among Christians is that grace was needed for the saving faith in the mysteries of revelation such as the Trinity and the Incarnation. Faith, in the theological sense, is belief in something on the word of God'.[38] It will therefore be obvious that, for the majority of lay people, the so-called 'word of God' and therefore use of the phrase 'grace of God' means nothing at all unless they have unquestioned faith. To believe unreservedly in the doctrines of the Trinity and Incarnation therefore implies accepting the fallible decisions of the early bishops who propounded these doctrines. Logically if you have 'faith' you can believe in any nonsensical ideas! Perhaps some of the early 'heretics' such as Arius (who claimed Jesus was not divine), Origen (who maintained that Jesus was subordinate to the Father) and Abélard (who was critical of the Trinity) were right after all and the 'authorities' wrong?

Significantly, Islam teaches that there is no obligatory doctrine about God. It dismisses theological speculation as *zanna*, or self-indulgent guess-work about matters which no one can either know or prove. Thus the Christian doctrines of the Incarnation and the Holy Trinity are regarded as examples of *zanna* and Muslims find such doctrines blasphemous. Nor did Muhammad ever claim to be divine, as the early Christians held Jesus to have been, but regarded himself as a mortal prophet. To have claimed otherwise would have been regarded as blasphemy in Islam as well as in Christianity. Biblical scholars are now coming round to believing that Jesus was no different.

At the time of the Reformation the doctrine of the Holy Trinity was again questioned. One of the most unfortunate dissidents was Michael Servetus (1511–1553), a Spanish physician who, mindful of how offensive the doctrine of the Trinity was to Muslims and Jews, published a book *On the Errors of the Holy Trinity* (1531). This argued that there was only one God the Father and, as a separate entity, his son Jesus. 'Not one word is found in the whole Bible about the Trinity nor about its persons, nor about the essence nor the unity of substance nor of the one nature of the several beings nor about any of the rest of their ravings and logic chopping'. He found himself handed over to John Calvin, but since most of the Protestant Churches had decided to accept the orthodox doctrine of the Trinity he was unlucky enough to be sentenced to be burnt as a heretic. In England, in the Thirty-Nine Articles of the Church of England (finalised in 1571) the reference to the Holy Trinity in the Creeds was preserved unchanged. We may here recall that part of John Wesley's success in preaching to simple people up and down the country in the eighteenth century was to ignore doctrinal complexities such as the mystery of the Holy Trinity. Perhaps preachers today would be heard with more conviction if they were to do the same and concentrate instead on Jesus's charismatic life-time mission.

By the time Gerald Priestland wrote his book (1981) he found the reaction of churchmen and the laity to the doctrine of the Trinity to be fairly sceptical. One of his friends was 'absolutely baffled. It's double-Dutch to me...' A Muslim friend said: 'there was really no hope of the average Moslem being able to make sense of the Christians' claim that they worshipped not three gods but one', and a Jewish rabbi told him that 'no religious Jew could possibly justify the Trinity or see how it could function...' Priestland recalled that the First Vatican Council's Dogmatic Constitution on the Catholic Faith (of 1870) declared that the Trinity is an 'absolute mystery' − something that has been revealed by God as true, but which is beyond human powers to understand. Perhaps this is just as well since the Blasphemy Act of 1697 made it an offence to doubt the Trinity! Priestland suggests that 'not only has too much piety and faith been invested in the doctrine; too much spiritual insight has been stimulated and expressed through it for us to afford throwing it away'. He concludes that 'the doctrine of the Trinity was like the Victorian piano in the front parlour; nobody played it nowadays, but nobody dared throw it out'![39]

It may reasonably be asked: what does it mean to say that Jesus was the Second Person of the Holy Trinity? A number of theories were advanced in the patristic period but were not acceptable and were therefore declared to be heretical. Professor Hick points out that the Chalcedonian formula 'merely reiterated that Jesus was both God and man, but made no attempt to interpret the formula'. He believes that the doctrine of incarnation is a traditional mystery: that Jesus was God the Son incarnate is not literally true, since it has no literal meaning, but it is an application to Jesus of a mystical concept whose function is analogous to that of the notion of divine sonship ascribed in the ancient world to a king. 'For more than a thousand years the symbols of Jesus as Son of God, God the Son, God incarnate, Logos made flesh, served their purpose well. Within the life of the church they have been for countless people effective expressions of devotion to Jesus as Lord'.[40] However, we now live in a different world. Few people today think of Jesus as God incarnate and skate over the language enshrined in sacred liturgy and song as a poetic relic of history. They no longer believe some of the old and familiar catchphrases like 'the Son of God taking our nature upon him' or the wording of Wesley's hymn 'Veiled in flesh the Godhead see'. Rather, they see Jesus as a charismatic prophet intensely aware of God and the Transcendent whose moral teaching and promise of a future life are of universal application and bearing witness to God's loving providence. They see him, in the words of Acts 2: 22, as 'Jesus of Nazareth, a man approved of God among you by miracles and wonders and signs, which God did by him in the midst of you'. Indeed, as the late Cardinal Basil Hume pointed out: 'St Matthew did not know that our Lord was God. From what he had heard, and no doubt from what he had seen, he knew he must have been sent by God'.[41] As Jesus himself had said: 'My doctrine is not mine, but his that sent me' (John 7: 16). Furthermore, today's ecumenical outlook has persuaded Christians of the inherent 'truths' and similarities of contemporary world faiths, and to treat them with respect and understanding. *Hitherto, if Jesus was believed to be literally God (as the second Person of the Godhead), it followed that Christianity alone among the world religions was founded by God in person 'and is thus God's own religion, uniquely superior to all others'.* Such was the implicit spiritual justification for European colonial conquest and exploitation.

In the light of biblical scholarship we now have a credible history of Jesus of Nazareth as a Galilean preacher and charismatic healer. Born in 7 BC as the son of Joseph and Mary, early editors of the original gospels of Matthew and Luke concocted a mythological prelude to Jesus's life story by telling of Mary's 'immaculate conception' and the virginal birth of this remarkable man (the circumstances of which followed the precedent of well-known contemporary pagan cults). Many of the details of the Nativity story (the mysterious 'star in the east', the visiting 'magi', the appearance of angels, the animals in the crib) were put together to form a charming and intimate scene, which has provided the inspiration for numerous artists from the earliest times. The Jews were at first quick to hail Jesus as the promised Messiah, in fulfilment of the biblical prophecy in Isaiah. Jesus himself, trained as a Jewish rabbi, was himself critical of the legalistic tradition of the Jewish priesthood and preached the gospel of a loving God, the need for repentance from sin, and the imminence of the arrival on earth of the Kingdom of God. He insisted that his message was directed only to Jews (as the 'chosen people'), but after his death the Church authorities deemed it necessary to preach the message of salvation to Gentiles worldwide (who proved to be far more receptive than the Jewish population). It was St Paul, above all other early missionaries, who spread the word throughout the Hellenised world and laid the foundation for its success. In fact, nowhere in the New Testament does Jesus claim to be God, and he could have had no conception of the later Church doctrine according to which he was elevated to the second person of a divine Trinity. Such a claim would have been impossible for a devout Jew. Indeed St Paul, considered by many to be the 'creator' of the religion now known as Christianity, and himself a Jew, never believed Jesus to have been 'God incarnate', and certainly no part of a theological construct such as the Trinity. The frequent use of the term 'Son of God' was a familiar one throughout the ancient world and was often applied to pharaohs, emperors and heroes. The term was always used metaphorically within Judaism. The various purported sayings of Jesus, such as 'I and the Father are one' (John 10: 30), 'He who has seen me as seen the Father' (John 14: 9) are now regarded by scholars as having been put into his mouth by a later editor of the fourth gospel. Thus Wolfhart Pannenberg in his book *Jesus: God and Man* (1968) says that: 'After D F Strauss and F C Bauer, John's Gospel could no longer be claimed uncritically as a historical source of authentic words of Jesus. Consequently, other concepts and titles that were more indirectly connected with Jesus's relation to God came into the foreground of the question of Jesus's 'Messianic self-consciousness'. However the transfer of these titles to Jesus... has been demonstrated with growing certainty by critical study of the Gospels to be the work of the post-Easter community'.[42] In Professor Hick's view 'We cannot rest anything on the assumption that the great Christological sayings of the Fourth Gospel (such as "I and my Father are one") were ever spoken in sober historical fact by... Jesus'.[43] But they were clearly believed in medieval times by – amongst others – the mystic Catherine of Siena (1347–80) in her work *The Dialogue*, where she puts in God's mouth the following words: 'Therefore of him [i.e. Jesus] I made for you a bridge. No man can come to me except by him, as he told you in the words 'No one can come to the Father except by me'.[44]

Jesus was in fact wholly human, as members of his family (who belonged to the Ebionite sect) readily appreciated. Yet his 'nature' was artificially defined, first, at the Council of Nicaea in 325 when a group of clerics *voted* him to be a god; at the Council of Chalcedon in 451 when he was *declared* to be consubstantial with the 'Father' in Godhead and existing in two 'natures', one human and one divine; and when he was *pronounced* to be the second person of the Holy Trinity at the Council of Toledo in 675. It is clear to scholars that the early Church authorities *interpolated passages* into the narratives of the evangelists to give the impression that the death of Jesus had been prefigured in the Bible and foreordained by God, and that he had instituted the ritual of the Eucharist (another borrowing from contemporary pagan cults and put into his mouth at a very early date, probably by St Paul, and copied by Paul's companion Luke). Jesus had exceptional charisma and preaching gifts, and he was always intensely aware of the presence of God. The Alexandrian priest Arius (250–336) – condemned for maintaining that Jesus was wholly human and excommunicated for this view in 321 – was seemingly correct in his assessment, while the Gnostic Cerinthus (who believed that the spirit of God descended upon Jesus at his baptism and left him during the Passion on the cross) could also lodge a plausible claim to have correctly interpreted the nature of Jesus.

Jesus's popular preaching aroused the jealousy of the Temple priests and the suspicion of the Roman administration who feared lest he was inciting sedition (one of his followers was a Zealot). With the collaboration of the Chief Priests he was arraigned before the Roman prefect of Judaea, Pontius Pilate, condemned and executed on Friday, 7 April, AD 30 by the usual method of crucifixion for those found guilty of sedition. After Jesus's death his followers kept together as a small religious movement, and gradually the Christian myth developed: God had descended to earth to be born of the Virgin Mary, and as 'his Son' had died to atone for our sins, and had risen again to heaven, and would return again in majesty on the 'Last Day'. When, some 200 years after the crucifixion, there was still no sign of the arrival of the Kingdom of God, the Church authorities had to formulate a theology which explained that the arrival of the Kingdom of God was synonymous with the establishment of the Church, while the realisation of the reign of God was deferred until the 'coming again' of Jesus and the expected 'final judgement'. The need today is to transmute a literal into a metaphorical understanding of the central themes of Christianity, and to recognise stories such as the Nativity and the Easter resurrection as poetical dramas designed to stir our imagination and emotions. Jesus's moral teaching, bearing witness to God's loving providence, and his promises of everlasting life in a heavenly kingdom (a common theme in other world religions) are of universal relevance for all time.

From the historic sources and the researches of theological scholars we may therefore conclude that:

1.   Jesus was officially declared to be a god, and *consubstantial* with God the Father, at a Council in Nicaea in 325, and the Nicene Creed was finalised at the Council of Constantinople in 381.

2.   The nature of Jesus was finally defined as *consubstantial* with the 'Father' in Godhead and existing in two natures, one human and one divine, at the Council of Chalcedon in 451.

3.   Jesus was regarded as the 'Word of God', the ultimate source of all human knowledge, who became flesh in human form.

4.   The doctrine of the Holy Ghost (or Spirit) was developed to form part of the Trinity of 'Father, Son and Holy Ghost', in whose name all liturgical forms of worship were conducted, at the Eleventh Council of Toledo in 675.

5.   The concepts of the Holy Trinity and of Jesus being God the Son incarnate have been seriously questioned by theological scholars in recent years, and the old 'certainties' which they represented have been found to be untenable in the modern world. It is important to note that during his lifetime Jesus emphatically *never* regarded himself as divine nor as the second person of a divine Trinity: such a claim would have been blasphemous and therefore impossible for a devout Jew. Jesus had no intention of founding a new religion. He would have regarded himself as having been sent by God as a prophet to pass on God's message to his chosen people. That is what members of his family believed. Thus the early Christian definitions of the specific nature of Jesus – divine, consubstantial with God and a member of the Holy Trinity – are meaningless today and can therefore be relegated to the pages of theological scholarship.

6.   Jesus may now unequivocally be considered to have been a charismatic human prophet intensely aware of God and the Transcendent, 'a man approved by God among you' (Acts 2: 22), whose moral teaching and promise of everlasting life are of universal relevance. Above all, Christians believe in the revelation of God given to the world in the person and teaching of Jesus. Early theological speculations as to his precise nature, which gave rise to bitter and often violent confrontations between bickering bishops, may safely be relegated to the pages of history (and to – no doubt – continued scholastic exegesis and disputation). Islam is surely correct in regarding such speculation as *zanna*.

NOTES

[1] As Professor Vermes points out: 'the representation of the Deity as 'Father' is a basic element of Old Testament theology'. It proclaims 'a parental relationship between God and individual members of the Jewish people' (Vermes, 2004, 223)

[2] Wilson, 1998, 33

[3] Ibid., 63

[4] Ibid., 33

[5] There were a remarkable number of tracts – so-called Gospels, Acts, Apocalypses and Epistles – written by contemporaries about Jesus. Some were forgeries. These are examined in detail by Professor Bart D Ehrman in his *Lost Christianities* (2003). We have referred to some of these tracts in section (b) above

[6] Quoted in Freeman, 2008, 59

[7] Ehrman, 2003, 178–9

[8] In his impressive scholastic work on *Arius* (2001), Dr Rowan Williams has traced the course of the Arian controversy. Arius's theology is discussed in detail on pages 95–116 of that work

[9] Amongst other matters discussed at the Council of Nicaea was the method of fixing the date of the festival of Easter. It was decided that Easter should be celebrated throughout the Christian world on the Sunday after the full moon following the vernal equinox. Furthermore, if the full moon were to occur on a Sunday coinciding with the Jewish Passover festival, Easter should be celebrated on the following Sunday. This decision accounts for the considerable variation, even today, in the date of Easter each year

[10] Williams, 2001, 79–81

[11] Ibid., 80

[12] Ibid., 81

[13] Ibid

[14] Ibid., 42

[15] Freeman, 2008, 59–63

[16] Ibid., 65

[17] This Council eclipsed a council which had been summoned by the Western emperor Gratian to meet at Aquileia in 381 organised by Ambrose, bishop of Milan, and intended to enforce Nicene orthodoxy on bishops of the Western Church

[18] Strangely the text seems to have disappeared until it was read out at the Council of Chalcedon in 451 (Freeman, 2008, 98)

[19] For a detailed account of the intensive debates leading up to the Councils of Nicaea and Constantinople see Freeman, 2008, 52–7, 78–104

[20] Freeman, 2008, 126–9

[21] Quoted in Butler, 1977, 97

[22] Freeman, 2008, 152

[23] Young, 1977, 28. She also recounts that 'Rightly or wrongly, deep emotions and profound intolerance stirred up councils, churches and armies of monks into horrific attacks upon one another, and to the excommunication and exile of upright and sincere church leaders. It is a distressingly human story' (page 28)

[24] Dill, 1919, 14–15

[25] Ibid., 30–1

[26] The other Trinitarian reference is Jesus's commandment to his disciples after he had risen from the dead and met them in Galilee when he instructed them to baptise their new disciples 'into the name of the Father and of the Son and of the Holy Ghost' (Matthew 28: 19). However, in this post-resurrection passage Jesus is recorded as saying: 'Go ye therefore, and teach all nations, baptising them...' We have noted elsewhere that Jesus was emphatic that his message was addressed to the chosen of Israel alone, and not to the Gentiles. Thus this passage in Matthew is almost certainly a later interpolation and can therefore be discounted.

[27] McGrath, 2007a, 250

[28] Freeman, 2008, 63

[29] The Athanasian Creed in full was as follows:
And the Catholick Faith is this: That we worship one God in Trinity, and Trinity in Unity;
Neither confounding the Persons: not dividing the Substance.
For there is one Person of the Father, another of the Son: and another of the Holy Ghost.
But the Godhead of the Father, of the Son, and of the Holy Ghost, is all one: the Glory equal, the Majesty co-eternal.
Such as the Father is, such is the Son: and such is the Holy Ghost.
The Father uncreate, the Son uncreate: and the Holy Ghost uncreate.
The Father incomprehensible, the Son incomprehensible: and the Holy Ghost incomprehensible.
The Father eternal, the Son eternal: and the Holy Ghost eternal.
And yet they are not three eternals: but one eternal.

As also there are not three incomprehensibles, not three uncreated: but one uncreated, and one incomprehensible.

So likewise the Father is Almighty, the Son Almighty: and the Holy Ghost Almighty.

And yet they are not three Almighties: but one Almighty

So the Father is God, the Son is God: and the Holy Ghost is God.

And yet they are not three Gods: but one God.

So likewise the Father is Lord, the Son Lord: and the Holy Ghost Lord.

And yet not three Lords: but one Lord.

For like as we are compelled by the Christian verity: to acknowledge every Person by himself to be God and Lord;

So are we forbidden by the Catholick Religion: to say, There be three Gods, or three Lords.

The Father is made of none: neither created, nor begotten.

The Son is of the Father alone: not made, not created, but begotten.

The Holy Ghost is of the Father and of the Son: neither made, nor created, nor begotten, but proceeding.

So there is one Father, not three Fathers: one Son, not three Sons: one Holy Ghost, not three Holy Ghosts.

And in this Trinity none is afore, or after other: none is greater, or less than another;

But the whole three Persons are co-eternal together: and co-equal.

So that in all things, as is aforesaid: the Unity in Trinity, and the Trinity in Unity is to be worshipped.

He therefore that will be saved: must thus think of the Trinity.

Furthermore, it is necessary to everlasting salvation: that he also believe rightly the incarnation of our Lord Jesus Christ.

For the right Faith is, that we believe and confess: that our Lord Jesus Christ, the Son of God, is God and Man;

God, of the Substance of the Father, begotten before the worlds: and Man, of the Substance of his Mother, born in the world;

Perfect God, and perfect Man: of a reasonable soul and human flesh subsisting;

Equal to the Father, as touching his Godhead: and inferior to the Father, as touching his Manhood.

Who although he be God and Man: yet he is not two, but one
Christ;
One; not by conversion of the Godhead into flesh: but by
taking of the Manhood into God;
One altogether; not by confusion of Substance: but by unity of
Person.
For as the reasonable soul and flesh is one man: so God and
Man is one Christ;
Who suffered for our salvation: descended into hell, rose again
the third day from the dead.
He ascended into heaven, he sitteth on the right hand of the
Father, God Almighty: from whence he shall come to judge the
quick and the dead.
At whose coming all men shall rise again with their bodies: and
shall give account for their own works.
And they that have done good shall go into life everlasting: and
they that have done evil into everlasting fire.
This is the Catholick Faith: which except a man believe
faithfully, he cannot be saved.
Glory be to the Father, and to the Son: and to the Holy Ghost;
As it was in the beginning, is now, and ever shall be: world
without end. Amen.

[30] McGrath, 2007a, 254–7
[31] Freeman, 2008, 100
[32] Quoted in McGrath, 2007a, 256–7
[33] For a full discussion of Abélard's clash with the Church authorities see Freeman, 2008, 188–193
[34] Armstrong, 1999, 350
[35] Kenny, 1992, 67
[36] Ibid.
[37] Perham, 2010,82
[38] Kenny, 1992, 65–6
[39] Priestland, 1981, 120–133
[40] Hick, 1977, 178–9
[41] Hume, 2002, 185
[42] Hick and Hebblethwaite, 1980, 184
[43] Ibid.
[44] Carrigen, 2007, 52–3. This claim is now thought by scholars to have been a later interpolation into the fourth gospel

(e)   Findings of biblical scholars and theologians

We are now in a position to summarize some of the conclusions of biblical scholars and theologians on the person of Jesus in the light of recent research and new textual discoveries. It has become clear that:

1. Jesus was born in a natural way, the son of Joseph and Mary, in the year 7 BC. He was one of twin sons, the other being named Didymus Judas Thomas.

2. After Jesus's death the legends of the 'Virgin birth' were composed by the early Church authorities to demonstrate the fulfilment of Isaiah's prophecy, thus turning the Jewish baby Jesus first into the promised Messiah, then into the Son of God, and finally into the position of God the Son, the Second Person of the Holy Trinity. Legendary features (such as the 'Star in the East' and the visit of the 'Three Kings') were added to embellish the account of the Nativity.

3. Jesus's preaching of the imminence of the arrival of the Kingdom of God had to be revised after his death. This 'arrival' was then held to be synonymous with the establishment of the 'Church'; the 'reign of God' was deferred until his 'coming again'.

4. The early Church authorities interpolated passages into the narratives of the evangelists *ex post facto* to give the appearance that:

(i)   Jesus had agreed that his message of salvation should be preached to the Gentiles as well as to the Jews

(ii) Jesus had predicted the details of his death and that this event was prefigured in the Bible and foreordained by God

(iii) Jesus had instituted the sacrament of the Eucharist (which St Paul claimed he had received by 'revelation' from Jesus and which was in fact based on contemporary pagan practices)

(iv) Jesus had established a 'Church' of which Simon Peter was to be the leader with the keys to open and lock the gates of the Kingdom of God. In fact, it is highly unlikely that Jesus ever contemplated 'founding' a new religion.

5. The early Church authorities:

(i) declared Jesus to be divine and consubstantial with God (325 and 381 AD)

(ii) defined the nature of Jesus in relation to God (451 AD)

(iii) formulated the doctrine of the Holy Trinity (675 AD)

(iv) formulated the doctrine of Jesus's resurrection based on the 'vision' of St Peter (Acts 10: 40–1), notwithstanding the fact that Jesus seemed unaware until the very last moment of his impending death and made no allusions to it in his parables

(v) established the historical narratives, doctrines and rituals which were to become the orthodox canon for the Christian Church, branding (sometimes unjustly) any churchmen or theologians who disagreed with their ex cathedra pronouncements as 'heretics'.

6. Jesus never regarded himself as divine nor as the Second Person of a divine Trinity. Some of his sayings (e.g. 'I and the Father are one') are now considered to have been later interpolations into the fourth gospel

7. Jesus is now considered to have been a charismatic human prophet intensely aware of God and the Transcendent, 'a man approved of God among you' (Acts 2: 22), whose moral teaching (bearing witness to God's loving providence) and his promises of everlasting life in a heavenly kingdom are of universal relevance even today

8. There is a widespread belief that, through the mechanism of the human conscience, humans are enabled to enter into a spiritual dimension receptive of the Transcendent. Religious believers (in whatever faith) will enter this dimension with their prayers in the hope of receiving spiritual support and enlightenment. Christians believe that through this medium they are indeed inheritors of the powers given to Jesus's disciples at Pentecost. Artists, musicians, writers, scientists and mathematicians may, consciously or unconsciously, derive inspiration from the Transcendent in their respective creative fields. And some of us may be able to enter into

other-worldly experiences through meditation and trance-like visions.

Many theologians and churchmen are frankly aware of some of these findings but are understandably reticent about making them public. They fear the disillusionment of the dwindling numbers of the faithful when they learn that many of the hallowed tenets of their religion are based on historical myths and questionable doctrines, some of them perpetrated by a small group of clerics when they began to formulate the doctrines and dogmas of their 'new' Christian religion in the second and third centuries AD. But it is surely time that responsible Christian ministers − from the highest to the lowest − make their congregations aware of the historical findings of twentieth century scholarship and theology.

(f)   The divisive history of the Eucharist

We have seen above (Section (b)) that Jesus is unlikely to have personally instituted the ritual of what came to be known as the 'Eucharist' and that this, together with the miraculous doctrine of Transubstantiation, was in fact a formulation by St Paul or the early Church authorities in their attempts to establish the 'orthodox' doctrines for their new religion. Indeed, the lack of clarity surrounding the interpretation of the so-called Eucharistic 'instruction', which is discussed below, argues strongly for a spontaneous Pauline origin. For most medieval Christians the 'Mass' (from the Latin 'missa est', pronounced at the end of the Service) was the embodiment of the Eucharist, and it was in practice amongst the most complicated of rituals largely depending on the ecclesiastical calendar which governed the various 'readings'.

Little did the authorities realise to what anguish, feuding and rebellion the interpretation of the words purported to have been spoken by Jesus at the pre-Passover *Seder* supper would give rise. In particular, what was the nature of Christ's presence in the Eucharist? Aelfric (*c.*955–1020), an Anglo-Saxon monk at Winchester who subsequently became abbot of Cerne, was author of two books of *Homilies*, in one of which was a Paschal homily *against* Transubstantiation (which was eventually published in 1566 during the Reformation). This is an interesting reflection upon the belief and practice of the pre-Conquest English Church. His contemporary, the scholastic theologian Berengar of Tours (999–1088) maintained that 'if Christ had truly died and was by the right hand of the father, then his 'presence' at the altar could not be his body or blood'. He was forced to recant and 'to swear to Christ's *real presence* – that Christ's body and blood are truly, in reality, present in the bread and wine'.[1] Aristotelian physics were then enlisted to provide an explanation of the mystery so that by the time of the Fourth Lateran Council (1215) the Council felt able to decree the doctrine of Transubstantiation – viz. that the bread 'changes in substance' into the body, and the wine 'changes in substance' into the blood of Jesus during the service of the Mass. Any deviation from this policy would be regarded as heresy and anathema (anyone so condemned could be liable to excommunication or indeed execution).[2] The Council also decreed that lay people should receive the sacrament of the Eucharist at least once a year at Easter.

The doctrine of Incarnation was another major issue for Christians by the sixteenth century. Catholic communities were divided over the Incarnation, in particular 'the nature of Christ's presence among his followers 1500 years after his death; what is meant for humanity and for God that Christ had a body or was embodied; and the import for the world of matter and for the human body of Christ's spoken words, 'this is my body', 'this do', and 'remembrance of me'.[3] The Chalcedonian (451) formula had concluded that Jesus was both God and man, but left the matter there with no attempt at interpretation. The doctrine of Incarnation – which starkly posed the question of the relationship between the world of matter and God – was at the very heart of the ritual known as the Eucharist and had implications for both the bread and the wine which formed the basis of the ritual. How were the words 'this is my body' and 'this do in remembrance of me' to be interpreted? As Professor Lee Palmer Wandel pointed out in her magisterial study *The Eucharist in the Reformation* (2006) 'Europe witnessed a vortex of conceptualisation of the Eucharist – not one or two or three, but hundreds – fragmenting communities at every level, from family to state, as individuals, predominantly preachers... gave voice to divergent understandings of what these words mean for worship'.[4] And it is noteworthy that sixteenth-century Christians could not even agree on a name for the Eucharistic ritual – some continued to call it 'Communio' (Latin) or 'Communion' (English), others 'Abendmahl' or 'la Cène' or 'Supper'. These 'deep divisions in understanding of the relationship between humanity and God and of how Christ is 'present' among the living community of the faithful' coincided with the arrival of European humanism and scholarship, and especially of Erasmus's new translation of the New Testament based on the earliest extant texts.[5]

The confusion in the Church centred on a number of important questions. It was asked: what is 'my body'? What kind of body did Jesus have: was he seated at the right hand of God or was he corporeally present among Christians on earth? Was Jesus's body human or different because of his divinity? Was Jesus capable of being in the bread at the moment his own words (or those attributed to him) were spoken by the priest and was he capable of being everywhere at the same time? The words 'this do' (in remembrance of Jesus) had by 1500 come to mean that the Church 'through councils, papal bulls, and episcopal decrees, had come to stipulate who was to participate, degrees of participation, the clothing of the celebrant(s) and their connotations, the gestures of the celebrant and their connotations, the times and places when and where the Eucharist could be celebrated, as well as the vessels, the specific site – the 'altar' – the lighting, the music, the incense – all the somatic dimensions of the ritual'.[6] Contrast this with the simple pre-Passover *Seder* meal, an *agape* celebration amongst friends, eaten in the guest chamber of a house designated by Jesus in Jerusalem. The brief record of the meal is totally silent on the many 'details' considered later to be so central theologically. 'Why did it matter, if an altar or a table was the site of the ritual? Why did it matter if the container for the wine was silver or tin? Why did it matter what the celebrant wore?'[7] There were many bitter debates, and in Professor Wandel's words 'the divisions that were unleashed as Christians sought to hear precisely God's Word tore apart not only European Christendom, but a Christendom that was extending across the globe... The power of those words ['do this in remembrance of me'] and of the divisions they engendered in the sixteenth century haunt us to this day'.[8] The squabbles resulted in (for example) the City Council of Augsburg (in 1530) instituting its own, unique liturgy, both theology and practice, and in 1533 the City of Nuremberg published its own Church Ordinance. By the end of the century three Churches had been recognised as doctrinally, liturgically, and ecclesiastically distinct: Lutheran, Reformed and Catholic. The Lutheran tradition was based on Martin Luther's concept of the Eucharist (see page 181 above), and was followed by both the kingdoms of Denmark and Sweden. *The Scots Confession* drafted (in Latin) by John Knox and adopted in 1560 was in fact only ratified after the abdication of Mary Stuart in 1567. On the Eucharist this follows Calvin's evangelical line – 'Not that we imagine any transubstantiation of bread into Christ's body, and of wine into his actual blood, as the

Romanists have perniciously taught and wrongly believed'.[9] Finally, the Council of Trent (1545–1563) issued (1551) decrees on the Eucharist, confirming the doctrine of transubstantiation, and Pope Pius V published the Tridentine Missal (1570) with its implications for the Mass throughout the Christian world.

In the 1960s the question of transubstantiation came under critical examination by Catholic theologians, of whom the late Professor Edward Schillebeeckx was the most prominent. He was aware of the growing hostility in Catholic circles to the 'ontological' or 'physical' interpretations of the Eucharist', and his book *The Eucharist* (1968) set out his views. He maintained that the sacraments should be understood as 'symbolic acts or activity as signs': in the Eucharist there was 'no need to invoke the notion of a physical change of substance of the bread and wine. Christ's intention was not to alter the metaphysics of the eucharistic elements, but to ensure that these pointed to his continuing presence within the church, as the community of the faithful'.[10] The official response of the Catholic Church was to assert that such ideas 'were acceptable, provided that they were upheld within the context of the traditional understanding of transubstantiation'.[11] In other words, no change in the traditional doctrine!

So long as credulity and superstition continue to play an important rôle in the mind-set of Roman Catholics, believers will be untroubled by scientific or theological objections to questionable articles of their faith such as transubstantiation or incarnation. But for many – including Catholics – it is time the Church re-examined its inflexibility, and papal 'infallibility', on matters of doctrine which for most people are now hopelessly out of date. As Father Timothy Radcliffe writes: 'The Eucharist is often called 'the sacrament of unity', and yet it is also that which divides the Body of Christ. That we do not share communion with each other is the source of much pain. It impairs our witness to Christ, in whom God gathers all of creation into unity'.[12] Indeed, it is hard to understand how Roman Catholic Churches can continue to deny offering the Eucharist to visitors from other Christian congregations: it is regarded by them, sadly, as a slap on the face.

Notwithstanding the undoubted historical divisiveness of the ritual surrounding the Eucharist, there can be no doubt that today the Eucharist remains the most important ritual in the Christian Church. Thus Michael Perham, Bishop of Gloucester, believes that 'the Eucharist draws me into an experience of the reality of God'. And he reflects 'on the mystery of how God takes the bread and wine that we place upon an altar table, and by the operation of the Holy Spirit inhabits that bread and wine in a way that is more than a symbol as we give thanks, break and share; and God continues to be present in a real sense beyond the celebration in the bread'. [13] For Christians, whether the Eucharist should be regarded as a symbol or as an experience of the reality of God must be an individual judgement.

NOTES

[1] Wandel, 2006, 21
[2] Ibid., 20–1
[3] Ibid., 12–13
[4] Ibid., 2
[5] Ibid., 3–5
[6] Ibid., 9
[7] Ibid., 10
[8] Ibid., 11
[9] Ibid., 188
[10] McGrath, 2007a, 438–9
[11] Ibid., 439
[12] Radcliffe, 2008, 13
[13] Perham, 2010, 31–6

5. RELIGIOUS PLURALISM

From medieval times the Catholic Church proclaimed its absolutism in forthright terms. The Council of Florence (1438–45) declared that 'no one remaining outside the Catholic Church, not just pagans, but also Jews or heretics or schismatics, can become partakers of eternal life; but they will go to the everlasting fire which was prepared for the devil and his angels, unless before the end of life they are joined to the church'.[1] This was enshrined in traditional Roman Catholic dogma as the expression *extra ecclesiam nulla salus* (i.e. outside the Church there is no salvation). It was this cast of thought that inspired the Church to support the Crusades and political persecutions; to send out missionaries into every corner of the world, and to assume that it was God's will that all mankind should eventually be converted to the Christian faith.[2] Such dogmatic ecclesiastical imperialism was ineluctably and gradually modified as a result of growing contacts with, and knowledge of other world faiths, and the realisation that the Christian faith is held by only a minority of the human race, so that by the time of the Second Vatican Council (1965) the Catholic Church was able to declare that 'God's providence and his evident goodness and his plan of salvation extend to all men...' and that the Church 'urges her sons... to join members of other religions in discussions and collaboration...'[3] Furthermore, biblical scholars are now convinced that the words attributed in St John's Gospel to Jesus where he says 'No one comes to the Father, but by me' and other comparable statements are in fact later interpolations by the Church authorities when they set about defining future Christian doctrines in terms of Jesus's incarnation and his position as the Second Person of the Holy Trinity – concepts totally unknown to Jesus himself.

With the Catholic Church at last recognising that Christianity holds no monopoly of faith nor exclusive key to salvation, most people agree with Hans Küng when he stated that 'a man is to be saved within the religion that is made available to him in his historical situation. Hence it is his right and duty to seek God within that religion in which the hidden God has already found him'.[4] From this it follows that we have to recognise 'that the universe of faiths centres upon *God*, and not upon Christianity or upon any other religion... that the different world religions have each served as God's means of revelation to and point of contact with a different stream of human life'.[5] As Cardinal John Henry Newman once said, there is 'something true and divinely revealed in all religions'. There is moreover universal accord amongst the great world religions that kenosis – love and self-sacrifice – is the foundation of morality amongst all mankind.

Religious pluralism (which was a cardinal belief of Mahatma Gandhi) – 'the idea that the great world religions are different human responses to the same ultimate transcendent reality' which is in itself beyond the scope of our human conceptional systems – has been ably discussed by Professor John Hick in his *The Fifth Dimension* (2004).[6] As he explains: 'This means that the different world religions – each with its own sacred scriptures, spiritual practices, forms of religious experience, belief systems, founder or great exemplars, communal memories, culture expression in ways of life, laws and customs, art forms and so on – taken together as complex historical totalities, constitute different human responses to the ultimate transcendent reality to which they all, in their different ways, bear witness'.[7] It is noteworthy that the founders of these world religions were profoundly spiritual figures with exceptional sensitivity to the Transcendent and whose experiences we understand by the term 'revelation'. The first millennium BC, a period often referred to as the Axial Age (800–200 BC), produced men of profound spiritual insight – the Chinese Confucius; the Indian Siddhartha Gautama (the Buddha) and Jaina Mahavira (the founder of the Jain tradition); in Persia Zoroaster; the Hebrew prophets Amos, Hosea and Jeremiah; the Greek philosophers Pythagoras, Socrates, Plato and Aristotle. The following millennium saw the lives of the Jewish Jesus of Nazareth and the Arabic Muhammad with the revealed God of the Qur'an.

Because of the lack of intercommunication between continents, people developed in different cultural worlds, and in consequence it is not surprising to find early experiences of divine revelation being manifested to human beings growing up in conditions of widely differing culture, language and climate. Hence the differences in spiritual beliefs and practices of the chief world religions. Thus some will concentrate on the mystical and prophetic kinds of faith, others on the more spontaneous liturgical and more structured forms of devotion. Of course no one can define 'Ultimate Reality', nor do we have the right to criticise the way different religions approach it. We may note here that although the supreme being is called by different names in different religions – God by Christians, Adonai by Jews, al-Lah (Allah) by Muslims, Param Atma by Sikhs and Rama (or Krishna) by Hindus – the varying terms are used to designate the Ultimate Reality of the universe which has been responsible for the creation of heaven and earth. But it is important to emphasise that the term 'God' is one of convenience, since some religions – e.g. Buddhism – deny that human language can describe a reality that lies beyond our system of concepts and reason. Thus the essential difference between Buddhism and Christianity is that the former is a *practice* and a discipline which offers a route to salvation, rather than the worship of a 'Creator God'. It is attractive because of its emphasis on non-violence and contemplation, and its concentration upon the suffering of humanity.

What is evident today, in an increasingly ecumenical climate of opinion, is that 'God' is being worshipped not only by Christians in numerous church settings and rituals, but also by Muslims, Jews, Sikhs and Hindus in their own special ways. Professor Hick is surely correct in recognising this pluralistic religious convergence, and he quotes from *The Bhagavad Gita* the words: 'Howsoever man may approach me, even so do I accept them; for on all sides, whatever path they may choose is mine'.[8] Thus we may recall that Gandhi (1869–1948), a devout Hindu, believed that 'religions are different roads converging at the same point. What does it matter that we take different roads so long as we reach the same goal? I believe in the fundamental truths of all great religions of the world. I believe they are all God given… No one faith is perfect. All faiths are equally clear to their respective votaries'.[9]

The Hindu tradition (the name Hindu, incidentally, being derived from the people who occupied the land drained by the river Indus), as expounded by the sacred texts known as the Vedas and the Upanishads, came to be dominated by the two great figures of Shiva and Vishnu, with Rama and Krishna as incarnations or avatars of Vishnu (Krishna being regarded as the eighth incarnation of Vishnu, and whose birthday is celebrated in the Hindu festival of Janmashtami). Together with innumerable lesser gods all are regarded as providing access to the ultimate reality of Brahman, the inner meaning of all existence. Hinduism has never insisted upon uniformity in matters of belief and practice because of the complexity of the ancient religion. Human beings, according to Hindu tradition, are imbued with the eternal principle known as atman, and are engaged in a spiritual journey towards unity with the Divine Soul. Everyone is regarded as being in samsara, the endless round of re-births from which ultimately it is hoped to escape and to achieve union with Brahman. The nature of each re-birth is determined by the law of karma – implying one's works or deeds in that particular incarnation, but, importantly, there is no supreme judge making a decision in each individual case. Ultimately, devotees are all moving towards a final liberation – i.e. the achievement of moksa.

It is important to make the point that, centuries before Christianity and Islam appeared in the world, the Hindu and other contemporary religions had preached the principle of re-incarnation. This would achieve the objective, according to the law of *Karma*, of rewarding or condemning an individual depending on his/her record in the life just lived. Ultimately, everyone has the opportunity to achieve final liberation and unification with Ultimate Reality or Brahman. By contrast, the Christian 'Final Judgement' at the end of this life is a blatantly histrionic affair which gives little hope to the wicked who will apparently then and there be cast into outer darkness and not accorded a fresh chance of behavioural improvement as would be the case with Hindu reincarnation. While one may have an open mind about a final judgement, worldly experience suggests that this has been a consistent threat by prophets and religious leaders to increase their hold over a frightened populace. Medieval frescos in rural churches of the 'Last Judgement' were designed to intimidate!

Spiritual leaders of the Indian subcontinent such as Siddhartha Gautama (born *c.*404 BC) (later known as Buddha – 'the enlightened'), the founder of Buddhism, and Mahavira, leader of the Jains, taught that there were two distinct worlds, the material and the spiritual. The goal of life is to achieve freedom from the material world, a world of *dukkha* or perpetual suffering, so as to attain *nirvāna*, a Sanscrit word meaning 'extinguishedness' or the extinguishment of desire, greed, acquisitiveness and the end of pain ('the supreme goal and the one and only consummation of our life, the eternal, hidden and incomprehensible Peace'[10]). This could be achieved by following a systematic lifestyle known as the Noble Eightfold Path, and by living a life of compassion for all living beings. Later a new form of Buddhist emerged, the *bodhisattva*, who put off his own *nirvāna* so as to help others achieve their own spiritual enlightenment. Both Buddhism and Jainism constitute small minorities in India. They each reject the gods of the Hindus, yet believe in a future life and its culmination in *nirvāna*. Buddhism has spread throughout the world, particularly in Tibet and Thailand, and it was once the state religion of China (where it has harmonised with traditional Chinese reverence for ancestors). In 2001 there were some 152,000 Buddhists in the UK. Buddhism insists that there is no one way to enlightenment and embraces many practices, from active meditation of monks to the chants of married Japanese Buddhist priests, but its underlying philosophy is reverence for the material world. Then there is the small (70,000 in number) but influential group in India known as the Parsees, followers of the Iranian prophet Zarathustra (sixth-century BC), who arrived in the country after Iran had been conquered by Alexander the Great. They seek no converts, and like Judaism being a Parsee is a matter of race and religion. They are renowned for their philanthropy.

In China Confucius (551–479 BC) and Lau-Tzu emphasised the harmony of nature and in order to stem the conflicts in everyday life (which they attributed to an imbalance of natural forces) they taught a regime known as the 'Way of Heaven'. Yet Confucius was not a conventional religious thinker. He was a member of the professional class and a talented administrator who loved history and music, but his students wrote down his views on life which were later embodied as his *Analects*, which covered subjects such as personal duty, family responsibility and society in general. He rejected dogmatics and encouraged his students to think for themselves. His golden rule: 'what you do not wish done to yourself, do not do to others' has moral overtones yet did not carry with it any religious implications. As a moral sage he had immense influence and Confucian Institutes are now being established in China and overseas. It has been pointed out that Confucianism 'does not display anything like the organised religious structure or developed theism of Judaism, Christianity or Islam, but 'this does not make Confucianism one bit less a religious world-view...' After the arrival of the Jesuit missionaries in the sixteenth century many Confucians 'embraced the Christian faith as something entirely compatible with their Confucian commitment'. This is surely still true today.[11]

Sikhism, founded by Guru Nanak (1469–1539) in the fifteenth century is a monotheistic religion which did not recognise any distinction between the Hindu gods and the Muslim god al-Lah. Thus the creed of Sikhism begins with the words: 'There is but one God: *Sati* [Truth] by name...' As Guru Gobind Singh, the tenth of the Sikh gurus, stated: 'God is the same, whether known as "Allah" or "Abhak". The message of God's scriptures is the same. All scriptures take the same form and emanate from the same source. All people are of the human race and should be recognised as one'.[12] The Sikhs abolished the Indian caste distinctions and adopted the surname 'Singh' (meaning 'lion') and the practice of unshorn hair. They worship the *Akal* ('Timeless God') in their gurdwaras (or temples), and founded the city of Amritsar in India as their capital, where they built the famous Golden Temple with its four domes to indicate that it is open to all peoples from every direction. Sikhism is a visionary religion and believes in the efficacy of meditation. For Sikhs there is a series of different stages of spiritual development before attaining the ultimate vision when they enter *sach khand*, the realm of truth, and join the elect in the company of the Creator. The Sikh community in Britain now numbers some 400,000 members.[13]

In Islam, amongst the mystics, there is a distinction between the ultimate reality, *al-Haqq*, and the revealed God of the Qur'an. Thus Muid ad-Din ibn al-Arabi (1165–1240) says: 'God is absolute or restricted as He pleases; and the God of religious belief is subject to limitations, for He is the God contained in the heart of His servants. But the Absolute God is not contained in anything'.[14] Islam, too believes in the goodwill of God towards humanity and in particular for those who obey him. Indeed, as Professor Hick recounts: 'Each surah, or chapter, of the Qur'an begins, 'In the name of God, *rahman hahim* ['most benevolent, ever merciful']'.[15] Muslims believe that it is not particular sins but 'the complete rejection of God' which leads a man to the torments of hell. The Qur'an maintains that God 'has laid down for you the same way of life and belief which he had commended to Noah, and which We have enjoined to you, and which We have bequeathed to Abraham, Moses and Jesus... Say [to the Jews and Christians]: "I believe in whatever Scripture God has revealed, and I am commanded to act with equivalence among you. God is our Lord and your Lord. To us our actions, to you your deeds. There is no dispute between you and us. God will gather us all together, and to Him is our returning."' Throughout the Qur'an 'there is a profound sense of the unfathomable mercy of God'.[16] For the history and early development of Islam see Chapter 3(i).

Islam has become a much-maligned religion in recent years – largely because of the atrocities perpetrated by radical Muslims following their own narrow political perception of the justification for 'jihad' against any 'infidels'. There is now a clear distinction between Muslims and Islamists, the latter calling for a totalitarian Islamist state with *jihad* – 'confronting the West and killing non-Muslims and Muslims' – as its foreign policy. But in fact the tenets of Islam – if faithfully observed – are of exceptional virtue and vision. The fundamental beliefs of Islam are as follows:

- the equality of human beings, irrespective of social status, colour, sex or territorial origin. Respect for those of other faiths (who are all equal before Allah)
- justice tempered with compassion and mercy
- the creation of a just and egalitarian society

- the just distribution of wealth in society and warning against
  the accumulation of wealth for personal benefit and hence
  the consumerism of modern capitalist societies
- the payment of *zakah*, an obligatory levy to assist the poor,
  widows and orphans, and even the manumission of slaves
- the freedom of conscience
- the oneness of humanity and for humanity to live in peace
  and harmony.

However, over the years Islamic prayers or *salah* have been
reduced to mere ritual, glossing over the obligations to weaker
sections of society because of the vested interests of the wealthy.
Most Muslims follow religious practices mechanically, and this
tends to transform their religion into a set of fixed rituals which
largely overshadow the vision of its founder. Thus it has been said
that 'the radical thrust of Islamic prayer has been lost and prayer
becomes a mechanical exercise, performed without knowing what
one is reciting from the holy Qur'an. Millions of Muslims do not
know the Arabic language and all prayers are said in that
language… The same can be said of other rituals such as fasting
and the hajj, which are no less mechanically performed, their
spiritual and liberative contents having been lost…'

Another factor which brings Islam into disrepute today is the
interpretation of the Qur'an by hard-line sects (such as the
Wahhabi, Ikwani, or Salafi), sometimes based on the *hadiths* (or
sayings of the Prophet) some of which are indeed spurious and
were compiled many years after the Prophet's death. For example,
the wearing by women of the hijab (head-scarf) or face-covering
(niqab or burka) is pronounced by such sects as being a religious
requirement. It is nothing of the kind. While calling for public
modesty on the part of both sexes there is no mention in the
Qur'an of the words burka or niqab, the wearing of which is
solely a matter of personal cultural choice. As Dr T Hargey has
pointed out, the particular dress of women is 'neither a Koranic
imperative or a religious duty'.[17]

The problem for Muslims in Britain and other non-Muslim
countries is that Islam has no ecclesiastical hierarchy like
Christianity and there is therefore no recognised leader who can

264

speak on its behalf. In Britain there are Muslims from many different backgrounds and ethnic groups (e.g. Bangladesh, India, Pakistan, Egypt), and there is often competition and rivalry between them. Several umbrella groups have been formed – e.g. to try to bring these diverse traditions together, but there is no overall leader with recognised religious authority who might counter Islamic extremism.

In sum, the vision of Islam is 'the creation of a just and egalitarian society where there will be no hierarchy or status; where there will be no accumulation of wealth in a few hands; where there will be no master and slaves, physical or intellectual; where there will be complete freedom of conscience and expression; where human dignity will not be trampled upon; where religious, ethnic, racial and territorial differences will not stand in the way of human unity; where dogmas will not divide human beings and restrict their freedom; where gender injustice will not be permitted and where all human beings will keep their heads high'.[18] In the light of prevailing political and social conditions in the Middle East there is clearly a long way to go before the vision of the Prophet Muhammad will be entirely realised, but optimists and people of goodwill look forward to that day, as they reflect upon the great contribution made to the world by Muslims in earlier centuries in the fields of scholarship, literature and art.

Another interesting group are the followers of the Bahá'i faith – the religion of Bahá'u'lláh, the name (meaning 'splendour of God') given to Mirza Huseyn Ali (1817–92), who in 1843 founded a new religion embracing Muslim, Christian, Jewish and Parsee elements. Supporters of this faith (who regard Bahá'u'lláh as a messenger of God and his writings as the Word of God) are untrammelled by the foundation myths and historical baggage of the major world religions, and concentrate essentially on a future vision of the world in which we live. They believe that they come to know God through those 'manifestations of God' through whom God's will is manifested, which have included the historical figures of Abraham, Moses, Buddha, Jesus, Muhammad and Bahá'u'lláh. They proclaim 'all established religions to be divine in origin, identical in their aims, complimentary in their functions, continuous in their purpose, indispensable in their value to mankind'. The Bahá'i faith seeks therefore to distil the essence of the major religions of the world without the accumulated layers of superstition, myth and ritual with which they are encumbered. It maintains that a new divine revelation – in the person of Bahá'u'lláh and which was equivalent to the second-coming of Jesus Christ – has begun the process whereby humanity is already beginning to transform society across the world. This task will lead to the establishment of the 'Lesser Peace' which will be followed in due time by the 'Most Great Peace' when all divisions between the peoples of the world will have disappeared and mankind will be truly one. Thus 'inculcating a consciousness of the oneness of humankind is a specific goal of the Bahá'i faith'.

Bahá'u'lláh's son and successor was Abdu'l-Bahá (1844–1921), who wrote a treatise called the 'Seven Candles of Unity' which specifies the various goals of humanity, such as 'political unity', 'unity of thought', 'unity of freedom', 'unity of religion' (this being 'the corner-stone of the foundation itself...'), 'unity of nations', 'unity of race' and 'unity of language'. Progress towards some of these may already be discerned in international political organisations and in the appeal of political freedoms and human rights. The concept of the 'unity of religion' may however be a stumbling block in that Bahá'i scriptures speak of 'repudiating the claim of any religion to be the final revelation of God to man...' and insisting on distinguishing between 'the essential and the authentic from the non-essential and spurious in their teachings, separates the God-given truths from the priest-prompted superstitions...' The Bahá'i religion maintains that 'the kingdom of God will not be heaven on earth; humans will still experience pain, struggles and suffering', but all this 'in a social climate that is far more equal and just, and far less violent and prejudiced, than the contemporary world'. Although the emphasis of the Bahá'i faith is on unification amongst the people of this world, they do in fact also believe in an afterlife. Thus 'the nature of the soul after death can never be described, nor is it meet and permissible to reveal its whole character to the eyes of men. The Prophets and Messengers of God have been sent down for the sole purpose of guiding mankind to the straight Paths of Truth. The purpose underlying Their revelation hath been to educate all men, that they may, at the hour of death, ascend in the utmost purity and sanctity and with absolute detachment, to the throne of the Most High...'[19]

As Professor Keith Ward has emphasised: 'At their best most religions offer a distinctive emphasis which can be reflected by others, and thereby given a different tone and colouring in its new contexts. The compassion for all beings which Buddhism and Jainism affirm so strongly, the reverence for humanity that characterises Christianity, the love of life of Judaism, the total dependence on the divine will of Islam, the inner harmony and mindfulness of East Asian spirituality and the profound sense of the unity of all things in the cosmic self which is found to such a degree in Hinduism – all these, and many more, are facets of spiritual reality which are discerned in the diverse faiths of the world'.[20]

All the world religions have undergone historical development, although Islam has probably changed less than the others and sometimes still exhibits instances of a medieval mind-set (such as stoning to death and beheading). Yet the essence of Islam is a spirit of tolerance and co-operation. This is seen particularly in the policies of Akbar, the third Moghul emperor (who reigned from 1560–1605), who was a respecter of all faiths. In Karen Armstrong's words: 'out of sensitivity to the Hindus, he became a vegetarian, gave up hunting – a sport he greatly enjoyed – and forbade the sacrifice of animals on his birthday or in the Hindu holy places. In 1575 he founded a House of Worship, where scholars from all religions could meet to discuss God. Here, apparently, the Jesuit missionaries from Europe were the most aggressive. He founded his own Sufi order, dedicated to 'divine monotheism' (*tawhid-e-ilahi*), which proclaimed a radical belief in the one God who could reveal himself in any rightly-guided religion'.[21] Alas, such an enlightened policy did not last and the policies of the later emperors led to conflicts between Muslims, Hindus and Sikhs. Over the years there have been conflicts between Church missionaries and other faiths in the mistaken belief that the whole world would ultimately become Christian.[22] It is now, at long last, beginning to be recognised that a 'one-world religion' is a chimera, and that the way forward is to conceive of a common quest or shared pilgrimage between religions in seeking the one ultimate Reality. As a Sufi poet wrote: 'On my way to the mosque, O Lord, I passed the Magian in front of his flame, deep in thought, and a little further I heard a rabbi reciting his holy book in the synagogue, and then I came upon the church where the hymns sung gently in my ears and finally I came into the mosque and pondered how many are the different ways to You – the one God'.[23] And in St John's vision of the heavenly city he implies that there is no Christian church, no Jewish synagogue, no Hindu or Buddhist temple, no Muslim mosque, no Sikh gurdwara, for all these exist in time, as routes through time to eternity. As Father Timothy Radcliffe writes: 'Our destiny is to make our way to our destination, which is life with God, our happiness'.[24]

In recent years there has been an attempt to bridge the differences, and encourage warmer relations, between the three Abrahamic religions of Jews, Muslims and Christians by the establishment of The Three Faiths Forum, on the initiative of Sir Sigmund Sternberg. The forum fosters links between professionals of each faith (e.g. doctors and lawyers) and attempts to mediate in conflicts in the Middle East and to promote tolerance in this region. In the same spirit it is to be hoped that the recent approach (2007) of 138 leading scholars from every branch of Islam addressed to the Pope, Archbishop of Canterbury and other Church leaders around the world 'to come together with us on the common essentials of our two religions' with a view to contributing to global peace, will produce fruitful dialogue and, with other like-minded initiatives, perhaps herald a climate of increasing understanding between people of all faiths. This, it should be said, is the essential purpose of the Bahá'i faith whose supporters will warmly endorse all such initiatives.

NOTES

[1]   Hick and Hebblethwaite, 1980, 178

2   This antipathy towards other religions was reinforced by customs deemed abhorrent to civilised values. For example, the Islamic practice under Sharia law of stoning and beheading culprits; the Hindu practice of *suttee* (where wives have to throw themselves alive on to the funeral pyre of their deceased husbands); and the Hindu practice of polygamy and infanticide. Efforts at evangelisation overseas began at the end of the eighteenth century under the influence of devoted Christians such as William Wilberforce which led to the formation of the Church Missionary Society for Africa and the East

3   Hick and Hebblethwaite, 1980, 80–6

4   Ibid., 179

5   Ibid., 182

6   First published in 1999. My quotations are from the 2004 edition. See also Ward, 2004, 220–237 and Peterson *et al.*, 2003, 267–285

7   Hick, 2004, 83

8   Ibid., 190

9   Ibid., 210

10   Conze, E., 1959, *Buddhism: its Essence and Development*, 40

11   See Berthrong, J., 1995, 'A Confucian-Christian?', in Forward, M. (ed.) 1995, 22–36

12   Fisher, M. P., 1995. 'Interfaith Vision at Gobind Sadan', in Forward, M. (ed.), 1995, 100

13   See Mohinder Singh, 1995. 'The Sikh Vision of the Ultimate', in Forward, M., (ed.), 1995, 250–6

14   Quoted by Hick, 2004, 95–6

15   Ibid., 76

16   Ibid., 77. It may also be noted that the Qur'an is fundamentally opposed to the actions of those Muslims who perpetrate acts of terrorism in its name. The Qur'an teaches that Islam is a religion of peace and not war. It teaches its followers to be tolerant and compassionate, to help those who are sick and infirm. It forbids the killing or maiming of an innocent person, and instructs that one should not take one's own life. Thus strapping explosives to one's body in order to kill others in an act of suicide in search of martyrdom is totally non-Islamic and contrary to the injunctions of the Qur'an which all Muslims must obey. The tragic events of 9/11 in New York and 7/7 in London sees Islam – a religion of peace – associated with murder and terrorism

17   T. Hargey, *The Times*, 25 June, 2009

[18] Engineer, A. A., 1995, 'Islam: The Ultimate Vision', in Forward, M. (ed.), 1995, 92–99

[19] Momen, W., 1995, 'Why I am a Bahá'í', in Forward, M. (ed.), 1995, 196–206; Stockman, R., 1995, 'The Vision of the Bahá'í Faith' in ibid., 266–274

[20] Ward, 2004, 233

[21] Armstrong, 1999, 303

[22] Thus as late as 1995 Dr Daleep Mukarji of the Christian Medical Association of India regretted the narrow evangelism and triumphalistic aspect of Christianity which offered a simple gospel of personal salvation in another world yet little reference to the problems and realities of the current world, and that there was little tolerance for people of other faiths

[23] Quoted in Braybrooke, M., 1995, 'One-World Faith?', in Forward, M. (ed.), 1995, 45

[24] Radcliffe, 2008, 153

6. OTHER FORMS OF SPIRITUALITY

One of the most perceptive students of religion in the nineteenth century was Emile Durkheim who maintained that all 'religions' are social phenomena. Thus in his view religion may be defined as a 'unified system of beliefs and practices relative to sacred things... which unite into one single moral community called a church, those who adhere to them'.[1] He drew a distinction between 'a religion handed down by tradition' and a 'free, private, optional religion, fashioned according to one's own needs and understanding'. The most significant feature of the past century has been a relentless shift in sentiment from 'traditional' religion to subjective-life spirituality. In society today individuals exhibit a greater concern for self-development and psychic well-being than for other-worldly salvation. When Horace Man conducted his census of *Religious Worship in England and Wales* in 1854 the percentage of the population attending church on the census Sunday was about 39%. Since then the picture has been one of relentless decline in church attendance. Congregational membership declined from 33% of the population in 1900 to 29% in 1930, to 24% in 1960, and then a more rapid decline to 12% in the year 2000.[2] In 2003 Steve Bruce forecast that 'three decades from now, Christianity in Britain will have largely disappeared'.[3] Peter Brierley's surveys extrapolate this decline to a possible figure of 0.9% of the English population still attending church in 2016.[4] The reasons for this decline in church attendance stem partly from the age profile of congregations: the average age of a churchgoer is now higher than the average age of the population, while the number of young people under 19 attending church has halved in the last 20 years to 25% of all churchgoers. According to Heelas and Woodhead 'when the current (older) generation of churchgoers die out, there will be very few people to take their place'.[5] Heelas and Woodhead state that some 4,600,000 people in Britain today 'are active in the congregational domain on a typical

Sunday, and around 900,000 in the holistic milieu during a typical week'.[6] This 'spiritual revolution' – i.e. the growth of 'holistic ('alternative', 'body, mind and spirit', 'New Age') spiritualities such as yoga, reiki, meditation, tai chi, aromatherapy, reflexology, wicca, etc. – has been gathering pace since the 1960s and now presents a serious challenge to conventional Christianity.

People are now searching for meaning in their lives so as to make sense of the many confusions in this world. But there is a danger that, by rejecting the discipline of the mainstream religions, individuals may be attracted to forms of spirituality that are inward-looking and concentrate on the individual's own soul and on their personal relationship to God, rather than being linked with a community of charity and good deeds. It can therefore lead to selfish personal self-obsession. In recent years young people have turned to such practices as Zen Buddhism, Transcendental Meditation and to Kabbalism in order to satisfy their search for personal spiritual fulfilment. As an alternative form of spirituality let us consider (for example) Yoga.

Yoga is derived from a Sanskrit word signifying 'union between mind, body and spirit' and dates from the Indus Valley civilisation some 4,000 years ago. It has developed many different styles over the years but essentially offers classes in physical exercises and meditation designed to bring inner peace to its participants. It is feared by some Christians who maintain that it is a form of pagan worship, and yoga classes have sometimes been banned from church halls. Even if yoga has its roots in Hindu faith this reaction seems incredibly short-sighted. Reiki, another practice, is an ancient holistic therapy which was revived by a Japanese doctor, Mikao Usui, in the late nineteenth century. It involves placing the hands on parts of the anatomy with the aim of alleviating pain and stress through relaxation. The results range from a 'feeling of calm' to an improvement in physical, mental or emotional problems. It can help the body's self-healing abilities, and can thus be regarded as a 'holistic' treatment.

A 1998 review found that by the 1990s, 31% of the population of Britain believed in 'God as Personal' compared with 40% who believed in 'God as Spirit or Life Force'. The 'Soul of Britain' survey in 2000 revealed that only 26% now believed in 'a personal

God' with 44% either reporting belief in 'some sort of spirit or life force' or 'there is something there'.[7] The same poll, incidentally, found that 31% considered themselves to be 'a spiritual person' while 27% regarded themselves as 'a religious person'.

An extremely informative and valuable study was undertaken by Paul Heelas, Linda Woodhead and others of the University of Lancaster and published in their book *The Spiritual Revolution. Why Religion is Giving Way to Spirituality* (2005) which seeks to examine the claim 'that traditional forms of religion, particularly Christianity, are giving way to holistic spirituality, sometimes still called 'New Age''. They took a small country town, Kendal in Cumbria, as the centre of their research, and the 'Kendal Project' has provided many hitherto unknown facts and expressions of views which are applicable to religion and spirituality throughout Great Britain.

A major problem to start with was how to define the concept of 'spirituality'. The participants were aware of Meredith McGuire's statement (1997) that 'we do not yet have the language or conceptual apparatus for refining our understanding of spirituality' and therefore sought to use distinctions which would emphasise the aspect of 'religious spirituality' on the one hand, and that of 'subjective-life spirituality' on the other, while acknowledging the inevitable overlap between the two. The difficulty with the category of 'subjective-life spirituality' is that the authors define it as 'those forms of spirituality in the West that help people to live in accordance with the deepest, sacred dimension of their own unique lives'.[8] These will include 'multifarious forms of sacred activity which are often grouped together under collective terms like 'body, mind and spirit', 'New Age', 'alternative' or 'holistic' spirituality, and include (spiritual) yoga, reiki, meditation, tai chi, aromatherapy...'[9] The researchers aimed to examine the claim that 'subjective-life spirituality' is in fact overtaking conventional religion.

There are a number of interesting discoveries that the 'Kendal Project' has thrown up which has a national significance. The 'traditionalist' churches in the area not surprisingly laid great emphasis on 'Jesus Christ who functioned as the immediate focus of devotion, reverence and deference, and as the inspiring model of perfect obedience and self-sacrifice'.[10] There was also a strongly-felt sense of moralism and 'general acceptance that the authorities of church and chapel are there to instruct people in how to live their lives'.[11] On the other hand, the 'holistic milieu' of Kendal and environs boasts an extraordinary collection of activities ranging from aromatherapy to Buddhism, circle dancing to the Alexander Technique, naturopathy to reiki. These activities take place in a variety of settings (including Kendal College, which has its own Holistic Therapy Diploma). The chief difficulty is to assess to what degree any of these holistic activities are genuinely 'spiritual'. In questionnaires to those practising such activities the respondents gave a variety of answers: 82.4% agreed that 'some sort of spirit or life-force pervades all their lives' while 73% expressed belief in 'subtle energy (or energy channels) in the body'. Asked to describe their 'core beliefs about spirituality' 40% equated 'spirituality' with 'love' or being 'a caring and decent person', 34% with 'being in touch with subtle energies' and 'healing oneself and others'. Importantly, 'very few associate spirituality with a transcendental, over-and-above-the-self, external source of significance', while a mere 7% believed that spirituality is 'obeying God's will' (contrasted with some 60% of churchgoers who believed that 'spirituality' *is* obeying God's will).[12] It was clear that practitioners of the various activities saw themselves as 'serving' their participants (rather than some higher spiritual authority or common good). But it is difficult to avoid the conclusion that many of the holistic therapies are essentially devoted to health and fitness and the relief of stress. There was evidently a complete contrast between the Christian congregational idea of spirituality ('God... knows what is best for us better than we know ourselves', 'Fix your eyes on him. Take them off yourself'. 'Lift us out of our own selves') and the ideas of the holistic milieu where 'the aim is to build on people's own resources, spiritual resources'.[13] Unsurprisingly, the researchers found that 'the congregational domain and holistic milieu constitute two largely separate and distinct worlds'.[14]

But to many people the important question is: why are people leaving the traditional churches and devoting their spare time to holistic therapies (which may, or may not, have any remote connection with 'spirituality' as most people understand the term)? Studies have shown that 'commitment to personal autonomy, independence, and freedom play an important role in disaffiliation from the congregational domain'. Many young people apparently leave the church 'because they do not like the way the church makes them *feel*. In some cases, it is simply that they feel nothing very much at all, except perhaps 'bored'. People may dislike their experience of church as 'dull', 'cold', 'formal', 'unexciting', 'dead', with attendance 'having nothing to offer me'. 'What's the point in going?', some of our students respond when we ask why they don't attend church, 'You don't get anything out of it, it simply does not touch my life, it's meaningless'.[15] The researchers found that 'few church services offer the strongly affective, intense experiences which young people can find elsewhere, whether by way of relationships, music, movies, clubs and so on'. One respondent remarked 'I didn't see my Christian upbringing as being spiritual. It was all about dogma, beliefs. Something outside me. There was nothing that ever touched me'. Her confirmation service proved to be her 'unconfirmation', for she felt nothing and experienced nothing throughout the service of this supposedly life-changing ritual. 'It was only when I began Transcendental Meditation many years later', she explained, 'that I found the spirituality I wanted... the spirituality within each individual'.[16] Yet despite individual stories of frustration there is evidence that certain types of Christianity – e.g. 'strict' and 'conservative' churches where 'an overarching framework of theistic authority is combined with concern for the healing, cultivation and enrichment of subjective life'[17] – are becoming popular and growing.

In conclusion, we may note Heelas and Woodhead's view: 'For religion which tells you what to believe and how to believe is out of tune with a culture which believes that it is up to us to seek out appropriate answers for ourselves. How can any other source tell me how to live my life, when only I can know from inside who I really am and what I may become? In short, subjective-life spirituality serves and reflects contemporary core values...'.[18] The Dominican Father Timothy Radcliffe nevertheless believes that there is an immense spiritual hunger amongst the young. He quotes the 1999 European Values Study which showed that a growing number of young people define themselves as religious. 'They are searching for a meaning to their lives. They are often more interested in 'spirituality' rather than doctrine, and they are nervous of belonging to any institutional form of religion which might limit their autonomy. In the words of Grace Davie, a sociologist who studies European religion, they believe without belonging. They are often more interested in other religious traditions than Christianity'.[19] How can Christianity respond to this indifference amongst the young to institutional forms of religion, and their preference for practising a subjective form of 'spirituality'? This is the Church's dilemma.

NOTES

[1]   Durkheim, 1963, 47

[2]   Heelas and Woodhead *et al.*, 2005, 139

[3]   Ibid.

[4]   Ibid., 140

[5]   Ibid.

[6]   Ibid., 149

[7]   Heald, 2000

[8]   Heelas and Woodhead *et al.*, 2005, 7

[9]   Ibid.

[10]   Ibid., 15

[11]   Ibid., 16

[12]   Ibid., 25

[13]   Ibid., 31

[14]   Ibid., 32

[15]   Ibid., 121

[16]   Ibid., 122

[17]   Ibid., 124

[18]   Ibid., 126

[19]   Radcliffe, 2005, 3

7. FRESH THINKING ON HISTORIC DOCTRINES AND WORSHIP

Christianity would be a straightforward, simple religion were it not for the doctrines of the Incarnation, the Virgin Birth, the Resurrection and the Trinity which for many are incomprehensible. And not only for the laity. In 2002 a survey by Christian Research revealed that, of 2,000 clergy questioned, only 3 out of 10 women priests believed in the Virgin Birth, while 7 out of 10 men and 5 out of 10 women, believed in the Resurrection. A spokesman for Cost of Conscience (which commissioned the survey) said 'There are effectively two churches co-existing uncomfortably in the Church of England – one that is overwhelmingly convinced of the historic truths of the Christian faith, and one that is, at best, dubious and, at worst, frankly disbelieving... The people out there in the pews have no idea this is going on'.[1]

We would do well to recall that, more than a century ago, George Eliot (1819–1880) rejected evangelical Christianity because she felt that the quality of a person's faith was judged by doctrinal correctness rather than a love for Christ. She regarded Jewish and Christian scriptures as 'histories consisting of mingled truth with fiction'. Who would now disagree with her?

In today's intellectual ambience, and after the evolution of scientific ideas over the past two centuries, the Trinitarian concept of an incarnate God is unintelligible to most people – whether believers or not – and has led to a resigned scepticism and a gentle but ineluctable drift away from the Church. Statistics for Church attendance demonstrate this only too clearly. How many of us, when attending Church Services, simply mumble the age-old phrases occurring in the Creeds and Penitential prayers without comprehending their meaning? Indeed, as has been ruefully pointed out: 'constant liturgical repetition, particularly in the small hours of the night, inevitably dulls the critical faculty, and has played a not insignificant part in breeding a conservative attitude to any attempts to examine some of the time-expired formulae of Christology'. As Michael Goulder has confessed, in the early days of his ministry 'Trembling beliefs do not alter themselves: they are reinforced daily by the repetition of the liturgy'.[2] Professor John Hick points out: 'In the past Christians have generally accepted the established language about Jesus as part of their devotional practice without raising the question of its logical character. They have not asked what kind of language-use one is engaging in when one says that 'Jesus was God the Son incarnate'.[3] This is an ongoing dilemma for the Church. How much of old-fashioned Christian doctrines could be jettisoned in order to attract younger, free-thinking recruits? How many devout worshippers realise that Jesus never claimed to be God incarnate and that his nature was 'defined' more than a century after his death by a group of self-interested clerics who roundly condemned their intellectual rivals as 'heretics'? One of these, the priest Arius (250–336) probably came nearer to the 'truth' about Jesus than any of his disputing – and grander – contemporaries.

In his remarkable book *Honest to God* (1963) the late Bishop John Robinson caused a major stir in ecclesiastical circles by suggesting that it was time to demythologize much of 'traditional' Christian doctrine such as the Incarnation, the Atonement and the Resurrection. And above all the concept of a theistic God. He had been impressed by Rudolph Bultmann's essay on the 'New Testament and Mythology' (1941) where Bultmann had suggested that the 'mythological' element in the New Testament represented a completely antiquated world-view and was so much unintelligible jargon to the modern man. Robinson believed that traditional Christianity had been formulated in terms of 'supranaturalism' with the deity acting as a theistic god whose omnipotence and omniscience is set out in Psalm 139. The whole world-view of the Bible is in such terms: 'we are still left with what is essentially a mythological picture of God and his relation to the world. Behind such phrases as 'God created the heavens and the earth', or 'God came down from heaven', or 'God sent his only-begotten Son', lies a view of the world which portrays God as a person living in heaven, *a* God who is distinguished from the gods of the heathen by the fact that 'there is no god beside me'.[4] But such a God 'is constantly pushed further and further back as the tide of secular studies advances. In science, in politics, in ethics the need is no longer felt for such a stop-gap or long-stop; he is not required in order to guarantee anything, to solve anything, or in any way to come to the rescue'.[5] As Julian Huxley wrote: 'The god hypothesis is no longer of any pragmatic value for the interpretation or comprehension of nature, and indeed often stands in the way of better and truer interpretation. Operationally, God is beginning to resemble not a ruler but the last fading smile of a cosmic Cheshire Cat'.[6] Robinson believed that Tillich was right to conceive of God, not in personal terms, but as 'the ultimate depth of all our being, the creative ground and meaning of all our existence'. God may therefore best be described as 'the ground of our being', and inseparable from this is 'the love of God in Christ Jesus our Lord'.

What direction did Robinson see for the future of the Church (insisting that it was not his intention to 'map a new programme')? First of all he saw the necessity to re-define the image of God. For the Jews, he maintained, the Christian Gospel was a stumbling-block, and, as Paul discovered when speaking to the Greeks on the Areopagus in Athens, it was to them folly ('And when they heard of the resurrection of the dead, some mocked...' (Acts 17: 32)). As Robinson says: 'For the Christian Gospel is in perpetual conflict with the images of God set up in the minds of men, even of Christian men, as they seek in each generation to encompass his meaning'.[7] Secondly, he saw the need for the abolition of (in Tillich's phrase) the 'superworld of divine objects': a source of incredulity rather than an aid to faith. In the late Bishop Hugh Montefiore's words: 'The old formulas continue to be used: they serve in worship, they comprise pictorial imagery useful for meditation, and they mark the continuity of our faith and devotion with that of our Christian ancestors. They preserve what may be meaningless to one generation but meaningful to the next'.[8] Robinson believed that we should be 'purging out the dead myths, and being utterly honest before God with ourselves and the world'.[9] For example, the traditional doctrines of the Incarnation, the Atonement and the Resurrection must all be re-interpreted.

Thirdly, Robinson foresaw an increase in the lay element in the Church (the laity being the *laos* or people of God in the world). He foresaw that 'tomorrow's layman must be a Church-man of conscious dedication and ministry to the things of the Kingdom. *How* he will exercise that laymanship is likely more and more to be through secular rather than religious groups. That is to say, it will be through structures, clusters, *ad hoc* and even (in the case of individual injustices) *ad hominem* associations... and one of the main differences will be that these clusters will from the beginning include those who are not religious and indeed not Christian'.[10]

Bishop John Robinson's book went through 15 impressions between 1963 and 1971 which testifies to its popularity and influence. But he was virtually ignored by the Church hierarchy who undoubtedly found his opinions 'unsafe'. Indeed, Bishop John Selby Spong records that 'Archbishop Ramsey later acknowledged his negative reaction to John Robinson as one of the major mistakes of his primacy'.[11] There have of course been a number of other prominent churchmen and theologians with liberal views who, like John Robinson, were well aware of the need for doctrinal reform. For example, the late Revd Dr Alec Vidler (Dean of King's College, Cambridge), who was described by his friend Malcolm Muggeridge as 'a man who believed with all his heart and doubted with all his mind'. In 1977 the publication of a book entitled *The Myth of God Incarnate*, edited by Professor John Hick, again caused consternation in theological circles largely because its title might suggest to the uninformed laity that the word 'mythical' was synonymous with 'untrue'. Another book was rushed out, entitled *The Truth of God Incarnate*, edited by Canon Michael Green, bubbling with indignation and peppered with academic point-scoring against some of the statements made by contributors to the earlier volume. Both sides, however, were quick to emphasize that the former book contained nothing new, Professor Hick pointing out that with the steady increase in human knowledge 'the pressure upon Christianity is as strong as ever to go on adapting itself into something which can be believed – believed by honest and thoughtful people who are deeply attracted by the figure of Jesus and by the light which his teaching throws upon the meaning of

human life'.[12] The contributors to the former book believed that
the conception of Jesus as God incarnate 'is a mythological or
poetic way of expressing his significance for us'.[13] Indeed,
Professor Hick has made it clear elsewhere that his idea of a true
myth is 'a story, or a description, that is not literally true but that
nevertheless expresses and tends to evoke an appropriate attitude
towards the subject of the myth'. For example, the stories of the
creation of the world in seven days; the fall of Adam and Eve and
their expulsion from the Garden of Eden; the Hindu myth of the
sacred mountain, Mount Meru, at the centre of the world; the
Jewish myths in the Hebrew scriptures relating to God's
miraculous interventions on behalf of his 'chosen people'.[14]

In her contribution to the book Dr Frances Young states:
'patristic discussion of Christology was conducted within the
framework of contemporary philosophical presuppositions – in
other words, like New Testament Christology. It was culturally
determined'.[15] The Christians of the early church 'lived in a world
in which supernatural causation was accepted without question,
and divine or spiritual visitants were not unexpected'. But in
today's world, dominated by the human and natural sciences,
'supernatural causation or intervention in the affairs of this world
has become, for the majority of people, simply incredible'.[16] In
other words, the present intellectual climate is entirely alien to the
whole Christian theology as traditionally conceived, and it is
therefore time for people to be told the historical 'truth' about
their religious faith.

As Professor John Macquarrie wrote in *The Truth of God
Incarnate*: 'It may at once be agreed that the story of a divine
being who descends to earth as man is technically a 'myth' and not
a straightforward history',[17] but what in his view was important to
consider was the metaphysics of incarnation against the
background of Christian theology. If, as suggested by Professor
Maurice Wiles,[18] the abandonment of the doctrine of incarnation
'would not involve the abandonment of all the religious claims
usually associated with it', then Macquarrie reasonably wonders
which claims would have to go: the doctrine of the Trinity? or of
atonement? and 'would the Eucharist be reduced simply to a
memorial service?'[19] Dr Don Cupitt has pointed out that the

classical doctrine of the incarnation belongs, not to the essence of Christianity, but only to a certain period of church history, now ended, and that doubts began to be voiced about the old Chalcedonian 'orthodoxy' during the nineteenth century. The Chalcedonian formula contained no explanation of the incarnation. Theologians recognised, for example, that orthodoxy claimed 'that in the incarnate Lord a divine will for which sin is a logical impossibility is hypostatically united with a human will for which it is a real and pressing temptation' and that this theory raised great problems. And there was also the problem of the hypostatic union being dissolved on the death of Jesus and presumably being re-instated at the resurrection. Can death dissolve what God has previously joined?[20] After 1500 years the Chalcedonian formula has effectively lost any meaning for us today. A vast cultural gap separates Jesus and his contemporaries from all things 'modern'.

Professor Hick quotes the historic example of 'the exaltation of a human teacher into a divine figure of universal power' in the person of Gautama, the Buddha or Enlightened One – a human being who had attained the status of *nirvāna* or enlightenment. 'The human Gautama came to be thought of as the incarnation of a transcendent, pre-existent Buddha as the human Jesus came to be thought of as the incarnation of the pre-existent Logos or divine Son... Gautama was the *Dharma* (Truth) made flesh, and Jesus was the Word made flesh: indeed the Burmese translation of the New Testament treats *Dharma* as the equivalent of Logos...'[21] It should be emphasised that Jesus was not considered to have risen from the dead because of his divine nature, but to have been raised by God alone. 'Accordingly *the first Christian preachers did not draw the conclusion that he was himself God but that he was a man chosen by God for a special role and declared by his resurrection to be Messiah and Lord* (Acts 2: 22, 36)'[22] Professor Hick contends that the words of the Nicene Creed that Jesus was 'the only-begotten Son of God, Begotten of the Father before all the ages, Light of Light, true God of true God, begotten not made, of one substance with the Father...' is as far from anything that the historical Jesus can reasonably be supposed to have thought or taught as is the doctrine of the Three Bodies from anything that the historical Gautama can reasonably be supposed to have thought or taught'.[23] Modern scholarship considers that 'the Fourth Gospel is a profound theological meditation in dramatic form, expressing a Christian interpretation of Jesus which had formed (probably in Ephesus) fairly late in the first century' and that 'we cannot properly attribute its great Christological sayings − 'I and the Father are one', 'No one comes to the Father but by me', 'He who has seen me has seen the Father' − to Jesus himself'.[24] Nevertheless he believed that Jesus was 'intensely and overwhelmingly conscious of the reality of God. He was a man of God, living in the unseen presence of God, and addressing God as *abba*, father'.[25]

We find ourselves today back where sceptics found themselves in the mid-nineteenth century, e.g. Charles Hennell's view that Jesus was a religious leader who suffered martyrdom and that 'the early church mistakenly interpreted the empty tomb as evidence of a resurrection, and thus initiated a relentlessly inflationary understanding of Jesus's identity that transformed him from a Jewish teacher to the Son of God incarnate' (1838), D. F. Strauss's conclusion that 'religion was ultimately an expression of the human mind's ability to generate myths in the first place, and then to interpret them as truths revealed by God' (1835), and George Eliot's belief that 'the moral aspects of faith could... be maintained without the metaphysical basis of Christianity. We can be good without God'. Modern scholarship has moreover cast doubts (as we have seen earlier) on many of the hallowed traditional beliefs of Christianity − namely, the virginal conception of Jesus, the Incarnation and the nature of Jesus, the Holy Trinity and the institution of the Eucharist.

How do the public react to all this? In Dr Frances Young's words: 'Genuine faith in Jesus Christ does not take the same form in all believers... There are a fair number of residual Christians who go on believing what they were taught as children and adolescents, but increasingly individuals who have not 'made the faith their own' drift away under the pressure of this non-religious age'. While for some the abandonment of Trinitarian theology 'would be a welcome release from an incomprehensible and cramping burden, for many others it would appear a serious break with Christian traditions... Trinitarian theology is the traditional way of our human attempt to express his Being whether in imaginative and analogical terms, or in abstruse philosophical definitions'. She concludes: 'the future seems to lie with pluralism in christology... Jesus Christ can be all things to all men because each individual or society, in one cultural environment after another, sees him as the embodiment of their salvation. He becomes, as he did for Paul, the unique focus of their perception and response to God'.[26]

There can be no doubt that the key to the survival of Christianity – particularly in its early days – has been its adaptability, what T. S. Eliot once declared as the ability of 'adapting itself into something which can be believed'. Thus it has been able to adapt itself to the needs of the wealthy Westernised world, no less than to those of the impoverished masses of the third world. It has indeed succeeded in being 'all things to all men'. For believers, the figure of the Crucified Christ has become a symbol of the suffering of humanity and of the love of God: a mysterious reminder in our daily lives of a link between the contemporary world and the Transcendent.

The position of the 'traditional' Christian has been summarised by Dr Young in her personal testimony when she recalls that despite the difficulties of the incarnational doctrine 'many of us remain Christian believers... when faced with difficulties or crises, we turn normally to prayer. In moments of joy, we instinctively offer thanksgiving. Sunday by Sunday we take ourselves to a place where the presence of other believers will assist us in praising and worshipping God who, we claim, is the author and sustainer of the universe. We confess our sins and accept forgiveness in the name of Jesus Christ; we battle against evil and suffering in the power of the Lord. We offer intercessions for the sick and pray about situations of physical conflict and war. None of these activities can be regarded as 'rational' in so far as they appear inconsistent with our fundamental assumptions about the world in which we live'.[27] The above passage was written thirty years ago, and the number of people attending conventional church services has steadily continued to decline. What is putting them off? Traditionalists like Dr Young, it must be noted, express a desire

284

'to praise and worship God', to confess our sins and accept forgiveness in the name of Jesus Christ', and to offer prayers for the sick. To contemporaries, however, the idea of praise and worship – *worship*? – of an unknown unworldly entity or ultimate reality, and of confessing one's 'sins' ('manifold sins and wickedness which we from time to time most grievously have committed against thy divine majesty, provoking most justly thy wrath and indignation against us' – a veritable 'song of the grovelling multitude') seems totally unreal and harks back to the period of a medieval morality play. Few, if any, will have read the colourful adulation of God in the book of Revelation. And how on earth can people be expected to believe that Jesus, an unknown Jewish rabbi, 'died for the sins of the whole world' in an act of atonement for the mythological 'original sin' of Adam and Eve? The thought for many is quite bizarre! Bishop John Robinson recognised that most people were understandably sceptical and that the 'full, perfect and sufficient sacrifice, oblation, and satisfaction for the sins of the whole world' supposed to have been 'made' on Calvary requires, I believe, for most men today more demythologizing even than the Resurrection'.[28] Most people today would answer Professor John Macquarrie's question as to what would result from abandonment of the doctrine of incarnation – that, yes, the doctrine of the Trinity and of atonement would have to go, and the Eucharist would indeed be reduced simply to a memorial service.

In the long perspective of Christian history there have been pressures which have led to doctrinal revisions. Prior to the Reformation the central act of Christian worship, the Eucharist, was regarded – through the act of Transubstantiation – as transforming the consecrated bread and wine into the real body and blood of Jesus. As a result of Reformation theology parts of the Christian Church came to regard partaking of the bread and wine at the Eucharist as merely *symbolic* of the real body and blood of Jesus. The books of the Bible are no longer regarded by most Christians (although certain Evangelical sects would disagree) as dictated by divine authority. We now have to accept a further adjustment and accept that Jesus was 'a man approved by God' (Acts 2: 21) with a role to play on earth as part of the divine plan for humanity, but not as the *later interpretation of him as 'God incarnate'* which is now realised to be a mythological or poetical way of interpreting his life on earth. We are again reminded of T. S. Eliot's words: 'Christianity is always adapting itself into something which can be believed'.

The nub of today's indifference to Christianity was precisely described forty years ago by Robert Adolf, when he wrote: '…unbelief seems to be the sign of our time. I do not mean by this primarily the cultural phenomenon of atheistic humanism. Rather, it is a question of disbelief among Christians, and it is not a rebellious disbelief. It is a great indifference, which develops in people who discover that they can be complete human beings without religious faith'.[29] To which Alistair Kee has added: 'Belief in God is not only impossible for the vast majority of people today, it is also found to be impossible for a growing number of Christians'.[30] For Claude Geffré 'religious indifference is the result of the lack of relevance of a particular historical form of Christianity to the basic questions modern man is asking about the future of the world'.[31] For the eminent philosopher Bertrand Russell 'the whole conception of God is… quite unworthy of free men. When you hear people in church debasing themselves and saying that they are miserable sinners, and all the rest of it, it seems contemptible and not worthy of self-respecting human beings. We ought to stand up and look the world frankly in the face. We ought to make the best we can of the world… A good world needs knowledge, kindliness and courage; it does not need a regretful hankering after the past, or a fettering of the free intelligence by the words uttered long ago by ignorant men…'[32] Yet there is undoubtedly an *instinctive* (even if not openly admitted) desire for some form of association with other-worldly spirituality. This has been true since prehistoric times. It affects different people in different ways: some have a strong affinity with the idea of a supernatural being or God actively concerned in the world, others a mild, matter of fact view of our traditional historic connection with Christianity, a muted scepticism about the obvious mythological parts of the faith – the majority indeed of those who declare themselves to be 'Christians' in official surveys but who seldom if ever go to church.

There are still theologians who hope that traditional forms of Christianity can, even now, be made attractive to today's sceptics. Thus the Dominican Father Timothy Radcliffe writes: 'If Christianity is to flourish in our society, and not become the practice of a dwindling minority, then we have to recapture some sense of it as 'a huge event' that grants me life, to which I simply *must* go'.[33] Unfortunately there is little sign of it being 'a huge event' in Britain today, and Radcliffe's book *Why Go to Church?* (2008) – attempting to show that the Eucharist is a drama in three acts whose 'huge event' is the transformation of the bread and wine into the body and blood of Christ – is so densely written that it is unlikely to inspire the 'man or woman in the street' with any sense of excitement! Indeed, sometimes one is reminded of a gloss in a medieval manuscript where the commentary spreads across all the margins of the page leaving only a few lines of the text in the centre! Not that Radcliffe writes badly: he writes brilliantly, as his books are always fluent, humorous and full of the knowledge and understanding of human foibles. How many *religious* authors could enliven their writings with references to films such as *Tsotsi* and *Brief Encounter* and books such as *Casino Royale*, *A Passage to India*, *The Mauve Tam-O'Shanter*, *Barchester Towers*, *The Da Vinci Code* and many others? But the *subject matter* just doesn't interest people any more. Moreover, one does not realise, when opening *Why Go to Church?* with its Foreword by the Archbishop of Canterbury, Dr Rowan Williams, that it actually constitutes a Roman Catholic Primer on the sacrament of the Eucharist – despite the disclaimer (page 13) that his book 'is not a commentary on the liturgy of the Eucharist'. If not on the liturgy, *per se*, then surely it's a commentary on the 'drama' in which Father Timothy is trying to interest the public! And because of that it is unlikely to inspire the laity. To take one example: Radcliffe states: 'Our confession of faith in the Trinity is not the assent to an obscure doctrine, remote from ordinary life, celestial mathematics: it is a declaration of the true nature of all love, our share in that perfect equal love of Father and Son which is the Holy Spirit. The doctrine of the Trinity challenges us to rid our loves and friendships of all that is dominating, patronising, selfish or exploitative. Intolerant forms of Christianity have lost the plot, literally'.[34] Just what does all that mean to the 'man or woman in the street'? For Radcliffe 'dogma matters. Orthodoxy liberates one from prejudice and petty-mindedness, and unlocks our hearts and minds'.[35] In fact, to the outsider, the closed mind of orthodoxy fossilises out-of-date prejudices and inhibits any hope of flexible thinking which, more than ever before, is essential in today's world. So it is unlikely that the orthodox and conservative doctrines surrounding the 'drama' of the Eucharist will meet with an overwhelming response from those who may be curious about the title of Radcliffe's new book! Furthermore, the language of the book illustrates one of the problems facing the Church today in its attempt to appeal to members of the public, namely, one of communication. Church ministers have a tendency to speak and write in an oblique and esoteric style which might be termed 'God-speak', reflecting their own particular spiritual mind-set. It baffles the laity. Apart from Father Radcliffe's passage 'our confession of faith in the Trinity...' (quoted above), which is probably unintelligible to most readers, we might quote a passage by the Archbishop of Canterbury, Dr Rowan Williams writing in the foreword to the same book. He writes (page ix): 'The drama at the core of our humanity is about our reluctance to be human; and the gift that the Church offers is the resource and courage to step into Jesus' world and begin the business of being human afresh – again and again, because our reluctance keeps coming back'. What, pray, does this mean? The 'man or woman in the street' just doesn't understand why he or she should be accused of a 'reluctance to be human' and what is meant by 'the drama at the core of our humanity'? Such a person would surely argue: 'but I am a member of my local community; I willingly participate in our community's affairs; I get on well with my neighbours; I try to help those in my community who may need help (e.g. with their children or if they are ill). Where is my 'reluctance to be human'? Or are such people not intended to be included in this sweeping archiepiscopal pronouncement? Bishop Tom Wright waxes lyrical about 'Jesus exploding into the life of ancient Israel... as the one through whose life, death and resurrection God's rescue operation was put into effect, and the cosmos turned its great corner at last' (see below). Father Radcliffe admits that 'we may lazily spew out bland churchy words' (page 55). One wishes sometimes that religious writers would *write in simple language* that the layman can understand without the need for an interpretive gloss!

In 2002 John Selby Spong, a former Episcopal bishop of Newark, USA, took up where his former friend and mentor, Bishop John Robinson, had left off. As devoted as was his friend to the well-being of the Christian Church, in whose service he has spent all his life, Bishop Spong maintains that the deity which we have hitherto thought of as a 'theistic God' is now out of date. He defines the 'theist God' as 'a being, supernatural in power, dwelling outside the world and invading the world periodically to accomplish the divine will'. Such a deity's interventions in the world, as vividly described in Bible passages, have been concerned with such matters as miracles, sickness and health, world weather patterns (hurricanes, floods, droughts), and supporting righteous warfare amongst nations. Although such a concept of God is now out of date, nevertheless the diminishing number of churchgoers today are largely still held in a time-warp of old liturgical language and are content not to think more than superficially about what they are saying in their prayers. Yet, contradictorily, there has started to be an anti-mythological trend amongst the public at the same time as there is support for fundamentalist sects in some areas of Evangelical Christians believing, against all historical evidence, in the literal truth of the Bible as the 'word of God'. Spong sees a rise in behavioural anxiety as a consequence of the declining influence of a theistic God, in relation to traditional family values, manifested in the increased use of drugs such as caffeine (in tea and coffee), alcohol and smoking. In Spong's view, the old myth of theism has now lost its appeal and we need a new vision. He believes that 'there is a reality we call God that is the source of the life we live, the power of the love we share, the Ground of Being that calls us to be all that we can be. I live today in the conviction that I am not separate from this God... Do not confuse this God with the God we served in the childhood of our humanity. This God is not identified with doctrines, creeds and traditions. The reality of this God is beyond all of that'.[36] He continues: 'I am free of the God who was deemed to be incomplete unless constantly receiving our endless praises; the God who required that we acknowledge ourselves as born in sin and therefore as helpless; the God who seemed to delight in punishing sinners; the God who, we were told, gloried in our childlike, grovelling dependency'.[37] In Spong's view there is no longer any place for the concept of 'original sin' or of the old sacraments such as baptism ('a sacrament designed to wash away the effects of a fall into sin that never occurred') and the Eucharist ('the re-enactment of a sacrifice designed to restore human life to something we have never been').[38] In his view the sacraments were devised as a deliberate attempt by the early Christian hierarchy to acquire power for themselves over their adherents. On 'original sin' Spong regards this as a myth. The idea of people being excluded from God's presence he regards as another example of hierarchical power. For Spong love is inseparable from God, who may be thought of – in Tillich's phrase – as the 'ground of being' – a God conceived 'not as a person, but as the source of personhood, the God defined in the book of Acts... as that presence or power in which 'we live and move, and have our being', (Acts 17: 28)'.[39] And 'being' is something one is: our 'presence'. Spong sees Jesus as 'a portrait of divinity into which a full humanity inevitably flows, not as the incarnation of a scriptural external deity on a divine mission of rescue'.[40] Contrast this with Bishop Tom Wright's belief that 'we are lost and need someone to come and find us, stuck in the quicksand waiting to be rescued...' (see below).

One of the problems identified by Spong concerns prayer. Bishop Robinson was clearly uncomfortable about the subject: 'Prayer is the responsibility to meet others with *all* I have, to be ready to encounter the unconditional in the conditional, to expect to meet God in the way, not to turn aside from the way. All else is exercise towards that or reflection in depth upon it'.[41] Not one of Robinson's most lucid descriptions! Nor is his remark: 'Prayer is openness to the ground of our being; and in it 'the readiness is all'.[42] Bishop Spong, on the other hand, asserts that the common view is that 'prayer consists of petitions and intercessions addressed to the deity... and that the deity can intervene to assist the one praying in a personal crisis...'[43] But he remains sceptical of the claims religious people have made for their prayers. 'I do not deny that love shared or concern expressed creates positive energy. I do not deny that positive energy has therapeutic power, that positive energy enhances life as being... But I make no claim beyond that'.[44] However, with a new conception of the nature of God 'prayers to God' are meaningless since they represent an attempt to speak to 'someone' for whom speech is impossible. Thus prayers should *not* represent 'a grovelling sinner seeking mercy from a divine judge'.[45] Prayer must either be dispensed with or redefined. He believes that God calls him to work 'to enhance the humanity of every person, to free the life present in every person, to increase the love available to every person, and to celebrate the being of every person'.[46] He prefers the words 'meditation' or 'contemplation' to the word 'prayer'. This concept of prayer is however unlikely to be universally popular since there is a deep-seated instinct in humanity to petition the deity in times of crisis and to pray daily to God as a routine part of Christian life. In this respect people are reluctant to dispense with the idea of a 'theistic God'. Gerald Priestland found himself bothered by prayers of intercession. 'Surely God will know best, if He has not decided already what we should have? Is not intercessory prayer going back to a kind of magical approach; to a belief that we can manipulate God if only we use the right words?' The gospel admonition 'what things soever ye desire, when ye pray, believe that ye receive them, and ye shall have them' is hardly to be interpreted as open-ended or it would be meaningless. One of Priestland's Roman Catholic respondents said 'Too often people are taught that prayer is reciting formulae together. Many people fall away from prayer because it has ceased to have any meaning for them. In my experience the starting point is not words but silence. It is only when one creates a space for stillness that one can become aware of something deeper...' This is indeed one of the central features of Quakerism, where silence can produce 'something new, unexpected and immensely valuable' and people witness 'an experience of transcendence – the transcendent activity of the inner light or Holy Spirit'.[47] It is interesting to note that some people – especially Muslims – dislike the beseeching tone of Christian prayers: in Islam there are no 'pleading' prayers – just 'praising' rather than 'supplicating' expressions of devotion.

Bishop Spong sees the continuing need for a meeting-place in a reformed Church – which he suggests might be called an *ecclesia* (meaning 'those called out'). He foresees the continuation of ritual acts to mark human transitions – baptism as a form of welcome, and festivals such as Christmas (centred on the Christ-story) and Easter (celebrating the breaking of the barrier of death), and a new Eucharist to mark Jesus's selfless love (rather than being based, as now, on sacrifice and rescue). But there would be no reference to the incarnation of a theistic deity. Apart from Bible readings there would be readings in services about famous religious people from the past, such as Origen, Aelred, Francis of Assisi and Bernard of Clairvaux. 'So this Christ-life, newly defined, will continue to be at the heart of our liturgy; it will be the focal point, the interpretative clue around which worship in the ecclesia of tomorrow will be organised'.[48]

With new ideas for the reformation of existing forms of Christian worship, such as those suggested by Bishops Robinson and Spong, what do people consider the reasons for *wanting* to believe in 'religion'? These can effectively be reduced to a few basic psychological and emotional instincts / desires:

- to counter the natural but generally suppressed anxiety or fear of death ('the dread of something after death, the undiscovered country from whose bourn no traveller returns...' (Shakespeare) by the re-assurance of immortality) (see below);

- to provide an emotional shelter at moments of distress or terror (to feel that one is not alone in shouldering the burdens of life, but can call on spiritual support to give one courage and endurance, especially at times of personal bereavement. (Sales of Bibles, for instance, increased sharply after the 11 September attacks in America, and Pentecostalists and Evangelicals often carry Bibles with them everywhere because of their defiant devotion to the 'word of God');

- to provide a channel for our desire to believe in a supreme entity who can respond to our prayer for help (played up by the churches 'putting on a great show of authority, presenting the idea in vivid images and mysteriously performed dogmas, reinforced by colourful liturgies and powerful hierarchies which in the past people accepted uncritically');[49]

- to provide re-assurance and support for those lacking intellectual security or social self-sufficiency;

- to build and preserve social cohesion (as suggested by Emile Durkheim (1858–1917), widely regarded as one of the founders of sociology). Thus Church supporters constitute recognised communities which in many instances (especially in rural areas) provide the framework for social cohesion, charitable and educational support, and stability.

And if Christians are concerned at the thought of death, what do they believe with regard to life after death? In the early years of Christianity the prospect of the arrival of the Kingdom of Heaven was very real and urgent; so, too, was the fear of judgement and damnation for the wicked. In St Matthew's Gospel Jesus says: 'But I say to you, that every idle word that men shall speak, they shall give account thereof in the day of judgement. For by thy words thou shalt be justified, and by thy words thou shalt be condemned' (Matthew 12: 36–7). Although the Kingdom failed to arrive, belief in a life after death nevertheless remained strong throughout the medieval period, when it was thought that people went either to Heaven or Hell – Heaven being the Kingdom where God reigned supreme, accompanied by the righteous, those who had been 'saved', and by the saints. Later came the idea of Purgatory where the souls of Christians were thought to be punished and purified before passing on to Heaven, but this idea was removed from Protestant theology after the Reformation. By the nineteenth-century belief in an after-life had waned, and agnosticism about the form of any such life has since become increasingly prevalent. It seems that even theologians now try to avoid the subject! Many people today probably share the attitude of the Roman emperor Marcus Aurelius (121–180), a man of singular virtue and a follower of Stoic philosophy, of the 'soul which, at whatever moment the call comes for release from the body, is equally ready to face extinction, dispersion, or survival'. But within Judaism, Christianity and Islam there is a belief that the soul continues to exist 'either living for ever as spirit, or being at some stage reunited with its physical body, or acquiring a new 'spiritual' body. The conclusion of the human story, according to their traditions, is eternal life in heaven, or in heaven via an intermediate state, or in hell'.[50] It may be noted that the Qur'an informs us that all the Prophets of God preached belief in the afterlife to their respective peoples, and the afterlife (*al-akhirah*) is an integral part of Islamic beliefs together with a day of judgement. Judaism believes in an afterlife but is deliberately vague about its precise nature and is more concerned with improving conditions in the present world.

The conventional Christian scenario presents immense difficulties, and most people are sceptical about it. As Professor John Hick points out: 'The faithful echo it in liturgies, hymns and ecclesiastical rhetoric, particularly within funeral services, but it does not, for most, form part of the operative set of convictions by which they live'.[51] But what form, one may ask, will the next life take? In any future life do we (for example) preserve our cultural identity, language and memory despite the fact that our physical body (with which these were intimately connected) has perished? Can we expect to recognise and to converse with our deceased relatives and friends? This is one of the 'comfortable' suggestions proposed by the Church, but without much conviction. We may recall that the philosopher Plotinus (204–270 AD) thought that memory was concerned with our life in time, and that as the soul grows towards eternal life it will remember less and less, and that ultimately we shall recall nothing of personality or of the things of this world. As Bertrand Russell pointed out, our memories and habits are bound up with the structure of the brain. But the brain, as a structure, is dissolved at death, and memory therefore may be expected to be also dissolved. Thus it is not rational arguments, but emotions, that cause belief in a future life,[52] and the most important of these emotions is fear of death. Christians, however, have been re-assured by Jesus about the immortality of the soul and should therefore look forward to the next life. Thus Cardinal Cormac Murphy O'Connor, former Archbishop of Westminster, sees 'the manner in which I live now as a kind of antechamber to an eternal life, the like of which I can have no full knowledge. Did not St Paul say: 'Eye has not seen, nor ear heard... what God has prepared for those who love Him'? Indeed, the only definite information we have of the next world is in the Gospel of St John where Jesus is recorded as saying: 'In my Father's house are many mansions: if it were not so, I would have told you. I go to prepare a place for you. And if I go and prepare a place for you, I will come again, and receive you unto myself; that where I am, there ye may be also' (John 14: 2–3).' For Dr Shahid Raza, director of the Imams and Mosques Council (UK), belief in *al-akhirah* (the afterlife) is vital. He believes it promotes morality, goodness and justice in this world. We know that Allah is watching over all our actions and we have to account for them in the afterlife. Rabbi Sir Jonathan Sacks, Chief Rabbi of the United Hebrew Congregations of the Commonwealth, maintains that 'the most attractive aspect of the Jewish belief in 'the world to come' is its inclusivity. You don't have to be Jewish to reach Heaven. The righteous of all nations, we believe, do so. That is why Judaism does not seek converts... Judaism is an intensely this-worldly faith. Our supreme religious challenge is to make this world with all its conflicts and collisions, a more gracious and compassionate place'.[53] According to Dr Tom Wright, former bishop of Durham, ''Resurrection' does not mean 'going to heaven when you die'. It isn't about 'life after death'. It's about 'life *after* life after death'. You die; you go to be 'with Christ' ('life after death'), but your body remains dead. Describing where and what you are doing in that interim period is difficult, and the New Testament writers mostly don't try. Call it 'heaven' if you like, but don't imagine it's the end of all things. What is promised *after* that interim period is a new bodily life within God's new world ('life *after* 'life after death'').[54] It is not however clear whether this new 'bodily life', which Dr Wright maintains will be in the 'new' world created within the *present* material universe, will bear any relation to one's dead body: there would be obvious difficulties if one had been cremated or otherwise physically disposed of unless one is to be given a 'new worldly' body! Sensibly, Christian theology avoids such difficult questions, so one can really only speculate about a future life. A gentle, simple and reassuring message is proffered in the late Pope John XXIII's *Journey of a Soul*, in which he says: 'Death is part of the future for everyone. It is the last post of this life, and the reveille of the next. Everywhere men fear death. It is the end of our present life, it is the parting from loved ones, it is the setting out into the unknown. We overcome death by accepting it as the will of a loving God, by finding him in it. Death, like birth, is only a transformation, another birth. When we die we shall change our state, that is all. With faith in God, it is as easy and natural as going to sleep here and waking up there'. And, as we have seen in Section 4(ii) above, many people on their deathbeds believe that they see deceased members of their families coming to escort them on the 'journey' to the next world.

Now it is reasonable to suppose that we may have to account for how we have lived our earthly lives and the extent to which we have grown spiritually whilst on earth. Any continuation of life would very likely be such as to enable us to advance our spiritual growth still further, and the obvious means to achieve such a result would be through re-incarnation, or re-birth, in the present world. This would provide an equal chance to everyone, no matter how long they had lived or the circumstances of their lives. Such is the belief of the Buddhist and Hindu faiths whose adherents believe that a number of re-births take place until such time as the soul has achieved final enlightenment or *nirvāna* and absorption into the ultimate reality of Brahman. The precise identity of each re-born human may perhaps be likened to the share of the 'divine fire' possessed – according to Stoic philosophy – by each mortal and round which we have accumulated a cloak of our earthly thoughts, emotions, desires and record of our actions in life. This cloak – like Plotinus's conscious memory – would fade away leaving the underlying reality of the divine spark to be re-born again. And very occasionally there may be faint memories of previous existences, as sensitively portrayed by the poet Wordsworth in his Ode on 'Intimations of Immortality from Recollections of Early Childhood' and by Henry Vaughan in his poem 'The Retreat'.[55] Each poet recalls that in infancy he was conscious of having formerly been part of a different – or heavenly – world, but when he grew up this blissful memory faded. For

Vaughan this earlier world – which life on earth temporarily interrupted – was 'eternity', for Wordsworth 'immortality', both under the benevolent gaze of God. Thus for both poets a temporary alienation from an earlier blissful state is the price of human personality and consciousness in the present life. This concept is a logical and attractive idea, and it may well be that the Eastern faiths have something important to teach the Western Church in this respect. On the other hand, perhaps the concept of reincarnation can be equated with Bishop Tom Wright's idea of 'life after death' which he considers to be an *interim* existence before attaining a new bodily life within 'God's new world': thus equating our *first* 'resurrection' with the Eastern faiths belief in reincarnation until such time as we have achieved final enlightenment or *nirvāna* and absorption into the ultimate reality of Brahman – or, in the case of a Christian, into the reality of God (i.e. within 'God's new world'). Historically, belief in a re-birth was common in *c*.500 AD amongst Buddhists and Hindus. It was also held by the Greek philosophers of the Pythagorean school and by the practitioners of Orphic rites. But in the West this belief did not persist, and disappeared after the arrival of Christianity and, later, of Islam. In India and East Asia, however, it continues to be a fundamental element of Buddhism and Hinduism. Perhaps Christian theologians might now consider reverting to the Pythagorean belief in reincarnation as a *temporary* state in the process of attaining a full resurrection?

The late Bishop John Robinson, Professor John Hick, Bishop John Selby Spong and others have urged that Christianity be de-mythologized to make it a plausible religion for the twenty-first century, and the distinguished biblical scholar Professor Geza Vermes has made a plea for a complete doctrinal re-structuring. How should this be brought about? One answer would be for the Church to re-convene the Church of England Doctrine Commission to recommend how existing doctrines could be revised and re-interpreted to make sense in the twenty-first century, and to recommend which might gently be consigned to history. A re-convened Liturgical Commission could then, on the doctrinal and theological foundation of the Doctrine Commission's reports, prepare a *New Christian Prayer Book* to take the place of the present book of *Common Worship* (which is supplemented in many Churches by a confusion of alternative prayers and former 'Series One' (1966) Services). This new prayer book could contain a variety of Services: a reformed Service of Holy Communion; a reformed Service of Common Worship; an unreformed Service based on the traditional 1662 Book of Common Prayer; and perhaps one or two others – for example, a Service of Music and Dance (for the younger generation and held not in a pew-filled Church but in open spaces within Church Halls[56]). The reformed Services would of course be based on a reformed Creed so as not to perpetuate now-outdated concepts (such as the Virgin Birth), and on text that avoids or qualifies mythical stories. A *New Christian Book of Intercessions* could be prepared alongside the new prayer book, to be used in conjunction with it. And the Church calendar would require amendment and the feast (for example) of the Holy Trinity quietly downgraded like the former feast of the Circumcision. A new prayer book would not necessitate any alteration to existing Hymn Books which would remain as examples of spiritually-inspired earlier Christological thought (such as the Wesley brothers' hymns). And we may envisage the spread of Gospel Music amongst congregations whose spiritual and emotional needs would be met by such expressions of devotion. Indeed, increased emphasis on music and singing may be the catalyst which begins to attract young people to a new and *unstructured* form of Christianity. In diocesan parishes 'reformed' Services would be the norm, but at Christmas and Easter the traditional festivals could be retained as joyous mythological pageants celebrating the birth and death of Jesus, whose moral and spiritual teaching would remain the essential focus of a revived Christianity. And it may be that the site of new Christian communal initiatives, embracing musical and art forms and linked to the preaching of the word of God, will be moved from old and inhospitable church buildings to modern church or community halls. Cathedrals could in future become the repositories of traditional liturgical Services based on the 1662 *Book of Common Prayer* and the King James Bible, accompanied by traditional choral chants, anthems and psalms. At the major festivals of Christmas and Easter the cathedrals would display their most glorious ceremonial, liturgical ritual and music, and well-known events such as the Carol Services with Nine Lessons from King's College, Cambridge, would continue to delight the public.

As Professor Hick says: 'The proper function of common worship is to be an enabling context of religious experience. When and to the extent that it is this, it constitutes a transforming awareness of the Transcendent. All of these are among the innumerable different settings in which the inbuilt religious propensity of our nature is evoked. And when evoked it leads to what we can only call faith or trust. But faith or trust in what? For some, trust in a personal God, for others trust in the ultimate structure of reality...'[57] Convinced Christians, such as Dr Tom Wright, former bishop of Durham, remain defiantly optimistic. In his view 'Christianity is not about Jesus offering a wonderful moral example, as though our principal need was to see what a life of utter love and devotion to God and to other people would look like, so that we should try to copy it... Nor is Christianity about Jesus offering, demonstrating or even accomplishing a new route by which people can 'go to heaven when they die'... Finally, Christianity is not about giving the world fresh teaching about God himself — though clearly, if the Christian claim is true, we do indeed learn a great deal about who God is by looking at Jesus'.[58] What, then, does Dr Wright consider Christianity to be all about? Dr Wright's 'new perspective' (if we may so call it) is that 'we are lost and need someone to come and find us, stuck in the quicksand waiting to be rescued, dying and in need of new life'. In his view 'Christianity is all about the belief that the living God, in fulfilment of his promises... has accomplished all this — the finding, the saving, the giving of new life — in Jesus... A great door has swung open in the cosmos which can never again be shut. It is the door to the prison where we have been kept chained up. We are offered freedom: freedom to experience God's rescue for ourselves, to go through the open door and explore the new world to which we now have access... we are not only to enjoy it as such but to work at bringing it to birth on earth as in heaven'.[59] Dr Wright affirms that 'This world is where the Kingdom must come, on earth as it is in heaven'. He assures us that 'though Christians believe that Jesus is now 'in heaven', he is present, accessible, indeed active, within our world...'[60] This is all of course a question of credibility. Does the 'man or woman in the street' understand the concept of 'exploring the new world' and 'bringing it to birth on earth as in heaven'? Highly improbable. 'The Kingdom of God is at hand', was Jesus's pronouncement to the Jews of his day. He believed the current Jewish prophecies were about to be fulfilled. As Dr Wright tells us 'The whole point of Jesus's work was to bring heaven to earth and join them together for ever...'[61] His disciples were agog with anticipation, but nothing happened. He was crucified and his disciples retired, demoralised, but did not give up. A century passed, and the new 'Church' had to explain away this delay. Two thousand years have now passed and the promised Kingdom of God seems a distant memory. Yet devout Christians still have hope. As Dr Wright declares: 'Jesus exploded into the life of ancient Israel, the life of the whole world, not as a teacher of timeless truths, nor as a great moral example, but as the one through whose life, death and resurrection God's rescue operation was put into effect, and the cosmos turned its great corner at last'.[62] For the ordinary 'man or woman in the street', the reaction to such an extravagant claim is likely to be a limp 'so what'? He or she might reflect on what has happened since Jesus's day: crusades, religious wars, religious persecutions and injustices, mass starvation in under-developed parts of the world and national disasters (earthquakes, floods and 'tsunamis' – bringing misery to thousands); genocide in various parts of the world; the history of Jesus's own people – the Jews – who were reviled for centuries by the Christian Church (and only recently has the Roman Catholic Church officially absolved the Jewish people for their part in the death of Jesus). They could well wonder how anyone could credibly assert that, since Jesus's appearance on earth, God's 'rescue operation' – this brave new world – was anything but fanciful! If Jesus, before he died, wept over the city of Jerusalem (which was to be destroyed forty years later), how much more might he have wept over the thought of the subsequent history of his own 'chosen people'! The nagging doubts remain, as does the reality of the steadily declining number in England who are convinced by the Christian optimistic exegesis even if they are receptive to other forms of 'spirituality'. As Father

Timothy Radcliffe ruefully admits, 'People are more interested in spirituality than in 'institutional' religion'.

Some years ago Professor Dennis Nineham argued that 'after the experience of ten or twelve hundred years, Christians had got it deep into their minds that their faith consisted in believing, in more or less the identical words, what people had believed in the days of the Creeds and the New Testament. Understandably it has taken the Church a very long time to realise that this is no longer possible and that we have got to devise new formulations. We have to ask ourselves 'What must the truth be *now* if people who thought like that so long ago put it as they did?'.[63]

The challenge for Christians today is their willingness to 'move from a literal to a metaphorical understanding of some of the central themes of the Christian story'. Many have already done this in relation to the myths of biblical creation. 'But can Christians now be expected to come to see Jesus, no longer as God incarnate, but as our brother, one of us although far ahead of the rest of us in his openness to God?'[64] Professor Vermes has written: 'Christianity considers itself the transmitter to posterity of the legacy of Jesus, albeit one that has been converted by the church into a gospel for the whole human race. Yet on reading the original message, thinking and honest members of the various Christian faiths may (should?) feel the need for a thorough re-examination of the fundamentals of their belief, ethics and piety, a reconsideration which may demand a complete doctrinal restructuring, a new 'reformation''.[65] But the overwhelming problem, as A. N. Wilson has correctly recognised, is that 'the ultra-orthodox Christians – whether Catholic or Protestant – are so anxious to preserve their religious faith intact that they do not dare to confront the conclusions of the last two hundred years of New Testament scholarship'.[66]

Church leaders ought to take this seriously, but they will no doubt find such root-and-branch ideas of reform which have been outlined above extremely painful and difficult to accept. The Roman Catholic Church has inherited a vast amount of 'spiritual baggage' from the doctrines of the Christian Fathers of the early Church – doctrines which have little relevance today – which they can hardly deny without losing 'face'. Who can imagine, for example, the Catholic Church giving up the doctrines of the Immaculate Conception, the Virgin Birth, the Incarnation, Transubstantiation or papal infallibility (the doctrine of which was defined at the First Vatican Council of 1870)? Or the Catholic condemnation of homosexuality and of the role of women in the Church as priests or bishops; or its condemnation of abortion and artificial contraception (the latter widely disregarded by Catholics in the developed world and an issue considered by theologians and clergy as having done more than any other to undermine the authority of the Holy See). Could the fading *imperium* of the Vatican Curia ever admit that any of these elements of its teaching have been mistaken? Any such reform would require a radical revision of traditional Christian worship with its liturgical language that assumes that Jesus was literally God. It would be necessary to understand and to face up to what is implied by the expression 'Christian myth'. In Dr Don Cupitt's view Christianity will have to become a 'de-mythologized' religion to be believed. For future generations iconic doctrines such as the incarnation of God in Jesus and the Holy Trinity will gradually be accepted as 'mythological', the hitherto familiar sacraments of the Eucharist (where participants are held 'to feed on the mystical body and blood of Christ' and believe thereby to receive divine grace), will no doubt continue to be periodically received by a dwindling minority of devoted followers, and in some of the 'reformed' branches of Christianity grace will continue to be mediated through the Bible preached metaphorically as the 'word of God'. The late Professor Maurice Wiles (d. 2005) in his book *The Remaking of Christian Doctrine* (1974) eloquently, but timidly, sketched out how traditional doctrines of the Church (such as the incarnation of God in Jesus) might be reinterpreted in 'a bold and creative use of the speculative imagination', and acknowledged that 'there will be some questions... that have been in the past and still are a cause of grave anxiety to the Christian theologian which he will no longer need to pursue. He will come to see them as questions which cannot be answered and which (despite what he has often been assured in the past) do not need to be answered in order to safeguard the religious realities of Christian faith'.[67] He did not specify which!

We have to face the fact that today's congregations are predominantly middle-aged. Parish incumbents lament the absence of men and young people at their Services. One middle-aged rector remarked sadly that at his Services he was himself often the youngest member of the congregation, and that attendance at worship consisted largely of middle-aged ladies but few young people. Is the Church now regarded as a feminine social club (and indeed as one of a number of social and voluntary organisations)? Where are the children? As David Voas has pointed out: 'The difficulty is in retaining the children who have churchgoing parents. So long as churchgoing is something that gets you laughed at, so long as there is a social stigma attached to being a churchgoing young person, it will be difficult to reverse the trend'. In contrast, young Muslims live in a different environment. 'Being religious is a way that you show you are different, that you are proud of your heritage. One of the ways young Muslims assert their identity is by being more observant than their parents'.[68] Do these examples not reveal a glaring missed opportunity for missionary outreach in the hundreds of Anglican primary schools? The Roman Catholic Church has for years been renowned for the resources it has put into the spiritual education of schoolchildren in an attempt to implant the seeds of faith into younger generations.

Finally, we should do well to recall the words of Dietrich Bonhoeffer, struggling in a Nazi prison to formulate ideas for how the Church might be reformed to make it fit for its mission in the twentieth century, when – shortly before he was led out to be hanged by the Nazis – he drafted a chapter for a future book which began:

'The Church is her true self only when she exists for humanity. As a fresh start she should give away all her endowments to the poor and needy. The clergy should live solely on the freewill offerings of their congregations, or possibly engage in some secular calling. She must take her part in the social life of the world, not lording it over men, but helping and serving them. She must tell men, whatever their calling, what it means to live in Christ, to exist for others'.[69]

In these thoughts he was following Martin Luther who believed that the Church as an institution was unnecessary for salvation. This belief is of increasing relevance as support for the institution of the Church wanes and both Catholic and Anglican Churches face mounting financial pressures.

And if support for the *institutional* Church continues to dwindle, may we perhaps see the appearance of a different practice of Christianity along the lines of the 'house churches' which are emerging in the new Christian communities in China? Here, groups of young, intelligent businessmen and professionals meet together in someone's house for prayer, hymn-singing (music downloaded from the Internet!) and the study of Bible texts. At the conclusion, the leader sums up the discussion. Ambitious young people in China today consider that the worship of God is 'the thing to do': 'in Europe the church is old. Here it is modern. Religion is a sign of higher ideals and progress. Spiritual wealth and material wealth go together...'[70]

In the evolving society of the future, with failing congregations, the inevitable closure of churches, the likelihood of fewer candidates for ordination, and an increasingly part-time clergy (like non-stipendiary ministers today), would the discarding of mythological doctrines, which still form the core of Christian institutional Services, and a concentration on the teaching of Jesus as a charismatic human being intensely aware of God and the Transcendent, and preaching a message of love and ultimate hope of salvation, be sufficient to re-kindle the interest of the passer-by? As Dr Frances Young (whose views we have quoted earlier) contends, the future seems to lie with pluralism in christology: individuals and societies, in their different cultural environments, see Jesus 'as the embodiment of their salvation' and he can therefore continue to represent 'all things to all men'. Devoted parish priests today, struggling to exercise pastoral supervision over a number of churches, should not despair. Doctrinal changes could be introduced gradually – almost stealthily. It would not take too much soul-searching gradually to erase the repetitive Christian mantras 'in the name of the Father, Son and Holy Ghost', 'the blessing of God Almighty, the Father, the Son and the Holy Ghost', and references to Jesus as 'God incarnate', to alternatives such as 'in the name of Jesus, our saviour', 'the blessing of Almighty God and the love of Jesus be with you and remain with you always', or, as Paul wrote to Timothy, 'grace, mercy, peace from God the Father and Christ Jesus our Lord', and to Philemon 'the grace of our Lord Jesus Christ be with your spirit'. And perhaps we might return to the historic greeting: 'The Lord be with you' and the gracious response 'And with thy spirit'! And how about Church Services? Would a *New Christian Prayer Book* (as has been suggested above) provide an opportunity to make the liturgy of the Church more user-friendly? When the Anglican Church decided to update the *Book of Common Prayer* – a process which began with the 'Additions and Deviations' proposed in 1928 and ended in the publication of *Common Worship* – it made a number of revisions to the traditional liturgical rules. In view of the insensitivity and initial unpopularity of the introduction of the new 'giving of The Peace' (so un-Anglican a practice, which many of Betjeman's 'hearty middle-stumpers' felt unable to accept and left their congregations!), the authors of any new prayer book should tread carefully!

Many people instinctively enjoy the sense of drama, of ritual, of richness in colour and imagery which is provided by colourful Church Services, irrespective (it has to be said) of their belief in the intrinsic meaning of such spectacles. Moreover congregational hymn-singing is becoming increasingly popular, with inspirationally uplifting hymns and songs such as 'O Lord my God! when I in awesome wonder...', 'Thine be the Glory', 'Great is Thy faithfulness' or 'Abide with me' which could be introduced as 'Songs of Praise' in novel musically-inspired forms of Service. Parochial choirs and instrumental groups, with perhaps dramatic players, could provide incentives for participation by young people. Meanwhile, parish priests across the country will continue to lead their Christian communities for worship as the 'people of God': to praise God for the universe in which we live; to pray to God for justice and peace throughout the world; and to ask forgiveness of our shortcomings as individuals. Continuing encouragement of local communities to participate in 'parochial' functions may be the means of retaining the identities and purpose of Christian parishes, many of whose participants seldom in

practice attend conventional Church Services (yet are firm
supporters of their communities). Progressive thinkers in the
Anglican Church such as Michael Perham, Bishop of Gloucester,
have pointed out that 'there is no one solution to the challenges
that face us. God wants to work with our communities as they are:
with the people in our churches and communities with their
particular aptitudes, gifts and foibles… the pattern of ministry and
mission appropriate for a grouping of rural parishes may be very
different from that for a suburban deanery. The worship that will
help older congregations in villages may be very different from
that appropriate for a youth congregation… [71] And again,
'Pioneering work is needed that goes far beyond creating
alternative worship services in established congregations and
church buildings. New forms of Church have to be allowed to
develop…' He envisages the Church reaching out to communities
of interest, e.g. 'youth congregations, café church, ramblers
church, school church and many more…' [72]

Whether a 'reformation' of church doctrines and Services (as
envisaged by the late Bishop John Robinson, Bishop John Selby
Spong and others) is ever put in hand, it would seem inevitable
that we shall see:
- A continuing decline in church congregations;
- A growing inability on the part of Anglican churches to pay
  their diocesan 'shares' (the former 'quotas');
- A growing inability to find people willing to act as
  churchwardens and members of parochial church councils;
- The closure and sale of smaller churches;
- The concentration of clergy on fewer, larger and financially
  viable churches;
- The increasing financial instability of the Church as an
  institution (both Anglican and Catholic);
- The building of multi-faith centres in co-operation with
  other religious faiths, where services/meetings can be held by
  all faiths. Initiatives such as 'The Three Faiths Forum',
  designed to form a 'trialogue' between the three Abrahamic
  faiths (Jews, Muslims and Christians), should be warmly
  encouraged;

- The possible re-convening by the Church of England of the Doctrine Commission to draw up a doctrinal statement for the twenty-first century. This should honestly acknowledge the mythical nature of some of its major doctrines; which of them can now be abandoned; and how the remainder can be interpreted for the new century. It should freely acknowledge the man-made doctrines relating to the nature of Jesus which were formulated by the early Church authorities and which are meaningless today, and should draw up a new Creed for Christianity which recognises Jesus as a mediator between God and the world, rather than an earthly incarnation of God. A re-convened Liturgical Commission should prepare a *New Christian Prayer Book* based on the person of Jesus and his expressed relationship with 'God the Father' and omitting references to the Holy Trinity, to God 'incarnate', to Jesus as a '(Jewish) sacrificial 'lamb of God' dying to redeem the 'sins of the whole world' (i.e. the whole concept of the atonement based on the myth of 'original sin' as conceived in St Augustine's sin-obsessed imagination) and other discredited concepts. However, if such a radical policy were to be implemented it would undoubtedly lead to the secession of Evangelicals and Fundamentalists from the Church of England, as well (possibly) as a number of dioceses in under-developed areas of the world (especially in Africa) where mythical imagery is an acceptable element in primitive spiritual and animistic beliefs;

- The likelihood of Roman Catholic biblical scholars, whose intellectual integrity is compromised by the Vatican 'Nihil Obstat' ruling (in other words, censorship), being obliged to consider resigning from their Church in protest,

- Finally, the possibility being considered of the disestablishment of the Church of England, which would lead (*inter alia*) to the removal of 26 bishops from the House of Lords. The *Act of Settlement* would also have to be repealed, with its control over the religious ties of the Royal Family. Church and State have evolved together since the Church (of which the Queen is 'Supreme Governor') became a powerful institution in its own right. But since the advent of representative democracy there is logically no place for the continuing presence of the Church *per se* in the governance of the country, and Royal Mandates for matters such as the Consecration of bishops will no longer be required. Disestablishment would also mean that the Archbishop of Canterbury would no longer be effectively appointed by a secular institution (through the current Prime Minister, as now) and could be elected (like the Pope) by his colleagues from the Worldwide Anglican Communion. This would remove the last vestiges of 'colonialism' in the Anglican Communion (of which some of its African leaders are still remarkably sensitive). If it were felt that the deliberations of the House of Lords would be impaired by the absence of the 26 bishops who now sit *de jure* in the Lords, there would be nothing to stop the government of the day from appointing one or more bishops to voice ecclesiastical points of view in debates, and appointments could also be made from leaders of other faiths. Disestablishment should not *in practice* affect the current duties and responsibilities of parish priests to serve their communities – by officiating at weddings and funerals, and by offering pastoral care to those in their parishes. Church schools should be able to continue their work as partners with State institutions, and linked to their respective Christian parishes.

A growing interest by the public in ecumenical co-operation, and the final abandonment of the former 'colonial' presumption that all nations should become Christian, could be of immense social and political value. Christians should be encouraged to follow Gandhi's lead and come to regard Christianity as simply one of a number of major world religions following different patterns but all with the same goal of ultimate union with God. Furthermore, it may soon become increasingly popular to follow Gandhi's belief that God is not a 'Person' (either male or female) but is beyond any personal / impersonal distinction as the ultimate morality underlying all things. Thus the Christian concept of 'God the Father' would be understood as an indescribable entity or all-pervading spirit, beyond human comprehension, eternal in space-time and hence not of this finite world, yet the creation of which

'God' was nevertheless responsible, and seeing in Jesus the mediator between this 'God' and the material universe. This does not however mean that we as Christians should in any way lessen our faith in Jesus Christ as a pointer to God and immortality, but the overriding emphasis should be on our love for Jesus while at the same time quietly dropping those time-expired doctrines which have no meaning for today's generation. And we should also freely acknowledge that – for the millions of people in the universe of widely differing cultures – there are other ways to the understanding of God.

NOTES

1   Ruth Gledhill, *The Times*, 31 July, 2002
2   Goulder, 1977, 64
3   Hick, 1977, 171
4   Robinson, 1971, 32
5   Ibid., 37
6   Ibid., 37–8
7   Ibid., 125
8   Ibid., 133
9   Ibid.
10 Robinson, 1972, 68
11 Spong, 2002, 247 (Preface, Note 2)
12 Hick, 1977, ix
13 Ibid., 28
14 See Hick, 2004, 235–246
15 Ibid., 28
16 Ibid., 31
17 Macquarrie, 1977, 140
18 Wiles, 1977, 9
19 Macquarrie, 1977, 144
20 Cupitt, 1977, 134, 142
21 Hick, 1977, 169
22 Ibid., 171 (my italics)

23 Ibid.

24 Ibid.

25 Ibid., 172

26 Young, 1977, 38–42

27 Ibid., 32

28 Robinson, 1971, 79

29 Adolfs, 1967, 83

30 Kee, 1971, 81

31 Geffré, 1983, 60

32 Russell, 2005, 18–19

33 Radcliffe, 2008, 5

34 Ibid., 73

35 Ibid., 72

36 Spong, 2002, 74

37 Ibid., 75

38 Ibid., 124

39 Ibid., 142

40 Ibid., 147

41 Robinson, 1971, 100

42 Ibid., 102

43 Spong, 2002, 191

44 Ibid., 198

45 Ibid., 199

46 Ibid

47 Priestland, 1981, 166–170

48 Spong, 2002, 213

49 Hick, 2004, 17

50 Ibid., 248. In Judaism, being 'gathered to one's fathers' implied that everyone went to a place named Sheol, 'a kind of storehouse of the not-alive, into which all went and from which none emerged' (Davies, J., 1999, 90). Only two human beings are recorded in the Hebrew Bible as going to 'heaven' – namely, Elijah and Enoch. For the rest 'resurrection' is a barely-mentioned concept

51 Ibid.

52 Russell, 2005, 43–4

53 For these various religious views on the after-life see Bess Twiston Davies, *The Times*, 4 November, 2006

54 Wright, 2006, 186

55 See Chapter 4 (ii)

56 Yet the Church must be cautious for, as the writer Fay Weldon admits 'I am made nervous by the happy-clappy, the joining

together in singing and swaying as in a pop concert. It's mass hypnosis – not appropriate. I am dismayed by the slipping over of services into group therapy, by the determined egalitarianism which seems to favour the tasteless over the tasteful: which reduces the priest to just another 'person like us' whose job happens to be that of a parson. He is not: rather a man of God, appointed to be just that, dedicating his life to the task. That's why we give him our respect' (Weldon, F., 'Converted by St Paul', in Chartres, C. (ed.), 2006, 137). In fact, what she describes (and dislikes) is exactly what has attracted young people to Charismatic/Evangelical-style gatherings in the past: the young *need* emotional and ecstatic experiences whether religion – or drug-induced

[57] Hick, 2004, 118

[58] Wright, 2006, 78–9

[59] Ibid., 79

[60] Ibid., 81

[61] Ibid., 87

[62] Ibid., 119

[63] Priestland, 1981, 22

[64] Hick, 2004, 245

[65] Vermes, 2004a, 417

[66] Wilson, 2003, xv

[67] Wiles, 1974, 120–123

[68] Quoted in *The Times*, 8 May, 2008

[69] Quoted in Robinson, 1971, 135

[70] Micklethwait and Wooldridge, 2009, 1–9

[71] Perham, 2010, 47

[72] Ibid., 78–9

8. AT THE CLOSE OF THE DAY

The foregoing chapters have given a résumé from an historian's point of view of the history of philosophical and religious thought which provided the background for the formulation of the Christian religion, of critical views of Christian theism, of the cloud of myth surrounding Jesus of Nazareth and of the place of religious pluralism. It ended by suggesting ways of fresh thinking on historic doctrines and worship. This last chapter sums up the strands of thought which have been discussed throughout the book.

Based on the findings of biblical scholars and theologians over the past century, together with a synthesis of widespread religious views, the following conclusions emerge:

1.   since it has now been established amongst leading academic theologians that the existence or non-existence of God lies beyond rational proof, belief in God can therefore only be a matter of faith;

2.   the cosmological fact that the existence of our universe has depended on an almost unbelievable degree of fine-turning of its various physical constants is such that the explanation of the universe could be the result of an act of a 'God' or 'Transcendent Power' whose intention it was to create beings like ourselves, although Professor Stephen Hawking conceives of such an entity as the embodiment of the laws of nature, rather than the 'personal' God of the monotheistic faiths. Alternatively, it could have been the remarkable result of pure chance;

3.   although the existence or non-existence of God cannot be proved, the powers of human consciousness nevertheless enable humankind to enter into a special dimension receptive of the Transcendent (in its multiplicity of different aspects including the concept known to many as 'God' or the 'ground of our being');

4.   our conception of God must change from the traditional vengeful, demanding and overbearing God of the Old Testament to a God that is the loving source of our lives (the 'ground of our being'); not so much a personal entity up in the sky to whom we pray, but rather a 'presence' in which 'we live and move, and have our being' (Acts 17: 28);

5.   Jesus of Nazareth was a man recorded in history (born 7 BC, died by crucifixion in Jerusalem AD 30) who is now considered to have been a charismatic prophet in the Hebrew tradition, intensely aware of God and the Transcendent, a mediator between God and the world, 'a man approved of God among you' (Acts 2: 22). He was not an earthly *incarnation* of God but, as Paul believed, 'God was in Christ' (2 Corinthians 5: 19). By his life and teaching Jesus offered contemporary people in the Near East a supreme example of ethical behaviour as well as the promise of a future existence in the 'next world';

6.   although doubts have been expressed by some scholars as to the reality of the person known as Jesus (specifically since there is a historical record of only 50 days out of the 37 years of Jesus's life, and an inexplicable ignorance in Paul's epistles concerning Jesus's early life and teaching and of his death and crucifixion), it is nevertheless reasonable to accept in explanation that many contemporary records of his life – both pagan and Christian (such as Bishop Papias's book *The exegesis of the Lord's oracles* (*c.*140)) – will have been lost;

7.   after Jesus's death the early Christian communities were beset by the rivalry of already well-established state religions (such as the worship of Cybele, the Phrygian *Magna Mater* or 'Mother of the Gods') and a variety of pagan religious cults (such as Mithraism), and the first action of their leaders was therefore to formulate their own detailed narratives, doctrines and rituals (some clearly based on pagan antecedents) which would constitute the basis of their newly established faith;

8.   Jesus did not himself therefore found the 'Church' or the Christian religion. It was Jesus's early apostles who composed a semi-mythological narrative of his life and teaching (i.e. the

gospels) which would be acceptable to the contemporary credulous age in which miracles were readily believed. Early Church leaders (soon to be known as bishops) then devised doctrines and sacraments as special 'means of grace', presided over by the clergy and therefore under the strict control, and for the ultimate financial benefit of the developing institutional Church;

9.	the Church authorities, up until the time of the early Christian Fathers, interpolated passages into the narratives of the gospel writers and other scriptures *ex post facto* to give the appearance that Jesus had said that his message should be preached to all people (not just to the Jews); that the death of Jesus was prefigured in the Bible and foreordained by God; that Jesus had initiated the Eucharist as a memorial to himself, to which many years later (at the Fourth Lateran Council in 1215) was attached – in a clear attempt to increase its liturgical importance and solemnity – the Doctrine of Transubstantiation; and that Jesus had established a 'Church' of which Simon Peter was to be the leader, with the keys to the gates of the Kingdom of God;

10.	Jesus's insistence on the imminent arrival of the Kingdom of God (which has still not materialised) led the early Christian authorities to devise the theory that this claim was synonymous with the establishment of the Christian 'Church';

11.	Jesus never considered himself to be God, or even a manifestation of God; it was the early Church authorities who (a) declared *by a conciliar vote* that Jesus was a God (AD 325, 381) and so gave rise to the Western Orthodox Creed (or 'Nicene Creed'), (b) defined Jesus's nature (AD 451) as *consubstantial with God* and as the 'Word of God', and (c) formulated the theory of the Holy Trinity of 'Father, Son and Holy Ghost (AD 675);

12.	the concept of the Bible as being *literally* the 'Word of God', rather than a collection of historical / mythical memoirs and inspired words of wisdom by prophets and sages, should be discounted;

13.	the teachings of Jesus as recorded (in part at least) in the narratives of the gospel writers and in St Paul's epistles provide the essence of today's understanding of the religion of Christianity;

14.   the recognition (at last) by the Roman Catholic Church that it holds no monopoly of faith nor exclusive key to salvation, should encourage Christians of all denominations to welcome dialogue with other faiths, which are similarly seeking (in their own diverse ways) to understand the reality of God;

15.   the indifference of today's youth to 'religion' and to formal Church Services demands a re-thinking of the concept of religious 'worship' and the offering of new forms of devotional expression;

16.   the inevitable decline in the number of Church supporters and congregations will lead to the abandonment of many smaller church buildings and the concentration of missionary effort on the larger and financially viable churches and cathedrals. We may envisage the building of multi-faith centres in co-operation with other religious faiths, along with inter-faith initiatives;

17.   the Church of England should re-convene its Doctrine Commission to draw up a doctrinal statement for the twenty-first century acknowledging the mythological nature of some of its major doctrines; which of these can now be abandoned; and how the remainder can be re-interpreted for the present century. It should prepare a new Creed for Christianity and a re-convened Liturgical Commission should prepare a *New Christian Prayer Book* based on the person of Jesus and his expressed relationship with 'God the Father' and omitting references to the Holy Trinity, to God 'incarnate', to Jesus as a (Jewish) sacrificial 'lamb of God' dying to redeem the 'sins of the whole world' and other discredited concepts;

18.   the possibility of the disestablishment of the Church of England may need to be considered, coupled with the repeal of the *Act of Settlement.*

These conclusions should be considered part of the wider debate about religious belief today, which was initiated by Gerald Priestland's BBC Radio programme and his subsequent book (1981). That programme, Priestland believed, brought comfort to that he termed the 'Great Anonymous Church of the

Unchurched'. The same approach was followed by John
Humphrys in his Radio 4 series entitled *Humphrys In Search of
God* and subsequent book *In God We Doubt* (2007). Perhaps the
present book, illustrating how many of the traditionally accepted
Christian beliefs can no longer be seriously entertained, yet leaving
us with a picture of Jesus as a much-loved charismatic prophet
with a message still relevant in today's world, will stimulate
people's thoughts once again.

How do the findings of this study impinge upon the
'conventional' Christianity in which the author and many others
were brought up? First of all the concept of a creator God, whose
existence cannot be proved but which is the bedrock of Christian
faith, has received weighty support from recent cosmological
studies which demonstrate the uncanny coincidence of the various
physical constants without which our universe could not survive
nor produce intelligent life. The existence of our universe, and of
us within it, 'rests upon a knife-edge of improbability'. Must it not
therefore have been deliberately designed? Or, was its formation
the remarkable result of pure chance?

The position of Jesus is very different. How many of today's
churchgoers, as they sit in the pews of their parish churches, realise
that a group of clerics presumed to decide in the year 325 by 218
votes in favour and 2 against that Jesus was 'God incarnate'; that
another group of clerics presumed to decide in 451 that Jesus had
two natures, one human and one divine (i.e. was *consubstantial*
with God) and yet another group of clerics pronounced (finally) in
675 that Jesus was the second person of a theoretical concept
known as the Holy Trinity? These 'attributions' have been
seriously questioned in recent years by biblical scholars as
untenable. Jesus *never* regarded himself as God, or 'God
incarnate', nor as the second person of a divine Trinity; such
claims would have been blasphemous and therefore impossible for
a devout Jew like Jesus. Jesus is now regarded by scholars as having
been a charismatic human prophet intensely aware of God and the
Transcendent, 'a man approved of God among you' (Acts 2: 22),
whose moral teaching, bearing witness to God's loving
providence, and his promises of everlasting life in a heavenly

kingdom still resonate today. Yet dutiful parishioners and cenobitic worshippers have repeated, day after day, the words:

'we believe in one God the Father Almighty... And in our Lord Jesus Christ, the only-begotten Son of God, Begotten of his Father before all worlds, God of God, Light of Light, Very God of very God, Begotten, not made. Being of one substance with the Father, By whom all things were made: Who for us men, and for our salvation came down from heaven, And was incarnate by the Holy Ghost of the Virgin Mary, and was made man... And I believe in the Holy Ghost, the Lord and giver of Life, Who proceedeth from the Father and the Son, Who with the Father and the Son together is worshipped and glorified...'

It is remarkable that the unquestioning faithful have accepted this mythological scenario for so long. As A. N. Wilson asserts: 'If it were even half possible that an historical personage existed who said the words attributed to him in the Gospels, there could be no greater insult to his memory than to recite the creeds, invented in a Hellenized world which was, imaginatively speaking, light years away both from Jesus and from ourselves. Nor could one insult his memory by claiming that he had founded a Church which for many years of its history was devoted so intently to prosecuting anyone who dared to question these creeds. Wars, crusades and inquisitions have been perpetuated in the name of Jesus'.[1] It can only be that, for the older members of the faithful, the comfortable ambience of traditional modes of worship and familiar if meaningless liturgical passages provide warmth and reassurance in the uncertainties of the contemporary world.

Incomprehension, intellectual doubts, and painful disillusionment were the respective criticisms of the Christian religion voiced by three individuals in Chapter 1. Clearly for some – especially the young (untrammelled in the present age by former traditional parental influence) – 'religion' and spiritual beliefs are foreign to their existential attitude to life and experience in the 'modern' world. They know nothing of the background and history of Christianity and religion for them is an irrelevance. For many distinguished philosophers and theologians through the ages intellectual doubts have been a common theme with often painful consequences (from excommunication to execution). For those whose scholarship leads to serious intellectual doubts about the doctrines of the Christian Church there is little alternative but to leave the ranks of its believers. And lastly, painful disillusionment has been the lot of many who have finally left the ranks of believers with sadness.

At the beginning of the third millennium there is no longer among the general public of Christian persuasion a belief in the infallibility of divine revelation as expressed in the 'scriptures' which was formerly accepted without question. This former assumption has today been eroded by the advances of scientific knowledge since the Enlightenment and by the findings of recent biblical scholarship. Improvements in education have meant that more people are now capable of thinking for themselves, and questioning what were formerly 'accepted' dogmas of the Church. Many have found these to be wanting, both in terms of fact and of credibility. They simply do not accept what has in the past been held to be the 'revealed truth'. We have suggested in Chapter 7 some ways in which the Church might be reformed to meet this challenge. Whether the will is there, time alone will tell. It is more likely that the task of doctrinal reform, after such a long period of doctrinal fossilization, will prove too daunting. Practical members of the hierarchy may well take the view: 'What does it matter if Jesus did not, in fact, institute the Eucharist; if he was not, in fact, divine; if all the early Church attributions at Nicaea and elsewhere are meaningless – provided *today's* Christians (or most of them) still believe in the mysterious power of the body and blood of Christ, and address Jesus as if he was still alive and active in today's world? If this indeed is what our dwindling band of supporters want for spiritual comfort and re-assurance (and also for our own continued existences as ministers), don't let us disillusion them!' In which case parish priests will doubtless continue with their mission, although well aware of the scepticism and indifference of those who understand the mythological foundation of much of the Christian faith.

As the shadows lengthen and daylight fails, elderly parishioners who have lived their lives in the unquestioned beliefs and rituals of the traditional Church will, one by one, move on – and, as T. S.

318

Eliot presciently wrote many years ago, Christianity will perforce once again be 'adapting itself into something which can be believed' – indeed to a model that will suit the circumstances of a new and less credulous age. As Paul said in his epistle to the Hebrews (Hebrews 13: 8): 'Jesus Christ is the same yesterday and today, yea and for ever'. It will be for the younger generation to decide whether the Christian religion in the West will gently subside into a small historical cult retaining its time-honoured mythological liturgical imagery, or whether, under new inspired leadership, it will boldly proclaim Jesus as the exemplar for us all, divested of the doctrinal strait-jacket imposed by the early hierarchy, and the prophet of a future heavenly and eternal life.

NOTE

[1] Wilson, 2003, 255

BIBLIOGRAPHY

Adolfs, R., 1967, 'Is God dead?', in Murchland, B. (ed.), 1967,
  The Meaning of the Death of God (New York, Vintage
  Books)

Andrews, E., 2009, *Who Made God?*

Armstrong, K., 1999, *A History of God* (London, Vintage)

Austin, M., 2005, *Explorations in Art, Theology and Imagination*

Beard, M., North, J and Price, S., 2005 (seventh printing),
  Religions of Rome

Bettenson, H. S. (ed.), 1946, *Documents of the Christian Church*

Bezzant, J. S., 1965, 'Intellectual Objections', in Vidler, A. R.
  (ed.), 1965, *Objections to Christian Belief*

Brandon, S. G. F., 1967. *Jesus and the Zealots*

Braybrooke, M., 1995, 'One-World Faith?', in Forward, M. (ed.),
  1995, *Ultimate Visions*

Brown, R. E., 1973, *The Virginal Conception and Bodily
  Resurrection of Jesus*

Butler, C., 1977, 'Jesus and Later Orthodoxy', in Green, M. (ed.),
  1977, *The Truth of God Incarnate*

Carrigen, H. L., Jr. (ed.), 2007, *Little Talks with God / Catherine
  of Siena*

Chartres, C. (ed.), 2006, *Why I am Still an Anglican*

Collins, F. S., 2007, *The Language of God*

Conze, E., 1959, *Buddhism: its Essence and Development*

Cornwell, J., 2007, *Darwin's Angel*

Crehan, J., 1976, 'Near Eastern societies' in Toynbee,
  A., Koestler, A., *et al.*, 1976

Cupitt, D., 1977, 'The Christ of Christendom', in Hick, J. (ed.),
  The Myth of God Incarnate

——, 1980, *Taking Leave of God*

Davies, J., 1999, *Death, Burial and Rebirth in the religions of
  antiquity*

Davies, P., 1992, *The Mind of God*

Dawkins, R., 1991, *The Blind Watchmaker* (Penguin 1991 edn.)

320

——, 2006, *The God Delusion*

Dill, S., 1919, *Roman Society in the Last Century of the Western Empire* (2nd edn.)

Durkheim, E., 1963, *The Elementary Forms of Religious Life* (trans. Swain, J.) (London, Allen & Unwin)

Eagleton, T., 2009, *Reason, Faith and Revolution: Reflections on the God Debate*

Ehrman, B. D., 2003, *Lost Christianities*

——, 2006, *Whose Word is it?*

Engineer, A. A., 1995, 'Islam: The Ultimate Vision', in Forward, M. (ed.), 1995, *Ultimate Visions*

Fenwick, P. and Fenwick, E., 2008, *The Art of Dying*

Fisher, M. P., 1995, 'Interfaith Vision at Gobind Sadan', in Forward, M. (ed.), 1995, *Ultimate Visions*

Forward, M. (ed.), 1995, *Ultimate Visions*

Frazer, J. G., 1949, *The Golden Bough* (abridged edn.)

Freeman, C., 2008, *AD 381 Heretics, Pagans and the Christian State*

Geffré, C., 1983, 'The Outlook for the Christian Faith in a World of Religious Indifference', in Jossua, J-P. and Geffré, C., (eds.) 1983

Goulder, M., 1977, 'The Two Roots of the Christian Myth', in Hick, J. (ed.), 1977, *The Myth of God Incarnate.*

Gray, J., 2007, *Black Mass*

Green, M. (ed.), 1977, *The Truth of God Incarnate*

Hampson, M., 2006, *Last Rites: The End of the Church of England*

Hardy, A., 1979, *The Spiritual Nature of Man*

Hawking, S. W., 1988, *A Brief History of Time*

—— and Mlodinow, L., 2010, *The Grand Design*

Heald, G., 2000, *Soul of Britain* (London: The Opinion Research Business)

Heelas, P. and Woodhead, L., with Seel, B., Szerszynoki, B. and Tusting, K., 2005, *The Spiritual Revolution*

Heywood, R., 1976, 'Illusion – or what?', in Toynbee, A., Koestler, A., *et al.*, 1976

Hick, J. (ed.), 1977, *The Myth of God Incarnate*

——, 2004, *The Fifth Dimension*

Hick, J. and Hebblethwaite, B., (eds.), 1980, *Christianity and Other Religions*

Holloway, R., 1999, *Godless Morality*

——, 2001, *Doubts and Loves*

——, 2004, *Looking in the Distance*

Hume, G. B., 2002, *Searching for God*

Humphrys, J., 2007, *In God We Doubt*

Hutton, R., 1996, *The Stations of the Sun*

Jenkins, D., 2002, *The Calling of a Cuckoo*

Jonas, D. F., 1976, 'Life, death, awareness, and concern: a progression', in Toynbee, A., Koestler, A., *et al.*, 1976, *Life after Death*

Jossua, J-P. and Geffré, C. (eds.), 1983, *Indifference to Religion* (Stichting Concilium)

Kasser, R., Meyer, M. and Wurst, G. (eds.), 2006, *The Gospel of Judas*

Kee, A., 1971, *The Way of Transcendence*

Kenny, A., 1992, *What is Faith?*

——, 2006, *What I believe*

Koestler, A., 1976, 'Whereof one cannot speak...', in Toynbee, A., Koestler, A. *et al*, 1976, *Life after Death*

Levin, M., 1998, *The Pool of Memory*

Maccoby, H., 1986, *The Mythmaker*

Mackie, J. D., 1952, *The Earlier Tudors*

Macquarrie, J., 1977, 'Christianity without Incarnation?' in Green, M. (ed.), 1977, *The Truth of God Incarnate*

McGrath, A., 2004, *The Twilight of Atheism*

——, 2005, *Dawkins' God*

——, 2007a, *Christian Theology* (4th edn.)

McGrath, A. with McGrath, J. C., 2007b, *The Dawkins Delusion?*

Micklethwait, J. and Wooldridge, A., 2009, *God is Back: How the Global Rise of Faith is Changing the World*

Momen, W., 1995, 'Why I am a Bahá'i', in Forward, M. (ed.), 1995, *Ultimate Visions*

Mooney, B., 2003, *Devout Sceptics*

Moule, C. F. D., 1978, *The Origin of Christology*

322

Obrist, W., 1983, 'Indifference to Religion: Symptom of a Mutation of Consciousness', in Jossua. J-P. and Geffré, C. (eds.), 1983, *Indifference to Religion*

Parrinder, G., 1976, *Mysticism in the World's Religions*

Penrose, R., 2010, *Cycles of Time*

Perham, M., 2005, *Glory in our Midst*

——, 2010, *To Tell Afresh*

Peterson, M., Hasker, W., Reichenbach, B. and Basinger, D., 2003, *Reason and Religious Belief*

Pliny: a self-portrait in letters (trans. and intro. by Betty Radice) (Folio Soc. edn., 1978)

Polkinghorne, J., 1998, *Science and Theology – An Introduction*

Priestland, G., 1981, *Priestland's Progress* (First Ariel edn. 1983)

Procopius, *The Secret History* (Folio Soc. edn. 1990)

Publius Virgilius Maro, *The Georgics* (trans. K. R. MacKenzie) (Folio Soc. edn. 1969)

Radcliffe, T., 2005, *What is the Point of Being a Christian?*

——, 2008, *Why Go to Church?*

Robinson, J. A. T., 1971, *Honest to God* (15th imp.)

——, 1972, *The Difference in Being a Christian Today*

Russell, B., 1965, *History of Western Philosophy* (9th imp.)

——, 2005, *Why I am not a Christian* (Routledge re-print)

Schlette, H. R., 1983, 'From Religious Indifference to Agnosticism' in Jossua, J-P. and Geffré, C. (eds.), 1983, *Indifference to Religion*

Simon, B., 2004, *The Essence of the Gnostics*

Smart, J. J. C. and Haldane, J. J., 2003, *Atheism and Theism* (2nd edn.)

Sommet, J., 1983, 'Religious Indifference Today: A Draft Diagnosis', in Jossua, J-P. and Geffré, C. (eds.), 1982, *Indifference to Religion*

Spong, J. S., 2002, *A New Christianity for a New World*

Staniforth, M. and Louth, A., 1987, *Early Christian Writings*

Stanton, G., 2002, *The Gospels and Jesus* (2nd edn.)

Stark, R. and Bainbridge, W. S., 1985, *The Future of Religion*

Thiede, C. P., 2004, *The Cosmopolitan World of Jesus*

Toynbee, A., 1976, 'Man's concern with life after death', in Toynbee, A., Koestler, A., *et al.*, 1976, *Life after Death*

Toynbee, A., Koestler, A., *et al.*, 1976, *Life after Death*

Turbutt, G., 1999, *A History of Derbyshire*

Vermes, G., 1973, *Jesus the Jew*

——, 2004a, *The Authentic Gospel of Jesus*

——, 2004b, *The Complete Dead Sea Scrolls in English* (revised edn.)

——, 2005, *The Passion*

——, 2006, *The Nativity: History and Legend*

——, 2008, *The Resurrection*

Vidler, A. R. (ed.), 1965, *Objections to Christian Belief* (re-print)

Wandel, L. P., 2006, *The Eucharist in the Reformation: Incarnation and Liturgy*

Ward, K, 1996, *God, Chance & Necessity*

——, 1998, *God, Faith & the New Millennium*

—— 2004, *The Case for Religion*

Warrior, V. M., 2006, *Roman Religion*

Weiler, A., 1983, 'Theories About the Causes of Religious Indifference', in Jossua, J-P. and Geffré, C. (eds.), 1983, *Indifference to Religion*

Wells, G. A., 1971, *The Jesus of the Early Christians*

Wiles, M., 1977, 'Christianity without Incarnation', in Hick, J., (ed.), 1977, *The Myth of God Incarnate*

Williams, J., 2006, *Angels*

Williams, R., 2001, *Arius* (2nd edn.)

Wilson, A. J., 2007, *Deluded by Dawkins?*

Wilson, A. N., 1998, *Paul: The Mind of the Apostle*

——, 2003 (Pimlico edn.), *Jesus*

Wooldridge, A. and Micklethwait, J., 2009, *God is Back: How the Global Rise of Faith is Changing the World*

Wright, N. T., 2003, *The Resurrection of the Son of God*

——, 2006, *Simply Christian*

Young, F., 1977, 'A Cloud of Witnesses', in Hick, J. (ed.), 1977, *The Myth of God Incarnate.*

INDEX

Bahá'í, faith, 264, 265, 266
Balthazar, 162
Baptist Church, 13
Barbelo, 205
Barnabas, epistle of, 37, 209, 211
Barth, K., 201
Basil, St, of Caesarea, 8, 233
Baur, F. C., 68
Bede, the Ven., 26, 134
Benedict IX, pope, 52
Benedict XVI, pope, 77
Benedict, St,, 8, 48
Bennet, Justice, 13
Bentley, Richard, 62
Berengar of Tours, 251
Bergson, H., 211
Bernard, St, of Clairvaux, 235,
    291
Betjeman, J., 1, 304
Biddle, J., 12
Blake, W., 65
Blue, rabbi, 182
Boethius, 46
Bonaventure, St., 54
Bonhoeffer, D., 302
Boniface VIII, pope, 56
Book of Common Prayer
    (1662), 78, 233, 297, 304
Borgia, Cesar, 58
Borromeo, St Charles, 61
Brierley, P., 270
Bruce, S., 270
Buddha, Gautama, 257, 260,
    281
Buddhism, 16, 75, 258, 260,
    266, 271, 273, 296
Bultmann, R., 74, 160, 201,
    277

Buren, P. Van, 73
Burne-Jones, E., 71
Caesarea Maritima, 211
Calvin, John, 58, 59, 97, 238,
    253
Carthusian monastic Order, 7
Caspar, 162
Cathars, 38
Catherine of Siena, 8, 127, 129,
    130, 241
Celsus, 19
Cerinthus, 28, 29, 32, 185, 242
Chalcedon, council of (451), 39,
    229, 241, 243
Chardin, P.T. de, 73
'Charismatic Churches', 79
Charlemagne, emperor, 51, 153,
    216
Charles I, king, 12
chi-rho, symbol, 150
Chrestos, 30, 155
Christmas, festival of, 33, 34,
    291, 297
Church attendance figures, 85,
    86, 87, 270
Cicero, Marcus Tullius, 18
Cistercian monastic Order, 8
Claudius, emperor, 154, 215
Clement, of Alexandria, 210,
    223, 231
Clement, of Rome, bishop,
    201, 206
Codex Tchacos, 167
Collins, F. S., 102, 107, 111,
    129
Common Worship, book of,
    78, 297, 304
Comte, A., 66, 98